Blood Vessels

BLOOD VESSELS

Vigilante Violence in the American West

PATRICK T. HOEHNE

UNIVERSITY OF OKLAHOMA PRESS : NORMAN

This book is published with the generous assistance of the McCasland Foundation, Duncan, Oklahoma.

Library of Congress Control Number: 205036264
ISBN: 978-0-8061-9610-7 (hardcover)

The views and opinions expressed herein are solely those of the individual author(s) and do not reflect the policy, opinions, or positions of the University of Oklahoma, its regents, officers, or employees.

The paper in this book meets the guidelines for permanence and durability of the Committee on Production Guidelines for Book Longevity of the Council on Library Resources, Inc. ∞

The manufacturer's authorized representative in the EU for product safety is Mare Nostrum Group B.V., Mauritskade 21D, 1091 GC Amsterdam, The Netherlands, email: gpsr@mare-nostrum.co.uk.

For Jackie and Charlotte

Contents

Acknowledgments

I have been fortunate enough to work with a number of supportive and encouraging mentors and colleagues. From the University of Nebraska-Lincoln, I would like to thank the members of my PhD committee: Bedross Der Matossian, Jeannette Jones, Peter Capuano, and Timothy Mahoney. I owe a great debt to my advisor, William G. Thomas III, for his patience, backing, and guidance. I am also grateful to the faculty and staff affiliated with the Center for Digital Research in the Humanities. My thanks to Carrie Heitman, Elizabeth Lorang, Jessica Dussault, Kaci Nash, Karin Dalziel, and Laura Weakly. Thanks also to Anthony Foreman, Donna Devlin, Elodie Galeazzi, Lina Homberger Cordia, Timothy Turnquist, and Veronica Duran. I only pursued a PhD after the encouragement of my mentors at Colorado State University, and remain indebted to Jared Orsi, Sarah Payne, and Robert Gudmestad for this. Finally, I am grateful to my former colleagues at the University of Southern Mississippi. My sincere thanks to Andrew Haley, Matt Casey, Ian Dunkle, Katya Maslakowski, Leah Parker, and Bradley Phillis.

Several archivists, librarians, and editors were also of tremendous help throughout this process. I would like to thank the entire staff at the Montana Historical Society, who were all so friendly and knowledgeable. I would also like to thank Diana Di Stefano and Jeff Bartos at *Montana The Magazine of Western History* for their work in editing and publishing my work on the Montana vigilantes, a portion of which appears in this book. I would also like to thank the staff and archivists at the Abraham Lincoln Presidential

Library and Museum, History Nebraska, and the Illinois Regional Archives Depository. And, of course, my thanks to Joe Schiller and the University of Oklahoma Press for seeing the value in this work and bringing it to publication.

I would like to express my sincere gratitude to the Harry Frank Guggenheim Foundation, which generously funded the final year of writing the dissertation that would become this book. I would similarly like to thank the University of Nebraska-Lincoln and the University of Southern Mississippi for providing support. I would also like to thank the Montana Historical Society for providing funding which made possible three weeks of archival research in beautiful Helena, Montana.

My greatest debt is to my family. My mother, Ellen, remains the best teacher I have ever had. Her encouragement, love, and faith have made me the person I am today. My father, Richard, has served as an inspiration throughout my entire life. He has been a model of duty and dedication. My sisters, Rebecca and Alexandra, remain my best friends. Thank you all for always being there for me. I love you all. My daughter, Charlotte, is my world. Although she has only been present for the final stage of the writing process, she has been a constant source of joy who makes the work seem light and every day a wonder. Finally, I owe special thanks to my wife, Jackie. Her love, patience, support, and humor have made the last few years the happiest in my life. She made this book possible.

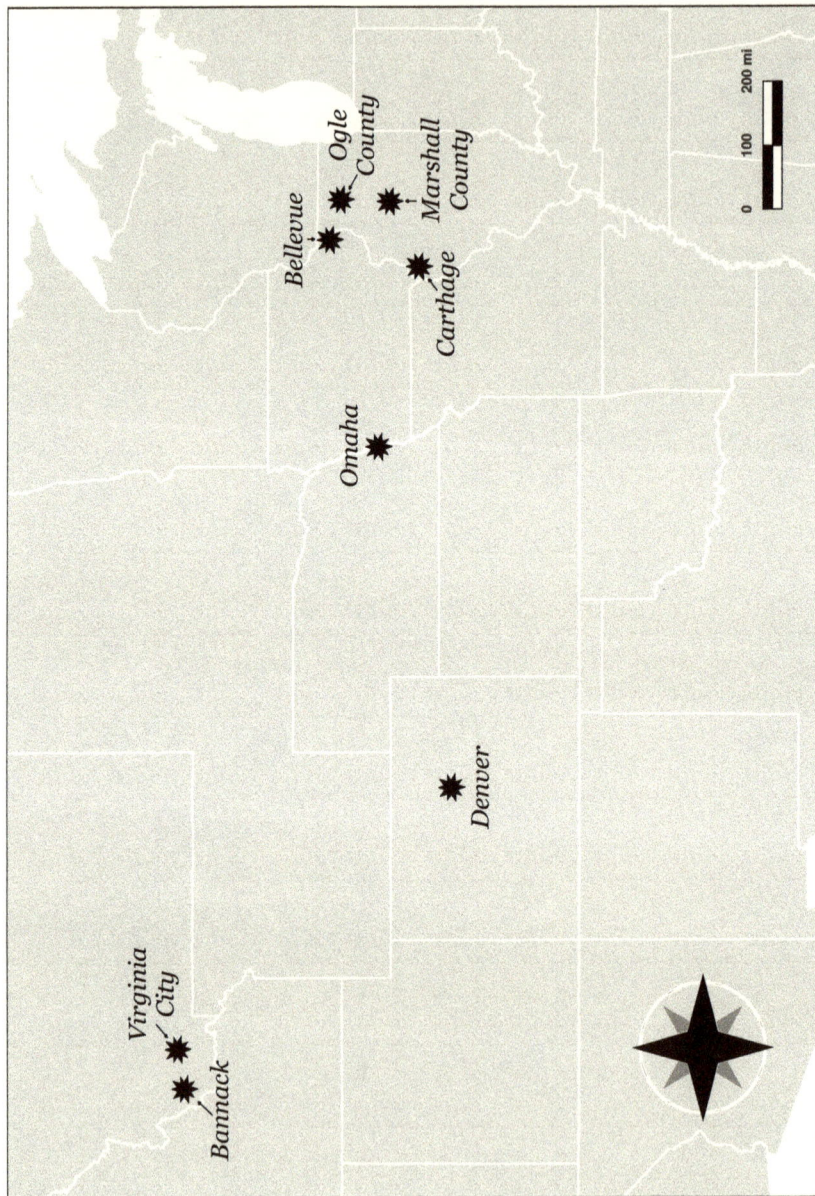

Locations in the United States, circa 1865, where violent episodes discussed in this book took place. Based on map from the *Atlas of Historical County Boundaries*, Dr. William M. Scholl Center for American History and Culture, Newberry Library, Chicago, Illinois.

INTRODUCTION

"I believe that a she-devil is just as bad as a he-devil, and should be killed just as quick as any other devil."

Colonel Thomas J. Babcoke stood before the Missouri State House of Representatives as he spoke. Applause punctuated the remark. The date was November 17, 1865, and Babcoke, a Republican member of the chamber, was facing accusations that Union militiamen under his command had lynched Judge Lewis F. Wright and four of his sons. The Wrights had allegedly harbored Confederate guerrillas implicated in the killing of an unarmed Union captain. Babcoke claimed that he had ordered his men to transport them to civil authorities in Rolla. They were not to be allowed to escape. "I told the men," he insisted before the House, "'Don't let them get away; stop them with Minie bullets; if you can't stop them any other way, stop them with Minie bullets!'" About five miles out, the militiamen had done just that. A percussive sound evoked the memory of the fatal volley, as legislators excitedly stamped their feet in response.[1]

Missouri's Democratic newspapers had already published reporting that contradicted Babcoke's account. They insisted that the killing of the Wrights had been a "slaughter, in cold blood." *The Daily Missouri Republican* printed a report that Judge Wright had been shot in the face at such close range that "blotches" of gunpowder could be seen on his burned skin. No less than 26 shots had perforated the 5 bodies, the *Republican* claimed, with 12 of those delivered to their heads.[2] The paper also accused Babcoke and his men of seizing an unnamed woman, "who is said to be still missing."[3]

Babcoke was defiant in the face of the accusations. "If they are corrupt and vile," he thundered on, "kill them. Just kill them as quick as the others. They just make trouble and expense, and it would be economy to kill them and let them sink as low down as they belong."[4] Throughout his address, Babcoke seemed, in the same breath, to both deny and justify the allegations. Publishing his remarks, Jefferson City's *The People's Tribune* moaned on November 29 that their readers would "see now that Babcoke and his friends not only admit the intentional killing of the Wrights, but exult over it."[5]

The *Republican* dug deeper. Unconfident that the Republican-dominated House would seriously try to investigate the killings, the paper groped into the past for some evidence that could injure Babcoke. What they found led them over a quarter-century into the past and hundreds of miles north. "And who is this Thos. J. Babcoke?" posed the *Republican* to its readers on December 20. Thomas Babcoke, the paper claimed, had not always been as he now appeared. Back in 1839, Babcoke had been Babcock, a Methodist preacher on the move from Indiana into territorial Iowa. He had developed a reputation for his powerful sermonizing, the paper noted. But coinciding with the reverend's appearance, "a quantity of bogus silver was put into circulation in that portion of the country." Agitated locals had begun to hold meetings and eventually, the paper stated, decided that Babcock, along with "a man named Bonny and another named Osborn," were the cause of the counterfeiting. In response, Babcock had fled the area. Not long after, the *Republican* noted, he had been caught up in mob violence in the small town of Bellevue, Iowa Territory, where locals had again moved against an alleged "gang of counterfeiters." The resulting collision had proved deadly.[6]

Babcoke published his response to the allegations in the January 26, 1866, issue of the *Missouri State Times*. "I was associated with said Bonney," Babcoke admitted, "but our business was detecting and breaking up the most formidable gang of counterfeiters, robbers and murderers ever known in the western States." Babcoke did not merely attempt to deny the allegations, he sought to reverse them into a story of his own heroism. He then went even further, claiming that "the editor of the *Republican* was then associated with S. Haight and others, furnishing counterfeit money for the gang." In support of his claims, Babcoke produced some legal documents from an 1846 counterfeiting trial connected to an 1845 murder investigation. Contained therein were references to Bonney, Heaight, a gang of Mormon alleged counterfeiters, and a family of horse thieves. Babcoke even included a certificate penned by then–Illinois governor Thomas Ford, which proclaimed that a legal effort to prosecute Bonney for counterfeiting had been organized to prevent him from investigating the 1845 murder.[7] Babcoke's revelations only added further layers of strangeness to the whole affair.

Just five days after Babcoke's response was published in the *Missouri State Times,* the Missouri State House of Representatives opened an official inquiry. The chamber organized a committee to investigate allegations "which," as the resolution stated, "if true, are of a character to render him unfit to occupy a seat on this floor."[8] That committee would determine if Col. Thomas J. Babcoke had orchestrated the lynching of the Wrights. To understand that act of violence, its members would look to the past, parsing the fragmentary revelations advanced both by Babcoke and the *Republican.* No longer could the killing of the Wrights be treated as some isolated incident. It now had to be located within a vast and tangled web of human connection, across which cascading sequences of violent, extralegal, and criminal actions flowed. A fuller and deeper understanding of how the Wrights met their deaths would only emerge through engagement with such linkages. The she-devils and he-devils waited in those details.

The history of extralegal collective violence is a human one. It is human beings—like the Wrights, Babcoke, and his men—who experienced violence employed beyond the sanction of the formal legal system, be it as perpetrators, targets, or witnesses. If they survived the encounter, they carried that experience with them as they moved across space and time. If those individuals engaged in subsequent incidents of violent action they did so informed by that prior experience. Through this movement and activity, such persons operated as vectors who established invisible linkages between violent incidents. Chain sequences emerged as further individuals gained their own experience with extralegal violent action and perpetrated the cycle. Linkages spread, tangled, and twisted. Sometimes, that violence caused entire clusters of participants to scatter forth to preserve themselves, engorging the flows along which further action could cascade. To trace the threads bound up in that tangled human web is to witness the violent beginnings of western cities like Omaha, Denver, and Salt Lake City. It is to glimpse the coagulation of American memory regarding vigilantism and supposed lawlessness. It is to excavate the genealogies of violence.

Rather than a collection of disparate, random episodes, this extralegal collective violence flowed across interconnected webs of human movement, exchange, and collision. Episodes of violent action rarely existed in isolation. They were not simply spawned from supposedly exceptional conditions, nor did participants generally innovate out of whole cloth. Instead, the violence moved and developed across those human webs as past experience informed responses to local conditions and realities. To pick up just one gnarled thread from that web is to follow that history, leading to a fuller understanding of not only the history of extralegal violence in the United States but the very mechanics by which such violence was reproduced and modified at the most granular level.

In this book, I trace one such thread. The primary narrative arc examines an unbroken, cascading flow of violent action as it crashed across the places now known as Illinois, Iowa, Nebraska, Colorado, and Montana between 1840 and 1865. That sequence contained extralegal events as significant as the Bellevue War, the mob killing of Mormon prophet Joseph Smith, and the bloody 1863–64 vigilante campaign in what is now Montana. The narrative flows as the violence itself did: across the direct human linkages that bound together every episode within this sweep. To make visible those human linkages is to develop a deeper understanding of each of those constituent events, while simultaneously advancing a more longitudinal analysis of the interconnected sequence of action.

Adopting a lens that is both wide and narrow offers new insights into the granular processes behind larger trends. This method accounts for the increasingly lethal nature of extralegal violence over the course of this period, the developing relationship between Americans and the formal, constitutional legal system, and the emergence of the propertied interests of small groups as a primary issue around which the violence was structured. My focus on the human element of the violence also provides a clearer window into the complexities and contradictions bound up in each episode of violent action. This approach demonstrates the degree to which legal identities could blur and shift, challenging romanticized tropes regarding frontier lawlessness and lawbringing.[9]

I did not choose the geographical and temporal ranges that bracket this account arbitrarily. Richard Maxwell Brown, one of the preeminent early scholars of American extralegal violence, argued that four "major peaks of waves of vigilantism" occurred in the eastern United States.[10] Brown, who located the first peak of vigilantism in the early 1830s, placed the second peak in the early 1840s and used the Bellevue War, which occurred in April 1840, as one of four examples of this wave. Similarly, the Bellevue War serves as the starting point for this narrative, with the survivors of that action later reemerging in connection with extralegal violence in Illinois, Nebraska, and, in the case of Thomas Babcock, Missouri. The conclusion of my book coincides with the end of the Civil War, in line with Brown's argument that the fourth "wave" of vigilantism "occurred in the immediate post–Civil War period (1866–1871)."[11] In keeping with this construction, however, I do not attempt to replicate Brown's notion of waves or East–West division but rather reframe the high ebbs as part of a larger cascade that flowed along human linkages. Those linkages did not end in 1865. However, the legal and constitutional changes wrought by the Civil War did change the nature of American extralegal violence in important and dramatic ways.[12] So, while the human linkages studied here would stretch on, the "transformations" ushered in by the Civil War and Reconstruction mark a natural point at which to conclude this analysis.

I selected the geographic contours with similar intentionality. The study of American extralegal violence has long been dominated by a discourse grounded in notions of regional exceptionalism, or an overreliance on the explanatory power of the supposedly unique conditions of a given locale. Violent extralegal action remains primarily associated with the American South and West, both in the popular and scholarly imagination.[13] That is not to say that regional conditions, such as the legal sanction of racial slavery, were not of consequence. They were. Rather, it is to say that regional exceptionalisms, when used as the primary explanatory force in the study of violence, fail to adequately capture either the granular complexities and dynamics or the larger, transregional processes, movements, and interconnections behind the production of that violence.

Unlike that in the South and West, extralegal violence in the American Middle West has received comparatively little scholarly attention. This is not because the region was devoid of violence.[14] In order to further challenge prevailing notions of regional exceptionalism and contribute to a fuller understanding of the history of this violence, this book traces a sequence of violent actions which began and developed in the Middle West before eventually flowing into the West.[15] Prominent instances of "western" vigilantism, such as the Montanan vigilante movement, emerged directly from this flow. My goal here is not to simply replace one sense of exceptionalism with another. Instead, it is to exhibit the boundary-defying human interconnections that shaped and informed action across porous boundaries.

In this book, I build off and attempt to reconcile the two major approaches to the study of American extralegal collective violence. The first approach typically studies a single violent event intensively, paying careful attention to local relationships, conditions, and dynamics. Local historians have produced much of what has been written on such incidents, and this book relies on excellent, in-depth studies like that penned by Susan Lucke on the Bellevue War.[16] Such detailed and focused accounts, however, often lack the scope to explore larger patterns and processes behind the production of violence. Moreover, this genre remains particularly susceptible to the influence of notions of exceptionalism. Older variants of this approach were sometimes written by those who lived through the violence or knew those who did. While still valuable, these older histories often dramatized, sanitized, and romanticized events, especially in cases of vigilantism.[17] Their triumphalist narratives have even become tangled up in concepts of local identity and tourism.[18] While academic presses have published major monographs on well-known incidents of extralegal violence like the New York City Draft Riots of 1863 or the San Francisco Committee of Vigilance, scholars have given less prominent episodes relatively little in-depth attention.[19]

Most academic historians of extralegal collective violence in the United States have, in recent decades, adopted a second, more longitudinal approach. Such scholars seek to identity the patterns and trends within large datasets over long stretches of spatial and temporal distance.[20] The studies produced by these scholars have yielded tremendous insight into the larger trends and developments within the practice of American extralegal collective action. My work on this book initially emerged out of a digital history project, the *Riot Acts* project, which explored some 2,200 incidents of violent action between 1783 and 1865.[21] Still, a longitudinal approach has limitations of its own. These studies, in covering such wide scopes, tend to rely on the explanatory power of large-scale suprahuman forces, such as economic conditions, social changes, or legal and political developments. While the significance of suprahuman forces must be accounted for and incorporated into any analysis of violent action, an overreliance on the explanatory power of such forces can result in a soft determinism. This often leads to the form, direction, and structure of an incident being portrayed as having developed outside of the power of its participants. Such an approach removes the human from the analysis of human violence.

This book combines the strongest elements of both approaches. A focus on individuals retains a sense of the agency and contingency that helped define each unique episode of violence. At the same time, the webs of activity produced by such individuals are used to identify and interpret larger patterns and developments across the broader terrain of American extralegal action. My approach offers a lens into the human relationships, experiences, hierarchies, networks, interests, and movements that ultimately informed each episode of action and facilitated the transfer of forms of extralegal violence across time and space. It challenges narrow and distorted romanticizations and exceptionalisms. Most important, the identification of the direct human linkages that bound violent incidents reframes both local and national narratives, revealing the degree to which interconnection and relationality defined entire sequences of action.

Before advancing further, it is important to discuss language. This is a somewhat fraught task. Christopher Waldrep, in his book on the history of the word "lynching," refused to define lynching or lynchers, insisting that "such terms cannot be defined and function as rhetoric."[22] Paul Gilje, in his work on American rioting, warned that "drawing fine distinctions between 'criminal activity,' 'uprisings,' 'rebellions,' and 'riots' would lead to a semantic jungle from which we might never emerge."[23] Part of the difficulty is that terms like "lynching" change in meaning over time. Today, lynching generally refers to racially motivated killing that may or may not be collective. When the term was first introduced during the Revolutionary War, however, it had no racial dimensions and referred only to an extrajudicial, nonlethal whipping.[24] To reflect this, I defer to how actors at any given time understood the contested and evolving definitions of "lynching" as a word, and I use this fluidity as a lens through which to better understand how those actors perceived the violence.

Most of the violence studied here will be categorized as extralegal collective violence.[25] While not a categorization employed by the contemporary actors engaged in the action, "extralegal" offers a useful construction with which to differentiate group violence from both criminal and legally sanctioned forms of violence. Extralegal collective violence, to modify Gilje's definition of rioting, involves a group of three or more individuals banding together and invoking either custom or some notion of unwritten rights to employ coercive force beyond that sanctioned by the formal legal system without attempting to permanently break from that system.[26] This category of extralegal collective violence is a broad one. Some examples of extralegal activity discussed in this book include vigilante killings, mob action, and the coercive efforts of informal protective associations. The action might be near-spontaneous or directed by a central committee. The severity of the violence could range from nonlethal whippings to wholesale campaigns of summary killing. It is in the perception of the collective violence rather than in the general particulars of its formation and execution that the categorization of "extralegal" becomes coherent and useful.

A nineteenth-century American engaged in extralegal violence would not understand their actions to be illegal insofar as they understood it as flowing from an informal and unwritten constitution of customary rights made even more potent by the libertarian "Spirit of the Revolution."[27] This notion of "popular constitutionalism" maintained that the citizens, rather than the system of formal, governmentally established courts, were the ultimate interpreters of republican law.[28] When groups of individuals banded together to commit extralegal violence, they consciously referred to themselves as "regulators," "vigilantes," and "lynchers" precisely because each term was loaded with revolutionary or republican meaning. This understanding led to the existence of both "formal" and "informal" systems of law and justice in the nineteenth-century United States, even as the line between such systems, and between public and private violence, often blurred. Chapter 1 dives more deeply into the thought and tradition behind such beliefs, while the chapters that follow note its continuous transformation.

It is also necessary to reflect on the methods I used to interpret sources, as well as their nature, quality, and availability. Any inventory of extralegal violence will remain incomplete. Silences, deliberate and accidental, haunt archives. It was generally the vigilantes who survived to offer full accounts of the violence. They were typically eager to justify their brutal methods by advancing narratives that invariably portrayed the action in simple terms devoid of nuance, instead favoring tropes of lawlessness and unrepentant criminality.[29] Those who might offer countervailing narratives had generally died, so it was the pro-vigilante accounts that dominated and shaped much of the foundational discourse surrounding prominent episodes like the 1863–64 Montanan lynching campaign.[30] These misrepresentations are, at times, amplified by absences of archival material lost to fires, floods, disposal, and disappearance.

To counter these distortions and difficulties, I muster surviving archival sources, including newspapers, legal records, diaries, reminiscences, and governmental datasets, to verify, challenge, and restore narratives. These accounts must be read critically, and this book will show that judges, surveyors, and newspapermen were not unbiased or objective actors but could be active enablers of the violence. Still, when layered together and used to track human networks, movements, exchanges, and dynamics, such realities do not prove a weakness but an invaluable strength. They contribute to a reconstruction of the violence as it was. I also reference local county histories heavily throughout this work. These published works, popular in the late nineteenth century, were, to quote Carol Kammen, "not really written, but rather, compiled by agents of the publishing company with the aid of people in the community."[31] Such local histories offer a rich trove of local memory, containing reminiscences and narratives that sometimes challenged or expanded upon more prominent accounts. While these sources must also be treated critically, they offer a further widening of perspectives. I then leaven this compilation of source material with the insights produced by the secondary literature to excavate a more accurate understanding of the sequences and constituent episodes of violent action bound up within this account.

It is also vital to consider the interplay between race and extralegal collective violence. By focusing on largely White spaces in the rural, antebellum Middle West and West, this account explores a sequence of collisions in which White actors constituted the overwhelming majority of both perpetrators and victims. This does not mean that race played a marginal or insignificant role in shaping the violence, nor does it signal that the violence was somehow detached from the racialized extralegal violence experienced elsewhere.[32] Non-White actors caught up in these episodes of violence almost invariably suffered intensified scrutiny and more violent treatment than their White associates, even if they were not the primary targets of any given episode of extralegal action. While the actions examined in this book primarily consist of White actors targeting other White actors, to ignore the racial dimensions of the violence is to produce an analysis of its dynamics that is fundamentally incomplete. Non-White and White actors faced different realities when confronted with extralegal violent action. This must be acknowledged, both to locate the violence studied here within the broader terrain of American extralegal practice and to develop an understanding of that violence that fully recognizes the complex dynamics behind its production.

Finally, it is important to note that while this narrative of cascading violence unfolds alongside the rapid westward expansion of the United States, it largely does not explore violence between settlers and Indigenous peoples. This is not because such violence was unconnected to the action analyzed here but because settlers tended to perceive and therefore order violence against Native peoples differently, even if the actual form of the violence resembled extralegal activity. An illustrative example comes from Omaha, Nebraska Territory, discussed in chapter 5. When settlers moved against alleged claim "jumpers," they took US muskets from the local arsenal but organized themselves and their violence under the auspices of the extralegal "claim clubs." When those same settlers, with those same arms, moved against Natives, they organized themselves as a formally constituted territorial militia.[33] As legal scholar Gregory Ablavsky notes, such militia combinations could remain mob-like and mete out retributive violence not dissimilar to vigilantism.[34] Despite these abundant similarities, the veneer of sanction, and subsequent organization and perception of the violence, mattered. The ambiguous logic that governed extralegal action against fellow settlers did not apply in the same manner to violence directed outward against Native peoples. This absence created more flexibility for settlers engaged in such violence to present their actions as quasi—if not fully—lawful. The result was a strain of violence closely related to, but ultimately distinct, in both calculus and perception, from extralegal collective action. Of course, even as the above example illustrates some of the distinctions between intra-settler extralegal violence and violence against Native peoples, it underscores how connected on a practical and human level these violent actions were. To explore those connections with the depth merited is beyond the scope of this book, which cleaves to the framework of extralegal action, but the topic is deserving of future inquiry.

The following narrative begins with the 1840 "Bellevue War," in what was then territorial Iowa. Chapter 1 carefully explores the relationships and dynamics behind the violence, demonstrating the importance of human linkages and networks for understanding the fundamental realities behind the production of those actions. It also provides insight into the prevailing intellectual foundations behind American extralegal action and explores the shifting currents that would cause episodes of violence to become more lethal. Chapter 2 follows one linkage into Illinois, where a family by the name of Driscoll responded to the Bellevue War by responding violently to the formation of a vigilante company in their area. A local judge, Thomas Ford, initially encouraged the vigilantism and would be forced to reckon with its bloody consequences.

Chapter 3 follows Ford's unlikely political ascent to the governorship of Illinois and examines his relationship with Mormon leader Joseph Smith. It then analyzes Ford's actions surrounding the 1843 mob killing of Smith, arguing that the governor's fateful choices cannot be understood independently of his earlier experience regarding the Driscolls.

Chapter 4 explores the collision of human linkages from the Bellevue War, the Driscoll affair, and the killing of Smith, all centered around a cluster of interconnected families. That family network, which migrated into the Middle West from the New River region on the Virginian–North Carolinian border, engaged in organized criminality throughout the area. Members of the network had fought in the Bellevue War, sheltered a survivor in the aftermath of the Driscoll episode, and had contacts in Mormon Nauvoo, Illinois. The cascading consequences of the violent incidents explored in the preceding chapters flowed across these linkages, damaging the network's operations and leading to fracture. This chapter recounts how counterfeiter and former Nauvoo resident Edward Bonney, who had once worked with the network, turned on the New River families and led an effort to see several members arrested and killed. Elsewhere, vigilantes drove members from their homes, sparking a westward flight.

Chapter 5 traces that flight first into Iowa, where continued criminal activity sparked another vigilante movement directed against one branch of the network. Some members of that family, including Cam Reeves, continued west, into what would soon become Nebraska Territory. James C. Mitchell, a former vigilante who had helped initiate the Bellevue War, also appeared in the area. This chapter narrates the rise of the powerful and violent claim clubs, which infiltrated territorial government and effectively ruled the territory for its first few years of existence. Both Reeves, the former criminal, and Mitchell, the vigilante, on account of their familiarity with the use of force, quickly rose to prominence within the territory and its ruling claim clubs. Territorial Nebraska's extralegal violence reflected both strains of influence.

Finally, chapter 6 tracks former members of the Nebraskan claim clubs into what would soon become Colorado, where they used their prior experience with extralegal violence to found the city of Denver and later organize a bloody campaign of vigilantism in September 1860. It then follows another claim club member, some Denver residents, fighters from Bleeding Kansas, and a former member of the San Franciscan committee of vigilance north into the territory now known as Montana. Instances of violence flowed along those linkages, cascading and comingling into a volatile combination. In the winter of 1863–64, those men helped organize and orchestrate one of the largest and bloodiest vigilante campaigns in American history.

This book begins its investigation at the same place and time as *The Daily Missouri Republican* began its own: in late 1830s Bellevue, a small hamlet nestled along the western bank of the Mississippi River. A man by the name of William W. Brown, recently of Elkhart, Indiana, had, in 1837, assumed the bad debt of a former fellow Elkhart resident, Rev. Thomas J. Babcock.[35] The affable and charitable Brown soon opened a hotel. Although the Panic of 1837 had damaged the regional economy, Brown prospered. Many locals knew him as an employer and generous lender. Others thought of him as a horse thief and counterfeiter. Around his inn, rumors, jealousies, and allegations began to swirl.

CHAPTER 1

Bellevue, Iowa Territory

"Sue the Devil and Have the Trial in Hell"

"White beans for hanging; colored beans for whipping!" Two men moved through a crowded room. One carried an empty box. The caller held a box full of white and colored beans. Six seated prisoners watched the men—and the content of their boxes—anxiously.

The room was, according to one eyewitness, "still as death" as the two men moved, the silence punctuated only by their metronomic footsteps and the rattling of the beans. Stopping before one of his fellow captors, the man holding the box of beans pierced the silence and repeated his refrain. He plunged his hand into the box, selected the desired legume, and deposited the vote inside the other, formerly empty container. The pair then made their way to the next captor, and then to the next, crying out at each stop: "White beans for hanging; colored beans for whipping!"[1]

About twenty hours earlier, a fierce firefight had roiled the town of Bellevue, Iowa Territory. An armed column of some forty men under the command of territorial legislature member Thomas Cox and Sheriff William A. Warren had marched on the hotel owned by one William W. Brown. There, Brown and his own armed band of twenty men awaited them, and the wooden hotel transformed into a redoubt. A red flag fluttered outside the building, emblazoned with a simple and defiant message: "Victory or Death."[2]

According to Cox and Warren, Brown and his supporters were a gang of horse thieves and counterfeiters. By this logic, their armed party was a lawful posse comitatus, or group of deputized citizens organized to serve a warrant. Brown's supporters rejected this claim. They held Cox and Warren's men to be nothing more than a drunken mob driven by political and material ambitions rather than by any legitimate consideration for public safety. Armed with muskets, pistols, and pitchforks, both parties steeled themselves to fight for control over a bitterly divided community. By the end of the day, eight men would lay dead or dying with even more wounded. And six captives would find themselves at the mercy of the victors, in the terrible jurisdiction of "Judge Lynch."

The battle at Brown's hotel—remembered as the "Bellevue War"—took place on April 1, 1840. The gunfight itself only lasted fifteen minutes.[3] Those fifteen minutes remained a source of local controversy for decades, inspiring heated debate even as the remaining number of participants and witnesses dwindled to null. The positions of the participants embroiled in this protracted controversy remained nearly identical to those adopted during the Bellevue War itself, divided between those who pronounced Brown's guilt and those who proclaimed his innocence. Outside of Jackson County, though, the bloodletting at Brown's hotel received little attention. On the rare occasion that later scholars did reference the Bellevue War, they either replicated one of the two competing local narratives or portrayed the violence simply as emblematic of larger national patterns.[4]

There is more, however, to this story of blood and beans. This is a history of a lethal exchange rooted in sexual violence, factionalism, jealousy, and loathing. It offers a window into the intersections between politics, patronage, and property along the rural middle western frontier. It is an example of an incident that produced over a half-dozen fatalities at a time when killing remained relatively rare within the American tradition of extralegal collective violence. Replete with references to rhetoric and procedure, this history provides an opportunity to examine the deeper intellectual roots of that turbulent tradition, locating the violence within the broader contemporaneous debates surrounding the natures of law, governance, and popular will.

The Bellevue War is an example of a violent tradition in flux, where the practices of customary constraint and new rhetorical license vied for dominance. This account analyzes the affair as an act of violence driven primarily not by concern for justice or law but personal ambitions and propertied interests. At the same time, it establishes that the extralegal action was indeed grounded within the context of genuine threats against community safety, even as these threats roiled among the murky waters of rumor and allegation. Such tensions meant that neither of the hostile parties could turn to the formal legal system for a satisfactory resolution to their concerns. The only acceptable justice would be their own. The principal actors implicated within the Bellevue War navigated this terrain by borrowing from older justifications for extralegal collective violence and a populist Jacksonian understanding of popular constitutionalism. My analysis traces the process by which these factors divided a community and erupted in an unusually violent killing affair, one that portended the potential for a grimmer shift within the entire American extralegal tradition.

The Bellevue War is also the departure point for a larger story, one that stretches across decades and hundreds of miles. The fighting at Brown's hotel was not some isolated affair but was one node in an interconnected network of violent activity that tethered some of the most prominent incidents of extralegal collective violence in American history. These linkages are not abstract. Actors who participated in the Bellevue War would, in the years that followed, reemerge in direct connection with violent extralegal incidents across Illinois, Nebraska, and Missouri. In doing so, they would engage with and influence the trajectories of others, who would, in turn, go on to participate in an even wider series of violent activity in regions farther afield. The violent impact of the Bellevue War was not, therefore, contained to fifteen minutes of gunfire and the subsequent dispensation of extralegal punishment. Incidents of violence possess genealogies, and it is with the Bellevue War that we will commence tugging at one genealogical thread.[5] To follow this thread is to reinterpret the history of extralegal collective violence in the United States.

*   *   *

William W. Brown, his wife Betsy Brown, and their young daughter Roxanna arrived in Bellevue, in what was then Wisconsin Territory, sometime in 1836 or early 1837.[6] At that time, Bellevue was a small village nestled in the bluffs overlooking the western bank of the Mississippi River. Prior to their appearance in Bellevue, the Browns had resided in Elkhart, Indiana, just south of the Michigan border.[7] William Brown wasted little time in establishing himself in his new community. On January 26, 1837, Brown assumed the bad debt attached to twenty-two lots held by a fellow former Elkhart resident, Methodist preacher Thomas J. Babcock.[8] The $2,000 bond signaled the beginning of Brown's ascendency in local affairs. By June 1837, Brown had been appointed as a justice of the peace for Dubuque County, Wisconsin Territory, a position he held until 1838.[9] In July of that year, Bellevue and its environs became part of the newly organized Iowa Territory.

By many accounts, William and Betsy Brown were well-regarded around Bellevue. Anson H. Wilson, who arrived in Bellevue in 1839, later described William as "a fine looking man, tall, well built, dark complected, of genial, pleasant manners, and a perfect gentleman in every way." As for Betsy, Wilson recalled her as "a small woman of neat appearance with a winning way, that made her very popular."[10] Even Sheriff Warren, who partook in the attack on Brown's hotel, admitted that Betsy was "a handsome and accomplished lady," while William, he allowed, was "a charitable man, benevolent to those in want, ever pleasant and kind to children, and really possessed of a humane and generous heart."[11]

With a reputation for charm and generosity, William Brown quickly became one of Bellevue's most prominent and successful residents. In May 1837, Brown got into the loan business after lending a farming partnership $6.50. Just three years later, the value of the money owed to Brown accounted for well over $7,000.[12] To put this figure in perspective, in 1840, a farm laborer in Iowa might have expected to make on average $0.30 a day.[13] By late 1838, Brown began to operate a hotel and grocery in Bellevue. In addition to selling dry goods and foodstuffs, he also offered meals and liquor. In cooperation with Samuel Burtis Sr., Brown operated a slaughterhouse to augment his meat supply at these locations.[14] Brown sourced additional income from a woodcutting business, employing men to fell lumber on federal land in the winter months. He sold this cordwood to passing steamboats. These various enterprises allowed Brown to invest in real estate, and he bought and sold several lots both in and around Bellevue.[15] Brown needed help managing these various ventures, so he took on a partner in his store—a young man by the name of James Thompson. Thompson, whom Warren later described as possessing a "fine physique, with a liberal education and excellent address," hailed from a wealthy Philadelphian family and had previously operated a business in Savanna, Illinois, until a robbery caused the operation to fold.[16]

For many of the town's poorer residents, Brown was a generous supplier of credit, supplies, drink, and work. Employment included opportunities both at the woodcutting operation and at the hotel. As contemporary Bellevue residents A. H. Wilson and Joseph Henrie both recounted, young Thomas Welch was one such beneficiary who worked in the stable of Brown's hotel.[17] So too, according to local historian James Ellis, was Aaron Day, who received from Brown "clothes and provision . . . and employment" after Day arrived in Bellevue "destitute."[18] This sort of patronage not only helped Brown secure customers and workers but allowed him to cultivate a robust and loyal network of local clients.

Bellevue's wealthier residents also engaged in lucrative trade with Brown. Lumber merchant John Sublett supplied Brown with building materials on multiple occasions. John's brother, William, purchased land from Brown. Many, including the Subletts, kept open accounts with Brown. Those who owed Brown money included John D. Bell, James Kemper Moss, Anson Harrington, James C. Mitchell, Henderson Palmer, Len Hilyard, James L. Kirkpatrick, and others. Local sheriff William A. Warren too had an open account with Brown, owing the hotel keeper $148.18. Brown further had business dealings with Thomas Cox, a member of Iowa's territorial legislature. Cox himself owed $41.97, while his brother John and brother-in-law James owed Brown $287.42.[19] For his part, Brown also borrowed from others. In spite of these financial ties—or perhaps because of them—some of Bellevue's wealthier residents grew resentful of Brown. "There were other men in business in Bellevue who were less successful and could not compete with Brown," recounted Henrie, "and were very jealous and claimed that Brown was getting rich too fast. J. K. Moss and the Sublets were the loudest in their denunciation of Brown's methods of doing business."[20] The implicit accusation in this grumbling was plain: William W. Brown owed his financial success, in part, to crime.

For some, the middle western frontier was a place where fortunes could be made. It was also a place where fortunes could be made up. Counterfeiting was endemic in the region. The Panic of 1837 and subsequent economic fallout had done severe damage to the banking system of the Middle West, leading to an acute shortage of currency that was exacerbated by trends in trade that saw more currency flow east than west. These realities created an environment where counterfeiting was not only lucrative but sometimes even tolerated so long as the unwitting recipients of any spurious notes or coins remained outside of the community.[21] To the victims who received the worthless currency, however, counterfeiting was perceived as a violation of property rights and a cause for extralegal violent action. Sometime in 1839 or 1840, for instance, the inhabitants of Johnson County, Iowa Territory, seized and flogged two men for passing counterfeit bills in their community. One witness found the sight of the whipping so terrible that he prayed that "God grant I never witness another."[22]

Property rights violations in the Middle West also frequently revolved around stolen livestock, with horses constituting a particularly common target. Not only were horses an indispensable asset in the rural United States, they were a mobile asset. A thief could steal a horse and quickly transport the animal for sale a county or more away. While some horse stealing was prompted by opportunity or desperation, more organized outfits of horse thieves were active throughout the Middle West. Counterfeiters and horse-thieving enclaves alike relied on networks for their operations. Established stations provided locations for thieves to deposit stolen horses, exchange bogus currency, and receive information.[23] Given the strategic overlap between horse stealing and counterfeiting, it was not uncommon to practice both crimes in tandem. One imprisoned alleged horse thief and counterfeiter, Samuel Cluse, recounted in an 1842 confession the cadence of such an operation. A certain man, Cluse explained, stole a horse in Indiana and "sold" it for counterfeit notes in a documented sham sale to a partner thief in Michigan. The second thief then sold the animal for good currency in another Michigan town. Cluse, who was active in Iowa, noted the heavy presence of his "clan" in the territory. A posse comitatus arrested one horse-stealing associate of both Cluse and the Stoutenburg clan of counterfeiters, Andrew J. Gregg, in Johnson County, Iowa Territory, in late 1838 or early 1839. Gregg had recently escaped jail in Coldwater, Michigan, a town purported to be one of the earlier residences of William W. Brown.[24] Residents of Jackson, Jones, and Linn counties organized an association for mutual protection against livestock theft sometime in January 1839 but to little apparent avail.[25]

Bellevue was not spared these trends. Beginning in 1838, a controversy relating to the alleged stealing of livestock rocked the town and undermined local confidence in the formal legal system. Thomas Davis accused his neighbor, Samuel Groff, of stealing his cattle under the cover of darkness. While Davis eventually recovered the animals from a ravine near the town, he continued to insist that Groff was guilty. When men from Illinois came to the area in search of a stolen horse, Davis again accused Groff and directed the Illinoisans to search his property, but to no avail. While Davis again had produced no evidence that his estranged neighbor was stealing livestock, he continued to take "every opportunity to denounce Groff as a thief." These repeated accusations flew in the context of a property dispute between the two neighbors, with Davis holding a piece of land claimed by Groff.[26]

On April 8, 1839, the two men met in Bellevue to settle the land claim controversy. Groff, evidently preferring to settle out of court, borrowed a musket. Resting the weapon on a picket fence, Groff waited for his accuser to appear. When Davis walked past Groff, Groff squeezed the trigger, and the musket ball severed the spinal column of his neighbor. Local authorities quickly arrested Groff, and a grand jury indicted him for murder. The case quickly became the subject of intense local controversy. Dubuque's *Iowa News* reported that "difficulty was experienced by reason of the community in general having formed and expressed an opinion" regarding the killing, making it "almost impossible to empanel an impartial jury."[27] The trial began the following month, with the attorney for the defense, R. D. Parker, arguing that the killing had been provoked by the repeated accusations by Davis against Groff. The jury found the argument persuasive, and after about four hours of deliberation, its members declared on May 9 that they found Groff not guilty of murder. Some of Bellevue's outraged residents were less convinced, and that night they hanged the jurors in effigy.[28] On the bust of one effigy juror were scrawled the words "Not guilty, your honor."[29]

The mock execution of the jurors in the Groff murder trial reflected a growing distrust of the formal legal system not only in Bellevue but across the United States. This skepticism regarding the efficacy or authority of the legal system emerged from a mixture of practical and ideological concerns. In rural places like Bellevue, many residents lived in isolated dwellings with no capacity to quickly sound an alarm or summon help in the case of an assault or robbery. A local sheriff might eventually attempt to respond to offenses already committed but was often in no position to prevent their occurrence. Even on the occasion that alleged criminals were caught, a lack of suitable jails further hampered the formal legal system. Many rural localities simply did not have a jail, and those that did often possessed relatively unsecure buildings. Contemporary references to captured horse thieves and counterfeiters in the Middle West were replete with mentions of escapes and jail breaks. In his confession, Cluse referenced both breaking out of jail himself and, on another occasion, assisting his friends in doing so using nothing more than hand tools.[30]

An ideological distrust of judicial authority amplified such frustrations. Throughout the 1830s, the Democratic Party had championed in its messaging a stated belief in popular sovereignty. Even the Democratic shift from caucuses to a more accessible system of conventions served to emphasize this belief, tying, in the words of legal scholar Larry Kramer, "decisions at each level to the popular will."[31] Building on the earlier Jeffersonian position, Jacksonian Democrats railed against what they perceived as aristocratic institutions and frameworks. Such supposedly anti-republican, elitist targets included the centralized bank, national economic planning, and the notion of "judicial supremacy"—the idea that legal authorities wielded final say over the meanings of the Constitution and the law. Rather, the Democrats, like Jefferson's Republicans before them, insisted on a belief in popular constitutionalism. That is, they maintained that it was the people, not the courts, who possessed ultimate authority over the law.[32]

This assertion stemmed in part from the older concept of an unwritten constitution, or, in the words of legal historian Farah Peterson, "a constitution of customary right." This unwritten constitution, rooted in the logic of the British legal tradition, concerned a relationship between the state and the people that limited governmental power and preserved what were perceived as ancient popular rights. A belief in this unwritten constitution predated and helped spark the American Revolution. It also persisted long after the ratification of the Constitution of 1787, visible at the popular level and in Jeffersonian ideology. It would be Andrew Jackson, however, who most forcibly reasserted the authority of this unwritten constitution over the formal legal system. Jackson's actions against the Cherokees in defiance of the courts were immoral, Peterson maintains, but should not be understood as "lawless." Rather, they signaled "the unwritten constitution reentering the weave of positive law."[33] Silent prerogatives, understood by Jackson to, in this case, include the forceful assertion of White supremacy, outweighed the protestations of legal elites.

This championing of the supremacy of the people—narrowly constructed—over the courts occurred in tandem with, and at times grated against, shifts within the American legal system itself. Reformers, particularly in the northern states, attempted to shift the posture of the penal system from, to borrow from Pfeifer, "retribution and deterrence to reform of the criminal."[34] This approach

included a sustained effort to abolish the death penalty. Many northern states narrowed their lists of capital crimes in the early decades
of the nineteenth century, and, beginning in the 1830s, some northern legislatures began debating the abolition of capital punishment
entirely.[35] Such reform efforts were part of a larger movement beginning in the late eighteenth century to professionalize the American
legal system and enshrine within it humanitarian and due process
rights. Especially in the Northeast, this movement sought to replace
a traditional system of punishment that emphasized spectacle and
communal notions of justice.[36]

Not all Americans celebrated these reformist transformations.
Some of those who recoiled at these changes to the formal legal system
combined the notion of popular sovereignty with historical precedent
to justify an entirely different paradigm of justice: Lynch law. Defenders of Lynch law—or the dispensation of extralegal collective violence
in pursuit of summary justice—argued that Americans reserved the
right in certain circumstances to take violent action beyond that generally permitted under law. Such circumstances were nebulous but
generally centered around perceived threats to persons, property, or
the communal order. The people, being in this framework the ultimate source of all constitutional law, were not in opposition to the law
when engaged in extralegal action but were rather simply exercising
an unwritten prerogative that was theirs by right. Democratic jour-
nalist Francis Grund articulated this position in 1837 when he wrote
that "Lynch law is not, properly speaking, an opposition to the established laws of the country, or is, at least, not contemplated as such by
its adherents; but rather as a supplement to them,—a species of common law, which is as old as the country."[37]

In fact, the roots of Lynch law were far older than the country. The
roots of lynching in the United States can be traced to an older English
tradition of crowd disorder, which employed riots, noise making, and
humiliating public punishments in response to perceived threats
against communal safety or morality.[38] English colonists carried
this tradition of crowd action with them when they settled in North
America. There, extralegal violence became increasingly associated
with disputes over property, even as practitioners continued to rely

on older justifications grounded upon notions of communal health. According to historian Paul Gilje, one-third of extralegal incidents in colonial America were related to land disputes.[39] Crowd disorder played a famously large role in the outbreak of the American Revolution, and it was during this time that a new word emerged to describe the administration of extralegal violence: "lynching."

While "lynching" as a term would eventually become associated with the extralegal killings of Black Americans, it was not initially associated solely with racially motivated violence. Nor, for that matter, did it necessarily refer to killing at all. The earliest mentions of lynching generally appeared in reference to nonlethal extralegal punishments like flogging or tar and feathering.[40] Named after Virginian justice of the peace and Revolutionary War militia officer Charles Lynch, "Lynch's law" originally referred to the extralegal whipping of pro-British loyalists by Lynch and his men.[41] While the post–Independence transition to representative government delegitimized "politics out of doors" in certain corners of society, many Americans continued to invoke the "Spirit of the Revolution" to justify their use of extralegal violence.[42] For Virginians seeking to impose on others their own notions of justice outside the law, references to "lynching" offered one such rhetorical justification. "Lynch law" as an expression and practice traveled with Virginian migrants throughout the South and into the Middle West, remaining a regional idiom for nonlethal extralegal punishment for several decades following the Revolution.

In the 1830s, the Democratic valorization of popular sovereignty occurred in the context of an increasingly violent and volatile United States.[43] In 1835, a mob in Vicksburg, Mississippi, hanged five gamblers following a shooting. The mass extralegal execution was shocking. It captivated the attention of the press. Newspapers across the nation published accounts of the "Lynch law," introducing the word "lynching" to a wider national audience.[44] Some papers, especially in the South, defended the killings. Apologists cast aspersions on the deficiencies of the formal legal system while asserting the right of the people to defend their communities.[45] Lynching, from this point on, would be increasingly associated with lethal violence.

The press's interest in the Vicksburg killings reflected a society that had grown more turbulent throughout the 1830s. In the cities, demographic, social, and economic changes led to a surge of destructive riot violence structured around racial and ethnic divides. In the rural South, planters used cruel, often ritualized killings to discourage slave revolts. Violent opposition to those who would challenge enslavement was not relegated to the South; anti-abolitionist riots also shook northern states, including one 1837 incident in Alton, Illinois, that saw a mob kill abolitionist Elijah Lovejoy.[46] In Missouri, tensions over identity and land led to the 1838 Mormon War, which ended with the expulsion of the Mormon population from the state following a glut of death and destruction.

For the moment, however, such grisly scenes remained the exception rather than the rule. While extralegal activity did surge throughout the 1830s, it was only the most bombastic and bloodiest instances of violence that captured the attention of the press and nation. The overwhelming majority of extralegal incidents continued to remain limited to nonlethal action. In fact, the known number of instances of lethal extralegal violence per 100,000 residents in the United States between 1831 and 1840, while higher than the four decades prior, was still lower than the rate of such violence between 1783 and 1790.[47] Most extralegal incidents continued to revolve around supposed threats to a community or perceived property violations, and were generally settled through whipping, banishment, property destruction, or some form of humiliating spectacle. In 1830s Iowa, this included the flogging of alleged counterfeiters, thieves, and claim jumpers, as well as the tar and feathering of one man falsely accused of abusing a person with an intellectual disability.[48] The general form and application of vigilante activity had not itself undergone many substantial changes in the 1830s and remained largely consistent with the traditional practice of such violence. It was, rather, the hardening rhetoric around this sort of extralegal violence that signaled the potential coming of a radical shift.

It was within these winds that the whispers against William W. Brown flew. Brown's large networks of friends and clients only served to make those whispers louder. Around 1839, Brown's associate and fellow Elkhart migrant, Thomas J. Babcock, came under suspicion of operating a counterfeiting operation in Farmington, Iowa Territory. Babcock, along with his cousin, another former Elkhart resident by the name of Edward Bonney, allegedly brought to Farmington a large quantity of bogus coins from Indiana, which they passed through the community. One Farmington resident, James Thomas, recounted that the "common and general belief" was that Babcock and Bonney belonged to a larger "gang of horse thieves and counterfeiters," and, under increasing public pressure, both men eventually departed the community for good.[49]

At the same time, residents of Bellevue became increasingly convinced that their own county was infested with criminals. Such anxieties, which resident A. H. Wilson later dismissed as "exaggerated," were nonetheless real and not limited to Brown's merchant rivals. Joseph Henrie, a Brown sympathizer, insisted that the "country at that time was overrun with horse thieves and counterfeiters."[50] With this mood of suspicion in the air, some of the locals began to complain about the conduct and character of the men employed by Brown as woodcutters. Sheriff Warren later claimed that the winter periods when Brown's woodcutters labored coincided with surges in the circulation of counterfeit currency.[51] Even Wilson, a defender of Brown, admitted that "he had a tough set of men about his hotel."[52] Brown, for his part, attempted to maintain local goodwill by promising to replace with good money any counterfeit received at any of his operations.[53]

The rumors about Brown's criminal activities did little, however, to seriously damage Brown's reputation among the masses. In the summer of 1839, the hotel keeper's popularity earned him his most powerful enemy yet—Thomas Cox. The fifty-two-year-old Cox was a local big man, in both a literal and metaphorical sense. He stood over six feet tall, weighed some 250 pounds, and had dark blue eyes perched above a long black beard.[54] A veteran of the War of 1812 and the Black Hawk War, Cox had been elected to Iowa's first territorial legislature and was, to use Sheriff Warren's language, the "war-horse" of Jackson County's Democratic establishment.[55] He possessed a forceful magnetism and an athletic, masculine reputation. Anson H. Wilson, hardly a Cox sympathizer, remarked that the colonel was "one of the finest species of physical manhood he ever met."[56] He was also a violent, unstable alcoholic.

Thomas Cox liked whiskey. The old soldier was reportedly "fond of company and whiskey, and never at his best among the first until he was full of the last."[57] Alcohol was an invaluable political asset for ambitious populists, and Cox had first won his seat, according to one Bellevue settler, by generously supplying liquor until "he became acquainted with nearly every one in the country."[58] This heavy campaigning took its toll. Cox would appear in public so drunk that he could not fully control his own facial muscles, with the juice from his tobacco chew leaking from his numbed mouth into his long black beard.[59] Perhaps unsurprisingly, Cox formed a friendship with the keeper of a local public house: none other than William W. Brown. Cox initially dismissed the rumors spread by Brown's rivals, viewing the hotel keeper, according to Sheriff Warren, as a "persecuted man."[60]

Politics changed all that. The summer of 1839 saw Cox prepare for reelection. Before he could campaign for a seat in the territorial legislature, though, Cox would need to secure nomination from a Democratic party convention. He felt good about his chances. Having liberally canvassed the county with his preferred method of "campaigning," Cox believed that he maintained a secure influence over his electorate. Subsequently he neglected the convention, which he dismissed as a "mere formality."[61] When the convention concluded, however, Cox found, to his "amazement," that he had been defeated by "a vote of two to one." His political calculus failed to account for the burgeoning popularity of a local hotel keeper. William W. Brown had secured the Democratic nomination for the territorial legislature.[62]

Colonel Cox was not the kind of man to accept such a defeat gracefully. His own ally, Sheriff Warren, characterized Cox as a "high tempered man." Enraged by what he saw as a betrayal, Cox began to rabidly denounce Brown, at least in private.[63] Grasping for evidence with which to strike at a man of whom he suddenly found himself "politically jealous," Cox found a ready-made rhetorical weapon in the grumbling of Brown's merchant rivals. Modifying a familiar cadence of accusation with a call to action, Cox, according to one contemporary, "told his friends, Brown was getting rich too fast to get it honestly and that he thought there was a gang of horse thieves and counterfeiters at Brown's, and he proposed driving them out of the country."[64] Coming from Cox, this was not empty bluster. The colonel had allegedly engaged in prior lethal extralegal action while he was a resident of Illinois. During a protective association meeting earlier in 1839, Cox referred to his Illinois victims when he claimed that "we rid the country of them and found the most effectual means to be the hemp."[65]

While Cox did not specify the incident in which he had taken part, Illinois was, throughout the 1820s and 1830s, a hotbed for "regulator"—an older term for vigilante—violence. During this period, groups of regulators targeted alleged thieves and counterfeiters across Clay, Morgan, Scott, Edgar, Washington, Jefferson, and Pope counties.[66] While lashing remained standard practice, the extralegal collective violence as practiced in Illinois was sometimes a rougher form of Lynch law. One English traveler reported in the 1820s that the regulators of Moore's Prairie, frustrated that a flogging had not sufficed to drive out one targeted family, seized the family patriarch, "punished him severely, and cut off his ears."[67] Regulator action could also, at times, result in the use of lethal force. In 1823 Pope County, a band of men assaulted the fortified home of the Sturdivant family, who were accused of counterfeiting. The ensuing firefight saw one man killed and two more seriously wounded.[68] Since Cox had publicly associated himself with this tradition of violence, his accusations conveyed a tangible threat.

This escalation caused Bellevue to divide into two distinct camps, made up of Brown's supporters and the coalition of his accusers. Those opposed to Brown generally came from Bellevue's middle class, which both resented and suspected the innkeeper's success. Brown found supporters among his closer business associates, workers, and many of the community's poorer residents. Such nascent factionalism emerged in the context of sustained criminality in

Jackson County. On September 14, 1839, two men with "muffled up" faces entered the home of Dennis and Mary Collins. One of the intruders beat Dennis with a club and threatened to kill him while his partner began to loot a nearby chest. When the pregnant Mary attempted to stop him from taking the valuables, the man knocked her to the ground and stomped on her crumpled figure. When she cried out in pain, her assailant threatened to "stamp her guts out." The brutal assault caused Mary to miscarry her unborn child, and locals did not initially expect that Mary herself would survive.[69]

Some locals accused two of Brown's woodcutters, Arnold Godfrey and William Fox, of having committed the crime. Just five days before the robbery, William Brown and Dennis Collins had settled a legal dispute.[70] Several witnesses, including Bellevue blacksmith Henderson Palmer, claimed to have seen Godfrey riding out of town on September 14 while wearing a green overcoat similar to that worn by one of the assailants. Others, however, swore that Godfrey had spent the night in their company miles away from the Collins's home. The Collinses were unable to positively identify their attackers, and with little proof otherwise, the matter was dropped. The accusations, however, hardened already bitter feelings between the Brown and Cox factions. The posture of Brown himself, though, seemed to be at least overtly a conciliatory one, with his ledgers revealing that he continued to engage in a healthy business with some of his rivals and accusers.[71] If nothing else, Brown remained a pragmatic businessman.

As the autumn months gave way to winter, Bellevue continued to experience intermittent controversies related to purported property rights violations. That winter, a Mr. Kendall of Wisconsin Territory reportedly had a horse stolen, and, accompanied by a Mr. Pitts of Galena, Illinois, had come to Bellevue in pursuit. Joined by Sheriff Warren, the two men could find no trace of the horse and set off again to search elsewhere. Again, locals leveled accusations against Brown's men. Warren claimed that a resident of Camanche had confided in him that three men had passed him counterfeit notes while transporting a horse with a description similar to the stolen animal. The three men in question were William Fox, Stephen Brown, and Levi

Brown. The trio had apparently returned with two different horses. Brown allegedly took possession of the horses from the men and sold one to Bellevue resident Thomas Graham. Warren claimed that this horse too was stolen but lacked any real proof. Nothing came of the affair besides increased mutual enmity.[72] Meanwhile, residents of Sand Prairie, Illinois, began to complain about the theft of hogs and cattle. One man, John Donner, tracked the hoofprints of his stolen cattle through the fresh fallen snow. The trail led him to Bellevue, but again, a lack of tangible evidence forced the man to leave empty-handed.[73] It was around this time that members of the anti-Brown faction may have begun to harass a more vulnerable member of Brown's network—Levi Brown.[74]

Levi Brown, one of Iowa's few Black residents, lived with his wife in a cabin on one of the islands opposite Bellevue.[75] Records reveal a close association between Levi Brown and William W. Brown. He was one of William Brown's woodcutters, while his wife labored as the crew's cook. In addition, his open account with William Brown totaled a whopping $347.82—one of the largest of the accounts found in the hotel keeper's ledgers.[76] While the actual dynamics of the relationship between the two men cannot be known, Levi Brown may have been attempting to provide greater security for his family in accepting the patronage of an influential White member of the community. In 1839, Iowa's territorial legislature had instituted a restrictive and racist "black code" intended to curtail the legal agency of Black residents and limit further Black migration into the territory. Not only did Black migrants need to produce a certificate of freedom, but they had to pay the deliberately onerous bond of $500 before settling in the territory. Perhaps most egregious and dangerous, though, was the law barring Black Iowans from testifying "in any court or in any case against a white person."[77] In neighboring Illinois, a similar "black code" had facilitated a rash of kidnappings directed against free Black middle westerners, who, like the Browns, lived along waterways. Historian M. Scott Heerman finds evidence of 118 kidnappings of Black residents in Illinois between 1830 and 1860.[78] Their captors generally trafficked Black victims of kidnapping downriver into southern states and sold them into enslavement. Given these perils, ties with influential White community members could prove not only advantageous but necessary for Black residents of the Middle West.

In this case, however, such ties became themselves dangerous. The anti-Brown faction had failed to damage William W. Brown in any substantial way through the allegations hurled against Fox, Godfrey, or any of his other White associates. Members of this faction may have perceived Levi Brown as a more socially and legally vulnerable member of William Brown's network and as a more promising prospect around which to build a case against the hotel keeper. Sheriff Warren would later claim that, following the Sand Prairie livestock thefts, a group of White Bellevue residents conducted a search of the area around Levi Brown's cabin. When they found some barrels of meat, the men seized and interrogated Mrs. Brown, Levi's wife. She denied having knowledge of any stolen meat and insisted that a man by the name of Driscoll regularly supplied the meat for feeding the woodcutters. Once again, for want of evidence, the White party released Mrs. Brown.

The implicit threat bundled into this allegation was not the same faced by William Brown's other men who had been similarly harassed. For Levi Brown and his wife, accusations of theft, even if they were baseless, presented an acute danger. The extralegal collective violence of the 1830s, influenced by the ideology of Jacksonian democracy, had become increasingly structured around the maintenance of White supremacy.[79] The mob violence directed against Black Americans, enslaved or free, was oftentimes far more brutal than action directed against White targets. While most famously typified by the southern mobs who burned several Black victims alive, such White supremacism was not relegated to violence in slaveholding regions.[80] In nearby Dubuque, just months after the Bellevue War, a Black man named Nathaniel "Nat" Morgan was accused of stealing some clothing. A "drunken rabble" seized Morgan, tortured him into a false confession, and flogged him to death with such viciousness that his back was "broken, and his ribs and sides all stove in!"[81] Accusations of crime, even if false or minor, could be a death sentence. The search of Levi Brown's property, the seizure of his wife, and the accusation of thievery were together undoubtedly intended as an aggressive shot across the bow. The message was clear: Associate with William W. Brown at your own risk.

By the coming of the new year, these factional tensions had torn Bellevue's social fabric apart. The holiday festivities had done little to soothe the conflict, with the "scowling countenances" of Brown's sympathizers discouraging public revelry on the part of the anti-Brown crowd.[82] Some members of that faction, unwilling to be intimidated out of Bellevue's social world, planned a large ball at Anson Harrington's hotel for January 8 in commemoration of Jackson's 1815 victory at New Orleans. One of the men in charge of planning the ball was thirty-year-old merchant James Comly Mitchell. A former sailor standing just 5'5," Mitchell possessed a "very dogmatic and aggressive personality."[83] He had previously done business with Brown and, in October 1839, had supplied the hotel keeper with three loans worth a combined total of $230.[84] By January, however, Mitchell had become a fervent supporter of the anti-Brown faction and openly declared "that none of the horse thieves and counterfeiters shall attend the ball."[85]

On the night of January 8, a warm glow and the sound of music drifted out from Harrington's hotel. Inside, Mitchell and company made merry. Outside, a group of men moved through the snow. They were not attending the ball. With a sleigh in tow, they made their way toward James Mitchell's home. The argumentative Mitchell had recently antagonized his brother, Joshua. James had supposedly refused to surrender to Joshua some property, so Joshua, taking advantage of his brother's preoccupation with the dance, sought to organize some men to seize the property under the cover of darkness. He found those men among Brown's supporters, who were disgruntled by Mitchell's insulting and accusatory conduct. James Thompson, Brown's young business associate, had a particularly acrimonious relationship with James Mitchell. Thompson had been drinking and readily joined the group. Absalom Montgomery, one of Brown's men and a juror from the controversial Groff murder trial, also joined in, as well as Samuel Burtis Jr., whose father had operated the slaughterhouse in partnership with Brown.[86] When the crew arrived at Mitchell's home, they prepared to load the contested property into their sleigh. They discovered, however, that the building had not been left unoccupied.

Thirteen-year-old Jane Hadley had been staying with the Mitchells but had not joined them in attending the ball that night. James Thompson found her lying in bed. He asked her who she was and how old she was. He then told her he would "come to bed" with her. Hadley tried to scream for help but later testified that Thompson threatened to kill her, a statement corroborated by Montgomery's own testimony. Underlining this threat, Hadley "felt pistols and bowie knife" press against her as Thompson forced himself on top of her. Hadley tried to fight back and push Thompson away but was not strong enough. "He choked me until I was blind," she later testified, "said if I told of it he would kill me."[87] The brutality of the rape caused Hadley to lose consciousness. Still, Hadley defied Thompson's attempt to threaten her into silence. When she "came to," she ran through the snow to the home of her father, Nehemiah Hadley, and reported the assault.[88]

Although it was an innocent child who suffered, James Thompson's rape of Jane Hadley was also intended as an act of violence directed against James Mitchell. Burtis later testified that Thompson, after having assaulted Hadley, told him that "he thought it was Mitchell's daughter when he went to the bed and wished it had been."[89] The ordering of the household for many middle-class men like Thompson and Mitchell revolved around the patriarch's ability to protect, provide for, and control his dependents. In this framework, a rape was considered an affront to the family patriarch as much as it was an act of sexual violence against the victim. Reflecting this, contemporary discussions of rape generally revolved not around female victims but instead around their male relatives.[90] That Thompson expressed regret at not having raped Mitchell's daughter reflects this androcentric understanding of sexual violence. Thompson had not raped a member of Mitchell's immediate family but had still violated a ward under Mitchell's roof. Mitchell would have to respond.

Word of the rape soon reached Mitchell, who left the ball and borrowed a gun. Thompson, expecting a violent response, offered Burtis a pistol and asked him to come with him to confront Mitchell. Burtis refused, prompting Thompson to label him a "damn coward."[91] Thompson and Montgomery left and began to make their way towards Harrington's hotel. They met Mitchell in the street. In the cold dark, Mitchell asked Montgomery who he was, receiving the response "it is none of your business." Montgomery, evidently possessing no stomach for a fight, walked past Mitchell. As Montgomery moved forward, he heard one of the men cry out "Now damn you, if you want anything of me, now is your time." Montgomery turned around to see both men grasping each other around the shoulder. A gunshot rang out. Thompson fell to the ground, exclaiming "he has killed me, shoot him." Mitchell remained standing, bleeding "profusely" from a knife wound on left side of his face.[92]

Word of the killing raced through the town. According to Warren, Brown and his men soon arrived. They were armed and calling for vengeance. They might have lynched Mitchell, but Warren insisted that he would take Mitchell into custody and justice would be served. This was enough for Brown, who convinced his men to leave. Brown then privately encouraged the sheriff to position a strong guard around the house where Mitchell was to be confined as "the boys were all getting drunk and there was no telling what might happen under the circumstances."[93] Brown also counseled Samuel Burtis Jr. not to testify for Mitchell at his examination. Brown told Burtis that if he did so, "he would be shot," but it is unclear if this was intended as a threat or as a warning from a place of genuine concern. Given Brown's advice to the sheriff, which betrayed a belief that he could not control his own supporters, the latter seems a likely possibility. Whatever Brown's true intentions, Mitchell's killing of Thompson had transformed the factional conflict into a violent one. According to Henrie, "wildest excitement was created by this incident, as the two men represented the two factions, and the break between the factions was considerably widened and both sides went armed at all times."[94]

These tensions did not abate over the weeks that followed. More than seventy years after the conclusion of the Bellevue War, the *Bellevue Leader* published a document that seemed to reveal the existence of a secret, formalized pact signed by members of the anti-Brown faction. The oath, dated March 9 and signed by Cox, Warren, Harrington, Moss, Sublett, and other prominent community members, pledged to "expell from the Town of Bellevue W. W. Brown . . . together with all others of like character and occupation."[95] While there were no surviving signees who could confirm or deny the document's authenticity, there is no question that the potential for violence charged the atmosphere in Bellevue. On March 17, an associate of Brown's, Dexter Hapgood, stole two ploughs off the deck of the steamboat *Elba*. Authorities arrested Hapgood, but the episode aroused the usual indignation among the anti-Brown faction.[96] Brown, ever the charmer, continued to do business with his rivals. On March 12, Brown bought flooring from John Sublett, one of the purported signees of the secret March 17 pact. On March 25, he issued a third loan to John Cox, the brother of the man with whom he had had his most dramatic falling-out.[97] Such olive branches would not suffice.

On the same day that Brown issued the loan to John Cox, Sherriff Warren, Anson Harrington, John Sublett, and William Dyas traveled to Dubuque to meet with lawyers. One of these men wrote up a list of charges against William Brown and those belonging to his network of associates, and Anson Harrington swore to their veracity. The charges concerned passing counterfeit, thieving, and robbing. Charles Harris, a justice of the peace, then issued a warrant for the arrest of Brown and his men. In arresting all the men in a single sweep, the anti-Brown faction hoped to prevent the men from testifying on each other's behalf. When Warren returned to Bellevue and attempted to read the warrant, Brown's men surrounded the sheriff, "making many bitter threats." Brown, ever the diplomat, addressed the angry crowd and emphasized that Warren was only doing his duty. The men then turned their anger against Anson Harrington, who had sworn to the charges in the warrant. Again, the Browns intervened. Betsy Brown warned Harrington that the pro-Brown men were out for vengeance, and he subsequently fled to Illinois.

The Brown family was now engaged in furious diplomacy to avert bloodshed. Betsy Brown called on the hostile Moss family that night, and on the following evening, William accepted a message from Warren by way of John Sublett, whom he "received . . . kindly." Brown informed Sublett that "he would willingly surrender himself and abide the decision of the law if this would satisfy the warrant" but insisted that the rest of the men named be left alone. He also offered to simply depart Bellevue if reimbursed with two-thirds of the appraised value of his property there.[98] Having received this offer, Warren, Colonel Cox, Sublett, and other prominent members of the anti-Brown faction huddled in Moss's store. Deciding to ignore Brown's offer, the committee directed Warren to summon a posse comitatus consisting of local residents. They would march on Brown's hotel in a show of force that they believed would be enough to compel Brown and all his supporters to surrender. News of the meeting leaked within hours, and Brown and his allies immediately began to fortify the hotel. They unfurled a red flag with a message of resolve inscribed in front of the wood structure. Now, this was a matter of "Victory or Death."[99]

Warren attempted to move quickly to raise a force with which to march on Brown's redoubt. This effort was a resounding failure. Some declined to involve themselves physically, offering only to send letters urging peaceful surrender, while "other good men looked upon Brown as a persecuted man and declined taking any part in the way of advice or otherwise." Brown continued to enjoy the sympathy and support of a large section of the local population, and they simply refused to take arms against him. On March 31 in nearby Sabula, the sheriff only managed to induce a single resident—James McCabe— to join his posse. Unable to raise his own force, Warren deputized Cox and instructed him to gather forty men by ten o'clock on April 1. Cox also initially struggled to find willing fighters. This frustration caused the colonel's temper to flare. Anson H. Wilson later recalled that when he refused to join the posse, Cox "threatened him that he might be the next victim after Brown."[100] Unable to draw on much local support outside the members of the anti-Brown faction, Cox called on his contacts from outside of the county and his former comrades from the Black Hawk War.[101]

William Brown would not face this force alone. Many of his supporters and woodcutters took up arms in his defense, including William Fox, Samuel Chichister, Stephen Brown, Richard Fuller, Levi Trask, James Smith, Patrick Connolly, A. J. McDonald, David Knox, and more. Others who arrived to defend the hotel included the beneficiaries of Brown's generosity and charity, including Aaron Day and Thomas Welch. Day, who had done well for himself and secured a land claim of his own, had reportedly declared that "if Brown had to go he would go with him."[102] Samuel Burtis Sr., Brown's old business associate, also set up in the fortified hotel. Levi Brown, despite the threats already leveled against himself and his family, similarly joined the defense. Betsy Brown too remained defiantly in the hotel. The defenders prepared about thirty muskets, in addition to pistols, knives, and a half-dozen pitchforks for hand-to-hand combat.

On April 1, the sun dawned over a town girded for violence. Brown's supporters manned the hotel's parapets and patrolled the surrounding streets. Connolly, holding the red "Victory or Death" flag aloft, marched up and down the street, bellowing that "if they wanted hell, to come on."[103] Four blocks away, Cox quartered his men in a building owned by Richard Burk. A deadly exchange almost erupted when Anson Harrington and reinforcements from Illinois attempted to join up with Cox and Warren's force, but Brown again restrained his men. Meanwhile, Cox and Warren produced another warrant for Brown's arrest, this one issued by posse member and justice of the peace George Watkins. Alone, Warren made his way to Brown's hotel to again attempt to serve the warrant.

Passing through the hostile lines, Warren found Brown, who received him "very gentlemanly." Warren, William, and Betsy moved to a private room, where William made the sheriff a new offer. He and his men would surrender if Warren, John Sublett, George Watkins, H. K. Magoon, and Jerry Jonas would all pledge to protect them "from any violence." Warren agreed to these terms and left to fetch the requested parties. On Warren's return, however, Brown ordered the other men back and, taking the sheriff aside, told him that he had been unable to convince his men to lay down their arms. Brown informed the sheriff that "they had determined to defend themselves the best they could." Warren feared he would be held as a hostage.

An alarm from the hotel's porch rang out, interrupting Brown. Cox, evidently impatient with the negotiations, had ordered his men to advance. Brown directed his men to their fighting positions, released Warren, and told him to stop Cox and then return. Events now threatened to spiral rapidly out of control. A sheriff could, by law, summon and command a posse comitatus. Warren, however, was no longer in command. Cox now led what had become an armed mob.

Women and children fled from the buildings that lay between the two bands, retreating to the safer outskirts of the town. James C. Mitchell, still under house arrest for the killing of Thompson, begged to join the posse. Warren denied this request but furnished him with weapons. Warren later claimed that Brown's men were drunk and that the armed party led by himself and Cox were completely sober. This assessment was challenged by Henrie, who described the so-called posse as drinking out of "coffee pots which were filled with whiskey" at Moss's store. Cox, Henrie continued, "was very drunk himself."[104] Instead of stopping Cox, Warren fell in with his men, and the party advanced to within thirty paces of Brown's hotel. Men with muskets peered out of their window embrasures on the hotel's top floor. On the porch, William Brown stood at the front door, his musket raised to his shoulder, and pointed at Thomas Cox. Betsy stood next to William, holding additional loaded muskets to hand to her husband. Cox, pointing his own pistol back at Brown, called on the hotel keeper to surrender and promised that if he did so, he would not be hurt.

Tension gripped the moment. One errant twitch from either man could send musket balls flying and cost lives. Brown, with his wife by his side, made one last attempt at making peace. He began to lower his musket. As the gun dropped, however, it misfired. A musket ball exploded out of the barrel, embedding into the ground.[105] Jolted by the shot, someone opened fire. It was unclear who fired first. Two men from Cox and Warren's party aimed their muskets at Brown and squeezed their triggers.[106] Two musket balls burst through William Brown's head: one through his temple and the other below his ear. He died instantly, his body crumpling to the ground next to his wife. The battle now began in earnest.

Brown's hotel soon filled with smoke as its defenders opened the throats of their weapons and launched hot lead at the party below. Several of the attacking party fell wounded; some, like William Vaughn, were severely injured. Aaron Day, the young man who had been saved from ruin by Brown's charity, stepped out of the smoke onto the hotel's porch, aiming his gun at local blacksmith Henderson Palmer, a member of the attacking party. His ball found its mark, and Palmer collapsed dead. Day attempted to fall back into cover but was himself struck by a ball and slumped onto the porch, his head hanging off the side. Not dead but wounded, his "groans and cries were pitiful to hear." A noncombatant, Andrew Farley, declared he could not "stand this any longer" and ran to carry Day away. As he attempted to lift the young man, he too was struck, his body falling limply on top of Day's. Cox and Warren's men pushed forward, forcing their way into the hotel and engaging in "hand-to-hand" combat with the defenders, who soon retreated to the building's upper level. Unable to ascend the stairs, the attacking party started a fire with the intention of forcing the defenders to choose between surrender or suffocation.[107]

Realizing the desperation of their situation, the defenders who were still able-bodied leapt from a window onto the roof of a shed and made their escape. Levi Brown and six others successfully managed to evacuate in this fashion. Victorious, Cox and Warren's party extinguished the flames and captured six still-living defenders who had been unable to flee. The corpses of attackers Henderson Palmer, John Brink, and J. Maxwell bled on the ground. The defenders had lost William Brown and Aaron Day. Attacker William Vaughn and defender Samuel Burtis Sr. both possessed wounds that would soon prove fatal. Other men, though they did not end up dying, bled

Illustration showing the attack on Brown's hotel. From John W. Barber and Henry Howe, *The Loyal West in the Times of the Rebellion* (Cincinnati: F. A. Howe, 1865), 521. Courtesy of the Library of Congress.

from wounds of varying severity. Tom Welch, Brown's young stable-boy, had been shot through the side, and the company thought he was dead. When Charley Kilgore saw Welch move, he reportedly exclaimed, "Well, Tom, you are not dead yet," and fired his pistol at Welch's face. Welch had lifted a hand to defend himself, and the ball passed through his hand, missing his head.[108] An attacker from Illinois then approached and kicked him three times before one of the Kirkpatricks intervened. Some of Cox and Warren's men loudly advocated for hanging the prisoners immediately, but Cox entreated them to wait until morning, after the dead and wounded had been addressed. Henrie took a horse to Dubuque to find physicians, while others rode to Galena. By this time, relatives had begun to appear at the scene, some weeping over the corpses of the fallen. Brown's captured men were placed under guard in the hotel.[109]

The "more prominent citizens" then held a meeting at James L. Kirkpatrick's house to discuss the fate of the prisoners. Warren and several others insisted that the men should be made to answer the charges set forth in the warrant and be surrendered to the formal legal system. Cox and Harrington disagreed, arguing that there was no jail to hold them and that there existed a genuine possibility of a counterattack or rescue by Brown sympathizers. Given the trouble Cox and Warren had in recruiting men, this presented a very real concern. Cox and Harrington, Warren recounted, continued making their argument, insisting that "no man's life or property would be safe, and as we now had them in our power . . . nothing short of death would satisfy the community." The group agreed to meet at 10 a.m. the following morning, when they would vote to decide the prisoners' fates.[110]

On the morning of April 2, two hours before the vote, a steamer from Dubuque arrived at Bellevue. Rev. Thomas J. Babcock, the alleged counterfeiter and Brown's old associate, stepped off the boat. Warren believed that Babcock had arrived to collect some property from Brown's store. Cox's men recognized Babcock and seized him. Babcock begged Cox for protection. The colonel directed his men not to hurt Babcock but then turned to address the preacher. "We will treat you well today," Cox spat, "but damn you, we will hang you tomorrow." The men led away the "trembling and praying" Babcock and placed him with the other prisoners. Cooler heads soon prevailed, however, and Brown's old associate was summarily released after making a vow to never set foot in Bellevue again.[111]

Attention now turned toward the prisoners. At 10 a.m., Colonel Cox addressed them. He blamed the previous day's loss of life on the men having not promptly surrendered and informed them that, as a consequence of their actions, the sheriff was now relieved of duty. The captors would decide and administer their own justice. One of the prisoners, Samuel Chichister, then addressed the assembly, begging for mercy in "a low and trembling voice," in what Warren described as "one of the most fearful appeals I have ever heard." Chichister insisted that the prisoners would admit guilt and accept punishment if their lives were spared. William Fox and Levi Trask both allegedly made confessions.[112] Crawford, the attorney who had drawn up the first warrant, then advocated again for the prisoners to be handed over to the formal legal system, even as he acknowledged the lack of a suitable jail and the possibility of a counterattack.

Harrington, whose life had been saved by Betsy Brown just days prior, then rose and began to advocate for killing every last prisoner. He argued, according to Warren, that "they were all desperate characters. They were lost to all sense of honor. They were past reformation. No man's life or property was safe with them at large." Harrington continued, invoking Christianity, law, community, and property rights as he railed to have the men killed. It was the "higher duty," Harrington insisted, that the men be hanged, their dangling corpses transformed into "an example" to others. He closed his bloodthirsty appeal with a proposition to hold a vote. The captors would have two choices: either the prisoners would be executed or they would be whipped and banished. A simple majority would decide. The assembled captors agreed to these terms. [113]

Using white and colored beans to vote, the captors, one by one, deposited their preferences in a ballot box. After the vote concluded, two men counted the tally. They presented their results to Cox, who announced that, with a three-vote majority, those in favor of whipping over execution had won. The captors then "lynched" their victims in the traditional sense, administering fifty lashes each to Fox, Fuller, Chichester, and Trask. Connolly received thirty-nine. Another prisoner named Bartlett received no lashes for unclear reasons.[114] Thomas Welch, who had fought for Brown, was not counted among the prisoners, probably on account of his already life-threatening wounds. The captors then placed the defeated party in skiffs and banished the entire lot from Bellevue.[115]

Competing accounts of the Bellevue War emerged immediately. On April 4, public prosecutor J. V. Berry wrote an urgent letter to Governor Robert Lucas from Dubuque describing a county in "a state of complete disorganization." Berry called the men under Cox's command the "most infamous mob that ever was assembled," and described Brown as a "peaceable citizen," warning that Cox, Warren, and Moss planned to divide the slain hotel keeper's property among themselves. Furthermore, Berry claimed that Mitchell, still ostensibly awaiting trial, was "now let loose rejoicing with the good and pious mob citizens at this freedom from all the restraints of regulated society, law and good order." Berry concluded his letter by begging the governor to bring "to justice base and foul murderers."[116] Two days later, Dubuque's postmaster, John King, penned his own letter to the governor, similarly deploring the "mob" violence that had transpired. "Brown fell like a *brave man*," King insisted, "defending *his wife* and *child* from insults, and his property from the ravages of a reckless and lawless mob." King went on to describe a Dubuque public meeting so large that not all in attendance could fit in the church where it was held. The meeting produced resolutions calling for the removal of all public officials involved in the attack on Brown's hotel. The postmaster argued that either a new sheriff be appointed for Jackson County to arrest the perpetrators or the territorial militia be raised and deployed. Echoing Berry, King also claimed that Mitchell "was immediately turned out of prison and is now walking the streets."[117]

Several newspapers, however, were more sympathetic to the narrative of the anti-Brown faction. Burlington's *Iowa Territorial Gazette* published an account on April 4 describing Brown as a "notorious scoundrel" at the head of "horse thieves, counterfeiters and robbers." The paper endorsed the extralegal methods of the assault, writing that "not only the persons who by law are clothed with power and authority should be active in fereting out and bringing to punishment the numerous villains who openly practice counterfeiting and horse stealing in some of the counties of the Territory."[118] Galena's *North Western Gazette and Galena Advertiser* similarly described Brown and his men as "Horse Thieves" in an April 10 account and endorsed the dispensation of extralegal punishment. Discussing the fact that the men were "lynched," the paper argued that "this was, undoubtedly, the most proper course to take. Such a punishment has often worked wonders in the reforming way."[119]

Governor Lucas did nothing to address the violence. Citing the *Iowa Territorial Gazette* article in his response to Berry, the governor, influenced by the anti-Brown newspaper reporting, made it clear that he believed the affair remained an issue for the courts to resolve and that he would not intervene.[120] In Bellevue itself, the triumphant party was, according to Henrie, "arrogant and abusive to all those who had not sided with them."[121] In August, Cox would win reelection to a third term in the legislature. Four years later, he would be dead, stricken with pneumonia and "liver congestion."[122] A grand jury indicted James C. Mitchell for murder on April 17, but he won a "not guilty" verdict on June 19. All the while, claimants filed suit against the Brown estate, crowding around the $11,644.87 inventory like crows greedily picking flesh off a ribcage.[123] None other than Anson Harrington was the probate judge. Betsy Brown remained in Bellevue for a few months during this settling of the estate, working with Shadrach Burleson, who had been a friend to the family. Sometime in the fall of 1840, she departed the town that had killed her husband and devoured her property, returning to a brother in Michigan.[124] Burleson, for his part, struggled to collect the debts owed to the Brown estate. Anson H. Wilson later asked why he did not simply sue to recover the money. "If you sue the devil and have the trial in hell," Burleson reportedly retorted, "what show have you got for a favorable verdict?"[125]

In fact, almost every critical player involved in the Bellevue War had reason to fear a "trial in hell." Cox and Warren did not lead a legitimate posse comitatus but a mob—a mob largely composed of men motivated by political rivalries and financial jealousies more than any organic concern for community safety. Any legal pretense their group possessed had vanished when Cox took command and marched on the hotel. At the same time, Brown did arguably pose a genuine threat to community safety, even if this was not what motivated the core of his opponents. Brown did associate closely with known counterfeiters like Babcock and rapists like Thompson, and some of his men would, in the years that followed, be connected to sophisticated horse thieving rings and murder. Still, Brown's rivals could hardly produce evidence against most of Brown's men, much less Brown himself, and mired genuine concerns in the muck of rumor and accusation. No party implicated in the killing that April day could claim innocence, even as partisans would, in the decades that followed, argue to their respective villainy or virtue. So twisted were their networks of interest, rivalry, and association that neither party could trust that the adjudication of the formal legal system would result in a favorable verdict. A violent confrontation may have been, especially for the anti-Brown faction, the only acceptable conclusion. They had failed to prosecute any of Brown's allies and would surely have met with a similar outcome in trying to prosecute all at once.

So, rather than "sue the devil," they shot him. Two musket balls in Brown's head and a slate of floggings resulted in material and political outcomes for the anti-Brown faction more favorable than any that could have been achieved in the courts. They were able to accomplish this by weaving into the older understandings of extra-legal collective action the newer Jacksonian rhetoric concerning the people, the law, and violence. The lionization of an extreme vision of popular sovereignty and the disparagement of the formal legal system—both at the local and national level—allowed the leaders of the anti-Brown faction to insist on a right to apply lethal force beyond that which should have been allowed either by law or the unwritten constitution of custom.

This insistence did not occur only during the actual killing event itself. The shift was also apparent—and arguably even more so—within the subsequent administration of nonlethal floggings. While the anti-Brown party had barely voted for whipping over execution, they had reserved for themselves the right to kill their captives. This sort of mass, intentional extralegal execution had, on rare occasions like the 1835 killings at Vicksburg, happened before, but still remained largely outside of the bounds set by custom. The Vicksburg killings had captured the attention of the press precisely because they had been so alien and shocking. Now, just five years later, the anti-Brown party demonstrated through their actions that the choice to execute on such a massive scale was not relegated to the slaveholding cotton frontier. So too was it theirs by right. They cast access to such lethal force not as an aberration or a grim necessity but rather, to borrow from the words attributed by Warren to Anson Harrington, as a means to perform a "higher duty."

The Bellevue War was a legal event as much as it was an extralegal one.[126] It contributed to the amending of an unwritten constitution and reverberated not just through Jackson County and its environs but across hundreds of miles and tens of years. Those who had participated in the Bellevue War scattered like hot embers swept by the wind from the ashpit, carrying the precedent of the violence within their memories and across their scarred bodies. Those embers would soon spark new fires, which would in turn belch out their own hot residue. The killings would not stop in 1840. Across the river, in Illinois, new conflagrations threatened to erupt around some of the late William W. Brown's surviving men, his associates, and the broader networks thereto tethered.

CHAPTER 2

OGLE COUNTY, ILLINOIS

"Swifter, Deeper Vengeance!"

Sometime around eleven o'clock in the evening on March 21, 1841, scattered embers blossomed into flames. Light radiated through the night as fire wrapped around the newly constructed courthouse in Oregon City, Illinois. Someone sounded an alarm, but little could be done to quell the flames. The "new and elegant Court House" was quickly reduced, according to one eyewitness, to "a shapeless mass of ruins."[1] The tragedy immediately aroused suspicion among local residents. Oregon City was the seat of northern Illinois' Ogle County, some fifty-eight miles to the southeast of Bellevue, Iowa Territory. The next morning, on March 22, the spring term of the circuit court was scheduled to begin, with Thomas Ford, associate justice of the Supreme Court of the Ninth Judicial Circuit, presiding. On the docket were the cases of Norton B. Royce, Franklin Dewey, and Samuel Thatcher, who all faced charges related to counterfeiting. Another man named Brown faced a single count of forgery, and a man named Isaac Dennison (alias Dennison Waters) faced a count of larceny.[2] Rumors among the public immediately swirled around the possibility of the fire being an act of arson meant to help the alleged counterfeiters avoid legal consequences. The next morning, the eyewitness who described the fire wrote that "no doubt remains but the mischief was done by their friends out side."[3]

The fire at the Oregon City courthouse, which occurred less than a year after the conclusion of the Bellevue War, would ignite a flurry of extralegal collective violence in northern Illinois. Traveling via human vector, the action would, in the years that followed, profoundly influence a wave of violence that would sweep across Illinois and quickly seep beyond its borders. This violence was not disjointed or connected only in the suprahuman sense of a nebulous "movement." Rather, it operated along a cascading series of human networks that expanded with each sequential episode. Analyzing the diffusion of violent activity across these networks not only reframes the activity of the northern Illinois regulators; it illuminates the mechanics by which extralegal collective violence reverberated.

The violence in northern Illinois belonged to a larger sequence of action that flowed from the Bellevue War. Much of the action would orbit around a family by the name of Driscoll. A member of that clan had been an associate of William Brown's, and the Driscoll family's understanding of the Bellevue War—intertwined with their own personal experiences with collective violence—would inform their reaction to the organization of a regulator movement in their community. This reaction led to escalation and transformed the violence in northern Illinois into a radical and widely publicized departure from the established norms and customs of American extralegal collective action. Such linkages bound up the violence within a larger flow—one that was shaped by previous instances of extralegal collective activity and, with every subsequent entangled act of violence, surged with the potential to inform future episodes.

If the courthouse fire had been intended to interrupt legal proceedings, it was unsuccessful. Court commenced on March 22, as planned, though in a different building. On March 26, a grand jury indicted Royce, Dewey, Thatcher, and Brown. On March 30, the court handed down additional indictments to brothers Richard and Thomas Aikens.[4] On April 1, a jury found Royce, Dewey, and Thatcher guilty of knowingly possessing tools with which to produce counterfeit coin, and the court sentenced each man to one year in jail.[5] The court then ordered capiases against the Aikens brothers and set bail before adjourning until the September term.[6]

The tidy appearance of the court records would seem to indicate that the formal legal system had seemingly proven itself capable of moving against the alleged counterfeiters in the wake of the fire. In reality, threats and irregularities had propped up this neat façade. The fiery destruction of the most visible local symbol of the law's authority had, in the opinion of many residents, exposed a system unable to preserve order. A mixture of fear and fury subsequently swirled around the courtroom proceedings. "Considerable excitement prevails," concluded the eyewitness in his newspaper account of the courthouse fire, "and I shall not be much astonished if Judge Lynch should appoint a special term for the more speedy redress of grievances."[7] Talk of Lynch law spread throughout Ogle County. Even Judge Thomas Ford, the ranking local legate of the formal legal system, began to spit threats of extralegal collective violence. A "small and scrawny" man with a "squeaking voice," the judge felt particularly vulnerable.[8] Responding to threats real or imagined, Ford declared from the bench, according to one newspaper source, "that if his family were molested or his property destroyed during his necessary absence from home in the discharge of his official duties, he would on his return assemble his friends and take summary vengeance."[9] When one of the jurors refused to agree to a verdict against the alleged counterfeiters, Ford noted that the other eleven jurors had threatened to "lynch him in the jury room."[10] The judge did nothing to interfere with this rough deliberation, and the obstinate juror quickly fell into line.

The sentencing of Royce, Dewey, and Thatcher did little to calm tensions. Sometime in the April days of the court's waning spring term, a group of fifteen local residents summoned Ford for a secretive meeting at the schoolhouse in White Rock. Ford allegedly counseled the men to "organize a company, which should call upon the men whom they knew to be lawless, take them by force from their homes, strip them to the waist, and lash them with a blacksnake." The judge recommended thirty-six lashes for a first-time offense and sixty for a second. The leaders, Ford advised, should be banished.[11] This rough prescription was consistent with Ford's legal thinking regarding punishment and deterrence. According to John Dean Canton, a lawyer who knew and worked with the judge, Ford insisted that flogging "was the most deterrent punishment ever inflicted for the punishment of crime."[12] The judge might have been a representative of the formal legal system, but his ruling seemed to stem from more personal concerns. The burning of the courthouse had evidently led him to believe that his own life, family, and property were at risk. He later insisted that "combinations of criminals" were "too strong for the ordinary machinery of government."[13] Judge Ford adjourned the circuit court shortly thereafter. It was "Judge Lynch" who now presided in Ogle County.

As the court records indicate, many of the same patterns of criminality that bedeviled Jackson County also applied in Ogle. Allegations of violated property rights—whether related to land, livestock, or coin—remained at the center of many local complaints. One account, believed by historian David Grimsted to have been written by regulator Phineas Chaney, maintained that the owners of "fast or really good horses never presumed to leave them unguarded for a single night."[14] William Cullen Bryant, a poet and writer traveling through the area, observed in a July 2 letter that "horse-thieves are numerous in this part of the country." There was a seasonal cadence to the thieving, Bryant claimed. "Most of the thefts are committed early in the spring," he wrote, "when the grass begins to shoot, and the horses are turned out on the prairie, and the thieves, having had little or no employment during the winter, are needy."[15]

As Bryant's observation suggests, some of this turn to criminality was linked to the Panic of 1837 and sustained financial distress in the region. Richard and Thomas Aikens, for instance, who were both indicted during the spring term of the circuit court, belonged to a family that, before the Panic, had been regarded not only "as rather good men" but "men of considerable wealth and influence." The Aikens men, led by their father, Samuel Aikens, had speculated heavily in land claims before the crash, however. The sudden collapse in land value brought ruin not only to the family but to "a number of their neighbors and acquaintances—men that regarded the old man Aikens with respectful consideration, and in whose thrift and ken they had every confidence." According to one local history, it was with this financial reversal—and the accompanying local resentment—that Charles, Thomas, and Richard Aikens "became reckless, and finally identified themselves with the outlaws."[16]

Desperation and opportunity soon led to the establishment of more organized criminal efforts. In neighboring Winnebago County, *The Rockford Star*—the regional Democratic paper—complained in December 1840 about the existence of a "regularly organized band of thieves and robbers from this State, entirely through the Territory." An unknown party had robbed the store of local merchant H. L. Buell four or five months prior. Some of the stolen goods later resurfaced in Milwaukee, Wisconsin Territory, prompting a search of homes belonging to "suspicious characters." One of these homes was allegedly equipped with a number of secret underground cellars and entrances. The investigating party discovered and seized a man who had been inside the strange dwelling, only for him to slip away, steal one of their horses, and escape. *The Rockford Star*, remarking on the situation, commented angrily that "if the laws of the land are not competent to bring these devils in human shape to justice it is high time for Judge Lynch and his Jury to arraign them before their bar of Justice that they may try what virtue there is in his sentence."[17]

As evidenced by the frustration expressed by *The Rockford Star*'s editor, the ability of the local government to maintain order remained a concern for residents. While Illinois had been a state since 1818, population expansion necessitated the frequent creation of new counties over the subsequent decades. Ogle County had only existed as a political unit since 1836. This expansion, coupled with the financial devastation wrought by the Panic of 1837, taxed the resources of local governments and resulted in subpar facilities. Some counties, like neighboring Winnebago, had no jails at all. *The Rockford Star* had complained in December 1840 that it was a "great pity that a rascal can't get justice done him after he is caught."[18] Shortly thereafter, in February 1841, the paper implored local residents to support the urgent construction of "a small, strong, stone building" to serve as the county jail.[19] Thomas Ford himself criticized the state of jails in northern Illinois, later writing that "the new counties, such as Ogle, were so poor in revenue, and so much in debt, their orders at so great a discount, that they were not able to build good jails."[20] The recent partition of the region into new counties had also produced less visible fractures in the stability of local political structures. In some recently organized counties like Ogle and Lee, new jurisdictional lines haphazardly crisscrossed already extant social networks, undercutting the local officials who could no longer monopolize authority over those networks. In other words, to borrow from Obert, the drawing of borders "decoupled" local authority from the organic mechanisms of linkage and loyalty in counties like Ogle, mechanisms that were necessary for the effective functioning of the formal legal system.[21]

Ogle County's nascent band of regulators levied complaints regarding the efficacy of formal mechanisms of law enforcement, similar in substance and cadence to those issued on the eve of the Bellevue War, to justify their own campaign of extralegal action. This rhetorical strategy was a common one. Many practitioners and defenders of regulator or vigilante violence justified their actions by pointing to the "weakness" of the formal legal system. The interactions between Judge Ford and the Ogle County regulators seemingly affirmed this position. Such a characterization, however, is misleading. "Weakness" implies a level of power below that which might be expected, an aberration from a normative or desired state. The formal legal system in the antebellum United States had by design a limited ability to effectively employ mechanisms of violent coercion.[22] This was reflected in a formal sense by the enshrinement of the right of private citizens to keep and bear arms in the Second Amendment, in the reliance of the state on armed citizen militias, and in a legal system that continued to rely on the posse comitatus for law enforcement at the local level.[23] In an informal sense, this thinking resulted in the continued toleration of moderate forms of extralegal collective violence on the part of the government and the continued engagement in such violence on the part of the people. The ability of private citizens to enforce the law as members of a public posse comitatus stemmed from the same headwaters as the ability of citizens to participate in a lynching. Both activities, grounded in an older tradition of Anglo-American legal thought and popular constitutionalism, were predicated on a citizen's ability to employ violent force.[24] That the people constituted the "power of the county" and could combine to wield that power in either a legal or extralegal fashion was a feature of the system rather than an unintended defect. Access to such violence was both a check on the power of the state and a matter of custom.

This decentralized system of law enforcement benefited the United States as the nation engaged in westward expansion in the decades following the Revolution. The formal legal system outsourced law enforcement to private citizens, facilitating rapid territorial growth—even as that growth outpaced extant bureaucratic structures—while maintaining republican principles.[25] The problem with this public–private arrangement was balance, something that Thomas Ford would admit years later. "The peaceable and orderly many," he wrote, "are so engaged in separate and selfish, but lawful projects of their own, that it is hard to get them to take part in putting down the disorderly few." It was only when affairs became "intolerable and insufferable," Ford continued, that "the power of the many is exercised, as the limbs of the body are exercised in a spasm, which waits for neither law nor government."[26] As seen in the Bellevue War, the practical challenges to property rights in the region made the quick redress that accompanied the private dispensation of justice appealing, contributing, as Ford noted, to increasingly severe "spasms."

In northern Illinois, the group of regulators quickly grew as its organizers activated their networks across Ogle, Lee, and Winnebago counties. In early summer 1841, a number of local bands from across the region confederated into a cluster of companies captained by local elites. Some residents were pressed or coerced into joining the regulators, with one June 30 letter remarking that "if a man refuses to join these companies, he is put down at once with the horse-thieves."[27] At a meeting, the primary outfit adopted for themselves an unusually straightforward name: the Ogle County Lynching Society.[28] The first target of the self-proclaimed lynchers was an Ogle County resident by the name of John Hearl, who had allegedly aided in the theft of a neighbor's horse. The lynchers seized Hearl and administered thirty lashes, "the blood following every stroke."[29] Their next victim was a man named Asa Daggett, purportedly a former Baptist preacher and an alleged accessory to horse theft. The "agonized appeals" of Daggett's sixteen-year-old daughter initially shamed the lynchers into departing without having administered the planned flogging. In return, Daggett swore that he would leave the area. That night, however, a group of lyncher dissidents returned, seized the disgraced preacher, and whipped him with ninety-six lashes until he surrendered a "confession."[30] The lynchers were careful to prevent the torture from morphing into a killing, and a physician named Hobart periodically examined the victim to prevent his premature death.[31] When the lynchers had finished whipping Daggett, they gave him five days to leave.[32]

The lynchers also targeted Daniel Ross, a man related by marriage to the Aikens brothers, who had been indicted during the circuit court's spring term. The band forced Ross "to hold on to the limb of a tree just high enough to allow his toes to rest upon the ground." Each time Ross tried to lower himself down, "the prompt and vigorous application of cow-hide on his seat of honor, compelled him to take the old position."[33] The lynchers threatened several others, ordering them to leave the region within two weeks. One "suspicious person" was given three months to "prove a satisfactory character." The group intended this violence to function as a form of public spectacle meant to communicate a message of resolve and warning throughout the broader region. In this spirit, they published in *The Rockford Star* on June 17 an account of the violence they had inflicted up to that point. Styling themselves the "Ogle County Volunteer Company," the lynchers attempted to stress their republican character, claiming they had acted "pursuant to orders" and had only employed force after they "found it necessary, according to the constitution of the company."[34]

This initial lyncher action was not without precedent in northern Illinois. Many settlers had, in the years prior, claimed land in the region before it had legally opened for sale. Lacking the title to what they considered their property, these squatters were vulnerable to "claim jumpers" and speculators who sought to claim the land for themselves. To protect themselves from these threats, early settlers in the area banded together into mutual aid societies called "claim clubs." These clubs adjudicated disputes over land and used extralegal collective force to eject alleged jumpers from claims held by members. The constitution and bylaws of the "Oregon Claim Society," founded in 1836, obliged all members to "turn out and enforce an observation of" the regulations of the club "or protect their rights of membership."[35] This experience was educational and had an impact on the attitudes of locals toward participation in extralegal violent action. Thomas Ford, referencing the problem of claim jumping, noted that it "soon became apparent to every one, that actual force was the only protection for this description of property."[36] Extralegal collective force would adjudicate that which formal law could not.

There was limited overlap between the known membership rolls of the Ogle County Lynching Society and the claim club. In fact, convicted counterfeiter Norton B. Royce appeared on the claim club's rolls.[37] Still, the organization of groups like the Oregon Claim Society had preestablished locally the framework for the acceptable use of extralegal force in response to alleged property rights violations.[38] This schema reflected the traditional understandings and limits of extralegal violence in the early United States. In constraining their initial campaign of violence to floggings and banishment, the lynchers adhered closely to already established practice. Soon, however, an upsurge in local resistance to the regulators would escalate the violence employed far beyond that dictated by custom. This resistance would center on a family by the name of Driscoll, whose own interpretations of the unfolding violence had been informed not only by their own experiences with extralegal collective action but by their association with a late hotel keeper by the name of William W. Brown.

John Driscoll was the patriarch of the Driscoll clan. He stood over six feet tall and weighed about two hundred pounds. According to one contemporary, the old man was "all muscle and sinew." This size and strength, atypical for a man during this period, was complemented by striking facial features. A shock of coarse grey hair topped his head and large, "shaggy-like" brows framed his eyes. A chunk of his nose was missing, "which had been bitten off some years before in a fight with some human ghoul." While his appearance was fearsome, contemporaries noted that Driscoll "was not an ignorant man, nor void of generosity or charity." In one instance, he and his sons ploughed the field and planted crops for one recently widowed neighbor. In the words of one member of the Ogle County Lynching Society, this was just one of the "many kind acts passed to his credit in the neighborhood where he lived."[39] John lived with Mercy, his wife of almost forty years, and his younger children at their home on Kilbuck Creek, which John had named after a creek he had previously known in Ohio. Some of his older offspring, such as sons David, William, and Pierson, had established their own homesteads in the surrounding groves. Other members of the Brody family, who were tied to the Driscolls through a high degree of intermarriage, had done the same.[40]

Violence shaped much of John Driscoll's life. He had been born to Daniel and Eleanor Driscoll roughly around 1780. Daniel, a Revolutionary War veteran, made his home in Bethlehem Township, in Washington County, Pennsylvania.[41] In 1791, when John was around eleven years old, violent opposition to the excise tax in western Pennsylvania erupted into the Whiskey Rebellion. Washington County was a hotspot for anti-tax agitation. There, in April 1786, a mob of frontiersmen with blackened faces captured and humiliated state excise officer William Graham. In September 1791, Washington County men dressed in women's clothing tarred and feathered tax collector Robert Johnson before stealing his horse.[42] The federal government eventually asserted control over the region. John Driscoll, however, spent his formative years surrounded by rituals of collective defiance and rebellion. Daniel Driscoll became caught up in the turbulence of the insurrection and was forced, alongside other men from Bethlehem Township, to sign an oath of allegiance to the United States on December 31, 1794.[43] Following the Whiskey Rebellion, the family migrated to Ohio, where John would marry Mercy in 1802. It was also around this time that the Driscolls became first linked to the Brody family, with John's brother William marrying Mercy Brody in February 1804.[44]

The rough performance of violent masculinity dominated the Ohio frontier. Three of Daniel's sons—John, Phoenix, and Dennis—repeatedly appeared in court to face charges related to assault and battery.[45] The brothers were ensconced within a frontier culture of male violence that was prevalent enough to seep into social custom, becoming at times a form of communal revelry. One contemporary, John M. May, later described a fighting tradition in which both the Driscolls and Brodys participated. "Every neighborhood," he recalled, "had its bully or chief fighter, and these were pitted against each other like game-cocks. These fights often ended in a general melee, in which whole neighborhoods were sometimes engaged against each other." May recalled two factions in particular, the "Clearforkers" and the "Blackforkers," named after the waterways near their respective places of residence. "Among the Clearforkers," he continued, "were the Brodies, Slaters, and Driskells." Stephen Brody, brother of Mercy Brody Driscoll, "was the champion" of the group.[46] Not content with factional brawls, John Driscoll developed a reputation for hard-drinking bravado and would often challenge the stronger local men to public fights. He tended not to lose. On one occasion in a tavern, Driscoll provoked a fight with a man named Isaac Pew. Driscoll won the fight almost immediately, landing a powerful blow against Pew before viciously biting off the man's ear. Pew would soon take his revenge, however, at a public muster, ambushing John and biting off part of his nose.[47] It was in this fashion that Driscoll's face became disfigured.

While this violent behavior was dramatic, it was by no means exceptional. The bloody behavior of the Driscolls, Brodys, and men like Pew did not signal existence along some violent fringe. Rather, such violence was an established manner of custom in the frontier Middle West. William Blane, who traveled through Illinois in the 1820s, noted that "fighting in the Backwoods is conducted upon a plan. . . . The object of each combatant is to take his adversary by surprise; and then, as soon as he has thrown him down, either to 'gouge' him, that is, to poke his eye out, or else to get his nose or ear into his mouth and bite it off."[48] Blane was describing the "degenerated" behavior of backcountry English migrants, and his account matches perfectly with the cadence of the exchange between John Driscoll and Isaac Pew. James Flint, reporting from 1819 Kentucky, similarly noted that he had "seen several fingers that had been deformed, also several noses and ears, which have been mutilated, but this canine mode of fighting."[49] "Gouging" as a practice had initially emerged in the southern backcountry.[50] As migrants moved from the South through the Middle West, they carried the violent custom with them and established its practice in new communities. Outside observers like Blane and Flint decried "gouging." The custom, though, functioned as a release valve, allowing frontier men to perform and defend their masculine honor without needing to resort to the often lethal violence of dueling.[51] In the account of the confrontation between Driscoll and Pew, there is no mention of weapon use, and the inflicted bite wounds reflected a rough degree of parity.

Gouging, then, was not the problem. The reputation of the Driscolls and Brodys was, however, not limited to that of drunken fighters. Allegations of criminal activity soon emerged against the families. In 1825, a Wayne County grand jury indicted John Driscoll for larceny. In March 1826, a jury in the county's court of common pleas found Driscoll not guilty, but the allegations did not stop there.[52] Authorities detained Stephen Brody in 1830 for stealing a heifer. Brody, bellicose as ever, plunged a knife into the leg of one of the local constable's men during the arrest. This violent resistance did not dissuade the constable's party, and Brody was detained for trial. The county's court of common pleas subsequently sentenced Brody to five years hard labor for the offenses.[53] The ties between the Brodys and the Driscolls saw the latter treated with growing suspicion. This only deepened after authorities moved to indict Benjamin Wellington (alias Benjamin Worthington) for stealing a yoke of oxen from General Reasin Beall.[54] Information surrendered in the subsequent legal action reportedly implicated the Brodys and Driscolls as complicit in the theft.[55]

On New Year's Day in 1829, John Driscoll stole a gelding. While there was no immediate pursuit in response to the theft, Driscoll attempted to keep a low profile after the incident. The following night, an associate named Joseph Morrison helped Driscoll hide by allowing him to stay in Morrison's home, despite "knowing him to be a horse thief."[56] These precautions proved insufficient, however, and authorities, already suspicious of John Driscoll, soon moved to arrest him. Driscoll, anxious to avoid capture, fled to his childhood home in western Pennsylvania. The Wayne County Court of Common Pleas repeatedly issued continuances for Driscoll's indictment, undoubtedly on account of its inability to locate and detain him.[57] For years, the court would issue continuance after continuance. In spite of this sustained legal threat, Driscoll at some point left Pennsylvania and returned discreetly to his family.[58]

Residents blamed the Driscolls and Brodys for the theft that continued to plague that region of Ohio. In 1833, some local men organized an extralegal outfit, the "Black Cane Company," in response to the alleged depredations. The group, so-named on account of the torched and oiled clubs its members carried, quickly targeted the two suspected families.[59] John's twenty-seven-year-old son Pierson, along with a Brody identified only as "Crop-eared Brawdy," were alleged to have burned down the barns of two of the vigilante group's leaders in retaliation.[60] This only served to further infuriate the Black Cane men. In November 1833, Pierson Driscoll, David Driscoll, James Brody, Reason Brody, and Lewis Kenney Brody all appeared before the Richland County Court of Common Pleas to face an indictment for arson.[61] A jury found Pierson alone guilty of the act, and the court sentenced him to seven years hard labor.[62] This was not enough to satiate the Black Cane men. In December of that year, a party led by the victims of the arson staged a nighttime attack on a cabin belonging to a member of the family. They found John Driscoll there and three men tried to seize him while he slept. Driscoll sprung out of bed, bowie knife in hand, "threatening with death every intruder who did not instantly leave the house."[63] The fury with which the large man arose terrified the attackers, who immediately turned and fled the building. Outside, however, the larger company managed to regroup. They knocked out the chinking between the cabin's logs, sliding their muskets through the gaps. Faced with the slaughter of his family, Driscoll surrendered. Not long after, however, he again managed to escape. This time, both the Driscoll and Brody families quickly left the area. By 1835, they settled in Ogle County, Illinois.[64]

The Driscoll family carried these experiences with them as they moved into Illinois. Having already been the targets of violent vigilante action themselves, the family was pre-disposed to oppose Lynch law. This opposition hardened following the events of April 1, 1840. Bellevue's Sheriff Warren would, in his later reminiscences, refer to an association between an unnamed member of the Driscoll clan and William W. Brown. The wife of woodchopper Levi Brown, according to Warren, reported that a man named Driscoll from Illinois supplied the meat for William Brown's workers. Warren also claimed that Levi Brown confessed to trafficking stolen goods out of Iowa and into Illinois with the same Driscoll.[65] While Warren did not specify which Driscoll engaged in business with Brown, it is known that, at the very least, John's son William Driscoll spent extended stays in Iowa.[66] It is certainly possible that the Driscoll in question was engaged in lawful trade with either Brown or his men. If the allegations against Brown were true, however, Driscoll trafficked stolen goods—horses, meat, or other property—out of Illinois and into Iowa Territory, where possession would be transferred to Brown's men.

Such an operation would have fit the typical pattern of horse thieving and counterfeiting, with perpetrators obscuring their footprints by working across jurisdictional, political, and physical boundaries. These assorted financial linkages, legitimate or illegitimate, meant that the Driscolls were very familiar with William Brown. So too would they have been familiar with his death at the hands of a mob for alleged crimes in which they were supposedly implicated. Meanwhile, at least one member of the Brody family was formally documented as engaging in criminal activity just across the river from Bellevue, in Jo Daviess County, Illinois. In November 1839, around the time many of the anti-Brown faction in Bellevue were complaining about horse theft and criminality, the governor of Wisconsin, Henry Dodge, wrote the governor of Illinois to demand the arrest and extradition of "David Wilson, Judge

Holmes, and Stephen Brawdy," who were wanted on charges of burglary and larceny.[67]

The Brodys themselves had moved out of Ogle County around
1839, settling in Linn County, Iowa Territory. The family left Illinois after Benjamin Worden allegedly caught John Brody with
stolen livestock.[68] In Iowa, the Brodys would forge connections
with the Leverich family, with Hannah Brody eventually marrying saloon-keeper James Leverich in 1842.[69] The Leveriches had ties
to organized counterfeiting in the territory, with James's brother,
Joel, earning the local moniker "Old Bogus Coon" for his alleged
trade. In his 1842 confession, horse thief Samuel Cluse would reference an "old 'bogus coon' Leveredge" who "made very good bogus,
and has been long suspected."[70] In one ironic twist, Joel Leverich
would, in 1841, serve as a commissioner, along with James L. Kirkpatrick, to establish a road between Linn County and Bellevue in
Jackson County.[71] Kirkpatrick had been in the party that attacked
William W. Brown's hotel and killed the proprietor over allegations
not dissimilar to those leveled against Leverich. The Leveriches possessed valuable ties to a much larger network of counterfeiters that
operated throughout the territory.[72] Hannah's brother Bill eventually entered into a violent political rivalry with the Old Bogus Coon,
fracturing the criminal alliance and perhaps making it possible for
other residents of Linn County to, by 1843, drive the Brody family
out and into Benton County.[73] Still, for at least a few years, the Brodys, who maintained their deep ties with the Driscolls, functioned
as an important conduit connecting criminal networks in Illinois
to those in the Iowa Territory. The Driscolls and Brodys might not
have fought in Bellevue, but they were active in the region in the
lead-up to that episode of violence. The Driscolls would not soon
forget the lessons gleaned from that bloodletting.

Opposition to the lynchers was already percolating in Ogle County.
After members of the Ogle Lynching Society flogged Asa Daggett, a
resident named William K. Bridge appealed to the formal legal system to reassert control over the county. Bridge, a well-spoken and
charitable Pennsylvanian later described by one local contemporary

as an "Adonis," attempted to induce authorities to produce a warrant to arrest the offending party. With the sheriff conveniently absent, the task fell to the local coroner, James Clark, who failed to serve the warrant to anyone.[74] With appeals to formal authority having failed, the opponents of the lynchers moved to covertly intimidate the leaders of the society. An unknown party set fire to the sawmill owned by the lyncher captain John Long and broke the legs of his horse.[75] Some amount of suspicion soon fell upon the Driscolls, and the lynchers responded to the arson by targeting a man linked to the family. The man in question, Lyman Powell, was physically disabled, but the Driscolls paid him to work at "threshing and other odd jobs." He was "really a harmless, inoffensive man," according to one local history, but had been targeted on account of his association with the Driscolls. Unsatisfied by Powell's responses to their interrogation, the lynchers "beat him cruelly with hickory withes" and stole his horse. Long, already shaken by the torching of his mill, received shortly thereafter a letter "defying the society to combat, and threatening personal violence."[76] Sufficiently intimidated, the lyncher captain resigned. His replacement, W. S. Wellington, similarly vacated his post after receiving a letter upon which had been scrawled the skull and crossbones.[77]

The Ogle Lynching Society then elected for its new leader John Campbell, a Scottish-born "fugitive Canadian patriot."[78] By this time, clear fracture lines had emerged in the region. An assemblage of some eighty men who opposed the actions of the lynchers reportedly staged meetings in the barns owned by William K. Bridge and a member of the Aikens family, where the group discussed how to respond to the vigilante violence. These meetings sent the lynchers into a panic. Baseless rumors that the anti-lynchers would "visit White Rock and murder every man, woman, and child in that hamlet" prompted the residents there to erect barricades and muster a militia that included any boy large enough to lift a weapon.[79] While the supposedly imminent danger never did materialize, the event escalated tensions. The reception of a letter, addressed to John Campbell and purportedly written by William Driscoll, which was "filled with the most direful threats," further intensified the situation.

Rather than stepping down in the face of these threats, as his two predecessors had done, Campbell organized the lynchers to move against the Driscoll family.

In short order, Campbell organized a little under two hundred men to march on John Driscoll's home in South Grove. The attacking column advanced to within a half-mile of the dwelling, but upon finding the house defended by armed men, they paused to prepare for an assault. Before these preparations could be completed, however, some twenty defenders armed with handguns sallied out of the building and began to dash toward the woods. John Driscoll mounted a horse "and was soon beyond pursuit." A man named Bowman soon approached the lynchers, introducing himself as the Driscolls' messenger. Bowman then delivered a message reportedly from William Driscoll, which stated that three hundred pro-Driscoll men from Sycamore, DeKalb County, would soon arrive.[80] The lynchers elected to take up positions in the area around the house and await the coming riposte.[81]

John Driscoll returned sometime around 3 p.m. He was not accompanied by an armed band but by three representatives of the formal legal system from neighboring DeKalb County. The group that accompanied Driscoll included Sheriff Morris Walrodd, lawyer E. L. Mayo, and Probate Judge Frederick Love. That John Driscoll, who had spent much of his life at odds with the law, had appealed for the intervention of the formal legal system reflected his pronounced unease regarding the lyncher activity. The three officers, the Driscolls, and Campbell met to discuss the situation. The lyncher captain began reciting allegations against the Driscolls, claiming that William Driscoll in particular was not only a thief, but a thief so base that he stole from his own associates. William was, according to Campbell, "the meanest thief on the face of God's earth." The insults and allegations incensed the Driscolls, who "stood by livid with rage and gnashed their teeth."[82] The impromptu summit did little to foster greater understanding and mutual goodwill, but the presence of the law officers, at the very least, helped avert a bloodletting. Perhaps constrained by Judge Ford's tacit approval for the lynchers, a temporary palliation was all they could hope to accomplish.[83] The lynchers departed, but not before Campbell warned John Driscoll that he and his family had twenty days to leave the region lest their next meeting not end so peacefully. Addressing David Driscoll in particular, Campbell swore that if "after that time you are found east of the Mississippi river, we will brand your cheeks with R. S., and crop your ears, so that none shall fail to know your character as a rogue and scoundrel wherever you are."[84]

This time the Driscolls made no preparations to flee from the specter of extralegal collective chastisement. Campbell's brazen threats had, in the words of Isaac N. Arnold (later counsel for Taylor Driscoll), "roused the tiger passions in some of these threatened men."[85] Shortly after the near-confrontation, several of the targeted families gathered at Bridge's farm to discuss the lyncher threat. The Driscolls, the Brodys, the Bridges, and another family named the Barretts were all later noted to have been in attendance. A lively debate commenced regarding the proper response to Campbell's threats. Some urged compliance and departure within the enforced window. Others lobbied for fortifying Driscoll's grove and preparing to "defend their position with their lives." One unnamed member of the Driscoll family, however, proposed a bolder solution. The former lyncher captains Long and Wellington had both been intimidated into stepping down from their positions. Campbell had proven more stoic. A decisive strike against lyncher leadership, though, could put an end to the hydra once and for all. Kill Campbell, and no one else would dare take his place.[86]

This extreme proposition signaled a major shift for the family. The Driscolls had spent years at odds with the formal legal system, but no evidence suggests that any member of the family was a killer. Indeed, the previous violent action in which the male Driscolls and Brodys had participated over the preceding decades was structured to moderate the severity of violence employed and constrain the use of force to nonlethal levels. Even in moments of acute danger, the Driscolls had previously limited themselves to engaging in targeted property destruction against their enemies. When past tensions escalated to the point of threatening the use of lethal force, as had been the case in Ohio with the Black Cane Company, the Driscolls had elected to comply and depart rather than to mount a deadly resistance. Something significant had changed in the risk calculus of those members of the family present at Bridge's farm. A bloody, unwritten warning had been issued at Bellevue, one with which the Driscolls were certainly familiar. If they did not decisively confront the leadership of the Ogle Lynching Society, they might have to pay for it with their lives.

According to a later county history, the unnamed Driscoll specifically cited Iowa when arguing for the assassination of Campbell. William Driscoll had apparently spent the previous winter in that territory, and the speaker made a vague reference to a violent encounter that had taken place there. The targeted killing of a leader "had been tried in Iowa," where it had "worked successfully."[87] The exact meaning of Driscoll's reference appears, at first, unclear. The only major vigilante activity that had taken place in Iowa in 1840–41—certainly the only recorded vigilante activity there that involved killing—had been the Bellevue War, and that exchange had gone far more "successfully" for Cox and Warren's party than it had for Brown and his men. In a reference to Cox and Warren, however, might lie Driscoll's meaning and the logic for the shift in his family's appetite for risk. In quickly dispatching the leader of the opposing force, Cox and Warren left Brown's men rudderless and demoralized in the ensuing fight. They also eliminated the popular figure around which a counterattack might have mobilized.

As established previously, at least one of the Driscolls associated with Brown and would likely have known or later learned of the interpersonal dynamics that preceded the fighting at the hotel. Brown had been too conciliatory toward his enemies in Bellevue, right up to the final seconds of his life. He had repeatedly attempted diplomacy with the leaders of the assaulting party, only to be the first to die in the ensuing confrontation. Cox especially had been a major driver of not only the organization of forces against Brown but of the final assault on the hotel. No attempt had been made on Brown's part to forcibly disrupt Cox's activities until it was too late. The Driscolls' understanding of those events, combined with their own personal history of being targeted in extralegal collective action, offers the best explanation for why it was a member of the family who moved to escalate the situation in such an extreme and uncharacteristic way. Their pitch was compelling enough to sway those present, and a plan was established. The Canadian had to die.

On Sunday, June 27, John Campbell and his family went to church. On their return the family ate supper, and the lyncher captain lay down for a nap until sundown, at which point he got up and made his way toward his barn. Between the Campbell home and the barn was a large hazel bush. As Campbell approached, two men stepped out from behind the foliage and asked for directions to Long's burned mill. Before Campbell could answer, one of the men shot him through the heart. Campbell stumbled around for a few seconds before collapsing, dead. John's wife Margaret ran out to the corpse and screamed that the Driscolls had killed her husband. Campbell's thirteen-year-old son Martin grabbed his father's shotgun and attempted to shoot the assailants but misfired. Campbell's killers escaped to the southeast and soon disappeared.[88]

The killing of Campbell did not have the intended effect. Rather than demoralize the lynchers, the shooting sparked immediate outrage and calls for revenge. Margaret Campbell identified one of the killers as David Driscoll—although she would later make conflicting statements and misidentify the Driscoll brothers on several occasions. Ogle Lynching Society member Phineas Chaney also claimed to have been the target of a second failed assassination attempt. Chaney based this claim on words allegedly spoken at school that Monday by Hettie Bridge, the young daughter of William K. Bridge.[89] William T. Ward, sheriff of Ogle County, arrested John Driscoll on suspicion of murder just after sunrise on Monday, June 30. Lyncher and posse member Ralph Chaney later recalled being struck by the scene of one of John's adult daughters meeting her father's eye as he was arrested. "There was that kind of look I can hardly describe, passed between them," Chaney later shared, "and as she held his eye she nodded her head to him. Nothing was said, but such a look I never saw in the world."[90] Before departing with the sheriff to the Oregon City jail, Driscoll calmly turned to Mercy, his wife of almost four decades, and said, "Take care of yourself, and do the best you can . . . only that, and nothing more."[91]

The lynchers—enraged and not content to let the formal legal system process the killing—seized William and Pierson Driscoll from their homes and brought them to the Campbell home. They presented the captive brothers to Margaret and her son Martin, who both confirmed that neither man had been one of John Campbell's killers. This apparently mattered little to the lynchers. Blood shared made the brothers as guilty as blood spilt. They kept the captives over- night at the Campbell home under guard. The lynchers temporarily seized the pair's youngest brother, thirteen-year-old John Driscoll Jr., but soon released him.[92] Other parties of lynchers attempted to cap- ture David and Taylor Driscoll, Richard and Thomas Aikens, and William K. Bridge, but these people had managed to successfully flee. On Tuesday morning, another group marched to the Oregon City jail and seized John Driscoll from the sheriff's custody above the law officer's "protestations." Judge Ford, who had supported the Ogle Lynching Society from the beginning, also reportedly disap- proved of the forceful removal of the already-detained John Driscoll from the jurisdiction of the formal legal system.[93] The judge quickly learned, however, that the wildfire of popular will was easier to spark than to control. The ineffectual handwringing of legal author- ities could not stop the frenzy now in motion. The lynchers prepared to transport their three prisoners to Washington Grove, a rural area where a large crowd from Ogle and the neighboring counties began to gather.

En route to Washington Grove, the lynchers tied a horse's halter around John Driscoll's neck to prevent his escape. Feeling the lit- eral and proverbial noose tighten, Driscoll made one last attempt to save his boys. He confessed to lynchers Phineas Cheney and Obed Lindsay that he had "been a very bad man, and that he had done many unlawful and vicious things." Driscoll admitted to having been a prolific horse thief but insisted that the guilt was his alone. Specifically referencing the episode of arson that had seen Pierson sentenced to prison back in Ohio, John claimed that he had been the one to blame and that his son was innocent. Still, despite all his sin, John Driscoll insisted that "he had never committed murder." Driscoll's confession did little, however, to sway his captors. The group arrived in Washington Grove around ten o'clock and were joined shortly thereafter by the party holding William and Pierson captive. Another captive, Bowman the courier, was also brought to the grove. A crowd of at least a hundred lynchers soon gathered around the prisoners.

A barrel of whiskey arrived from a nearby distillery. The crowd freely and greedily drank the liquor.[94] It was a motley assemblage, with one newspaper account noting that there were "ministers, doctors, lawyers, farmers, and mechanics" in attendance.[95] A group of William Driscoll's friends arrived from Sycamore, in neighboring DeKalb County, to vouch for his innocence but were drowned out by the increasingly boisterous crowd. Following the arrival of additional men from Rockford, the lynchers began the proceedings. They elected E. S. Leland—a future circuit court judge—to head the trial. Leland seated himself on the ground at the foot of a large black oak tree while over one hundred lynchers formed a ring surrounding him.

The lynchers first led John Driscoll into the ring. They recited a litany of charges against the elder Driscoll, accusing him of being an accessory to the murder of Campbell as well as of belonging to a fraternity of horse thieves. On the former charge, the lynchers claimed that Driscoll had been at the Campbell home the day prior to the killing.[96] John Driscoll denied these charges. He reiterated that he had been a thief in Ohio but insisted that he had lived an honest life in Illinois. After the lynchers concluded their interrogation, they led the old man out of the circle to await his fate.

Next they brought in William Driscoll, who was similarly interrogated. Leland specifically inquired about William's alleged comments in which he had supposedly laid out the merits of killing the lyncher leader. Driscoll denied having given his brother instructions to kill Campbell, but Henry Hill, another Ogle resident, swore otherwise. William then admitted to using the language but insisted he had only done so as a dark joke. The lynchers went on to assert that William's early knowledge of the killing verified his involvement. Some of William's friends from Sycamore attempted to make their voices heard and explained that William had in fact seen the news scrawled on mail addressed to Chicago. Postmaster John R. Hamlin struggled to swear to this version of events, even as the ring of lynchers hissed and shouted him down. A group attempted to seize Hamlin and eject him from the circle, but Leland permitted him to speak. William himself then spoke. He maintained that he was innocent of everything but a joke, insisting that "he had lived honestly and done no injustice to any one." It was no use. Leland addressed the circle of lynchers and demanded they render a verdict.[97]

Over a hundred throats howled out a guilty verdict from the ring. According to one contemporary newspaper account, the charges were an amorphous combination of conspiracy to murder, accessory to murder, and retroactive guilt for the "many other criminal offenses previously committed."[98] Despite the protestations of William's supporters and the fact that neither Margaret Campbell nor Martin Campbell had identified either Driscoll as one of the killers, the lyncher tribunal sentenced the two men to death in a second, unanimous vote. Pierson and Bowman were ordered released for want of evidence, a paucity that must have been severe given the standards under which John and William had been found guilty.[99] According to the later pro-lyncher account in *The History of Ogle County* written in 1878, the tribunal originally sentenced the father and son to hang, but the pair requested to be shot rather than "hanged like dogs." The lynchers, over a few dissenting mutters, acquiesced and granted John and William an hour's reprieve before their execution.[100]

The grim proceedings lurched forward. One of the lyncher captains, a Methodist preacher named Jacob Crist, made his way to the liquor barrel and, taking the dipper, lustily guzzled whiskey. He then knelt down by the prisoners and commenced praying "loud and noisily." William joined Crist in prayer, while old John Driscoll remained detached, seemingly taking "no notice of what was transpiring." Meanwhile, William's friends moved through the crowd in a desperate bid to stir up sympathy for the condemned. They hoped to postpone the killing or even commute the sentence to a more traditional banishment. This appeal had an effect, and some members of the crowd began to agitate for clemency. The summary execution of unarmed prisoners, after all, continued to represent a radical departure from established custom. Even the victors of the Bellevue War, while asserting their right to put the lives of their own prisoners up for a vote, had refrained from executing their captives. Flogging and banishment remained, for many Americans, far more recognizable and palatable forms of collective punishment.

Several lyncher leaders moved to calm the crowd. One, Charles Latimer, delivered a snarling address, railing that "nothing but blood would palliate the crimes that had been committed." Latimer, according to a later pro-lyncher account, "maintained that the people were justified in taking the course they had, that their safety demanded it . . . that if the murderers could not be found, those who planned the foul deed must suffer in their stead." Another lyncher, Jason Marsh, attempted to shame those inclined to show the Driscolls mercy by labeling them "weak-kneed." These addresses convinced some of the crowd that the Driscolls should be killed, and, with the reprieve expiring, the lynchers prepared their muskets.[101] Others, however, continued to balk at the still-alien idea of executing their captives and milled around behind the rest of the group, their weapons leaned up against the trees. Marsh shouted that "all must join in" and threatened to have any resting guns "whipped up against the trees." The lynchers—some reluctantly—all fell into line.[102]

The lynchers divided into two companies, each numbering roughly fifty men. They then blindfolded John Driscoll and forced him to kneel. The first group took aim and, after a signal, opened fire. John Driscoll, shredded by the concentrated fire, immediately collapsed dead. The lynchers then forced the visibly terrified William to kneel beside the bleeding remains of his father. The next firing squad took up its position, and William quickly met the same gratuitous death as John. One newspaper reported that the lynchers proceeded to pick through John's and William's remains for "money and valuable papers." The lynchers then deposited the corpses in a rude, shallow grave and dispersed. Some lynchers—their bloodthirst apparently not slaked by the killing—went on to torch the Driscolls' homes and "expelled the widowed and orphaned families."[103] One newspaper account seemed to imply that the lynchers had acted, at least in part, out of a desire for illicit material gain, commenting that "the Driscalls were owners of valuable farms, which are under a high state of cultivation, and covered with extensive crops of growing grain." The lynchers, the paper reported, had "forbidden, under pain of death, any persons from harvesting the crops."[104] The killing of John and William, and the subsequent expulsion of their families, may have been motivated, at least in part, by a desire to vacate such valuable farmland.[105]

The killings at Washington Grove shocked many members of the local community. The lynchers had rejected both law and custom in executing their victims. Even in the wake of the 1835 Vicksburg lynchings, this kind of summary extralegal execution remained an alien occurrence for most Americans. The manner of the execution had itself been exceptionally brutal, with one later account claiming that the two men's skulls were so perforated that the blindfolds alone had prevented their heads from separating into "fragments."[106] Lyncher leaders had struggled to justify their actions to the uneasy crowd during the killing itself, and revulsion and disquiet regarding the lyncher action persisted in the days that followed. "Quite a number" of the local residents wished to see the lynchers prosecuted for murder, and some bolder persons signaled their displeasure publicly—albeit cautiously—directing unfriendly "looks and shrugs" in the direction of individual lynchers.[107]

The Rockford Star, the Democratic paper that had previously published the proceedings of the lynchers, printed a denouncement of the killings in its July 1 issue. If such actions were "tolerated," the paper argued, "no man's life or property is safe; his neighbor, who may be more popular than himself, will possess an easy, ready way to be revenged by misrepresentation and false accusation." Just over six months prior, the same *Rockford Star* had printed calls in favor of summoning "Judge Lynch and his Jury." Now the paper declared that "we wash our hands clear from the *blood of Lynch law*." In the same issue, a piece signed by "Vox Populi" labeled the lynchers "Banditti like" and "fiends in human shape." Taking aim at the use of lethal force, the anonymous writer asked if the community had degenerated to such a state where "a few desperadoes shall rise up and inflict all manner of punishment, even DEATH, upon whomso-ever they please?" Vox Populi ended with an appeal for the people to "rise *en masse,* and assert the laws of the land, and enforce the same against the murderers and lynchers!" It would be the last issue of *The Rockford Star* ever published. The lynchers, eager to discourage local retribution, responded to the denouncements on July 6. That night, a mob ransacked the offices of *The Rockford Star,* leaving, accord-ing to one Wisconsin Territory newspaper, the "type and fixtures so much injured and mutilated, that the paper has been obliged to discontinue."[108]

The reactions of other regional newspapers were mixed. The destruction of *The Rockford Star* muted more direct local criticism of the killings, and some of the accounts subsequently published in early July were more sympathetic to the lynchers. A letter published in the July 3 issue of the *Chicago American* characterized the sum-mary execution of the Driscolls as both "high-handed and revolt-ing" as well as "absolutely necessary."[109] An editor for the *Chicago American,* not content to couch their reactions in careful language, savaged the legal system directly. In the July 13 issue, they railed that "the slow and uncertain retribution of the legal code in its opera-tion, itself the sport of technicality, of perjury and every species of corruption—seems indeed, a mockery, and the ghost of the princi-ple and the blood of victims cry loud, long—plausibly, (may we not say justly) for swifter, deeper vengeance!"[110]

Criticism of the lynchers, while temporarily muted, did however persist, and intimidation soon proved insufficient to quiet all criti-cism. On July 13, the editor of Kenosha's *The Southport Telegraph,* unwilling to take a firm stance, meekly wrote that "the Supremacy of the law should doubtless be the resort for the punishment of crime in all cases where it is practicable. But there may be extreme cases in which the people have an undoubted right to take the law in to their own hands in self defense. No doubt there will be an honest difference of opinion."[114] A week later, *The Southport Telegraph*, in a dramatic reversal, condemned the affair and wrote that "Lynch law is the stepping stone to anarchy, misrule, and uncontrollable violence. To say that the laws of the states, are inadequate to perform the demands of human justice, is libel upon our government and institutions."[111] In late July, Illinois Attorney General Josiah Lamborn similarly denounced the lyncher violence and defended the efficacy of the formal legal system in the state.[112] On July 21, the *Peoria Register* placed blame on Judge Thomas Ford directly. Referencing the extralegal collective violence threatened by the judge during the spring term of the circuit court, the paper asked the reader if they might "not consider the tragedy in Ogle county as the first fruits of that strange and startling declaration, and is not Judge Ford in some measure responsible for its consequences?"[113]

News of the lethal lynching of John and William Driscoll soon spread beyond the region where the affair had occurred. Mob executions remained a rare occurrence in 1841, and the violence in Ogle County attracted the attention of newspaper editors from across the country, who subsequently republished accounts of the bloody spectacle. The story of the lynching of the Driscolls appeared in such large publications as the *New-York Tribune* and *Alexandria Gazette*, and accounts of the violence were published in states as far away as South Carolina, Vermont, and Connecticut.[114] Significantly, it was not the criticisms of the lynchers that reached a national audience. These distant papers generally republished accounts penned by the *Chicago American*, which had adopted a pronounced editorial slant in favor of the killing. Readers across the nation were presented with the notion that lynchings could not only be lethal, they could be necessary and good. It was the call for "swifter, deeper vengeance" that spread across the United States.

Back in Ogle County, the lynchers made no effort to impede the coroner's inquest and subsequent grand jury indictment of 106 men for the murder of John and William Driscoll.[115] On September 24, the murder trial began. None other than Judge Thomas Ford presided. Ford had helped set the entire affair into motion, and while the violence had grown too extreme for his liking, he now had to clean up the mess. In many ways, however, ceding power to the mob had directly benefited the judge. Ford had feared for the safety of his family and his property following the burning of the Oregon City courthouse and had used the specter of extralegal collective violence as a protective ward. Even though the men who brutally lynched John and William Driscoll had made good on Ford's threats, their actions did not directly implicate the judge. Years later, Ford would continue to insist that the lynchings "put an end to the ascendency of rogues in Ogle county."[116] Now, with the messier segments of the affair having been handled extralegally, Ford could use his power within the formal legal system to provide the episode with a neat, official conclusion.

The entire trial was a farce from the start. The grand jury that had indicted the lynchers included within its ranks several of the same lynchers listed as defendants. The brother of one of the defendants served as the grand jury's foreman.[117] That so many lynchers voted to indict themselves would indicate, as historian David Grimsted speculated, that Thomas Ford orchestrated the entire trial to preemptively absolve his allies and "preclude any possible later action."[118] The questionable legal maneuvering, at the very least facilitated by Ford, was unquestionably at the initiative of the lynchers. One of the defense attorneys, John Dean Caton, himself confirmed this, later writing that "I unhesitatingly advised that an indictment should be procured against all who were present at the execution, feeling perfectly assured that they could be acquitted then, while a change of condition, of population, and of public sentiment might, without a judgement of acquittal standing upon the records, give them trouble at some future time."[119] This maneuver was far from discrete. *The Southport Telegraph* was able to correctly surmise that the indictment was "probably brought about by the individuals themselves, and their friends in order to prevent their being troubled with the matter hereafter."[120]

Even the prosecution was in on the scheme. At some point early in the proceedings, a Peoria lawyer by the name of Lincoln B. Knowlton requested to join the prosecution. Knowlton was apparently serious about prosecuting the case. State's Attorney Seth V.

Farwell, however, refused Knowlton's request and dismissed him as a drunk, while Ford would later label him as "a kind of attorney-general for the horse thieves."[121] Unimpeded by Knowlton, Farwell would not challenge the irregular course of the proceedings. He was uninterested in prosecuting anyone.

When the murder trial did get underway, merely addressing the sheer number of defendants took most of the court's energy. "Most of the time occupied in the disposition of the case," according to the later *History of Ogle County*, "was consumed in calling the names of the defendants."[122] One newspaper account of the trial reported that "the very fact of the great confusion occasioned by so many names in the indictment, left the accused without any evidence to contend against." A few witnesses were introduced, but defense attorney Caton dismissed their limited knowledge of the affair as nothing more than "rumors." Judge Ford summarily instructed the jury that "rumors were not evidence."[123] The more valuable witnesses, according to the newspaper account, "were found, upon close examination, to be a part of the accused themselves, and of course could not testify."[124] Caton later bragged that the prosecution "utterly failed to prove that any person had been killed, much less that any of the prisoners had taken any part in killing anybody."[125] Caton's success, of course, is less impressive in light of the prosecution's total lack of effort. Ford then allegedly went even further, telling the jury explicitly that he did not see how over one hundred men could murder one.[126] The jury, with very little deliberation, returned a verdict of "not guilty." In all, 106 killers left court without the designation of "murderers."

Even following the mass acquittal, however, debate over the lynchers' actions continued to rage across the region. In the October 8 issue of Ottawa's *The Illinois Free Trader*, an anonymous writer going by "Amor Legum" railed that the lynchers "had violated the laws of their country, the laws of humanity, and the laws of God, in sending the unhappy victims of their wrath into eternity, without an opportunity of making a defence, or time to prepare for death." The writer presented an impassioned and educated argument against "mobocracy," quoting English jurist William Blackstone, who wrote that "the public peace is a superior consideration to any one man's private property; and as, if individuals were once allowed to use private force as a remedy for private injuries, all social justice must cease, the strong would give law to the weak, and every man would revert to a state of nature."[127] "Lynching," Amor Legum continued, "springs from the vindictiveness of excited passion, organizes its mob, seizes its victims, and hurries them beyond human help, tries them in hate, condemns them by acclamation, and murders them in passion."[128]

The lynchers had their apologists as well. The week before Amor Legum published their piece, a writer going by "A Spectator" had penned an article in the *Free Trader* defending the lynchers and their actions. "Individually," the author argued, "they could not protect themselves—mob law they repudiated—they therefore resorted to a counter organization, ordained new rules of evidence, and a new mode of proceeding, such, and such only, as in their judgement were effectual to protect them."[129] The bold assertation that the lynchers had the right to adjudicate their own rules of evidence and mode of proceeding represented a particularly radical understanding of popular sovereignty. Spectator sent a second article to the *Free Trader* shortly after Amor Legum published their denunciation of the killings. In a furious response, the anonymous author attacked Amor Legum directly, insisting that "those who executed the Driskalls were a whole community; they were a community whom the laws could not and did not protect; for all the laws protected them, they might be and were pillaged, robbed, and murdered."[130]

In a letter dated October 20, Amor Legum responded, accusing Spectator of misrepresenting Blackstone as "an advocate of Lynch Law" before arguing that if the community had combined to lynch the Driscolls, surely they could also have combined to try them by jury. The writer then specifically cited Ford's successful March–April prosecution of the counterfeiters to underscore the capacity of the northern Illinois formal legal system to settle criminal controversies. However, the writer continued, Judge Ford and the lynchers had "desecrated the temple of justice, and perverted the law" in securing an acquittal. "To complete this tragic scene," Amor Legum lamented, "the actors performed the solemn mockery of acquitting themselves, by going through a form of that very law that they had condemned, despised and violated; and now have evaded punishment, because the law protects them from again being tried."[131] The cynical blending of legal and extralegal tactics had been, in the understanding of Amor Legum, a grave sacrilege, all the more offensive on account of its success.

The exchange between the two anonymous commentators captured a larger debate in miniature—the continued struggle between those who advocated for the supremacy of the formal legal system and those who asserted the ultimate primacy of the people over the law. The lynching of John and William Driscoll would prove to be a significant episode in the evolution of this struggle. The lethal lynching of captives—sparked in part by the vigilante-adverse Driscolls' own reaction to the bloodletting of the Bellevue War— helped further establish an important extralegal precedent, one that newspapers disseminated across the nation. These press accounts parroted justifications for the extreme violence employed by the lynchers—justifications premised upon increasingly entrenched notions of an extreme vision of popular sovereignty and defended through already established Jacksonian rhetoric. It was views similar to those of Spectator rather than those of Amor Legum that were spread widely.

The press was only one vector, however, by which the significance of the Driscoll lynching diffused. As had been the case in the Bellevue War, the movement of human beings and their networks ensured that the violence would not remain confined to Ogle County. Actors implicated within the violence of northern Illinois would, over the years that followed, informed by their experiences in that episode, go on to profoundly shape subsequent incidents of extralegal collective action elsewhere in the state. This would occur at the interpersonal level across networks, as those fleeing the wrath of the lynchers carried with them the contagion of suspicion, extending the threat of extralegal collective violence to their contacts. It would also occur at the highest levels of state government. Less than a year after he engineered the acquittal of the members of the Ogle County

Lynching Society, Judge Thomas Ford would be unexpectedly elevated to high political office. It would be along such human linkages that the Ogle County lynching would have its most profound and severe impacts, enlarging the genealogical flow that had wound through Bellevue. From the corpses of the Driscolls bled a volatile brew that would seep across Illinois in the years that followed. It would include alleged thieves, counterfeiters, and professed prophets. The state was primed for an explosion.

CHAPTER 3

CARTHAGE, ILLINOIS

"Are We Indeed to Have a 'Lynch' Governor?"

At four o'clock p.m., on May 14, 1842, Adam Wilson Snyder made a fateful contribution to the political future of Illinois. He died. Snyder had been battling an affliction of the lungs, and heart failure brought an end to his misery. For the state's Democrats, Snyder's death came at an inopportune time. He had been the party's gubernatorial candidate for the state of Illinois and was slated to compete against Whig Joseph Duncan in just two and a half months. The Democrats now had to scramble to procure a serviceable candidate. They found one in a backcountry judge with a recently elevated public profile. Just eleven days after the death of Snyder, Thomas Ford found himself the Democratic candidate for governor.[1]

The political ascendancy of Thomas Ford occurred during a turbulent period in Illinois. Under the leadership of their prophet, Joseph Smith, the Mormon faithful had established a presence in the western reaches of the state.[2] Smith and his followers, informed by their own bloody experiences with extralegal collective violence, challenged and manipulated the formal legal system of Illinois to advance their interests and defend themselves against hostile combinations. This led to tensions between the Mormons and their "gentile," or non-Mormon, neighbors, who accused the Mormons of twisting the law to obfuscate sustained violations of not only property rights but established social and sexual mores. The specter of open sectarian violence soon loomed over Illinois. Thomas Ford would react to this threat with an attitude informed by his

Portrait of Joseph Smith, Peoria, Illinois, circa 1879. Photograph by W. B. Carson. Courtesy of the Library of Congress.

prior experience with extralegal collective violence, expanding the impact of the 1841 Ogle County lynchings far beyond the environs of northern Illinois. A mob would, in 1844, kill Joseph Smith and his brother Hyrum in the jail of the western Illinois town of Carthage. Thomas Ford had personally promised Smith protection, but his actions, informed by his previous experiences, made the extralegal killings possible.

To analyze the relationship between Ford and Smith—and the outcomes that would result from it—is to investigate spiraling sequences of individual choices and interpersonal encounters. As each man, in pursuit of his own goals, engaged with and reacted to the other, he participated in a continuous process of exchange, recalculation, and judgement. As both leaders navigated uncertain and consequential terrain, they weighed this ever-shifting calculus against their own personal experiences. The actions of either man cannot, therefore, be understood in isolation, nor can they be separated from each other's past.[3] From a higher vantage, this analysis advances the narrative of a genealogical flow in motion. Out of the relationship between Thomas Ford and Joseph Smith would spring profound consequences, not only for both men but for the larger populations under their leaderships. The aftershocks of the brutal termination of that relationship in June 1844 at the Carthage jail would irrevocably alter the fabric of western Illinois and, eventually, of the western United States.

Most of the Illinoisan Democratic press quickly rallied around Ford as their new candidate. *The Illinois Free Trader* had, not even a year prior, published Amor Legum's scathing condemnations of the legal farce in Ford's courtroom that saw the Ogle lynchers acquitted. Now, the same publication lavished praise upon the judge, insisting to readers that Ford was a "man of strong native mind, well disciplined by close and arduous application in the investigation of legal questions—high-minded and honorable—of strict integrity— sustaining an irreproachable character."[4] Other Democratic publications similarly lauded Ford for honesty and an unswerving adherence to his principles, with one paper proclaiming that "nothing on earth could induce him to falter in discharging his duties without favor or prejudice, personal or sectional."[5] Some Democrats went so far as to bestow upon Ford the sobriquet "the honest judge."[6] That "the honest judge" had hurled threats of lynching from the bench in Ogle County—and facilitated the questionable legal maneuvering that followed—did not apparently factor into this glowing assessment.

Ford's Whig adversaries also did not, for their part, immediately seize on the judge's connection to the Driscoll killings. They might have feared that publicizing the affair too widely could recast the small judge as a decisive Jacksonian man of action. Instead, the Whigs initially organized their attack around shattering Ford's coalition. In the northern reaches of the state, Ford's opponents accused the judge of opposing the completion of the Illinois and Michigan Canal and labeled him a "northern man with southern feelings."[7] Ford had vexed northern Illinois voters by rejecting a scheme devised by some residents of the upper counties to secede from debt-addled Illinois and join Wisconsin Territory. This did not stop the Whigs, Ford complained, from simultaneously "endeavoring to make the people believe that I am in favor of giving up to Wisconsin a portion of our territory in the north."[8]

It was among Ford's supporters, however, that the Whigs found some of their most incendiary ammunition. Before Ford had found himself on top of the Democratic ticket, then-candidate Adam Snyder had secured the support of Joseph Smith, the charismatic leader of a growing religious sect that had recently arrived in the state. To Smith's followers, the Mormons, he was a prophet. To his critics, Smith was a charlatan and blasphemer. Smith had led his followers west in search of an American Zion, but their eventual settlement in northwestern Missouri had led to tensions with the neighboring non-Mormon settlers. In 1838, the bloody "Mormon War" erupted. A series of violent confrontations left both combatants and innocents dead, and on October 27, Missouri governor Lilburn Boggs issued his infamous Missouri Executive Order 44, more commonly known as the Mormon Extermination Order, which directed the state militia that the Mormons "be exterminated or driven from the state if necessary for the public peace."[9]

Smith and his followers fled Missouri and sought shelter in neighboring Illinois. There, in 1839, they purchased the tiny hamlet of Commerce, located along the Mississippi River in western Illinois's Hancock County. The Mormons quickly transformed the small and sleepy village into a city, renamed Nauvoo. Illinoisan leaders initially welcomed the sect's settlement, seeing the Mormons as a much-needed source of economic stimulus and a potential pool of votes. Stephen A. Douglas, an ambitious young Democrat, helped the Mormons secure for Nauvoo an exceedingly permissive charter that granted the city an unusual degree of political sovereignty and even its own militia—the Nauvoo Legion.[10] Douglas also cleverly exploited the recent Mormon experience with bloody extralegal violence, insisting in one speech, according to a Whig newspaper, that "the duty devolved upon HIM, to protect the Mormons from a mob which was arming to attack them."[11] In return for Douglas's efforts, Smith directed his followers to throw their support behind the Democrat Snyder in the 1842 gubernatorial election. When Snyder unexpectedly died, Ford inherited Smith's endorsement.[12]

The Whigs saw in Ford's Mormon supporters an opportunity. Duncan loudly denounced the excesses of the Nauvoo city charter, with the *Quincy Whig* reporting that their candidate would repeal the charter, disband the Nauvoo legion, and put the Mormons "on equal footing with all other religious denominations in the State."[13] These attacks were buoyed by a growing anti-Mormon sentiment in Illinois. That July, the disgraced and excommunicated former mayor of Nauvoo, John C. Bennett, published a series of accusations directed against Smith and his religion. Writing in the *Sangamo Journal*, Bennett alleged that the "*beast* and *false prophet*" Smith had played a role in the attempted assassination of former Missouri governor Lilburn Boggs. Even more salaciously, Bennett revealed that Smith had secretly engaged in the polygamous practice of obtaining multiple "spiritual wives."[14] With the Whig attacks threatening to draw a close association between Ford and the controversial sect in the public mind, Ford moved to distance himself from the Mormons. "I reside at a great distance from these people, and know nothing about them," he insisted in a written public circular, "and I have never read those charters until very lately. It is my opinion . . . that they ought to be amended, so as to place them upon an equality with our other citizens."[15] Ford's ambivalence toward the Nauvoo charter disturbed the Mormons but did not break Smith's endorsement.

With Ford seemingly on the backfoot and already associated with the Mormons, the Whigs pivoted and attempted to shatter Nauvoo's support for the Democrat. The 1841 Ogle County lynchings provided them with the potential material to do just that. By mid-July the Whigs had begun to spread rumors of Ford's involvement with the Ogle lynchers, and on July 30, the *Quincy Whig*, published in Adams County just south of Nauvoo's Hancock County, ran a piece reminding readers that it had been "hardly one year, since Thomas Ford made his celebrated speech at Oregon City, that he would follow certain obnoxious individuals and 'hang them upon the first tree' he came to, 'Law or no Law.'" The bloodletting in Missouri remained an exceedingly painful memory for much of Nauvoo's Mormon population, and they were consequently extremely sensitive to the threat of mob violence and Lynch law. Explicitly invoking the "lynching and the murder of the Driscoll's, at Washington Grove," the piece undoubtedly sought to drive a final wedge between Ford and his Mormon supporters.

Nauvoo's Mormon residents were aware of the violence that had taken place in Ogle County the year before. Nauvoo newspaper and church mouthpiece *Times and Seasons* had reported on the killings in August 1841. The editors had denounced the lynchings using strong language, writing that "every reflecting mind must at once stand appalled at such unwarrantable and unconstitutional proceedings." Such mobs threatened not only their victims, the editors had argued, but the republic itself. "If the main pillar of the constitution, viz: the Judiciary is tottering," they maintained, "and the citizens after delegating that power into such hands as they choose, and then again take it into their own at pleasure, and use it as their excited passions may dictate . . . the glorious constitution of America . . . will fall, and in its ruins crush its best and noblest friends."[16] While the 1841 *Times and Seasons* article had made no references to Ford, the *Quincy Whig* attempted to clearly illustrate the connection a year later. "Is such a man to be made Governor of this State?" the 1842 *Whig* piece asserted, "Are we indeed to have a 'Lynch' Governor? And is the very captain of the 'Lynchers' to sit in the highest place of our State?"[17]

The Whig attack was well-calculated, but Smith's endorsement, and the Mormon vote, held firm. The promise of a friendly governor outweighed any hesitancy to support a "'Lynch' Governor." On August 1, 1842, Ford cruised to victory over Duncan by a margin of five thousand votes. One thousand votes from that winning tally came from Hancock County, where the Mormons overwhelmingly backed Smith's choice.[18] It was only on August 5, four days after his victory, that Ford's response to the reports of his relationship with the Ogle lynchers appeared in print. Publishing a letter dated July 18 and addressed "to the people of Illinois" in the *Peoria Register*, Ford denied "having been in favor of Lynch law in Ogle county" before limply claiming that he was too far away from home to produce the evidence necessary to demonstrate his innocence. The newly elected governor went on to insist that he had "a number of enemies among the horse thieves and counterfeiters of the north, who have not been able to swerve me from a strict discharge of my duty as a judge, by repeated threats of violence to my person and property." Ford dismissed Lincoln Knowlton, the lawyer who had been prevented from joining the prosecution in the trial of the lynchers, as a "drunken lawyer from Peoria" and maintained that he "had no power to compel" the prosecution to accept Knowlton's services. Ford carried this claim of personal powerlessness into his discussion of the lynchers themselves, arguing that he had attempted to stop the killings but "had no force, and the power was all on the side of the Lynchers."[19]

Ford's insistence on his own powerlessness and his supposed opposition to the work of the lynchers is not supported by the existing accounts of the Ogle County violence. He may have opposed the application of lethal force, but he had encouraged the use of extralegal force all the same. Ford's claims of innocence and disapproval also do not fit with his own central role in securing the acquittal of the lynchers through what could be charitably termed "irregular" legal maneuvering. Still, with the Whigs soundly defeated, the issue seemed to fade. The legacy of those Driscoll killings did not, though, disappear. The memory of the violence lived on within the new governor-elect, just as the memory of Missouri lived on within the Mormon prophet who had nevertheless endorsed him. Neither man knew it, but Ford's and Smith's personal histories of extralegal violence would continue to shape their relationship over the years to come. The consequences would prove considerable.

On December 8, Thomas Ford delivered his inaugural speech as governor in Springfield. Addressing the state senate, Ford's remarks largely revolved around the fiscal health of Illinois. Reckless government spending had submerged the state in debt, and the new governor devoted much of his time to a discussion of the canal, expenditure, revenue, and banks. Near the end of his remarks, Ford briefly touched on the question of the Mormons and Nauvoo's city charter. "The people of the State have become aroused on the subject," he noted, "and anxiously desire that those charters should be modified so as to give the inhabitants of Nauvoo no greater privileges than those enjoyed by others of our fellow citizens."[20]

The circumstances surrounding the Mormon settlement had only grown more complex since Ford's electoral triumph. The previous May, an unidentified assailant had attempted to assassinate former Missouri governor Lilburn Boggs in his home. The would-be assassin shot Boggs in the head and neck, but the former governor, to the surprise of many, survived. Boggs had issued the Mormon Extermination Order during the Mormon War of 1838, and rumors quickly spread that Joseph Smith had ordered the attempted murder. Many Mormons had indeed celebrated the news of the shooting of a governor at whose hands they had suffered. *The Wasp*, a Nauvoo newspaper edited by Joseph Smith's brother William, published a letter on May 26 terming the attempted killing a "noble deed." At the same time, William Smith dismissed the rumors swirling around the alleged involvement of his brother and the Mormon faithful. "The last account we have received is that he is still living and like to live," the editor wrote, "and if he has been shot at all it was by one of his own negroes."[21] Boggs evidently disagreed with that assessment, and, on July 20, signed an affidavit for the arrest of Joseph Smith on charges of being "accessary before the fact of the intended murder."[22] Subsequently, Missouri governor Thomas Reynolds requested that Illinois officials extradite Joseph Smith.

Outgoing Illinois governor Thomas Carlin quickly responded to Reynolds's request. On August 2, a day after the Mormon vote had helped catapult Ford and Carlin's Democrats to victory in the gubernatorial election, Carlin signed an arrest warrant for Smith. The Nauvoo City Council responded by using a creative reading of their city's charter to reimagine habeas corpus in their own favor. As historian Benjamin Park notes, the city council proclaimed "that even if a resident of the city was arrested outside of Nauvoo, for crimes that took place elsewhere outside of Nauvoo, and by a warrant signed at any jurisdictional level above Nauvoo, the accused still had the right to be returned to Nauvoo for a hearing."[23] The

Mormon militia, the Nauvoo Legion, prepared to defend their prophet and gave teeth to the city council's declarations. The Mormons interpreted these events through their own experience with extralegal collective violence and justified their actions accordingly. Wilson Law, a member of the Nauvoo City Council, wrote in an August 17 letter to Joseph Smith that "every movement of this generation reminds me of the history of the people who crucified Christ, it was nothing but mob law, mob rule and mob violence all the time, the only difference is that the Governors then were more just than the Governors now."[24] Illinois officials angrily denounced Nauvoo's leadership and their interpretation of habeas corpus but could do little else. Smith, for his part, went into hiding.[25]

Following Ford's inauguration, Stephen A. Douglas and US district attorney Justin Butterfield managed to convince the Mormons to appeal to the new governor.[26] Ford, after consulting with six members of the Illinois Supreme Court, wrote to Smith on December 17, informing him that justices were "unanimous in the opinion that the requestion from Missouri was illegal and insufficient to cause your arrest."[27] Ford promised Smith protection, and the Mormon prophet consented to submitting to state officials, arriving in Springfield on December 30 for a hearing. On January 5, 1843, Judge Nathaniel Pope threw out the Missourian extradition order.[28] The Mormons celebrated the verdict and praised the new governor, with Smith writing to Butterfield on January 16 that "the innocent been rescued from the power of mobocracy." Smith remained cautious against further legal trouble in the wake of the extradition attempt, but Ford's actions seemed to have suggested to the Mormon prophet that he had found in the new governor an ally. "I am in hopes," Smith continued in his letter to Butterfield, "that Gov'r Ford will not gratify the spirit of oppression and mobocracy."[29] Smith now reimagined Ford, the man denounced as "'Lynch' Governor" just months before in the *Quincy Whig*, as a potent ward against mob law.

Smith was correct that his enemies would persist in their attempts to see him extradited. In June 1843, the circuit court in Daviess County, Missouri, requested that Illinois extradite Smith to face charges of treason. On June 17, Ford signed the warrant for Smith's arrest. Smith escaped apprehension after a Nauvoo habeas corpus hearing but was furious over what he perceived as a betrayal on the part of the governor.[30] "I prophecy in the name of the Lord God," Smith wrote in his journal, "that Governor ford by granting the writ—againt me. has damned himself politically and his carcase will. stink on the face of the earth food for the carrion crow & Turkey buzzard."[31]

Word soon reached Nauvoo that officials might use the militia to arrest Smith. The Mormons' panic overshadowed their anger, and they again petitioned the governor and begged for his support. By the end of July, Ford made it clear that he would not order out the militia. Writing to the governor of Missouri, Ford took a legalistic stance, arguing that for him to authorize the deployment of the militia, "there must be either a requisition from the president an actual or threatened invasion, or some emergency to warrant the governor in exercising this power. Not one of these contingencies has arisen."[32] Smith and the Mormons again rejoiced at what they saw as another deliverance from the Missourians, and Smith subsequently directed his flock to back the Democratic candidate for the congressional race in the Sixth Congressional District that August while openly declaring himself a "personal friend" of the governor's.[33]

Joseph Smith's decision to direct the Mormons to back a Democrat in August 1843, however, provoked a wave of anti-Mormon sentiment. Incensed by what they saw as the Mormon manipulation of Illinois's legal and political systems, a group of anti-Mormons met in Carthage, Illinois, on September 6, 1843. There, they drafted a preamble insisting that a man such as Smith "cannot fail to become a most dangerous character, especially when he shall have been able to place himself at the head of a numerous horde." Labeling Smith an aspiring "despot" and "would be Mahomet," the anti-Mormons singled out Nauvoo's interpretation of habeas corpus, the Nauvoo Legion, and the Mormon practice of bloc voting, which, they maintained, resulted in "men of the most vicious and abominable habits, imposed upon us, to fill our most important county offices." Furthermore, the anti-Mormons declared, Nauvoo had become a den of thieves who, shielded by the city's court system, could operate with near impunity. "Citizens from the adjoining counties have been denied the right to regain property stolen and taken to Nauvoo," the anti-Mormons wrote, "even after they have discovered both the thief and the property." Ready to act on their own, the anti-Mormons vowed to defend their rights "peaceably if we can, but forcibly if we must." Even more explicitly, they swore that "if the Mormons carry out the threats they have made in regard to the lives of several of our citizens, we will, if failing to obtain speedy redress from the laws of the land, take summary and signal vengeance upon them as a people."[34]

Smith's teachings and Nauvoo's charter had long served as an irritant to the non-Mormon inhabitants of Hancock County and its environs, but the allegations of property rights violations were especially important as the anti-Mormon faction considered engaging in extralegal collective action. The engagements that saw William W. Brown and John and William Driscoll killed had all blossomed from disputes ostensibly rooted in the violation of property rights, and the defense of such rights provided one of the most potent rhetorical justifications for citizens, to borrow phrasing from the anti-Mormons, to "fall back upon their original and inherent right of self defense."[35] The anti-Mormons were certainly eager to rationalize organizing against Nauvoo. There is little reason, though, to believe that the complaints about Nauvoo serving as a hotbed for such violations were entirely fabricated, even if they were undoubtedly exaggerated.[36] Because of the use and abuse of habeas corpus in Nauvoo, coupled with and springing from Mormon anxieties regarding persecution by secular authorities, criminals could and did exploit residency within the city as a means of escaping prosecution.

One such individual was Edward Bonney. This was the same Edward Bonney, who with his cousin Thomas Babcock—the old associate of William W. Brown—had fled Farmington after locals determined the men to be counterfeiters. That experience, however, was apparently not enough to compel Bonney to cease the practice. On July 5, 1842, authorities had arrested Bonney near Warren, Ohio, along with associates Obadiah Cooley and Henry Kellogg for, according to one newspaper account, "being engaged in the manufacture of counterfeit coin." The trio, the account continued, had in their possession $2,070.50 of "spurious coin" along with tools for the production of counterfeit.[37] Bail was set at a whopping $1,000 each for Bonney and Cooley, and a still hefty $500 for Kellogg. After spending almost a month in the Trumbull County jail, Bonney eventually managed to secure bail. On November 1, a grand jury indicted the three men on charges related to counterfeiting.[38] On November 3, the court prepared to hear *The State of Ohio v. Edward Bonney, Obadiah Cooley & Henry Kellogg.* Edward Bonney, though, was nowhere to be found.[39]

The counterfeiter had fled west. Authorities in Ohio attempted to pursue him, submitting a requisition for extradition to authorities in Indiana.[40] Bonney needed to find a refuge where such extraditions could not haunt him. He found this sanctuary in Nauvoo. Bonney's brother, Amasa, was himself a Mormon and Nauvoo resident. While Edward was not particularly interested in Joseph Smith's religion, he was certainly interested in following the Mormon prophet's example in the navigation of legal affairs.[41] Edward Bonney was a fugitive from justice, but this did not relegate him to some underworld fringe. He quickly became one of Nauvoo's most influential residents. On April 4, 1844, Smith would elevate Bonney to his Council of Fifty, a body organized to help establish a theocratic "Kingdom of God" and support Smith's quixotic campaign for the presidency of the United States. Bonney was one of only three non-Mormon members of the council.[42] On June 18, Smith would appoint Bonney as one of his aides-de-camp in the Nauvoo Legion.[43] For Bonney the fugitive and counterfeiter, Nauvoo was not just a place to hide. It was a place where it was possible to thrive.

Certain members of the Mormon faithful also participated in criminal activity, infusing a strain of religious justification into their criminal operations. Such behavior emerged from the Mormon experience with extralegal collective violence, evolving in part from the actions taken by the militant "Danite" bands during the 1838 Mormon War in Missouri.[44] The Danites had been instructed by their leadership to "consecrate" and seize the property of their enemies during the conflict.[45] While many of the allegations of

Nauvoo criminality came from non-Mormons, the existence of such activity was also recognized at the highest levels of Church authority. In April 1843, Joseph Smith's brother Hyrum had disclosed the existence of an organized band of thieves operating out of Nauvoo. Hyrum Smith claimed that former Mormon David Holman had confessed to him that "there are a band of men & some strong in the faith of the Doctrine of Latter Day Saints. & some who do not belong to the church, were bound to by secret oaths &c that it is right to steal from any one who does not belong to the church if they gave ¼ part to the temple. if they did not remain stedfast—they ripped open thir bowels & gave them to the cat fish." Mormon leadership did not appear to condone such activities, with Hyrum Smith denouncing the Nauvoo band as "the very gadianton robbers of the last days," referring to a villainous group from the Book of Mormon. Joseph, for his part, followed Hyrum's address with strong words of his own, declaring that "I despise a theif above ground."[46] Still, it was the leadership's own political and legal strategies, driven by anxieties regarding persecution and secular authority, that had created an environment where such operations were possible. The anti-Mormons of the region were keenly aware of this.[47]

That winter the situation had further deteriorated. A group of men led by non-Mormon Hancock County resident Levi Williams had, on December 2, arrested two Mormons, Daniel and Philander Avery, for alleged horse theft in Missouri, a move that the Mormons considered a kidnapping.[48] At the same time, rumors began to spread that the Missourians would again attempt to extradite Joseph Smith. The Mormon prophet dashed off two letters to Governor Thomas Ford on December 6 and December 11, imploring his protection and asking if the Nauvoo Legion should be called out in response to the detention of the Averys. On December 8, the Nauvoo City Council took the Mormon reimagination of the law to a new extreme, declaring that any person found guilty of attempting to arrest Joseph Smith would be jailed for life. The governor could pardon such persons, but only with the express approval of the mayor of Nauvoo. The attempted Mormon inversion of Illinois's legal–political hierarchy did not stop there. The city council, within two weeks, passed yet another law. This one decreed that all writs issued outside of Nauvoo similarly required the approval of the city's mayor.[49]

Ford responded to Smith's first letter on December 12, instructing the Mormon prophet not to call out the legion and to behave peaceably toward the Missourians. The tone of the governor's response was cool.[50] Ford was growing increasingly impatient with Smith and the controversies that seemed to constantly embroil the religious leader. Ford also disapproved of the Mormons' flouting of Illinois's political and legal structures. The anti-Mormon backlash that followed the 1843 August elections had underscored the political danger of associating too closely with Nauvoo. Public outrage in response to the December actions of the Nauvoo City Council reaffirmed this danger. "When these ordinances were published," Ford later wrote, "they created general astonishment. Many people began to believe in good earnest that the Mormons were about to set up a separate government for themselves in defiance of the laws of the State." On perhaps a more personal level, Ford also noted that the Mormons had that winter, in his estimation, "bec[o]me more arrogant and overbearing."[51]

Smith noted the change in Ford's tenor but continued to place his faith in the governor.[52] This decision was seemingly validated on February 14, 1844, when Ford responded to anti-Mormon demands that the governor move against the Mormons. Dismissing some of the demands—such as forced Mormon disarmament and the deployment of the state militia—as "absurd and preposterous," Ford warned the readers of the rabidly anti-Mormon newspaper *The Warsaw Signal* against escalating tensions into violence. Smith publicly celebrated the governor's letter as proof of Ford's sustained goodwill and protection.[53] "There seems to be a prospect of peace," the Mormon prophet declared in the February 21 issue of *The Nauvoo Neighbor*, and he promised that he and his followers would "honor the advice of Governor Ford." Smith had taken Ford's words as a promise, when they were in fact a warning. The same proverbial sword that separated Nauvoo from its enemies kept one edge of its blade directed toward the city and the man who had built it. "I wish in a friendly, affectionate, and candid manner," Ford had written, "to tell the citizens of Hancock County, Mormons and all, that my interference will be against those who shall be the first transgressors."[54]

Meanwhile, visible fissures had begun to emerge within Nauvoo itself. Some prominent dissidents held personal grudges against Smith.[55] Others opposed Smith's controversial political and legal maneuvering.[56] Still, others turned to dissent in the face of increasingly loud whispers surrounding the prophet's marital teachings. Joseph Smith had begun to practice polygamy in secret. Rumors of marital heterodoxy had followed the Mormons since the 1830s, but as historian Benjamin Park argues, the actual practice of plural marriage, while "murky," likely began in Nauvoo in 1840.[57] Although Smith continued to deny the existence of the doctrine publicly, he secretly introduced the practice to other members of the Mormon elite. By 1844, Smith alone had over thirty secret wives, "and almost one hundred other men and women had entered the controversial order."[58] In May, dissidents Francis Higbee and William Law attempted to take legal action against Smith on charges of defamation and adultery, respectively.[59] By June 1844, however, the dissidents acquired an even more powerful weapon in their campaign against the prophet: a printing press.

On June 7, the dissident newspaper titled the *Nauvoo Expositor* published its first and final issue. The language was strong. "We are earnestly seeking to explode the vicious principles of Joseph Smith," the publishers wrote, "and those who practice the same abominations and whoredoms; which we verily know are not accordant and consonant with the principles of Jesus Christ and the Apostles."[60] Outraged, Smith convened the Nauvoo City Council and secured a unanimous vote to forcibly shut down the *Expositor*. That evening, a moblike combination of some two hundred men, pursuant to the council order, torched and smashed the *Nauvoo Expositor*'s printing press.[61] The sacking of the press generated immediate outrage from both the dissidents and the non-Mormon residents of the region. While the *Nauvoo Expositor* had in its single issue cautioned the region's anti-Mormons to "'keep cool'" and refrain from violence, anti-Mormons now roared for Nauvoo to be brought to heel. "Can you stand by," thundered Thomas Sharp, editor of *The Warsaw Signal*, "and suffer such INFERNAL DEVILS! To ROB men of their property and RIGHTS, without avenging them. We have no time for comment, every man will make his own. LET IT BE MADE WITH POWDER AND BALL!!!"[62]

The sound of war drums reverberated through Hancock County as both the Nauvoo Legion and non-Mormon militias prepared for violence. On June 18, Smith declared martial law in Nauvoo. That he had no actual legal authority to do so was, to the prophet, immaterial.[63] Governor Ford could no longer afford to not intervene. On June 21, Ford arrived in Carthage, the county seat of Hancock. He had not raised the militia but found in the town, in his own words, "an armed force assembled and hourly increasing."[64] Ford immediately reorganized the armed mob as a militia under his control. In addition to the Carthage militiamen, armed men arrived from the town of Warsaw and the counties of McDonough and Schuyler. Ford addressed the men, eliciting promises from them and the officers that the militias would support the governor "in strictly legal measures, and to protect the prisoners in case they surrendered."[65]

Ford then hurried off a letter to Joseph Smith, relaying to him that "I think before any decisive measure Shall be adopted that I ought to hear the allegations and defences of all parties. By adopting this course I have some hope that the evils of war may be averted."[66] Ford wrote again the following day, demanding that Smith and the other accused surrender themselves to the authorities in Carthage, or he would deploy the militia. Ford was in danger of losing control of the situation, and he knew it. "The whole country is now up in arms," he had written in that same letter, "and a vast number of people are ready to take the matter into their own hands. Such a state of things might force me to call out the Militia to prevent a civil war. And such is the excitement of the country that I fear that the Militia when assembled would be beyond legal control."[67]

Joseph Smith, fearing for his life in the face of the swelling mob, had initially refused to surrender and fled across the river to Iowa Territory. After receiving pleas from his frightened followers still in Nauvoo and assurances of safety from Ford, Smith returned to

Illinois. Pursuant to the governor's orders, Smith directed the Nauvoo Legion to surrender all its state-issued arms, which amounted to roughly 250 firearms and three artillery pieces.[68] Ford and Smith undoubtedly understood this gesture as a symbolic one, with the ultimate goal not of disarming Nauvoo but of easing tensions. The Mormons, as Ford would later note, still possessed sufficient private firearms to fully equip the Legion.[69] Smith then bid an emotional farewell to his family and, along with his fellow defendants, departed for Carthage. They arrived on June 24, just before midnight. The next morning, Ford, along with General Minor Deming, paraded Joseph and Hyrum Smith in front of the militia units that had assembled in Carthage.

The review started well enough, but when the group passed the local militia known as the Carthage Greys, the unit's militiamen began to behave mutinously. Ignoring the protests of their officers, the men refused introductions, began to hiss loudly, and cried out "down with all imposters!"[70] Samuel Otho Williams, a second lieutenant in the Carthage Greys, wrote in a letter to a friend that the men were "hissing and arming and making all sorts of hellish sounds. I tried to stop it but could not."[71] The men of the Carthage Greys loathed Joseph Smith and the Mormons, and they were eager to advertise their feelings. On top of this the militiamen were suspicious of their own authorities, with Lieutenant Williams noting that the men believed General Deming to be a *"Jack Mormon"* and had hissed at him during an anti-Mormon meeting in the town a few days prior. Following the review, a rumor spread that Ford had ordered that the Greys be arrested. "A number of the Company," Williams reported, "immediately mounted a wagon and made a speech to the troops and the remainder loaded their muskets with *Ball* cartridges and swore that they would die sooner than give up their arms."[72] While Ford soon cleared the misunderstanding and momentarily calmed the Carthage Greys, it was increasingly apparent that many of the men ostensibly under his command were more mob than militia.[73]

Later that day, the defendants appeared before Justice of the Peace Robert Smith—captain of the Carthage Greys. Joseph and Hyrum

Smith found themselves facing charges of treason related to the establishment of martial law in Nauvoo and therefore would need to appear before the circuit court judge to be assigned and post bail. Justice of the Peace Robert Smith simply adjourned proceedings before this could be done, assuring that Joseph and Hyrum Smith would be confined to Carthage and unable to return to Nauvoo. Ford refused to intervene in this biased and conflict-of-interest-tainted maneuvering, later offering the meek excuse that "the justice of the peace and constable, though humble in office, were acting in a high and independent capacity, far beyond any legal power in me to control."[74] The Smith brothers were then imprisoned in the small, two-story Carthage jail to await trial.[75]

On June 27, Ford gathered his militia officers and implored them not to march on Nauvoo. The governor had previously agreed to march on the city to search for counterfeiting operations and "also to strike a salutary terror into the Mormon people by an exhibition of the force of the State."[76] Now, Ford began to realize the danger of such a course of action. Although the Mormons had surrendered their state-issued arms, they could still field a large, well-equipped, and zealous fighting force. The non-Mormon militia forces that had mustered around Carthage and Warsaw were eager to avenge depredations both real and imagined, and many wanted blood. Some of the anti-Mormons were so rabid for a fight, as Ford himself would later admit, that they were even conspiring to launch a false-flag attack on the non-Mormon forces in order to trigger an assault on Nauvoo.[77] "The only danger is to be apprehended from our own camp," General Minor Deming had written in a June 26 letter to his family, "from the exasperated state of some of our citizens, who desire to demolish the city. . . . The loss of one man in our ranks will demolish and expel from the state every citizen of Nauvoo."[78]

As Ford had made clear in his correspondence with Joseph Smith in the days prior, he knew he had little control over his own militiamen. Ford believed, Lieutenant Williams recorded, "that if we once got into Nauvoo that he could not restrain the troops and that we would burn the place."[79] General Deming had recorded similar doubts regarding the quality of the militia officers and men in a letter to his family, complaining that he was "completely absorbed in the turmoil of a camp of inexperienced officers and excited citizens."[80] The mood remained more mob than military. Ford's entreaties to those "inexperienced" officers to rethink the march against Nauvoo only confirmed the governor's inability to control the men. While officers from Schuyler and McDonough counties mostly agreed with Ford, the majority of the Hancock County officers voted to march on Nauvoo in defiance of their commander-in-chief's wishes. Those in favor of the march carried the vote. Ford began to panic. The very real possibility of a bloody civil war loomed over Illinois.

At this juncture, Thomas Ford made a series of choices that have mystified chroniclers ever since. The governor ordered his own militia force to disband, save for two companies.[81] One company would accompany Ford to Nauvoo, where he would exhort the Mormons to behave peaceably. The other company would stay in Carthage to guard the jail where the Smith brothers were incarcerated. That company would be none other than the insubordinate and feverishly anti-Mormon Carthage Greys, under the command of the same Captain Robert Smith who had manipulated legal proceedings as justice of the peace to keep the Smiths in jail without the possibility of posting bail.[82] While General Deming would still be officially in command of the Carthage militia, the men had already made their attitude toward his leadership clear.[83] The Carthage Greys had already become openly mutinous at the mere sight of Joseph Smith even while in the presence of not only the general but their commander-in-chief. Ford's decision not to march on Nauvoo with the full force of the assembled militia had only further enraged the men. Eudocia Baldwin Marsh, who had two older brothers in the Carthage Greys, later recalled that the men reacted with "rage and disgust" when Ford disbanded the larger force. "Strong hope had been entertained," she explained, "that a show of determination, backed by strength, would secure the enforcement of law in the county, and possibly even banish the offenders."[84] On June 26, Ford had promised Joseph and Hyrum Smith that he would take the brothers with him for their protection when he left for Nauvoo.[85] The next morning, though, Ford reneged on that pledge. In a later account, he would hurry over the reasoning behind this reversal, offering only the vague explanation that his officers had "offered such substantial reasons for their opinions as induced me to change my resolution."[86]

Ford's decision to go back on his word and leave the Smiths in the custody of the Carthage Greys was shocking and seemingly counterintuitive. The governor could have just as easily disbanded the Carthage Greys and assigned one of the militia units from Schuyler or McDonough to guard the high-profile prisoners. Ford would later offer the limp defense that the decision was one of pure practicality, as the militiamen from outside of Carthage "were very much dissatisfied to remain." The Carthage Greys, on the other hand, "could board at their own houses, and would be put to little inconvenience in comparison." [87] Such anemic excuses might have sufficed if Ford himself had not already recognized the severity of the crisis and the real danger of armed conflict. The men and officers from Schuyler and McDonough had proven themselves to be better disciplined and willing to follow the governor's orders. The officers and men of the Carthage Greys, on the other hand, had repeatedly behaved in an insubordinate, threatening, and moblike manner. They should have been the last choice to guard vulnerable, highly sensitive prisoners. Yet Ford, by his own admission, left that unit as Carthage's sole armed force—under the command no less of a man who had already demonstrated not only his contempt for the Smiths but his willingness to subvert the rules to the brothers' detriment—during a moment of pronounced tension and instability, for the mere purpose of avoiding a little "inconvenience."

To borrow from Stuart Rulan Black, "Ford disbanded those he had organized under the government, and seemingly turned the militia back into a mob."[88] Indeed, by dismissing the more loyal militia units and leaving the town himself to travel to Nauvoo, Ford vacated the power of the state in Carthage. By Ford's own design, the openly hostile Carthage Greys—the very manifestation of anti-Mormon popular will—were left as the only remaining source of power and authority in the town. That Ford would choose this path would, at first blush, seem to indicate a stunning degree of naivety or raw foolishness on the part of the governor. Thomas Ford, for all his ı

faults, was not unintelligent, however. Nor, as events in Ogle County had proven, was he the scrupulous legalist as he is so often depicted in accounts of the affair. The governor had found himself sucked into a violent maelstrom for which his limited conventional political education had left him woefully unprepared. Still, there was a logic behind his decisions.

There is only one lens through which Ford's actions at Carthage appear intelligible and coherent. Stuck in such unenviable circumstances, Ford did not know what to do. So, he fell back on his own past experience.[89] Thomas Ford had faced the acute personal dangers of state powerlessness in the face of violent fracture before, and in yielding to the fury of popular will, he had in that circumstance emerged unscathed. That episode had been the sole experience that even somewhat prepared Ford for what he faced in Hancock County. It is through the prism of the governor's own prior experience with extralegal collective violence in northern Illinois, therefore, that Ford's seemingly bizarre and discordant moves in Carthage can be interpreted.

As a judge in Ogle County, Ford had experienced state impotence firsthand. He had watched his courthouse burn. He had feared for the lives of his family members and for his property. He had partaken in the exchange of bloody threats as his courtroom proceedings degenerated. Unable to accomplish anything through official channels besides securing a few minor unsatisfying convictions, Ford had ceded judicial authority to the lynchers and removed himself from the area as their violent work commenced. Then, when popular will had been made manifest, and John and William Driscoll lay covered under a thin veil of caked dirt and dried blood, Ford had returned, with his problems now solved and an ability to plausibly deny any involvement in the episode. All he had to do was secure a batch of acquittals for the killers, and the entire affair was seemingly settled for good. The experience had a profound effect on Ford's understanding of the relationship between popular will and state power. "For if a government cannot suppress an unpopular band of horse thieves, associated to commit crime," he would later write, "how is it to suppress a popular combination which has the people on its side?"[90]

Now, as governor, Ford knew the stakes were far higher. Events in Carthage had plainly exposed his feebleness during the crisis. After attempting to insert himself into the middle of the conflict and keep the peace, Ford realized that he had placed himself in opposition to the popular will of most of the militiamen ostensibly under his command. This, in the governor's mind, meant that his power was effectively negated. As Ford later reflected, the situation in which he had found himself in 1841 and now again in 1844 was the result of an American legal–political system where state power was intentionally limited as a deterrent against tyranny. In empowering the people to protect themselves against the abuses of the state, though, the Constitution failed to provide the state sufficient means to prevent the abuses of illegal or extralegal combinations of the people, such as organized horse thieves or lynch mobs.

Indeed, for most agents of the state to wield any substantial armed power, they were forced to rely on popular combinations of local armed citizens in the forms of the militia and the posse comitatus. They were as such beholden to the popular will that motivated those citizens. "Attacks upon liberty," Ford would later reflect, "were not anticipated from any considerable portion of the people themselves. . . . And if such a thing had been thought of, the only mode of putting it down was to call out the militia, who are, nines times out of ten, partisans on one side of the other in the contest."[91] If an agent of the state failed to concede to the realities of that arrangement, Ford was aware, those citizens would simply act outside of the formal legal system in order to enforce their will. Whether an armed band was called a militia, a posse comitatus, or a lynch mob, all ultimately prioritized local interests over state concerns. "The militia may be relied upon to do battle in a popular service," Ford continued, "but if mobs are raised to drive out horse thieves, to put down claim-jumpers, to destroy an abolition press, or to expel an odious sect, the militia cannot be brought to act against them efficiently. The people cannot be used to put down the people."[92]

Ford undoubtedly sensed that his personal involvement in the matter was doing little to calm the situation in Carthage. Should the situation deteriorate while he remained present in a position of leadership, moreover, the larger Illinoisan public would most certainly assign the blame to him. Ford's protection of Smith over his gubernatorial tenure, coupled with his previous unwillingness to challenge Nauvoo's use of habeas corpus, would undoubtedly resurface and become a source of great embarrassment in any sort of bitter legal struggle, undermining Ford's ability to react to any subsequent posttrial tremors. Regionally, the acquittal of the Smith brothers would likely provoke devastating violence, but so would their sentencing. Ford, based on his understanding of popular will, the behavior of the Carthage Greys, and his own earlier experiences in Ogle County, did not believe he could count on the militia to contain that violence. In short, to quote historians John E. Hallwas and Roger D. Launius, "Ford found himself in an impossible position."[93]

Ford's prior experience in Ogle County and the situation in Hancock County had convinced the governor that he could not stop the manifestation of popular will. All he could do was try to get out of its way and attempt to manage its course and consequences from the sidelines. In removing himself from the center of the action, Ford may have believed he had his best opportunity to carefully direct the flow of violence, even if he did not believe he could prevent its occurrence. It is worth speculating that Ford believed that ceding power in Carthage to the most moblike element of the region was a means of mitigating bloodshed. If extralegal punishment—which Ford was now not confident he could prevent—was visited upon the Smith brothers by forces ostensibly in state service while the governor and militiamen from several neighboring counties were present, it might appear that the state of Illinois itself was responsible for the violence. Such a perception potentially portended a broader-scale conflict between the Mormons and the larger population.[94]

Instead, Ford had chosen to leave only Carthage units to defend the jail while dismissing the militias from the neighboring counties and preparing to vacate the town himself. In taking these actions, Ford may have been attempting to ensure that Carthage alone would appear directly responsible for any action taken against the Smiths. The town was to be a lightning rod: a means of potentially directing Mormon fury toward a single target in the pessimistic scenario that the powerful Nauvoo Legion responded to mob violence with violence of its own. Ford likely hoped that any potential punitive expedition from Nauvoo might be satisfied with a strike against Carthage, leaving the rest of western Illinois unscathed. While the governor would never be willing to admit to such a desperate calculus in his later writings, it is the only logic by which his actions become coherent.

With no palatable options, Ford, just as he had back in 1841, ceded authority to the mob. On the morning of June 27, he departed the town with a company of dragoons. Four miles outside of Carthage, while en route to Nauvoo, Col. Nathaniel Buckmaster attempted to communicate to Ford that he believed "that an attack would be made upon the jail."[95] Ford disregarded the intelligence. The party was still close enough to Carthage to have turned back and bolstered the jail's security, but Ford had chosen his path. Although the governor had by now effectively surrendered the Smith brothers to the mercy of an angry mob, it is doubtful that he wanted the Smith brothers killed or that he even considered that eventuality a real possibility.[96] It is true that the lynchers had killed John and William Driscoll in the other incident of extralegal collective violence in which Ford was complicit, but that killing had been preceded by the Driscolls themselves allegedly having drawn first blood. Killing still remained relatively rare within the practice of American extralegal collective action, even as the genealogical flow that now cascaded into Hancock County hinted at a new paradigm. Ford had also secured promises from the officers and men of the Carthage Greys that they would "do their duty according to law." According to Lieutenant Williams, some two hours after he had left Carthage, Ford sent Capt. Robert Smith a message that "he expected him to do his duty," at least until, by Ford's own admission, the governor was safely out of Nauvoo.[97] The captain responded in the affirmative.[98] Ford expected Captain Smith and his men to preserve the lives of Joseph and Hyrum Smith. Ford probably anticipated the meting out of collective violence against the Smith brothers, but it is also probable that he believed that the militiamen would limit themselves to nonlethal action. Traveling to Nauvoo while leaving Joseph and Hyrum Smith in the custody of a glorified mob undeniably put the governor at risk, but, as Ford would admit in his own account, he "supposed a regard for my safety and the safety of my companions would prevent an attack until those to be engaged in it could be assured of our departure from Nauvoo."[99]

Back in Carthage, General Deming had departed the camp and left the other officers in command.[100] In Quincy, a lightning strike had killed the general's brother, Edwin, and Deming was anxious to attend to the affairs of the deceased. Captain Smith of the Carthage Greys ordered a squad of six men to guard the jail. The squad was to be rotated every three hours. The rest of the company remained at their quarters some five hundred yards from the jail.[101] Captain Smith ordered two boys to take a position on top of the courthouse as lookouts, with directions to watch for the approach of bodies of men. The captain was especially concerned about any movement coming from the direction of Nauvoo.[102]

Around 4 p.m., the boys spotted an armed body of men some two miles out, approaching the jail from the northwest. The lookouts hurried to Captain Smith, who took no action. A half hour later the armed body, which Hamilton figured to be 125 men strong, breached the timber and began making their way single file toward the jail. They were now only three-quarters of a mile away. The boys again rushed to find Captain Smith, but according to Hamilton, "could not find the captain; and . . . told another officer, who after considerable delay found the captain who ordered the company to fall into line."[103] The Greys, some of whom were only "half-awake," began to slowly assemble into proper military formation. The lethargy and lack of urgency was too much for one member of the unit, Tom Marsh, whose brother was one of the guards stationed at the jail. "Come on, you cowards, damn you, come on," he shouted at his fellow militiamen, "those boys will all be killed!" An officer attempted to shove Marsh back into formation, but he broke free and sprinted toward the jail. The other members of the company, however, ignored

Marsh's frantic pleas. They continued to slowly assemble, strangely unphased by the armed body rushing into their town. "I have always thought," the young lookout Hamilton would later admit, "the officers and some privates were working for delay."[104]

While the Greys continued their unhurried preparations to march, the rest of Carthage erupted in panic. Rumors spread that the unidentified armed force was a party of Mormons intent on rescuing their prophet from the jail. "By this time," recounted Eudocia Baldwin Marsh, "the square was the scene of the greatest excitement and confusion. Men ran about, some shouting, 'The Mormons are coming, the guard will all be killed'; others, 'The Danites are coming for the Smiths.' They did nothing but shout." Eudocia Marsh was Tom Marsh's sister, and she too feared for the life of her brother stationed at the jail. Disgusted by the inaction that surrounded her, she denounced the men as "cowards" and ran after her brother.[105]

Just before Eudocia Marsh could make it to the prison, the unidentified armed band surged into the area. They were not Mormons but men from Warsaw, a town to the south of Nauvoo and west of Carthage. Earlier that morning, the Warsaw militia, which had been preparing to march against Nauvoo, had received the governor's order to disband. The Warsaw men were enraged by the governor's orders, and prominent local anti-Mormons like Thomas Sharp, editor of *The Warsaw Signal*, had given furious speeches against "being made the tools and puppets of Tommy Ford."[106] George Rockwell, an anti-Mormon resident of Warsaw, would later write to his parents that some of the dismissed militiamen, now irritated and listless, became suspicious that "this disbanding was a plan to let the prisoners escape as they frequently had done before, and feeling unwilling to be trifled with any longer, they determined to take the matter into their own hands."[107] The members of the Warsaw militia-turned-mob then blackened their faces "with powder and mud" as a crude means of disguise and began their march toward Carthage.[108] They were soon intercepted by a messenger from the Carthage Greys. John Hay, whose father was a Warsaw resident who refused to join the mob, would later maintain that it was a common belief that the courier "brought an assurance from the officers of this company that they would be found on guard at the jail where the Smiths were confined; that they would make no real resistance,—merely enough to save appearances."[109] Thomas Ford himself would similarly later write that "a communication was soon established between the conspirators and the company; and it was arranged that the guard should have their guns charged with blank cartridges, and fire at the assailants when they attempted to enter the jail."[110]

When the men of the Warsaw mob charged the jail, sure enough, resistance was token. The guards fired blanks into the large crowd and were summarily overrun. Despite the theater, neither rioter nor guard received any real injuries. As Lieutenant Williams would later report, the guard's losses would account to a sword and musket, and the men "were not hurt except some bruises."[111] Joseph and Hyrum Smith, who had been secretly supplied with pistols by friends, used their bodies to block the door of their room from opening as attackers forced their way into the building. The crack of gunshots punctuated the din as mobbers took aim at the wooden door and fired. One of the balls hit Hyrum Smith in the head, and he dropped to the floor, dead. Joseph Smith, seeing his brother fall, unloaded his pistol into the surging mass of blackened faces. Under return fire, he then retreated toward the room's window. More members of the mob, gathered outside, saw Smith appear. They raised their weapons and opened fire. Balls ripped through Smith from behind and below, and the Mormon prophet tumbled out of the jail.[112] Joseph Smith was dead.

The purposefully delayed Carthage Greys were still about 150 yards away from the jail when Smith fell.[113] The young lookout William Hamilton, who had abandoned the slow-moving company and rushed to the jail, had witnessed the fatal fall of Joseph Smith. He later recollected that he had time to inspect the corpses of both Joseph and Hyrum before the Greys finally arrived at the scene. Their arrival put the cynical, conspiratorial farce on full display. They marched up, Hamilton would recount, "in good formation, marching in good time, with guns properly at shoulder and flag flying, as if on dress parade, or ready for business."[114] With the prisoners already dead, the Greys simply turned around and returned to camp to disband.

Thomas Ford learned of the killings about two hours after sundown. He had arrived in Nauvoo earlier that day and had addressed a crowd of several thousand of the city's inhabitants. The governor's powerlessness in the face of possible extralegal violence was clearly on his mind as he delivered his address. Ford would later summarize his own words, recounting that he had told the people of Nauvoo, in part, that should they chose violence, "the public hatred and excitement was such that thousands would assemble for the total destruction of their city and the extermination of their people; and that no power in the State would be able to prevent it."[115] After receiving assurances from the assemblage that they would obey the law, Ford departed the city. Two miles outside of Nauvoo, the governor and his party met with two messengers bringing word of the killings. Ford began to panic that "an exterminating war" was at hand.[116] As his mind raced through the implications of the killings, Ford, to his horror, began to reflect on the timing of the mob's attack. He had previously convinced himself that no danger would befall the Smiths while he was in Nauvoo, but the mob had lynched the Mormon prophet and his brother while Ford was still in the heart of the Mormon stronghold. This, to an increasingly terrified Ford, equated to an attempt on his own life. "Upon hearing of the assassination of the Smiths," he would write, "I was sensible that my command was at an end; that my destruction was meditated as well as that of the Mormons; and that I could not reasonably confide longer in one part or in the other."[117]

Ford immediately ordered the messengers be put into custody and prevented from reaching Nauvoo. The governor and his party then departed for Carthage, hoping to get far away from Nauvoo before word of the killings could reach the city. Upon their arrival in Carthage around 10 p.m., they found much of the town already deserted. Once the inhabitants of the town realized that the Smiths were dead, there was, to quote Eudocia Marsh, a "panic." Fearful that the Nauvoo Legion would descend and put them to the sword, most of the inhabitants fled. A few men, like Marsh's brothers and Lieutenant Williams, remained behind to defend their property. Ford, angry and afraid, "remained," in the words of Eudocia Marsh, "only long enough to denounce the people for their folly."[118] Lieutenant Williams noted that the governor "stated that he believed our town would be in ashes before the morning." That was enough for Williams and most of the other remaining inhabitants, who summarily deserted their posts and fled.[119]

Ford then quickly left Carthage and began to travel toward Quincy, where he hoped to regroup and reconstitute, if necessary, a new militia force. Confusion and dread prevailed throughout the region, and Ford had to halt several militia units who were preparing to march toward Carthage. Marsh and her family encountered a frantic Ford at Kendall's hotel, some nine miles outside of the town. Hearing the shouts of men and braying of horses, Marsh initially believed that the Mormons had arrived to massacre them but, to her relief, discovered that the governor and his men had paused at the inn to water their steeds. Ford was not, however, a calming presence. "He assured mother," Marsh would write, "that the avengers would be there before morning, and he could not leave us to be murdered. 'You must get up and state on,' he said, and so we did."[120] Ford and his party reached Quincy around 8 a.m., on June 28, and the governor "immediately issued orders, provisionally, for raising an imposing force."[121]

The feared Mormon reaving, though, did not materialize. Willard Richards, a companion of the Smiths who survived the attack on the Carthage jail, had sent a letter to Nauvoo immediately after the killings. He had urged his fellow Mormons "*Don't rush out of the city*—don't rush to Carthage; stay home, and be prepared for an attack from Missouri mobbers."[122] Ford had intercepted Richards's letter on his way back from Nauvoo, and, on his arrival in Carthage, directed Richards to add a segment to the letter proclaiming the governor's sustained promise of protection for the Mormon people.[123] Richards noted that the "governor will render every assistance possible" and even maintained that "the guards were true as I believe."[124] While some members of the faithful yearned for retribution, Nauvoo's elite lacked an appetite for further escalation. When the bodies of the Smith brothers arrived in Nauvoo on June 28, a sense of grief and despondency rather than a thirst for vengeance dominated the city.[125] That morning, W. W. Phelps—who would deliver the eulogy for Joseph Smith—and Ford's representative, Colonel Buckmaster, addressed the Nauvoo Legion "and all excitement and fury allayed."[126] Mormon resident Vilate Kimball wrote to her absent husband on June 30 that "every heart is filled with sorrow, and the very street of Nauvoo seam to morn. Whare it will end the Lord only knows."[127] The civil war that Thomas Ford feared had, for the moment, been averted.

Against all odds, Thomas Ford's strategy of ceding state authority to popular will had seemingly, once again, carried the day. No widespread armed conflict had erupted in Hancock County, and the political irritant that was Joseph Smith had been removed. Despite this, Ford walked away from the killings at the Carthage jail unhappy with the outcomes he had helped facilitate. It was not exactly that the governor mourned the death of Joseph Smith, a man he later characterized as "the most successful imposter in modern times."[128] It is clear, though, from his shocked and panicked reaction to the news of Joseph and Hyrum Smith's deaths that the governor had not anticipated a lethal lynching when he left the brothers to the mob in Carthage. That the mob had gone so far as to kill their targets put the life of the governor at risk. Moreover, the outright killing—as opposed to some form of extralegal humiliation or banishment—of two persons under state protection was a prominent humiliation for Ford's administration. As for the militiamen and officers who had aided the mob, Ford proclaimed bitterly that "they have added treachery to murder, and have done all they could to disgrace the state, and sully the public honor."[129] Still, it was Ford who had promised the Smiths protection, and it was that broken vow that would be remembered in retellings of the affair.

While the Mormons heeded the governor's pleas that they not mobilize for a punitive strike, many of the faithful in Nauvoo came to blame Ford for the death of their prophet. In his eulogy for Joseph Smith, W. W. Phelps lamented that the brothers had "fallen victims to the popular will of mobocracy," and placed the governor's name alongside a litany of infamous traitors that included "Cain, Nimrod, Korah, Judas, Herod, Boggs, Ford."[130] The July 1 issue of the *Times and Seasons* similarly bemoaned the fact that the Smiths had surrendered "under the solemn pledge of the faith of the State, by Gov. Ford, *that they should be protected!* But the mob ruled!!"[131] The official *History of the Church* would later go so far as to maintain "that the Governor, on arriving at Carthage, ordered the entire mob into service."[132] The Mormons clearly and correctly recognized that Ford was guilty of yielding to popular will and abandoning his personal and legal obligations to their prophet. The criticisms stung Ford, who in his later reflections would confess that he stood "a fair chance, like Pilate and Herod, by their official connection with the true religion, of being dragged down to posterity with an immortal name, hitched on the memory of a miserable imposter."[133]

In the immediate aftermath of the killings, however, an injured sense of honor was the least of Thomas Ford's concerns. Although Ford and Mormon leaders had momentarily staved off the specter of war, the deaths of Joseph and Hyrum Smith inflamed already stark tensions. Anti-Mormons continued to agitate for a broader conflict, threatening Mormons located in settlements outlying Nauvoo in hopes of provoking a crisis that would end in the overall expulsion of the Mormon people. "I am continually informed of your preparations and threats to renew the war, and exterminate the Mormons," Ford wrote in an exasperated communication to the people of Warsaw dated July 25. "One would suppose that you ought to rest satisfied with what you have already done."[134]

No party, of course, was content to "rest satisfied." The Mormon prophet was dead, but his people remained. This alone was enough to inspire those on both sides of the factional divide to prepare for a fight. Resentment, anxiety, and loathing had only compounded with the killings, and although civil war was not immediate, it was by no means averted. *The Warsaw Signal*, referencing Ford's own actions during the lynching of the Driscolls back in Ogle County, retorted that "if the conduct of His Excellency in a certain affair that transpired on Rock River, some years since, is correctly reported, we think that, were he now a citizen of Hancock he would be as loth to take his advice as any of us."[135] Here, the paper was more incisive than perhaps even its editors realized. What transpired in Hancock could not be divorced from the prior killing in Ogle. Thomas Ford had acted with an attitude shaped by his experiences as a judge in Ogle County, ceding power to the mob at a critical juncture. In this way, what had happened to Joseph and Hyrum Smith cannot be understood independently from what had happened to John and William Driscoll. That episode, in turn, cannot be understood separately from the killing of William W. Brown back in Bellevue. The bloodlettings were not independent but were rather interlinked within an expanding web of human action and movement. The aftershock of the Smith, Brown, and Driscoll killings would continue to roil. The violence did not begin with the killings at the Carthage jail. Nor, for that matter, would it end there.

CHAPTER 4

MARSHALL COUNTY, ILLINOIS

"Seize the Opportunity, and Cry Out Rogue!"

On October 29, 1845, hundreds of men, women, and children mingled outside the jail in Rock Island, Illinois. A wet and gloomy October morning lurched over the crowd, but the rain did not deter the mass of curious onlookers who milled about the gallows. A melody floated through the damp air as a band, the Green Mountain Boys, performed music they had composed "expressly for the occasion." At around one p.m., a guard assembled in front of the jail. Three well-dressed young prisoners left the building and began to make their way forward. The guard positioned themselves in a hollow square around the gallows, and the three men ascended the scaffold, where the sheriff and several others joined them.

The sheriff, after reading the order for execution, offered the prisoners an opportunity to speak. One of the young men stepped forward. He was slender, on the short side, and outfitted in gentlemanly attire. His hair, long and parted down the middle, framed sharp, gleaming eyes, which scanned the crowd that thronged before him. The man bowed. "Ladies and gentlemen of this respectable audience," he began, "I appear before you as a dying man, about to be launched into eternity, and request that you will listen to what I have to say, before I leave this world forever." And so began John Long's final appeal.[1]

It had been a little over a year since a mob had killed Joseph Smith at the Carthage jail. Smith's death had done little, however, to calm tensions between the Mormons and their gentile neighbors.

Daguerreotype of
John Long. Thomas M.
Easterly, "Unidentified
Man," daguerreotype.
Courtesy of the
Missouri Historical
Society.

Sporadic fighting and targeted acts of terror gripped western Illinois
as both sides, once again, prepared for greater bloodletting. The tensions took place against the backdrop of sustained anxieties regarding
the criminality that supposedly radiated out from Mormon Nauvoo.
That summer, a court had ordered two Mormon Nauvoo residents,
brothers William and Stephen Hodges, to be hanged for the murder
of Mennonite minister John Miller and his son-in-law Leiza at West
Point, in Lee County, Iowa Territory.[2]

The Hodges brothers had been arrested after an investigation led
by none other than Edward Bonney. Bonney, who had evaded the
law after being caught counterfeiting in Iowa and Ohio, had settled
in Nauvoo. There he had quickly found favor with Joseph Smith and
became Smith's aide-de-camp in the Nauvoo Legion, as well as one
of the few non-Mormon members of Smith's Council of Fifty. After
Smith's death, Bonney had fallen from the Mormon Church's graces
and found himself ejected from the council in early 1845.[3] Deprived
of Nauvoo's protection, Bonney used the Hodgeses' case to reinvent

himself once again. The old rogue refashioned himself as a private investigator working to expose Nauvoo's criminal networks. It was through Bonney's efforts that John Long, along with his brother Aaron Long and associate Granville Young, now found himself facing execution for the murder of Col. George Davenport.

"Is Mr. Bonney here?" John Long asked the assemblage gathered before the scaffold. Here he paused, scanning the crowd for the face of his accuser. Long had begun his speech by accepting responsibility for the Davenport murder but insisted that his two companions were innocent. He, William Fox, Robert Birch, and Thomas Brown had killed Davenport, Long proclaimed. Now, he sought the man whose testimony had caused him and his fellow prisoners to face death. "If Mr. Bonney is here," Long continued, "it is my request that he step forward." A voice from the crowd relayed that Bonney was, in fact, not present. "Well then," exclaimed Long, "if Mr. Bonney is not here, it knocks 650 pages from my speech! That man Bonney has been held before you, gentlemen, as one of the best men that ever lived. But I now tell you that he is the chief among thieves and robbers, and was accessory both before and after the fact to the murder of Miller."[4]

Like the execution of the two Hodges brothers, the grim proceedings during which Long spoke were of the legal variety. The state, not a mob, conducted the execution. Still, this sanctioned violence too was intimately connected to the sequence of extralegal action that had transpired over the five years prior. Long's pointed accusations were revelatory, offering a sliver of insight into the mounting damages wrought by the continued shocks of extralegal action to the human networks connected to the affairs. Long knew Bonney. They had operated in the same circles for years. William Fox and at least one of the Long brothers had cut wood for William W. Brown, while Bonney and his cousin, Brown's associate Thomas Babcock, ran a counterfeiting operation in Farmington, Iowa Territory. Exiled from Iowa, the men operated out of Nauvoo until the mob killing of Joseph Smith unsettled the city's dynamics and upended their operations. Stresses led to fractures. John Long may not have faced his doom at the hands of a mob, but the compounding consequences

MURDER OF MILLER AND LIECY.—page 26.

Illustration of the murder of John Miller and his son-in-law, Leiza. From Edward
Bonney, *The Banditti of the Prairies* (Chicago: D.B. Cooke & Co., 1856), 27.
Courtesy of the Library of Congress.

of violent extralegal action had still shaped the twisting path to his
noose.

This is, in part, the story of how these violent events brought
Young and the Long brothers to the scaffold on that rainy October day. The episode, however, is just one part in a larger narrative
of the collapse of the kinship network to which the Long brothers
belonged. The Longs were part of a cluster of associated families
consisting of the Reeveses, Phippses, Harts, Birches, and others that

had migrated into the Middle West from the Virginia–North Caro-lina border. That network possessed significant ties to every episode of violence analyzed in this larger investigation. Members partook in the Bellevue War, sheltered refugees following the Ogle lynch-ings, and were active in Nauvoo in the events leading up to Smith's death at the Carthage jail. The true extent of these connections would only become visible as repeated instances of violent action ravaged the region and unsettled the bonds of secrecy, caution, and loyalty. This unsettling led to even more violence, as vigilantes and mobs targeted branches of the families for their alleged connections to organized criminality and drove them farther afield.

To trace the story of these interconnected families is to unravel this chaotic tangle of connection and collision. It is to look both backward and forward, establishing more clearly the astonishing extent to which prior incidents of violent action had been con-nected, while at the same time tracking the subsequent episodes of mob action and killing, both extralegal and legal, that occurred as a result. The trials of that kinship network offer a lens through which we can follow a great human movement westward out of Illi-nois, through Iowa Territory, and into the unorganized territory that would soon become known as Nebraska. This fraught journey would be pocked with additional episodes of violence as the sur-vivors navigated the residual consequences of the action in Illinois while encountering new and sometimes hostile circumstances.

When the Ogle County lynchers seized John and William Driscoll in the summer of 1841, William K. Bridge had taken flight. Bridge had been one of the first residents of the region to resist the lynchers, and it had been in his barn that the Driscolls had allegedly formu-lated the plan to kill John Campbell. Furthermore, it was William's daughter, Hettie, who had, according to lyncher Phineas Chaney, revealed that Bridge and his associates had supposedly made addi-tional plans to end Chaney's life. When the lynchers captured the Driscolls, they also attempted to locate and seize several additional targets, including William Bridge. Had those targets not managed to escape, they too would have faced the same lyncher tribunal that saw John's and William's mangled corpses deposited into shallow graves. This initial escape did not guarantee safety, though, and as *The Illinois Free Trader* noted, "Detachments were sent off in every direction in pursuit of David Driscall and Bridge. They have not yet been taken, but it is considered next to impossible for them to escape."[5]

Desperate to escape the fury of the lynchers, Bridge had fled south to Marshall County. There he sought shelter at the home of a man by the name of George Reeves.[6] The Reeveses' home, not far from the Illinois River, was nestled "in the mouth of a deep ravine into whose dim recesses the sun seldom penetrated." A thick wall of timber, brush, and vegetation further concealed the property and its inhabitants. In this secluded wooded maw, the Reeveses had erected a dwelling place and several outbuildings.[7] There the roughly 46-year-old George lived with his wife, 41-year-old Elizabeth Doughton Reeves. Together they had 6 children: 19-year-old Joseph Cameron, who went by "Cam"; 17-year-old Preston; 15-year-old Sophronia; and younger children William, Jesse, and George, aged 11, 7, and 3, respectively.

The Reeves family offered Bridge sanctuary. The family was unable to hide the hunted man indefinitely but managed to protect him until tempers had sufficiently cooled back in Ogle County. A search party eventually found Bridge hiding in the garret of the Reeveses' home and brought him back to Ogle County to face charges related to his connection to the killing of Campbell. There a justice of the peace named William J. Mix discharged Bridge, according to one local history, "for want of sufficient evidence."[8] The lynchers, for their part, similarly failed to move against the man. The extralegal killing of the Driscolls had angered a significant number of the locals. One 1845 newspaper account later claimed that when authorities brought Bridge to Oregon City following his arrest, an armed band under the leadership of Adolphus Bliss and Corydon Dewey "proceeded to Oregon in wagons, with their implements of death, with the determination to rescue Bridge at all hazards, if they people offered him any abuse."[9] Bridge had escaped both legal and extralegal retribution, but at the cost of increased scrutiny now leveled at the family that had sheltered him.

Questions began to swirl around the nature of the relationship between Bridge and the Reeves family. That Bridge had fled to the Reeveses' secluded home, and that the Reeveses had readily harbored him, contributed to a growing chorus of murmurs. A later history of Marshall County reported that some locals believed the Reeveses were enmeshed in a large network of horse thieves and counterfeiters that stretched across the region. Those locals alleged that thieves brought stolen horses from the Rock River region of northern Illinois down to the Reeveses' home, where they would be concealed until they could be safely fenced. Thieves operating within Marshall County and its environs, however, made sure that "horses stolen here were swiftly taken abroad."[10] Decades later, the participants in various "Old Settlers" meetings, at which older residents commemorated the early histories of their settlements, still "recited" how George Reeves "secreted stolen horses and other property as well as thieves," was the "reported accomplice of a gang of horse thieves and counterfeiters," and "entertained horse thieves."[11]

By October 1841, these rumors had reached the Illinois attorney general, Josiah Lamborn, who had decried the lynching of the Driscolls in northern Illinois that summer. Now he had apparently come to believe it prudent to release the names of suspected criminals as a means of compelling them to depart from the region before tensions could erupt into the further application of what Lamborn termed "the disastrous method of linching." "There are many guilty persons at large in the community," he wrote in a letter to the *Illinois State Register*, "and it is a much safer way to drive them from the country or from the evil of their ways, by publishing them to the world, than by a resort to the passions of an infuriated mob, as has been too frequently the case." Lamborn specifically accused Matthew Spurlock, Garland O. Wilson, a Gleason, a Bigelow, a Wilkinson, a Hotchkiss, and "many traveling rascals who go by various names, and whose business it is to carry information, run of stolen property, distribute bad money &c., among these are Birch, Brown, Bartlett, Bridge and others." In a detailed account, Lamborn accurately described the networks of horse thieves and counterfeiters as "extensively connected together" and led by "permanent residents with the appearance of respectability," who would "make their houses the stopping places for those who do the active business of committing crimes." One such station, he wrote, "of the most abandoned description, is located in Marshall county, under the superintendence of George Reeves."[12]

Lamborn's strange attempt at shaming Reeves into vacating the area failed. Less than a month after the publication of Lamborn's letter, George Reeves received a patent for his more than seventy-nine acres of land in Marshall County.[13] Lamborn's accusations did not immediately trigger a local effort to remove the Reeveses through the kind of extralegal methods he ostensibly had been attempting to prevent. The local element of the formal legal system similarly failed to take action against George Reeves in any meaningful way.[14] Authorities undoubtedly did not possess sufficient evidence to make a move, while residents evidently lacked at that moment the will to organize an extralegal effort to evict or otherwise punish the Reeveses.

There are several plausible explanations for this lack of action. Locals might have tolerated the Reeveses' criminal activities if they themselves were not victims.[15] If the Reeveses had been counterfeiting or passing counterfeit, the cycle of passing spurious notes or trafficking stolen goods to outsiders would have injected muchneeded real money into the local economy. Like other communities in the Middle West, the people of Marshall County had suffered from a continued dearth of currency in the wake of the Panic of 1837. *The Gazette*, published in Marshall's county seat of Lacon, had bemoaned the economic state of northern Illinois just a few months prior, writing that "in trade there is very little doing—our merchants and other business men concur in the belief that the season was never so dull before in Peru." Peru was an important transportation and commercial hub located along the Illinois River to the north, and *The Gazette* blamed the economic issue on a lack of currency, continuing to note that "the gradual withdrawal of the circulating medium has been perceptible to every one for the last six weeks. All are complaining of the scarcity of money."[16] So long as the Reeveses did not make local enemies by violating the property rights of their neighbors, the county's residents may well have been content to ignore the alleged activity as it continued.

Indeed, the Reeveses took pains not to aggrieve their neighbors and, despite the rumors, fostered something of a positive social reputation among at least a portion of the local population. One local history, critical for the most part of the Reeveses, admitted that George Reeves "was a kind neighbor, scrupulously just in his dealings, ever ready to accommodate, and kind in sickness . . . suave and gentlemanly in appearance, seldom excited or thrown off his guard, and prompt to repair an injury or accommodate a neighbor." The family did not exist along the fringes of local society, and Elizabeth and George's teenaged daughter, Sophronia, was in fact a popular youth. The same local history noted that "Sophronia had many friends in Henry and was much thought of."[17] Even as whispers flew and rumors spread, these factors alone might have been enough to prevent, at least for the moment, extralegal action against the family.

Even if a subset of Marshall County's population wanted to move against the Reeveses, it would not have necessarily been easy to do so. The Reeves clan belonged to a sprawling network of interrelated families who dwelt around the larger region. That kinship network had in the years prior chain migrated into the Middle West from the New River Valley, which extended from southwestern Virginia into North Carolina. Some of these southern migrants developed something of rough reputation in their new environs, with the local history of Marshall County singling out one of the interrelated families—the Harts—as a "family of semi-outlaws" belonging to "the class known in the South as poor white trash, and were idle, vicious and pugnacious, quick to take offense and prompt to resent an insult."[18] If they could not command the overwhelming support of the area's other residents, local would-be vigilantes might have hesitated to trouble the Reeveses over the possibility of inviting retribution from such nearby members of the related New River families.[19]

To unravel the tangled webs of relation and alliance that bound the Reeves family to so many others in the Middle West is to trace the connections between various episodes of extralegal violence and alleged criminal operations woven by members of the network. This unraveling also makes visible the degree to which the aftershocks of violence could unsettle such networks, producing fluid situations where identities and relationships could be strained and, at times, renegotiated. It helps us to reckon with the production and aftermath of extralegal violence in terms of human mechanics and human cost. To understand any of that, however, the New River family network itself must be understood.

Elizabeth Doughton was born in 1799 in Grayson County, Virginia, to Joseph Doughton and Mary "Polly" Reeves Doughton.[20] Elizabeth eventually married her first cousin, George Reeves, who lived just across the border in nearby Ashe County, North Carolina.[21] Elizabeth and George's common grandfather, George Reeves, had migrated into the New River Valley from central North Carolina around the end of the 1760s, potentially pushed into the backcountry by the same forces that sparked the pre-revolutionary War of the Regulation.[22] The violence brought many other settlers into the New River Valley, with former regulators fleeing west following the defeat of their movement.[23] The Reeves and Doughton families, both of which had been among the first of those settlers to arrive in the area, erected homesteads and quickly established kinship bonds not only with each other but with many of the other migrant families. Grandchildren of those earlier settlers, Elizabeth and George remained in the New River Valley for the first decades of their adult lives. It was there that they started their family, with Elizabeth giving birth to children Cam, Preston, Sophronia, William, and Jesse.

While members of both the Reeves and Doughton families at times occupied prominent positions, legal records indicate that members of the Reeves family in particular had an often turbulent relationship with both their neighbors and the formal legal system. In 1808, an Ashe County jury found one George Reeves—probably the uncle of both George Reeves and Elizabeth Doughton—guilty of assault and battery. The next year, a jury found him guilty of slander. In 1811, William Tolliver, this George Reeves's brother-in-law, shot and killed him. The case inflamed local passions, and Judge

Samuel Lowrie found it necessary to transfer it to a court in Wilkes County. He ordered the sheriff to transport Tolliver "safely" out of Ashe County under a guard of "eight men from the proper offices of the militia."[24] Reeves men and women faced Ashe County juries with an extraordinary frequency, and few years passed without some legal action taken against a member of the family.

Another George Reeves, potentially the husband of Elizabeth Doughton Reeves, began to appear in the court's records in 1813, when he would have been around eighteen years old. Many of the charges leveled against members of the Reeves family included allegations of violent crime. In 1814, William Reeves Jr. faced allegations of forceful trespass, and assault and battery, while Jesse Reeves escaped false imprisonment charges that same year. John Reeves faced assault and battery allegations in 1815, while in 1816, George Reeves faced accusations of both trespass and assault. That same year, William and John Reeves stood accused of assault and battery, and John Reeves "and others" faced a riot charge. Charges related to assault and battery on the part of the Reeveses continued to work through the legal system over the following years, even seeing Ann Reeves accused of the crime in 1817. Charges relating to trespass and riot similarly continued to appear in the records. In 1819, a jury found William and John guilty on a charge of trespass, while a jury found George guilty of assault that same year.[25] Although a fire destroyed many of the Ashe County Superior Court records for the years that followed, it is likely that the Reeveses' stubborn pattern of criminality persisted through the 1820s. Criminal activity linked to the Reeves family was not confined solely to Ashe County, and in Elizabeth's home county of Grayson, Virginia, a John Reeves escaped charges of horse stealing in 1818 after the state entered a nolle prosequi.[26]

Perhaps eager for a fresh start or just a new opportunity, George, Elizabeth, and their children left the New River Valley between the late 1820s and early-to-mid-1830s and embarked on a journey into the Middle West. This migration would see the family travel far from the region of their births but would not take them into circumstances that were entirely unfamiliar. Several families from the New

River Valley, connected by association and often by a degree of inter-relation, had similarly migrated into the Middle West in the years prior. Familiar multifamily networks were quickly established where the New River migrants settled. One group of Reeveses settled in the adjacent Greene and Lawrence counties in Indiana. William Reeves, uncle to both George and Elizabeth Doughton Reeves, moved into the area with his family sometime in the late 1820s.[27] He appeared in the 1830 census as a resident of Greene County, alongside familiar names like William Phipps.[28]

Other New River families followed, and soon another group set-tled in Owen County, Indiana, adjacent to Greene County. There they established the Grayson township, undoubtedly named after the New River Valley county in Virginia.[29] Brothers Jesse and William Phipps, first cousins to both George and Elizabeth Reeves through their mother, Elizabeth Reeves Phipps, both led their families into the region in the early 1830s.[30] Like the Reeveses, the Phippses appeared frequently within New River Valley legal records, and Jesse alleg-edly brought a defiant attitude toward the law with him into his new environs.[31] One local history of Owen County characterized Jesse Phipps as "an early comer, whose reputation was none of the best." The history continued to note that Phipps "kept a house which for a number of years was the general resort of a class of roughs who set at defiance the laws of both God and man."[32] That "class of roughs" probably consisted of members of Jesse Phipps's extended family and other New River Valley migrants who, like the Long family, also had settled in the region. The New River Valley families continued to strengthen ties and intermarry while in Indiana, with Jesse's son John Meshack, better known as "Shack," marrying Marry Elizabeth "Polly" Long, while Polly's sister Jane married Troy Phipps, Shack's first cousin and William Phipps's son.[33] Jane and Polly's father, Jesse Long, also settled in the region, as did his brother, Owen Long.[34]

Some members of this kinship network soon moved out of Indi-ana, possibly in search of fresh opportunities and available land to meet the demands of the sustained migrations from the New River Valley. Brothers Lenoir and Terrell Reeves, sons of William Reeves and first cousins to both George and Elizabeth, settled in Putnam

County, Illinois, sometime in the early 1830s.[35] Local histories indicate that it was through this connection that Elizabeth, George, and their children first migrated into Illinois. Mistaking Lenoir and Terrell for George's brothers, one history noted that George and his family first lived with their cousins in Senachwine Township before settling in the adjacent Marshall County.[36] It was a pattern of scouting, migration, and settlement not unlike that practiced by their relations in Indiana in the years prior. Other New River families also established homesteads in Illinois, including the Hart and Robinson families.

The maintaining and strengthening of familial ties was a vital concern for the assorted constituent families of the New River network as they attempted to establish themselves in their new environs. This could be accomplished through intermarriage, as demonstrated by the joining of the Phippses and Longs in Indiana. It was also accomplished through visitation, the giving of aid, and social interaction. Female members of the network seemed to play a critical role in the maintenance of network ties. One local history of Putnam and Marshall counties would single out Elizabeth in its explanation of the connections between the Reeveses and the Harts. "Mrs. Reeves was a Dowton," it explained simply, "and connected with the Harts."[37] The statement is as revealing as it is misleading. While kinship was important, Elizabeth and her husband were so closely related that they shared many of those ties in common. That Elizabeth served as the primary conduit between the two families had undoubtedly more to do with her active efforts to support good relations between the groups. Elizabeth Reeves likely traveled between homesteads, offering news, social interaction, and perhaps most importantly, medical aid. Her later obituary would note that she "for more than fifty years had been a practical female physician."[38] Given her medical skills, Elizabeth likely provided critical assistance to members of the network during the delivery of children and times of sickness, reinforcing bonds between the various families and keeping the network healthy in both a literal and metaphorical sense.

The importance of such interactions may have been what allowed some of the New River women to enjoy positions of authority within their networks. A local history of Clay County would character- ize Betty Long as "the leading and guiding spirit of this gang of outlaws—she was the president and dictator."[39] The local history of Putnam and Marshall counties would similarly note that Eliza- beth Reeves was "the ruling spirit of the family, and its evil genius."[40] While such an obviously biased characterization was intended as an attack against Elizabeth, it also hints at perceptions regarding her standing within the family.

The same history also highlighted the leadership of an unnamed Hart woman during a dispute between the Harts and another family by the name of Baker. A Baker had challenged a Hart to fight, and "Hart perhaps feared the result and was inclined to back down, but when his wife heard of it she declared with an oath, if he did not fight Baker and whip him too he should not live with her another day." Her chastisement worked, and the male Hart not only fought but "pounded his antagonist severely, easily winning the fight."[41] The examples of both Elizabeth Doughton Reeves and the unnamed female Hart speak to the importance of women in managing and at times directing relations, not only within the family, but with exter- nal groups of interconnected kin and, in the Hart example, unre- lated outsiders. Women helped shape the mechanics and dynamics of the networks along which both violence and alleged criminal- ity would flow. According to Edward Bonney, one member of the extended New River network, Granville Young, would later state plainly his belief in the importance of women in the success of criminal operations. "There is nothing like a woman, to keep a man out of a scrape," Young would reportedly proclaim. "She is quicker- witted than a man, and has more self-command in a tight place."[42]

Over the first half of the 1830s, there was reason for optimism. The New River families had successfully established a patchwork of homesteads in Indiana and Illinois. The familial network that had structured the patterns of migration and settlement now offered a framework for mutual support. Able to rely on their kin and connections as they established themselves, some members of the network, like George and Elizabeth Reeves, began to acquire land and property. Owen County's Jesse Phipps, for his part, reportedly became "a man of considerable property." Owen Long, of the same county, opened his township's first mill.[43] The migration into the Middle West had delivered opportunity and now seemed to promise prosperity. That all changed, though, with the Panic of 1837. The financial crisis had an especially ruinous impact on the Middle West, creating acute shortages of currency.[44] Crop and land prices plummeted, while counterfeiting and horse theft spiked. Desperation abounded.

It was a watershed moment. The Panic of 1837 saw some members of the family network move farther afield in search of work or coin. Some began to engage in organized criminal activity. New River native John "Old Coon" Birch, for instance, would later remark to Edward Bonney that his own son, Robert, had left home and become itinerant and involved in crime sometime around 1837.[45] Others forged connections with other networks associated with counterfeiting and horse theft. Either John or Aaron Long, both sons of Owen Long and cousins to Polly Long Phipps, left Owen County, Indiana, and eventually wound up in Bellevue, Iowa Territory. There he found employment as a woodcutter for a local hotel keeper. According to Sheriff William A. Warren, Long worked for William W. Brown.[46] In that capacity, Long met—if he did not know him already—another son of North Carolinian migrants to Indiana: William Fox.[47] The sheriff would allege that both Fox's and Long's work for Brown extended well beyond the chopping of cordwood, and maintained that the young men were engaged in criminal activity under Brown's direction. Long did not appear in the account of the Bellevue War published in the immediate aftermath of the fight, either because he was in the group of Brown's fighters that escaped the burning hotel before it fell, or because he did not participate in the battle. Still, the connection between Long and Brown stuck, and in 1845, one newspaper would later refer to Long as "a pupil of the celebrated villain Brown, who was killed at Bellevue."[48] It is well documented that Warren and Cox's anti-Brown men captured and flogged William Fox.

While Warren insisted that both Long and Fox were acolytes within Brown's alleged criminal circle, the chaotic violence of the Bellevue War deprived both young men of a generous employer and saw their names soiled. Circumstances were already grim, and this alone may have exacerbated desperation and driven the men toward criminality. Warren himself would later note that, following the battle and flogging, Fox would reappear near Bellevue "covered with dirt and rags" to beg for the return of his pocketbook, which he had entrusted to Betsy Brown, the wife of his former employer.[49] Another Bellevue resident, going by "Old Settler," would later write that he saw Fox again not long after the armed contest, and Fox "swore he never would do another day's work while he lived, but would rob, murder or steal for a living. They had ruined his character and the sooner he was dead the better it would be for him."[50] John Long would later also seem to verify this statement, maintaining in 1845 that "what first set Fox to robbing" was being "taken, shot and whipped in company with another, for a crime of which he was innocent." Indeed, John Long also would claim that his own initiation into a life of crime occurred in 1840, the same year as the Bellevue War.[51] Regardless of whether the Bellevue War led to criminality or criminality led to the Bellevue War, connections between members of the New River family network and alleged organized criminal activity increasingly surfaced in the years that followed.

In late May 1841, an unknown party robbed a store in Clay County, Indiana. A newspaper account noted that public suspicion immediately "rested on an individual by the name of Long, who lived just on the line of Owen and Clay Co., and who had long been suspected of horse stealing, robbing, counterfeiting, and the like villainies." The Long in question was Owen Long, father to Aaron and John Long. A party searched Long's house, where they discovered one bolt of cloth allegedly from the robbed store along with a great quantity of supposedly counterfeit notes. The account noted that one of Long's two sons attempted to intervene to prevent the discovery of the spurious bills. "A roll as large as a man's leg fell from the clock," the paper reported, "which was snatched up by one of Long's sons, who was standing by and thrown into the fire and destroyed." Authorities took Owen, Aaron, and John Long into custody, along with "another scoundrel called Phipps."[52] It is likely that this unnamed Phipps was one of Jesse Phipps's sons: Shack or Eli Shadrach, better known as "Shade." It is also possible that the Phipps in question was William Phipps's son Troy Phipps, who had married Jane Long. A later history of Owen County noted that all three "gained considerable notoriety on account of their many daring acts of lawlessness."[53]

That the locals had been so quick to target the New River families in the wake of the robbery speaks to an already established degree of distrust in the community. One early settler, Elias Cooprider, would later claim that the New River families relied on their connections to frustrate the local legal system, maintaining that "when any of this gang, composed of the Longs, Phipps, and others were arrested and brought to court, their confederates would swear them out."[54] The robbery was surely not the first criminal act rumored to be linked to members of the family, fairly or not, and local resentment was evidently building. The arresting party's readiness to seize not only Owen, but Aaron, John, and their unnamed Phipps kinsman, may have been an attempt to preempt the men from providing alibis for Owen Long. For one of the Long brothers, the incident marked the second time in a little over a year that he had been accused of operating within an organized criminal network. It would not be the last.

The alleged criminal activity of the New River kinship network was not confined to Owen County. In Illinois, members of the New River family forged connections with criminal networks at some point prior to William Bridge's flight to the Reeveses' home. While the Reeveses were careful to leave minimal evidence of such associations, the fact that the panicked Bridge elected to seek sanctuary with the family in the wake of the Driscoll lynchings speaks to some already established level of trust and association. The Reeveses, moreover, were not the only New River family that Illinois attorney general Josiah Lamborn named, in October 1841, as constituents of the state's underworld network. Lamborn also made reference to a "Birch," and while he did not provide a first name, he was likely referencing the family of John Birch. The Birch family lived in Clark County, Illinois, around fifty miles to the west of the New River network cluster in Owen County, Indiana. According to a statement allegedly made by John Birch, he and Owen Long "were raised together in old North Carolina." The Birches, much like many of the other associated New River families, came under increased scrutiny during this period. One history of Clark County would later claim that the Birch family "was, of course, a constant object of suspicion, but no clue could be got of their transactions or connection with the deeds of crime that were constantly being perpetrated."[55]

As local suspicions and resentments grew, Birch's son, Robert, the Long brothers, and William Fox all became increasingly mobile operators.[56] Crime became their primary pursuit. Their Middle Western thieves' cant, as recorded by Edward Bonney, reflected their lifestyles and occupations. They "raised" horses when they stole them and created counterfeit—or the "ready"—when they acquired it. To mark a target for criminal action was "to get up a sight." If an individual was "nepoed," it meant he was murdered. For an individual to warrant trust as a fellow hand, he had to be "of the right stripe."[57] Still, slang aside, the young New River men attempted to present themselves as gentlemen, and by almost all accounts, they were handsome and well-dressed. According to Bonney, Robert Birch in particular "was very loquacious, and could play the bar-room dandy to perfection."[58]

"The boys," as these roving young New River men called themselves, widened the reach of the criminal network and established contacts throughout the larger region. Notably, they established a number of contacts in a fast-growing Illinois community that had recently become home to a new controversial religious sect. The town of Nauvoo offered the men several distinct advantages. Located on the Mississippi River, it offered ready access to transport. Perhaps even more important, Nauvoo's abuse of habeas corpus allowed the settlement to function as a sanctuary for those eager to evade the law.

Edward Bonney, who had himself migrated to Nauvoo for that exact reason, would later write that "in the case of an arrest at Nauvoo the accused were immediately released by the city authorities, and the cry of *'Persecution against the Saints'* raised, effectually drowning the pleas for justice of the injured, and the officer forced to return and tell the tale of defeat."[59] This was not a complete dramatization. Nauvoo's authorities, to borrow from historian Benjamin Park, partook in a "rejection of American law." In one instance, Joseph Smith had ordered a writ of habeas corpus be drawn up to preempt any attempted arrest of a man accused of repeatedly defrauding the US government.[60] Whatever Smith's motivations, it was clear that Nauvoo was not a city that gentile lawmen could easily navigate.

In addition to these factors, there was already a criminal element present in Nauvoo with which the New River men could cooperate. Some of these Mormon criminals were former Danites or had been influenced by their teachings, and infused their illicit actions with religious zeal.[61] John Long would later claim, according to one newspaper account, that it was an "Alanson Hodge" who first introduced him to counterfeiting.[62] The writer either misheard what Long said, or Long himself possibly misspoke, but he was probably referencing either Alanson Brown or a member of the Hodges family. Brown and the Hodgeses were all Mormon residents of Nauvoo, and all had documented histories of participation in criminal activity that ranged from horse stealing to fraud to larceny. Alanson Brown's son, Thomas, was also linked to criminal activity.[63] Church leadership excommunicated the elder Brown in 1841 and would do the same to Curtis Hodges Sr. in 1843, but Hodges would quickly return to fellowship and receive a patriarchal blessing from Hyrum Smith in May 1844.[64] The New River men were at any rate associated with both the Browns and the Hodgeses, and at some point became involved with another Mormon family, the Reddens, who were also linked to criminal activity.[65]

In addition to allying with their Mormon associates in an around Nauvoo, members of the New River network maintained contact with another cluster of criminals in Lee County, Illinois, led by Adolphus

Bliss, Daniel Miller Dewey, and Charles West. Unlike some of the Mormons like Brown and the Hodgeses, this trio was far from a fringe element in their local community. Both Bliss and West served as local officials, with the former being a justice of the peace and the latter a constable. Dewey operated a tavern named "The Travelers Home."[66] While it is unknown when exactly cooperation between the groups began, they appear to have emerged, at least in part, due to shared linkages to Bellevue and William W. Brown. Thomas J. Babcock—Brown's associate, counterfeiter, wayward minister, and cousin to Edward Bonney—was married to Lovina West Babcock, the sister of Charles West.[67] The Wests, Bonney, Babcock, and the Browns had all been former residents of Elkhart, Indiana, and their ties predated the Bellevue War. Even after leaving Elkhart for Bellevue, Brown maintained contact with West, and his probate records reveal a financial transaction between the men, addressed to Charles West at "Blisses Grove."[68] Fox and at least one of the Longs had of course worked for Brown, with Fox joining the fight at his hotel. The connections forged in Bellevue strengthened the ability of the mobile New River men to operate in the northern reaches of the state, and their positions within their community provided, for the time, robust cover for illicit conduct.

Nearby in the north, the Reeves family had, despite Attorney General Lamborn's efforts, seemingly managed to evade the trouble that had befallen their fellows in Iowa Territory and Indiana. At least, no mob or confederation of lynchers had organized to expel the family by force. By 1842, however, the Reeveses became increasingly audacious in their own criminal operations. It is possible that the family had been emboldened simply by the lack of response in the wake of Lamborn's public allegations. It is also possible, though, that the family was responding to the same pressures that had encouraged other members of their familial network to take greater risks. Those pressures had started with the Panic of 1837 and compounded with the subsequent allegations of criminality directed against members of the network. The network, which had previously supported and helped establish members in homesteads and marriages, weakened as allegations, vigilantes, and economic devastation drove members from their families and support systems, prompting a rise in desperation and injecting further volatility into the situation. Desperation in the wake of the Ogle lynchings was what had driven Bridge to seek refuge with the Reeveses, and his eventual detection had exposed their home as a sanctuary. Now some of the Reeveses' own desperate kinsmen, cut adrift from their homes and familial settlement clusters, operated and roved nearby. Lacking established homes, these men were incentivized to engage in more dangerous and mobile work that might have forced the Reeveses to increase their own appetites for risk. Such circumstances unsettled the established and careful cadences by which successful organized criminality was possible.

Regardless of their precise motivations, the Reeveses soon began taking risks that they had carefully avoided in prior years. According to one local history, Long, Birch, and Fox began to frequent the Reeve home around 1842, "and a long course of successful crime had made the perpetrators reckless." Elizabeth and George's eldest son, Cam, evidently began to emulate his older kin, especially his "intimate friend" Robert Birch, and locals began to blame "burglaries and much petty thieving" on the teenager.[69] Making matters much worse, it was also around 1842 that Elizabeth began to "pass counterfeit money at stores in Henry and Lacon." The timeline aligns with John Long's later claim that his own counterfeiting operation suffered from "a general breaking up" in 1842, and Elizabeth's actions might have represented a downstream consequence of that collapse.[70] While George redeemed any spurious notes detected as having been spent by Elizabeth locally, her boldness represented a grave miscalculation. Communities in the cash-strapped post-Panic Middle West could tolerate counterfeiters operating in their midst, but only on the condition that the manufacturers of the bogus coin did not circulate their forgeries locally.[71] Local public opinion, which had protected the Reeveses after Lamborn's initial accusations, now began to turn against the family.

While relationships between the Reeveses and their neighbors deteriorated, there was no immediate move to expel or punish the family. Still, anxieties regarding criminality increasingly loomed over Marshall and Putnam counties. In late May 1843, an unidentified thief broke into a warehouse in Henry and stole "dry goods and groceries to the amount of about $100."[72] A few days later, *The Gazette* bemoaned a supposed nationwide rise in crime, stating that "it really appears that the world is becoming one vast charnel house, where wickedness and crime may gloat and revel in unchecked holiday. . . . By what demon's dark spell has blight breathed upon the lilies of the soul? What curse is upon us?"[73] Cam Reeves, however, grew ever more wild and disregarded the darkening of local moods.

On Sunday, June 4, a camp meeting was held three miles outside of Lacon. That night, J. C. Coutlett, who was in attendance, noted that his watch dog had begun "to growl and bark and exhibit unusual ferocity." The dog's behavior eventually irritated Coutlett to the extent that he "got up and flogged" the poor creature.[74] He should have listened to his dog's warnings. That night, someone entered Coutlett's tent and stole a black dress coat, two silk dresses, and about twelve dollars along with "various other articles of less value." The next day, a party arrested two of the Reeves boys—likely the older teenagers Cam and Preston—and brought them before a magistrate, "but the only satisfactory evidence adduced was that the said young men were on the camp ground on Sunday; and they were discharged." That very night, a thief or thieves targeted another warehouse, this time in Lacon, and stole around two hundred pounds of sugar. Two days later, on Wednesday, June 7, an unidentified party ventured out into Henry Prairie and broke into the home of Augustus C. Ashermann and stole a small black leather trunk stuffed with valuables. The haul included $22, an expensive gold watch allegedly worth $250, six land titles, notes and certificates valued at $750, and a pistol with ammunition.[75]

The temperature was rising fast. After lying low for a few days, Cam and a companion, John Allison, fled Henry Prairie. Locals deputized a man named Thomas Collum to pursue the pair. With the help of a local constable from Perkin, Collum managed to apprehend the young men some ten miles outside Peoria. Reeves and Allison quickly enlisted the aid of two Peoria lawyers, Lincoln B. Knowlton and Norman H. Purple. Lincoln Knowlton was the same lawyer who had attempted to intervene in the sham trial of the Driscolls' killers back in Ogle County but had been stopped by Judge Ford and State's Attorney Seth V. Farwell. That incident had been enough for Ford to publicly lambast Knowlton as "a drunken lawyers at Peoria" and "a kind of attorney-general for the horse thieves."[76] The lawyers, lawmen, and prisoners then departed along the Illinois River by boat. While onboard, Reeves and Allison threw overboard the clothing that they had stolen. When Collum and the constable attempted to have Reeves and Allison transported to Lacon for questioning, the lawyers challenged their authority, noting the lack of a warrant. Knowlton and Purple succeeded in directing the party to the settlement of Henry, where they "reiterated the declaration that the pursuers of Reeves and Allison had no authority for their detention." The argument worked, and Collum and the constable set the two young men free, who promptly "fled to parts unknown." Knowlton and Purple's instrumental role in freeing the pair drew sharp criticism, and the newspaper account of the affair grumbled that their services "were secured by the payment of a '*brass*' watch and a young horse."[77] While less direct than Ford's earlier attack on Knowlton, the implication was clear.

The news that Cam Reeves and John Allison had managed to escape provoked outrage in the county. The previously cautious Reeveses had grown too bold. They were now perceived by many as not just criminals but a predatory threat to the local community. While the residents of Marshall County had been able to look the other way back in 1841 when Lamborn accused George Reeves of harboring horse thieves, they were now alienated and angry, and saw the Reeveses as threats to both their private property and communal safety. County residents had developed a vague understanding of the New River network and its criminal operations, and one local paper explained that the "conviction upon the public mind" was that "Geo. Reeves formed a connecting link to the chain of horse thieves, if not counterfeiters, believed to be spread over Illinois and other portions of the west and north west." Public opinion turned sharply against the family. Because the formal legal system had failed to punish the Reeveses, a group of local men decided that the time was right to rid the area of the family through rougher means. As the Lacon paper put it, the "immediate cause" of the outrage might have been the recent actions of Cam Reeves and John Allison, "but the general exciting cause was existence of the Reeves establishment, and the necessity of its extermination."[78]

On Friday, July 16, an extralegal committee made up of residents of Marshall and the adjoining counties sent the Reeveses a notice demanding that they attend a meeting the following day at Robinson's Grove, Illinois.[79] The next day, George, Elizabeth, and their children—sans Cam—arrived at the grove, which was about a mile from their home, sometime before ten o'clock in the morning. Over one hundred men awaited them there. The vigilantes were "armed, some with shot guns, others with rifles."[80] The meeting had been "informally organized," and the ad hoc vigilantes at first lacked a captaincy or command structure. The vigilantes were uncertain about what to do next, so they appointed Henry Prairie resident Hall S. Gregory as chairman and mounted him on horseback to symbolize his authority. The leaders of the mob then organized a committee made up of local elites, who began to debate and attempt to convince others as to what the course of action should be. Dr. James Swanzy, a physician from Bureau County, held forth, according to a newspaper account, "with much warmth, depicted the fears and injuries to which the country had been subjected on account of Reeves, & ended by recommending a resort to violence." The press sanitized Swanzy's actual demand. He wanted an extralegal execution.

At some point during these proceedings, George Reeves sent for Dr. Robert Boal. Hailing from Lacon, Boal was another physician and acquaintance of Abraham Lincoln's. He would later claim that he had attended the meeting with the express purpose of preventing "violence or bloodshed." The Reeveses sat on the ground on the outskirts of the mob. Elizabeth held an infant, and Boal noted that she and the children appeared "in deep distress." According to Boal, Reeves told him that "he was induced to come out to the meeting under a solemn pledge that his person should be safe, and his family and property suffer no violence, but he now believed they intended to kill him." George Reeves knew what had happened to the Driscolls at the hands of the mob. It could no longer be assumed that American mobs would not kill. Reeves begged Boal to use his standing to prevent the mob from killing him in front of his wife and children. Boal promised to do so but told him that "guilty or innocent, the temper of the community was such that he must make up his mind to leave the country at once, and forever." To this Reeves agreed.[81]

At this point, the enraged Swanzy, according to Boal, exclaimed "there is the d—d rascal, I once found him riding a fine English mare of mine which had been stolen." "Doctor," Reeves replied, "I thought I had explained that matter to your satisfaction, for we have often since drank whisky together in the grocery at Hennepin, and I supposed we were good friends." Reeves's appeal had no effect on Swanzy. He roared at the top of his lungs, "all who are in favor of shooting the d—d rascal, and giving him Rock river justice, follow me." Swanzy's reference to "Rock river justice" was an invocation of the lynching of the Driscolls. Locals' memory of that mob execution loomed large over the moment and now threatened to drive the crowd toward killing. Boal claimed that at this moment, about one-fifth of the assembled vigilantes cocked their firearms and turned toward George Reeves. Gregory, the chairman of the committee, maneuvered his horse between the Reeveses and the gunmen.[82]

Dr. Boal realized that he needed to intervene before the killing began. The mob had grown incensed by Swanzy's emotional and bloodthirsty reference to the Driscolls, but Gregory, in putting himself between Swanzy's men and the Reeveses, had created a momentary pause, and the confused crowd attempted to make sense of the chaotic scene. Boal, sensing an opportunity to address the mob, mounted a wagon and began to speak. Boal, according to the contemporary newspaper account, "said that if it were true that Reeves was guilty of horse stealing and harboring thieves, the greatest punishment that the law could inflict would be imprisonment in the penitentiary; and that to deprive him of life would be greater than the crime."[83] The physician also noted Reeves's willingness to enter into exile and argued that it "was the best and easiest mode of getting rid of him."[84] After hearing this, some members of the crowd expressed concern that they could not or would not take George Reeves's word. The threat of a lynching had not passed.

Dr. Peter Temple, a dentist, then spoke. According to a contemporary newspaper account, Temple "deprecated anything like a resort to violence, and recommended the observance of order; and concluded by suggesting that a committee of twenty men be appointed to pack their household furniture—conduct them to Henry and cause their departure on the first boat on its downward passage." The mob found Temple's compromise solution agreeable, excepting "a few violent spirits who thirsted for the blood of Reeves."[85] With the details of the punishment agreed upon, the vigilantes and their victims made their way to the Reeveses' home.

After the vigilantes loaded up all the family's furniture, Elizabeth Reeves requested a moment to enter the emptied home. The vigilantes agreed to this. She walked into the home alone and approached her fireplace. It had been an unusually cold and "backward" summer in Marshall County, but the coals were still burning hot.[86] Reeves reached out and passed her hands through the haze of emanating warmth before plunging them toward the source of the heat. She seized some of the hot coals and hurled them into a nearby pile of straw. The dried stalks ignited at once, and greedy licks of fire began to creep throughout the dwelling. Reeves made her way to the chimney, where she removed a stone and retrieved a small bag from behind it. She exited through the doorway to face her husband and children, and the armed band of vigilantes. Behind her noise and heat rose, as a flaming maw began to consume the Reeveses' home.[87]

Elizabeth Reeves did not attempt to hide her rage. According to a newspaper account, she was "a perfect hurricane of passion," while the local history of the county would claim she "raved like an enraged tigress."[88] She could do little, however, other than deny the vigilantes the pleasure of torching the house themselves. George remained quiet. The vigilantes then forced the family—still minus Cam—to the embarkation point at Henry. There, in the evening hours, they boarded the steamer *Dove* with what remained of their goods and property, and departed.[89]

Hiding in a thicket along the river, Cam Reeves watched as the *Dove* carried his family into exile. Earlier, Cam hid in a swamp two miles north of Henry and successfully evaded the vigilantes who attempted to hunt him down throughout the day. He had, though, received word of his family's banishment, probably from a local sympathizer, and, according to a newspaper account of the affair, "desired to witness the departure of his parents, brothers and sisters."[90] Cam crept to the water's edge only a hundred yards away from the landing, concealing himself in the thick foliage that grew along the river. It was a risky move, bordering on foolhardy. Still, he remained camouflaged by the tall reeds and again avoided detection.

Having seen his family depart, Cam stealthily made his way back into Henry. The teenager was hungry. He snuck into a home in town, where the sympathetic inhabitants gave him something to eat. As Cam tried to leave the house, however, his luck finally ran out. A less sympathetic party spotted Cam as he departed, and vigilantes gave chase. The young Reeves, though, was athletic and "too fleet for his pursuers." Cam ran about two miles to Webster, where he boarded a boat and attempted to conceal himself. When the boat passed by Henry, the vigilantes hailed it and boarded the vessel when it landed. After searching for half an hour, the vigilantes finally found Cam hidden "in the deck cabin, covered with blankets and rope." They took him to Ottawa, Illinois, and imprisoned him there. The next day, John Allison—his compatriot during the alleged thievery earlier in the month—voluntarily surrendered himself to authorities.[91]

Reeves and Allison would not remain in jail for long. On Wednesday, June 27, the jailer, a man by the name of True, was out of town. The two young prisoners, sensing an opportunity to escape, pried out a large loose stone from the wall of their cell. They bashed it against the jail's wall until they had created a hole large enough to squeeze through. Reeves and Allison crawled out of the freshly made aperture and vanished into the dark of the night.[92] Suspicion and anger prevailed in the aftermath of the escape, with Lacon's

Gazette noting that it was "supposed they must have had some assistance in effecting their escape."[93]

Crime in the immediate region had not subsided with the move against the Reeveses, which only compounded the situation. Just three days after the family's banishment, an unidentified party had broken into a store in Marshall's adjacent Putnam County and stole $300 worth of money and goods. In Marshall County, existing and would-be vigilantes began to threaten associates of the Reeves family, both real and imagined. As early as June 24, *The Gazette* reported that although there was a lack of any "tangable charge," vigilantes had already issued threats to target others "according to the code applied to Geo. Reeves."[94] Eventually vigilantes issued a warning against one unidentified party to "leave the country in ten days, under pains and penalties."

One anonymous resident, going by "A Looker-On," published a letter in *The Gazette* condemning "this summary way of doing business, and that without proof of guilt." While the writer endorsed the action that had been taken against the Reeves family, he stressed the branching consequences of further extralegal action, arguing that it would mean that "a tender wife, an aged mother-in-law, and other dear connexions are made to drink the very dregs of distress." Going even further, the anonymous writer insisted that extralegal violence could quickly become a means by which unscrupulous members of the community could silence and destroy rivals. "Who in this community but may have enemies," the writer asked, "and how easy a matter in times of high excitement, for enemies to seize the opportunity and cry out rogue! rogue! condemnation is the way-cry, and utter ruin the consequence."[95] The Reeveses were gone, but the legacy of the violence against the family would linger.

The loss of the Reeves station dealt a blow to the New River network's criminal operations. The family's secluded home had provided an ideal shelter for thieves in the field and a conduit for the traffic of stolen goods. Still, criminal operations in northern Illinois did not abate. Members of the New River network allegedly continued to work with Ogle County counterfeiters Norton B. Royce and William Bridge, who had for their parts not been intimidated out of the business by the lynching of the Driscolls or the banishment of the Reeveses.[96] The network had been damaged but for the moment remained robust. On September 18, an unidentified party robbed the Rockford store of William McKenney, making off with some $800.[97] Shortly thereafter, thieves successfully hit a mail stage on its route between Galena and Chicago.[98]

The criminal networks associated with the New River families would, in the early months of 1844, also receive a seemingly promising addition with the arrival of Edward Bonney in Nauvoo following his flight from authorities in Ohio and Indiana. Bonney had by this point been caught counterfeiting at least twice, but he was still a highly experienced counterfeiter and a charismatic, clever operator. His quick ascent to Joseph Smith's Council of Fifty, along with his connections to both the New River and Lee County criminal networks, confirmed his value. Bonney, according to John Long's later testimony, wasted little time in establishing a counterfeiting operation in Nauvoo.[99] Long's opinion was not relegated to condemned men. Mormon and fellow Council of Fifty member William Clayton would in his journal similarly name Bonney as one of the "bogus snakers of Nauvoo."[100]

The ties that bound together this loose criminal confederacy would begin to unravel, however, with the detention of Joseph Smith in the Carthage jail that June. As Smith attempted to evade legal repercussions for his role in the destruction of the *Nauvoo Expositor*'s printing press, he agreed to a bogus trial organized by Nauvoo city councilman and justice of the peace Daniel H. Wells. Smith organized the June 17 trial to give the appearance that neutral non-Mormons led the legal effort in order to lend an air of legitimacy to the inevitable dismissal of charges. Wells was himself a non-Mormon, influential in Nauvoo and an ally to Smith, while none other than Edward Bonney—himself also a non-Mormon and close ally to Smith—would serve as the prosecuting attorney.[101] This transparent attempt to evade justice failed to satiate Smith's opponents, and in less than a week, the Mormon prophet surrendered to Governor Ford at Carthage.

With Smith imprisoned, Ford and his militia marched on Nauvoo. While the original plan had been to search the city for counterfeiting operations while demonstrating a show of the state's force, Ford had determined that such a search was imprudent and could not be attempted without sparking a violent collision. Bonney, however, had no way of knowing about the governor's new plan. All he knew was that, with Smith imprisoned, an armed and hostile force was marching to reassert the authority of the state over the community. Desperate, Bonney turned to his New River network associates for aid. John Long would later testify that Bonney "had two presses for counterfeiting money in Nauvoo, in his cellar, and when the people became exasperated, and were about to attack his house, I went in the night and carried the presses to a distant part of the city."[102] Long's covert removal of the presses turned out to be unnecessary, with Ford making no effort to hunt down counterfeiters during his short stop at Nauvoo. Still, it was a sign of things to come. Even the brief absence of Joseph Smith had left Bonney vulnerable, and the death of the Mormon prophet deprived the counterfeiter of a vital ally and protector. Without its prophet, Nauvoo was no longer a sanctuary.

Following the killing of Smith, Bonney fell out of favor with Nauvoo's leading circles. On February 4, 1845, Bonney lost his position in the Council of Fifty.[103] Estranged from the Mormon Church's new leadership—much of which had now consolidated around Brigham Young following a succession crisis—Bonney left Nauvoo in spring 1845.[104] He settled in Montrose, a settlement located in Lee County, Iowa Territory.[105] Although increasingly antagonistic to the Mormons following his fall from Nauvoo's elite circles, he allegedly maintained his associations with the various criminal networks that operated in and around the river city.

According to John Long, Bonney was also involved in horse stealing, although he did not himself engage in the actual theft of the animals. In October of 1845, Long would claim that Bonney had "men now employed in stealing horses in Missouri; he furnished them with money, half counterfeit and half good."[106] Mary A. Hines, whose husband, John P. Hines privately claimed to be affiliated with the region's criminal network, would similarly later write that he "told me he had made lots of money for Bonney at different times."[107] According to Col. J. M. Reid, Bonney "was an unmitigated scoundrel and the scheming projector of all the operations of the hand, which resulted in getting money."[108] Reid's brother, Hugh T. Reid, was a contemporary resident of Lee County and had previously served as Joseph Smith's defense attorney. Though Bonney was not often "personally present at the perpetration of a crime," Reid continued, "putting little facts and circumstances together, and still greater revelations which have since come to light; there is little doubt that he was an accessory generally before and always after the fact."[109]

Bonney's situation grew even more precarious in the spring months of 1845. In Lee County, Illinois, authorities arrested Adolphus Bliss and Daniel Miller Dewey. It had not been the first time Bliss had run afoul of the law. In early 1841, he had faced counterfeiting charges. Dewey had helped pay his security, and the grand jury failed to indict him.[110] This time, however, the men would not be so fortunate. Authorities soon also arrested Bliss and Dewey's associate, Charles West, who was the brother-in-law to Bonney's cousin, Thomas Babcock. West, unwilling to tolerate a stay with his associates in prison, turned state's evidence. With the aid of West's testimony, the Lee County Circuit Court found Bliss and Dewey guilty of robbery in the spring term and sentenced both men to stays in the state penitentiary. West's disclosures, though, did not stop there. In addition to implicating familiar names like Ogle County's William Bridge, West turned on members of the New River network, reportedly naming William Fox and Robert Birch as the real perpetrators of the robbery for which Bliss and Dewey had been imprisoned.[111] The secretive array of loosely knit networks, which had for years facilitated clandestine criminal operations throughout the region, could endure no more shocks.

Given Bonney's criminal and familial connections to West, the disgraced constable's disclosures constituted a clear threat to the counterfeiter. Now bereft of the protection and support of influential men and deprived of Nauvoo's sanctuary, Bonney was one admission away from the jail sentence he had spent the past several years struggling to avoid. The situation further deteriorated on May 10, when William and Stephen Hodges, along with at least Artemus Johnson and Thomas Brown, killed two Lee County, Iowa Territory, men in a botched robbery.[112] All four men were Mormons and had documented connections to Nauvoo's criminal element. Aiding the killers was another foursome of Mormons: Ervine and Amos Hodges, William Hickman, and Return Jackson Redden.[113] The killers were not immediately identified, but the botched robbery left Bonney vulnerable. The West Point murders had occurred only a few miles from Bonney's new home in Montrose, Iowa. This was no coincidence. Bonney himself was likely involved in the selection of the targets. John Long would later insist that Bonney was an accessory to the murders.[114] According to J. M. Reid's later account, moreover, Bonney had ridden on a steamboat with the victims and had been heard to remark "that from their big German boxes and general surroundings that they were a better class of Germans than generally came to the county, and *that they must have plenty of money!*"[115]

The bungled West Point job, coupled with the implosion of the West, Dewey, and Bliss ring in the north, indicated that the proverbial walls were closing in on Bonney. A surge of outraged local excitement accompanied the murders, and in Bonney's own words, "The citizens of the surrounding country turned out 'en masse,' organized themselves into companies, and scoured the country."[116] Local investigators eventually scrounged two clues, "a cloth cap . . . trimmed with fur, and without a frontispiece," and a series of tracks leading to Montrose—Bonney's new town of residence.[117] Where another might only have seen risk, the counterfeiter perceived a window of opportunity.

Bonney, sensing his chance and his danger, approached Lee County sheriff James L. Estes and stated that he had seen one of the Hodgeses across the river at Nauvoo wearing such a hat. Bonney then quickly made his way to the Mormon city, where he, undoubtedly relying on his familiarity with the brothers, engineered the bloodless surrender of William and Stephen Hodges. Brown and

Johnson had fled.[118] The brothers had put their trust in their old associate, Bonney, and in the Mormon leadership's resolve to shield the Mormon faithful from gentile prosecution. Sheriff Lee soon arrived in the city and placed the pair under arrest. Unfortunately for the brothers, Nauvoo's new Mormon leadership showed no appetite for protecting the members of an obvious criminal element. Mormon apostle John Taylor derided the Hodges family in the May 10 entry of his journal as "notorious for thieving."[119] *The Nauvoo Neighbor*, for its part, falsely insisted on May 21 that "*these two young Hodges are not Mormons, nor never were:* neither are Johnson or Brown."[120] The Hodgeses had been deprived of the protection of Mormon leadership, and Sheriff Lee successfully extradited William and Stephen to Iowa Territory. By Bonney's account, the Hodgeses attempted to secure several witnesses to swear them out of trouble, compiling a list that included William Fox and the Long brothers.[121] The effort was to no avail, and the court quickly sentenced them to hang.[122]

The day before the court sentenced William and Stephen, authorities arrested Amos Hodges in Nauvoo for stealing. Taylor would write in his journal that he was "afraid" that Amos was "connected with a gang of villains that are lurking about, stealing on our credit. It seems when our enemies are quiet abroad, the devil is exerting himself in our midst."[123] According to Bonney, who had his own private reasons to attempt to defame Brigham Young, Hodges planned to rob a Nauvoo merchant named Beach with the help of two members of the New River network: William Fox and Robert Birch. According to Bonney, Hodges consulted with Young before the operation commenced, and the Mormon leader warned the intended target. Beach subsequently hired armed guards, who foiled the plan and nearly shot Fox and Birch in the process.[124] While the New River men escaped, Amos Hodges was not so lucky. Authorities arrested Hodges for theft, and unsympathetic Mormon leadership, according to Taylor, intervened to prevent his release.[125]

Ervine Hodges, outraged that the Mormon Church did nothing to save William and Stephen from execution and prevented Amos's release, threatened the life of Brigham Young.[126] According to the diary of Zina Diantha Huntington Jacobs, a widowed plural wife of the late Joseph Smith's and a future plural wife of Brigham Young, Ervine was "a man of unbounded temper." On the night of June 23, one day after the sentencing of his brothers, an unknown party repeatedly stabbed and clubbed Ervine to death, as recorded in Jacobs's diary, "not far from Pres B Youngs in the field."[127] Shortly thereafter, authorities released Amos Hodges, who subsequently disappeared. He too was likely murdered.[128] On July 15, William and Stephen Hodges hanged in Burlington.[129] All four Hodges brothers, in just a matter of weeks, had vanished or were dead.

Bonney's maneuvering during the Hodges incident had proven successful. In gently guiding suspicion toward Mormon Nauvoo, he had managed to redirect attention away from himself and the prickly fact that the Hodges brothers' footprints had first led to his own town of residence. Bonney planted his schemes in ground made fertile by anti-Mormon bigotries, and his audience was all too eager to embrace his narrative of Mormon corruption. An upsurge in violence between the Mormons and their gentile neighbors had once again gripped the region, and a miniature civil war again looked possible. Rumors of Nauvoo's sanction of criminality flourished in this atmosphere. Now, even if the Hodges brothers had tried to implicate or betray Bonney as West had done to Bliss and Dewey, he could dismiss their admissions as underhanded, spiteful, and fictive allegations hurled by members of the hated Mormon religion.

Bonney had, in helping secure the downfall of his former associates, protected himself from the consequences of the botched and bloody Lee County robbery. Still, he remained exposed through his connections to the battered yet still operational New River criminal network. If a member of the New River network was to learn of Bonney's betrayal of the Hodges brothers, that knowledge would likely lead to retribution. The risk that a member of that network might turn state's evidence themselves and disclose to authorities information relating to his illicit activities must have also continued to weigh on Bonney. The Hodges episode, however, presented Bonney with an avenue for shielding himself from these risks. Bonney had discovered a path to reverse his fortunes and secure immunity, all without turning state's evidence. That is not to say, though, that he could do so without continuing to betray his own associates. Bonney—the at-times miller, counterfeiter, councilor, and aide-de-camp—had reinvented himself before, but survival now demanded a more radical transformation. Enter Edward Bonney, lawman.

On July 4, while William and Stephen Hodges awaited their executions, a party composed of members of the New River network moved to execute another robbery. Their target was Col. George Davenport, a resident of Rock Island, Illinois. The band operated under the assumption that Davenport and his family would be out of the house and attending a holiday festivity. Davenport's family had indeed left to make merry. The elderly colonel, however, did not feel up to celebrating, so he remained in the house.

As Davenport rested, puffing on a cigar and reading in his parlor, he heard a noise from somewhere in the house. When the colonel rose to investigate, a door swung open, and he found himself confronted by three armed intruders. Both parties were equally surprised to see the other. One of the thieves panicked and fired his pistol. The ball smashed through Davenport's thigh. After they regained their composure, the three robbers restrained and blindfolded Davenport, demanding to know where he stowed his money. The colonel gave up a few hundred dollars, but this was less than the thieves had expected to find. They beat and strangled the old man in a vain attempt to induce further disclosures. Eventually, the intruders fled, leaving Davenport to soak in his own blood.[130]

Colonel Davenport would not survive the injuries he sustained during the robbery, but he lived long enough to give a description of his three assailants. Bonney quickly and very publicly inserted himself into the affair. Because of the small role he played in the Hodges incident, Bonney was able to secure a recommendation from Lee County's Sheriff Estes for Rock Island County's sheriff. Immediately after he arrived, Bonney began writing to local newspapers, giving an account of his investigation.[131] The open publication of his moves would seem counterintuitive for an investigator, but Bonney had reason to widely publicize himself and his efforts. If Bonney turned on the New River network, its members would surely expose his own criminal past. It was vital for Bonney to establish himself in the public mind as an investigator and lawman should such circumstances come to pass, as it would be easier to dismiss the revelations as little more than a spiteful smear. A prominent role in such a campaign also promised to elevate his profile among the emergent Iowan middle class in river towns like Keokuk who entertained deep anxieties regarding the threat posed not only by outsiders from Nauvoo, but, to borrow from historian Timothy Mahoney, by the local "settlers, squatters, ruffians, and mixed-blood people."[132] Such tensions sometimes flared into episodes of extralegal mob violence between the groups, and Bonney may have hoped that a public strike against the "ruffians" could again boost his standing following his fall from influence in Nauvoo.

More immediately, things were becoming heated in Montrose, where Bonney and his family resided. A mob there destroyed the home of one Potter, who operated a ferry supposedly used by members of the criminal network. Potter, probably a Mormon, fled to Nauvoo in the wake of the violence.[133] Bonney had no desire to share in Potter's fate and was quite happy to play the public role of lawman. By late July, the *Chicago Democrat* was publishing astonishing disclosures—probably fed to the publication by Bonney—linking Fox and Birch to not only a rash of horse stealing and robbery, but to the killing of lyncher captain Campbell during the Driscoll affair back in 1841. The anonymous informant was sure to link Fox and Birch's illicit operations to other familiar, already tarnished names like Dewey, Bliss, the Aikens brothers, Bridge, and others, exposing a web of organized criminality that spanned the region.[134]

Bonney's betrayal of the New River network was swift. Over the weeks that followed, he prowled through the Middle West, using his knowledge of the network's operations and interconnections to track down the men allegedly connected to Davenport's murder. Many of the men had fled far afield in the wake of the botched robbery, so Bonney had to carefully navigate the extended New River network to ascertain their locations. In the presence of the guarded and secretive company of professional thieves, Bonney had no trouble demonstrating that he was, to borrow language from the New

BONNEY AT MOTHER LONG'S.—page 92

Illustration of Edward Bonney at a Long family residence during his "investigation."
From Bonney, *The Banditti of the Prairies*, 107. Courtesy of the Library of Congress.

River men themselves, of "the right stripe." In his own later account
of the affair, Bonney would claim that he was able to pry answers
from members of the network through nothing more than careful
investigation, charm, and some counterfeit bills. In reality Bonney undoubtedly relied on the level of knowledge and trust he had
already cultivated as an associate of the loose criminal network.
As Mary Hines—widow to a claimed associate of that criminal

circle—would later write, "Bonney was a member of that band, for no member of the band would talk with any stranger unless he could prove himself a member by secret words and signs."[135]

Through Bonney's efforts, authorities arrested William Fox in Wayne County, Indiana. Fox, along with Shack Phipps, had prior to this been arrested in Bowling Green, Indiana, for horse theft but had been freed after both men's fathers posted bail.[136] In pursuit of Long and Birch, Bonney left Fox in the custody of Thomas B. Johnson, a former US marshal for Iowa Territory. Fox, however, managed to escape Johnson and vanished.[137] Bonney had more luck with Robert Birch and John Long, and he orchestrated their arrests in Lower Sandusky, Ohio.[138] Both men were successfully transported to Iowa Territory for trial. Authorities arrested John's brother, Aaron, at their father's residence at Sand Prairie, some six miles outside of Galena, Illinois. John Baxter, another alleged accomplice, was arrested in Wisconsin.[139] Granville Young, William Redden, and Grant Redden were arrested at the Redden residence on Devil Creek in Lee County, Iowa Territory. Authorities attempted to arrest Return Jackson Redden in Nauvoo, but a Mormon mob frustrated this effort.[140]

Robert Birch, terrified of a possible lynching, quickly broke and turned state's evidence.[141] A grand jury passed down indictments on all the men on October 6, and the Long brothers and Young went to trial. Fox had already escaped, and both Birch and Baxter secured changes of venue. Authorities released Grant Redden, while William H. Redden received a sentence of one year in the state penitentiary for his minor role as an accessory.[142] Thanks in large part to the betrayals of Birch and Bonney, a jury found Young and the Longs guilty in the matter of Davenport's murder and sentenced them to hang on October 29.

For a moment, it seemed as if Bonney had managed to evade retribution for his role in the arrests. Then, a resident of Keokuk, Iowa Territory, by the name of Silas Heaight, appeared before a grand jury in Fort Madison and secured four indictments against Bonney: three connected to counterfeiting and one in connection to the murders for which the Hodges brothers had hanged.[143] Heaight had previously resided in Farmington, Iowa Territory, where he had known Bonney's cousin, Thomas J. Babcock. Babcock and Bonney had run a counterfeiting operation out of Farmington until angry locals broke up the business.[144] Bonney's past had caught up with him, but Bonney had been apprehended before. Keeping hold of him would be the real trick.

John Long, Aaron Long, and Granville Young hanged on October 29, their deaths not postponed by the fresh allegations against Bonney. Bonney, fearing arrest, did not show his face at the execution.[145] John Long went to his death loudly proclaiming Bonney's guilt from the bully pulpit of the scaffold. In a macabre punishment that extended beyond the extinguishing of the men's lives, authorities donated the bodies of the Long brothers and Young to local doctors for dissection. John Long's skeletal remains would remain on public display until 1978, when locals finally buried him in Dickson Pioneer Cemetery.[146] Birch would eventually break out of jail and vanish, while Baxter, after a long legal battle, had his death sentence commuted to life in prison.[147] Interestingly, the presiding judge at Baxter's first trial was none other than Norman H. Purple, who as a lawyer had defended and helped secure the release of Cam Reeves just a few years prior.[148]

The legal effort against Bonney soon faltered. Bonney's charm campaign and publicized "detective" work had won him many supporters, including Governor Thomas Ford. The governor became convinced that Heaight's efforts amounted to little more than a cheap attempt at revenge on the part of a battered criminal element, and he even sat in on Bonney's trial in the December term of 1846. Bonney would win an acquittal. Ten of the jurors would write to Treasury Secretary R. J. Walker in the wake of the trial, demanding that Heaight lose his position as a confidential agent of the department. To this letter Ford attached a certificate, proclaiming that he "was fully persuaded from the evidence adduced, that the prosecution was put on foot, so far as Haight and the other witnesses against Bonney were concerned, to be revenged on him for ferreting out and bringing to punishment the murderers of Col. Davenport."[149]

Bonney had managed a fait accompli. By sacrificing his associates in the Nauvoo and New River criminal networks, Bonney had reinvented himself as a detective and lawman, blunting any attempts by former comrades to disclose his own criminal activity. Bonney would eventually publish a popular account of his exploits in 1850, cementing his reputation as an investigator. Bonney, of course, did not include any reference to his own past as a counterfeiter or fugitive from justice, nor did he mention his prior connections with the men he helped arrest. An eager public lapped up the retelling, anyway, and at least eight editions of Bonney's account would be printed.[150] The specter of Bonney's betrayal, however, would haunt him for the rest of his life. William Beckman, a later neighbor of Bonney's who as a boy had played checkers with him, later recalled that Bonney's "house had wooden shutters at all the windows which were all closed as soon as night came, and he would not go out of the house after dark."[151] Not even Edward Bonney could escape that.

The New River network in Indiana and Illinois all but collapsed. The repeated shocks of extralegal violence, which culminated in Edward Bonney's betrayal, had damaged the network beyond recovery. Surviving members of the New River network were outraged by Bonney's treachery but could do little to rescue their kin and associates or punish the turncoat. One member of the network allegedly sent the judge who presided at the Davenport murder trial a vicious letter, threatening to send "a bullet through [his] infernal, old, empty skull." The letter went on to threaten "the hell bound jury" and Bonney, who the writer promised would "come up missing when least expected."[152] Such threats, however, remained just that. Some of the ablest members of the network were now dead, imprisoned, or in hiding. Entire families, like the Reeveses from Marshall County and the Longs from Owen County, had been forced to leave their homes, while others found their reputations injured beyond repair. The New River family network had survived its connections to the Bellevue War and the lynching of the Driscolls. It had endured repeated allegations of criminality and had even survived direct action taken against its branches. Now many members of the network had decided to abandon their settlements in Illinois and Indiana and push farther west in search of fresh starts and new opportunities.

Nauvoo's Mormons, with whom members of the New River network had worked and associated for years, were also pushing across the river and into Iowa. They too could no longer bear the repeated shocks and threats of extralegal violence. Sustained allegations linked to the Hodges case and other cases of suspected criminality, coupled with existing anti-Mormon bigotries, had continued to fuel tensions in the region surrounding Nauvoo in the years after Joseph Smith's death. Starting in 1845, another rash of bloody extralegal violence rocked the region. Ford once again ordered troops into Hancock County. Gen. John J. Hardin helped negotiate a truce, under the terms that the Mormons would leave the state in the spring of 1846.[153] Led by Brigham Young, most of the Mormon flock migrated across the river over the months that followed, abandoning Nauvoo.

A few members of the New River network attempted to profit off of this exodus, purchasing lots in the vacated city. Both Shack and Shade Phipps and Hiram Long began to purchase Nauvoo property starting in May 1846.[154] Eventually they too abandoned the city. Rabid anti-Mormons, not satisfied with the withdrawal, continued to attack the remaining Mormons in the area, resulting in more deaths as armed sorties finally pushed on Nauvoo itself. Governor Ford, true to his belief in the power of popular will vis-à-vis the state, did little. "We did not think it worth while to arrest any one implicated in previous riots," Ford relayed in a whining 1846 address to the Illinois Senate, "knowing as we did, that, as the State could not change the trial to any other county, no one could be convicted in Hancock."[155] Once again under the supervision of Thomas Ford, the mob reigned triumphant.

Cascading episodes of violence would similarly haunt many of those members of the New River network who attempted to remain in Illinois and Indiana. In 1852, the "Birch War" would break out in Clark County, Illinois, when local vigilantes targeted Robert Birch's family and alleged associates following rumors that he had returned to the area. "Several parties," reported one local history, "were severely whipped." Although Robert Birch had disappeared, the rest of his family found themselves forced to flee their home.[156] Around 1850, back in Owen County, where so many members of the New River families had initially settled, a group of regulators would flog Shack or Shade Phipps. In the account of one local history, the regulators "took him out and lynched him under a large beech tree."[157] Luckily for Phipps, these regulators continued to subscribe to an older mode of lynching rather than the increasingly popular Rock River variation. Sufficiently chastised, the Phippses also soon left the area.

Many of the surviving branches of the New River network rendezvoused, like the Mormons, across the Mississippi River in Iowa Territory. In the three adjacent Polk, Warren, and Madison counties and in Monroe County, these members attempted to regroup and establish new settlements while preserving their network ties. The Reeveses, Harts, Phippses, and Longs could be found in this area. The families would attempt to rebuild their lives following the violence that had driven them from Illinois and Indiana. Even Owen Long would make it to Monroe County before dying in 1848, having lived through the execution of his sons just a few years prior. George Reeves helped settle his estate, which only contained about $100 worth of "goods, chattels, and effects."[158] Long's probate records totaled only a few pages. The brevity of these accounts reflect a story of devastating losses wrought by the cascading shocks of extralegal and legal punishment. Owen Long was a man who lost his sons, his property, and whatever measure of wealth he may have once possessed. He had been reduced to a handful of cheap possessions, and now, after an early death, was buried under the soil of a prairie far from the rivers and vales of his youth.

Most of the New River families slouched toward Iowa bearing scars that, while of varying intensity, mirrored those of the late Long. The families of that network possessed, to their ultimate downfall, a shocking series of connections to several violent extralegal events. Members had been present at the Bellevue War, were active in Nauvoo, had sheltered survivors of the Ogle lynchings, and engaged in

criminal operations across the Middle West. Through these connections the network absorbed a series of blows, starting with the
extralegal targeting of certain members, escalating to the targeting
of entire families like the Reeveses, and culminating in the collapse
of the network following Bonney's betrayal. To examine this collection of associated families is to see not only the connective tissue
by which the previously examined episodes of violence were bound,
but the stunning scale of that connection. Their experiences also
illustrate how violence does not cease when kinetic action itself ends
but how it can cascade across direct human linkages, shaping and
informing further incidents. The New River families would attempt
to rebuild in their new settlements in Iowa. They would not find
peace there.

CHAPTER 5

Omaha, Nebraska Territory

"There Is No Law Here"

It was an old and gnarled knot that tethered together the New River families. The ties of blood and association that bound their network had endured as the families migrated into the Middle West from the South. Those same ties had enabled the establishment of a series of connected settlements and eventually a robust criminal operation. When that operation collapsed, legal and extralegal retribution frayed and damaged the knot, but the kinship network nonetheless survived. Attacks on the New River families' prior habitations drove them across the Mississippi River into Iowa, where they again established settlements and operations in accordance with familiar patterns. Their kin were dead, their homes torched, and their property lost, but the knot that held them together remained. Edward Bonney had not undone it, nor had mobs, vigilantes, or courts. In 1848, in Des Moines, Iowa, two bullets from the gun of Cam Reeves finally severed that knot.

Prior to the shooting, James Phipps had lunged at Cam Reeves with a large stone.[1] How exactly the fight started is unclear. Phipps was a member of the New River family network. He had been born in Grayson County, Virginia, into a family connected to the Reeveses through a high degree of intermarriage and association that stretched back over generations. With Phipps was James Hart, whose own family had lived alongside the Reeveses in Marshall County, Illinois, prior to the 1843 banishment of the Reeveses at the hands of local vigilantes. The members of the New River network had continued to maintain and strengthen kinship linkages following their flight into Iowa, and ties between the Harts and the Phippses had been bolstered through the union of James Phipps and Eliza Hart in September 1847.[2] It was Phipps, not Reeves, behind whom James Hart now threw his support.

Responding to Phipps's attack, Cam Reeves, now a young man of around twenty-six years of age, took aim and squeezed the trigger of his gun. His shots found their marks. James Phipps found himself "seriously" wounded, and James Hart was "slightly" injured.[3] Blood had been shed, and blood had been sundered. The rending of the Reeveses from the larger New River family network occurred at a moment of acute tension between the family and not only with their kin, but also with the broader community. Allegations of organized criminality led to the downfall of the New River families in Illinois and Indiana, but the chastisement that accompanied those allegations had been apparently insufficient to reform the Reeves family. Within "a year or two" of the Reeveses settling in Linn Grove, Warren County, Iowa, residents of the surrounding area began to allege "that the Reeves crowd was a horsestealing outfit, if not murderers to boot."[4]

Just a few short years after a vigilante mob had expelled the family from Marshall County—and came close to lynching George Reeves in the process—the Reeveses again watched as local public opinion turned sharply against them. That summer a group of Warren County locals had attempted to combine into a vigilante company in order to expel the Reeveses. Numbering only some sixty men, they failed to drive the seasoned Reeveses from the land. Still, their efforts seem to have precipitated the break between Cam Reeves and his New River associates in Des Moines. The fight between Reeves, Phipps, and Hart had transpired shortly "after this occurrence."[5] Having just fled a deluge of legal and extralegal retribution for their familial connections to organized criminality, some members of the New River network may have resented the Reeveses for having drawn scrutiny so quicky. The specter of Lynch law loomed over the families yet again.

Authorities, lacking suitable facilities in Des Moines's Polk County, quickly spirited Cam Reeves to the jail in Oskaloosa.[6] The shooting hardened the attitudes of many locals toward the Reeves family. Calls for vigilante action again resounded in the region. Cam's younger brothers—Preston, William, Jesse, and thirteen-year-old George—spooked by the ineffectual expulsion attempt, by the renewed calls for vigilantism following the Phipps and Hard shooting, or by both, fled their rural homestead and took shelter in Des Moines.[7]

The Warren County vigilantes called for reinforcements. In nearby Madison County a group of eighteen men organized into the mounted "Black Oak Grove Vigilants Company" and elected Samuel Guye as their captain. These men rode to the Reeveses' Linn Grove, where they found the Warren County vigilantes already assembled. The vigilantes captured George and Elizabeth Reeves, who once again found themselves at the mercy of a hostile mob. The combined force left some of its members to guard the captives, and the next morning the remaining members prepared to march on Des Moines. Word of this movement reached Des Moines before the vigilantes could. Panic erupted in the settlement as the Reeves brothers rallied their sympathizers, and rumors spread of the group's bloodthirsty intentions. The warlike sound of "fife and drum" pierced the cold air as a group of Des Moines men armed themselves in preparation for what was to come.[8]

The westward flight of the New River families into Iowa preceded a larger surge. A sustained hunger for cheap land and a desire to profit off the traffic created by the discovery of gold in newly annexed California drove a glut of Americans to pour into the western prairies and Great Plains starting in the early 1850s. In a familiar cycle this mass human movement outstripped the capacity of the formal legal system to establish itself with sufficient rapidity and strength in the newly acquired regions. As was the case in the old Northwest, the federal government would informally outsource responsibility for law enforcement and regulation to private and extralegal combinations.

These circumstances brought about a cluster of bloody extra-legal violence deep in the heart of the Great Plains. In Kansas, speculative and landed interests would collide with the issues of slavery and sectionalism to create a violent conflict between armed pro- and anti-slavery factions. "Bleeding Kansas" quickly captured national attention for its visceral reflection of sectionalism and for its raw brutality. So fixated were observers on Kansas that, just to the north, a second cluster of unprecedented extralegal violence went largely unnoticed.[9] In Nebraska, the twin territory created alongside Kansas in 1854, the power of extralegal combinations would, for a few years, eclipse the power of the formal legal system, the militia, and even the territorial government itself. Consequently, the territory would see a campaign of organized extralegal violence unlike any experienced before in American history, as those groups maneuvered to advance the private interests of their members through brazen infiltration, subversion, and force.

While the narrative of this extralegal action in Nebraska attracted little national attention at the time and has been neglected since, it is indispensable for understanding the development of American extralegal violence post-1848. Human beings moving into and out of the territory served as a primary artery along which violence flowed across the plains. Individuals associated with extralegal Nebraskan outfits would play instrumental roles in the rise of cities like Omaha and Denver, shaping the early urban geography of the West with knife and noose.

To examine this movement across the Iowan plains and into Nebraska is to establish clearly the significance of earlier instances of middle western extralegal action in shaping the violence there and beyond. Direct human linkages bound the violence in Nebraska to previous and subsequent incidents of violence elsewhere, forming the very contours along which this entire sequence of violence would flow. Individuals who had participated in the Bellevue War, the Mormon Wars, and anti-horse-thief campaigns—perpetrators and targets both—would reemerge in Nebraska. They would influence the course of the action there, navigating dangerous property disputes, compromised legal trials, extralegal organizing, and increasingly lethal lynchings and would use the knowledge they had gleaned from their previous experiences with collective violent action. Those prior experiences proved invaluable in the turbulent atmosphere of time and place, and would allow those persons to assume highly visible, central positions in moments of violent action. Those already seasoned by prior engagement with Judge Lynch would influence and inform others, who would in the years that followed carry onward the genealogical legacy of that violence.

This is not, however, a narrative of a linear march west. It is a window into deepening flux. "Lawbringing" did not march across the plains in a Turnerian fashion, with the extralegal combinations establishing the rough framework against lawlessness upon which the formal legal system would establish itself.[10] Those with both prior vigilante and criminal experience would play prominent roles in shaping the form and direction of extralegal violence in early territorial Nebraska. There, the boundaries that ostensibly separated the legal, extralegal, and illegal would blur and warp as private interests, rampant speculation, territorial governance, violence, threat, and rhetoric swirled. Criminals would become lawmen; lawmen would become lynchers. Old ties would snap, and surprising new alliances would emerge. Such unexpected combinations helped produce a cluster of organized violent action and subversion that seemed to blend organized criminality with the rhetoric and tradition of American extralegal action. These linkages did not follow some straightforward rule of progress but flowed through and along a twisting web of human interconnections, guided by self-interest and self-preservation.

*   *   *

The cadence of the Reeveses' criminal operations in Iowa, according to local histories, had reflected the hard lessons gleaned from the family's knowledge of the Driscoll lynchings and their own expulsion from Illinois. According to local historian A. J. Hoisington, the Reeveses were careful to avoid angering the neighbors that resided around their residence at Linn Grove. "The Reeves had not stolen any horses in that vicinity, nor permitted others to do so, for prudential reasons," Hoisington wrote, "but to the south, southeast, and southwest, they were believed to be doing a wholesale business."[11] Mere allegations of criminality, after all, had been insufficient motivation for the residents of Marshall County to turn violently against the family. In that case, it had been only after the Reeveses had begun committing crime locally that public opinion turned against the family with enough momentum to trigger a vigilante movement.

While prudent and grounded in past experience, these precautions now proved insufficient. Many of the vigilantes who moved against the Reeveses in 1848 were already impoverished. Hoisington's history noted that about one-third of the Warren County vigilantes did not own horses and had to march on foot. One of these men, a resident by the name of Mason, did not even own shoes. Although the weather was cold, the man marched barefoot through "frequent puddles of frozen water."[12] Such economic hardships likely amplified the resentments that the alleged criminality of the Reeveses created, and the mere rumor of threats against their already meager property might have encouraged such men to take decisive action without the sanction of the formal legal system.

Enhanced operational prudence may have failed to shield the Reeveses from the wrath of some of their neighbors, but the family was not bereft of allies and sympathizers in the region. Sophronia Reeves, who was by 1848 a woman of around twenty-two years of age, had played an outsized role in winning over hearts and minds for the family in Des Moines. Sophronia had been a popular teenager back in Illinois, and even local histories critical of her family noted that she made many friends in the town of Henry and enjoyed a favorable reputation there.[13] In Des Moines, she again won over many of the residents. In 1847, Sophronia was able to secure a marriage to a rising member of the local middle-class elite, Alfred D. Jones. Jones had been elected

Polk County surveyor and had laid out the town of Des Moines. He was also an attorney, had served as a clerk of the Polk County District Court, and ran in local Democratic political circles.[14] The marriage established an important connection between the Reeveses and Joneses' network, which included some of the more influential elements of the Des Moines social and political worlds.

When news of the vigilante movement against the Reeveses reached Des Moines, these connections mobilized to aid the family. Polk County sheriff George A. Michael, later characterized by Jones as being one of his fellow "young gentlemen about the town," departed Des Moines with warrants to arrest six of the vigilantes. When the sheriff reached Four Mile Creek south of Des Moines, he saw the company marching on the settlement and apparently lost his nerve. He tied his horse to a sapling and pretended to lie in a drunken slumber. The ruse failed, and the furious vigilantes seized Michael, "took away his arms, all his official papers, and compelled him to accompany them on his horse, fully explaining to him what they wanted and were going to do, not only with him but with the Reeves."[15]

Meanwhile, in Des Moines proper, Col. Thomas Baker organized preparations for the defense. Baker was a prominent local Democrat and another contact of Jones's. Jones, according to his own later account, enjoyed "a business connection" with Baker, "first as student in law, and afterwards as his partner in practice."[16] Baker's efforts to scramble together an armed band created a sense of urgency that the sight of the vigilantes marching on the town from the south soon amplified. According to Hoisington, fevered reports raced through the settlement that "the town itself was to be destroyed and all the citizens compelled to leave for the sin of harboring the Reeves boys and their friends. It was also freely reported that some of the citizens of the fort, being found over on North River, were captured and killed."[17] Baker cobbled together a group of armed citizens while the Reeveses took refuge in Joseph Crews's saloon. Baker's ad hoc militia sent out scouts with instructions "to be careful that they were not captured and hanged to the nearest tree." When the scouts failed to promptly return, Baker's men dispatched additional scouts "to learn if possible their untimely fate."[18] None had fallen victim to the approaching column, but the episode laid bare the panicked and ill-prepared posture of Des Moines's defenders.

Not all residents of Des Moines were willing to take up arms to defend the Reeves family, especially in the wake of Cam Reeves's shooting of Hart and Phipps. The members of this faction "refused to join Colonel Baker and his excited band and quietly agreed among themselves that if the Vigilants only wanted the Reeves gang they were welcome to come and take them away."[19] Now only the Racoon River separated the vigilantes from Des Moines. When the vigilantes reached the water, they halted and dispatched two men to scout the town. After the scouts learned that the Reeves men were sheltering at Crews's saloon, they returned to the larger company.

Emboldened, the vigilantes forded the shallow river and made for the saloon. Mounted men led the assault, riding "rapidly, carrying their guns ready to fire, in their right hands and guiding their horses with their left hands." The vigilantes without horses trotted behind. Colonel Baker and his men, cowed by this show of force, did not emerge to give battle. Unchallenged, the vigilantes quickly surrounded the saloon. Preston Reeves, sensing the hopelessness and danger of the situation, tried to flee the building and make for the Des Moines River. His speed, however, proved no match for his mounted pursuers, and he was quickly captured. His brothers remained in the saloon.[20]

The vigilantes, hoping to keep the episode bloodless, communicated to the besieged brothers that "if they would quietly surrender, give up their arms, go with the Vigilants to their homes, load up their chattels and leave the country forever they would not be harmed." The Reeveses, unwilling to endure another banishment and perhaps distrustful of the proffered guarantees, refused to surrender. They promised to "fight to the last." With negotiations at an apparent impasse, the vigilantes threatened to torch the saloon, leading to the proprietor demanding that the Reeveses surrender. Once the brothers secured guarantees for their safety, they finally did so. Their captives in tow, the vigilantes departed Des Moines in triumph. When they again forded the Raccoon River, they released Sheriff Michael and restored to him his arms and papers, completing the bloodless humiliation of the pro-Reeves faction.[21]

The vigilante companies, having led their prisoners to the family's home at Linn Grove, forced the Reeveses to once again prepare for exile. The next morning all the Reeveses—sans the still-imprisoned Cam—"loaded their wagons, and with live stock and everything movable, trekked southward, escorted by both Vigilant companies." At one point some of the Warren County men "who had suffered from the depredations of the Reeves gang" grew frustrated with the bloodless punishment and seized George Reeves. They tied the old man to a sapling and flogged him until they were stopped by more scrupulous members of the Madison County party, who demanded that they abide by their earlier promises.[22] Ordering the Reeveses to depart the state, the vigilantes returned to the family their firearms and disbanded. The Reeveses pushed south, stopping briefly at the Mormon station of Mount Pigsah in Union County, Iowa, before crossing into Missouri.[23]

Not only had the Reeveses now endured two exiles in the span of just five years, Cam's shooting of Hart and Phipps in Des Moines had sundered the family from the New River network on which they had long relied. The Reeveses were adrift, but the extralegal ban on their returning to Iowa was not rigorously enforced. Elizabeth Doughton Reeves spent the winter of 1848–49 in Missouri, and in 1849 returned to Iowa, where she settled in Madison County near what is now the town of Winterset.[24] Census records indicate that the matriarch lived there with her sons William, Jesse, and George, and Cam, who had managed to evade serious legal repercussions for his shooting of Hart and Phipps back in Des Moines. Alfred and Sophronia Jones also migrated to the area, appearing on the same page of the census.[25]

Despite having endured yet another extralegal chastisement, the family's illicit maneuvering did not abate. At one point Elizabeth and Alfred Jones defrauded Franklin Robinson, the son of Elizabeth's late sister, Mary Doughton Robinson. Franklin Robinson had fought in the Mexican–American War as a private with the Missouri Mounted Volunteers, for which he was to receive a land warrant. In May 1849, Robinson, caught up in the fever of the Gold Rush, departed the region for California before he received the warrant. Before he left, Robinson made arrangements with Jones to receive the warrant in Robinson's name. Instead, Jones, when he received the warrant in 1852, transferred it to Elizabeth Reeves, who in turn gave Jones the warrant in 1853 so that he could preempt a claim for himself in Pottawattamie County, Iowa.[26]

The elder George Reeves did not appear in these various records. The old man resurfaced, alone, in Cass County, Iowa, where local histories noted that he was the first settler of Washington Township, where "no living thing was there to dispute his title, save the wild animals and game." George built a lonely cabin but did little else to improve the land. According to the same local history, "George did not have one of the best of reputations, and was not to be relied on."[27] He developed a reputation for drunkenness and died in his wagon sometime in the early to mid-1850s.[28] Cam, for his part, also spent some time away from his immediate family during this period. He drifted between Iowa and Missouri, where he had married Elizabeth Evans. He appeared in the 1850 census both as a member of his mother's household and as a member of his mother-in-law's household in Benton, Osage County, Missouri.[29]

In April 1853, Alfred Jones surveyed and platted the settlement of Council Bluffs on the western border of Iowa.[30] The settlement was nestled along the Missouri River, which separated Iowa from the Unorganized Territory, land that the federal government had not yet legally opened up for American settlement. The region beyond the western shore of the river was home to a number of Native peoples, including the Omahas, Otos, Kansas, Poncas, Pawnees, Missourias, Lakotas, Cheyennes, and Arapahoes. Across from what would become Council Bluffs, the US military had once maintained a presence on the western bank at Fort Atkinson but had abandoned the site in 1827. A small number of fur traders had also built and operated stations in the region. In the winter of 1846, Mormons fleeing from Nauvoo and the violence of the Illinois Mormon War had reached the area and formed an encampment known as Winter Quarters. While most of the Mormon group continued west following the thaw, in 1847, another group of Mormons used materials from the abandoned Fort Atkinson to establish a short-lived farming operation in the area intended to support further emigrants.[31]

Council Bluffs itself was established at the site of the Mormon settlement of Kanesville, formerly known as Miller's Hollow. Kanesville was a product of the extralegal flow of violence that had driven so many west, and was established as a station for Mormons fleeing from mob violence in Illinois. Mormon leaders had planned for Kanesville to operate as a temporary hub rather than a permanent settlement, and they had not even drawn up blueprints for a town.[32] Its purpose was to outfit Mormons for the westward trek to Utah, but the settlement became unexpectedly prosperous following the 1848 discovery of gold in California and the subsequent stampede of eager miners west. Orson Hyde, who had been a member of the Smith's Quorum of the Twelve Apostles, operated a newspaper out of Kanesville—*The Frontier Guardian*—that simultaneously attempted to keep local Mormons informed on matters related to the Mormon Church and Utah, while also promoting the development of the town itself.[33] Eventually Mormon leadership grew concerned that too many of Kanesville's residents were growing overly comfortable at what had been established as a temporary waystation. In 1851, leaders ordered the Mormons there to abandon the settlement and continue moving to Utah.[34]

While not all the Mormon settlers acquiesced to this departure, many did. Much of the settlement was vacated, clearing the way for the 1853 incorporation of the settlement known as Council Bluffs. Some gentiles realized that prominence at such a key outfitting hub could provide opportunities for political and financial advancement. One such gentile, an attorney by the name of Alvarado C. Ford, became in 1852 the editor and eventual owner of the rebranded *The Frontier Guardian and Iowa Sentinel*, the ownership of which Hyde had initially transferred to Jacob Dawson earlier that year.[35] Ford had tried his luck searching for wealth in California but had fled from criminal charges there only to be arrested in 1850 in New

York for "being a fugitive from justice, from the State of California, and also with having counterfeit money in his possession."[36]

Greed and opportunity drew ambitious and sometimes unscrupulous wealth seekers like Ford to the area. Violence sometimes accompanied such circumstances. Thomas Brown, a Mormon who had been linked to both the Miller and Davenport murders back in Illinois, reappeared in the area during its Mormon settlement. Return Jackson Redden, who had been similarly linked to the New River network and criminal operations, also resurfaced.[37] Brown, who had managed to threaten the lives of the Quorum of the Twelve during his tenure in the area, died in murky circumstances in early 1848. Sources differ wildly on whether his death was at the hands of a fellow Mormon horse thief, in a brawl, or as a consequence of an accidental shooting.[38]

On May 13, 1853, Baltimore Muir supposedly murdered and robbed a man by the name of Samuels. Both men had been part of an emigrant train from California. An angry mob quickly located and seized Muir, even though "no money that could be fairly considered as belonging to Samuels, was found on his person." The Californian emigrants, undoubtedly accustomed to the swift and lethal tribunals of the mining districts, organized a lynch court. Alvarado Ford served as Muir's attorney in the matter, "and made the best possible effort he could under the circumstances." Still, the jury quickly found Muir guilty. In a sign of the changing nature of extralegal violence, and possibly of the influence of the Californian element, they sentenced the accused to death. At sunset, extralegal executioners fastened a noose around Muir's neck, flung the rope over a tree's branch, and tied the rest to a mule. The animal dragged him up and "into eternity."[39]

Undeterred by the rough nature of the region, Alfred Jones joined in the speculatory excitement. It was in Council Bluffs's Pottawattamie County that he, with the cooperation of his mother-in-law, used their ill-gotten land warrant to claim a tract. Council Bluffs, though, was not Jones's primary interest. What interested the surveyor most lay beyond the river, in the Unorganized Territory. Kanesville had provided an illustrative example. What was supposed to have been nothing more than a temporary camp had stumbled into prosperity by the accident of its favorable location. The area beyond the Missouri River sat at the intersection of two thoroughfares, one by the water of the "Big Muddy" and one across the Great Plains. So long as traffic continued across the region, the control of strategically located land along the river offered potentially lucrative opportunities for speculation and investment. Jones wanted to stake the land before any competitors could. While surveying Council Bluffs, he began to make note of favorable locations for claims on the western bank of the Missouri.

In November 1853, Jones cast his die. He embarked across the river in "a small, leaky scow," accompanied by brothers Thomas Allen and William Allen. The Allens had previously lived in Illinois, and although it is unclear whether they belonged to the Mormon faithful, they had joined the greater Mormon flight from Illinois in the 1840s. The Allens and their families had been part of the Mormon Summer Quarters community in the Unorganized Territory and had thereafter settled in Kanesville.[40] Thomas rowed the small vessel while "Bill" bailed out the water that constantly poured into the craft.[41] Upon reaching the safety of the opposite riverbank, the men set to work staking claims and blazing lines to delineate what they now claimed to be their land. Jones then "laid his claim foundations regularly, completing the requisites for making a good and valid claim according to the laws and customs among squatters in others new portions of the public domain."[42] When the men completed their work, they again launched their leaky boat into the icy waters of the Missouri and returned to Iowa.

Travel aboard a questionable watercraft, however, was not the only risk Jones faced in staking a claim on the western bank of the river. Jones and the Allens had staked claims that were unauthorized and therefore unregulated. No force of law, besides the squatter custom adhered to by Jones, protected or even recognized the claims. Any person or persons could simply squat on the claim and take it for themselves. If Jones wanted to keep the land he now claimed as his property, he would need to be able to guard it.

On March 3, 1854, the US Senate passed the controversial Kansas–Nebraska Act, which would create both the Kansas and Nebraska Territories. On March 27, Jones sold half of his Pottawattamie claim for $1,000 and prepared to invest in his claims on the western bank of the river.[43] In May, the Kansas–Nebraska Act passed in Congress, and on May 30, Franklin Pierce signed the act into law. While Nebraska was now an official territory, and settlers could legally file to acquire public lands under the Preemption Act of 1841, the government had undertaken no survey of the territory, nor had it established a land office. Settlers could therefore not file for preemption, and squatting remained the only means of holding title.[44] Still, settlers began to cross the river in earnest, hoping to stake claims and speculate in the new territory before all the best land was taken. Plans were drawn for a new settlement that was to be called Omaha, after the Native Omaha people.[45]

In this unregulated environment, a claim was only as good as one's ability to hold it. Jones discovered this in the summer of 1854, when a "big Frenchman" by the name of François Guittar squatted on Jones's Nebraskan claim.[46] Guittar, who operated a store in Council Bluffs, was a tough and seasoned outdoorsman. He had his start in the fur trading business at the age of just fourteen years and had lived and trapped in the region since 1827.[47] The bookish, middle-class Jones did not stand a chance. According to Rachel and William Snowden, who themselves settled in the territory that June, Guittar easily "succeeded in scaring Jones off."[48] With no formal legal or regulatory recourse, the claim appeared to be forfeit.

Alfred Jones had little chance of evicting Guittar from the claim alone. He was not a fighter. Luckily for Jones, though, his brother-in-law was. Cam Reeves was no stranger to violence or risk. Jones sent word to his brother-in-law, promising, according to the Snowdens, that Reeves "could have half the claim, if he would hold it." This time, it would be a Reeves doing the banishing. Reeves answered Jones's call for aid. Armed with a shotgun, the horse thief "persuaded" Guittar to retreat across the river and back to Council Bluffs. Two weeks later the men met in the streets of that settlement, and a fistfight ensued. Guittar was strong and initially maintained an upper hand. Reeves spent so much time on the ground that "his shirt was torn from his back by rubbing against the rocks and stumps." Still, Reeves had more stamina than his opponent. The melee raged on until Guittar exhausted himself. Reeves won the fight. That settled the affair, and Guittar and Reeves eventually drank together and made peace. Jones had his land back, and the Reeveses had come to Nebraska.[49]

Cam Reeves settled in Nebraska on July 10, 1854, following his eviction of Guittar from Jones's claim.[50] Just a few days later, on July 22, Jones and several other squatters gathered at Omaha to form the "Omaha Township Claim Association." The squatters agreed to "unite [themselves] under the above title for mutual protection in holding claims upon the public lands in the territory of Nebraska and be governed by the claim laws." Club laws laid out regulations to govern the staking, holding, and vacating of claims. They also violated federal law. The squatters agreed to allow members of the organization the right to claim up to 320 acres of land, double the amount allowed under the Preemption Act. The squatters also pledged to band together to enforce the rulings of the club. They then elected officers and selected Jones to serve as their presiding officer and judge.[51] The extralegal organization founded on that July day would soon be known by a new name—the Omaha Claim Club.

Reeves may have retaken Jones's claim, but his beating of Guittar had not eliminated the threat of future "claim jumpers." As soon-to-be Omaha Claim Club member James M. Woolworth would explain, "Where the land has not been surveyed, the United States law affords no protection to a squatter, against a jumper; that is, a person entering upon his claim and asserting his right to it."[52] Mutual protection and extralegal enforcement presented squatters with the only means of securing title in such conditions. The violence that Reeves had visited upon Guittar would have to be institutionalized in an extralegal combination to prevent and, if necessary, resolve similar instances.

The claim club was not a Nebraskan innovation. Such organizations had existed for years in the United States. As scholar Ilia Murtazashvili argues, claim clubs were "the most important initial source of private property institutions as individuals fanned out across the nation's vast lands during the nineteenth century."[53] The Reeveses themselves had some familiarity with claim clubs, with George Reeves's cousin, Lenoir Reeves, having belonged to a claim club organized in Des Moines prior to the family's banishment.[54] The Omaha Claim Club was itself modeled primarily on the example of such Iowan organizations. The club's 320-acre claim allowance, for instance, was not a novelty but reflected the custom and practice of many of the Iowan clubs.[55] In adhering to an already established model, the Nebraskan squatters were able to rapidly organize a structure with immediate familiarity and informal legitimacy, extralegal though it was.

Claim clubs unquestionably responded to a pressing and necessary need. In an environment devoid of formal regulatory structures and recourses, they seemed to embody an extralegal yet republican constitutionalism. There was a dark side, however, to these organizations. In Iowa, as historian Allan Bogue argued, claim clubs at times employed their extralegal force not for true and defensive mutual protection, but to aggressively advance the financial interests of club leaders and speculators to the detriment of would-be petty squatters. It is imperative, to borrow Bogue's sage warning, to "not confuse the symbols of agrarian democracy with its substance."[56] In Madison County, Iowa, George Guye, the son of Samuel Guye—who had led the mounted vigilante company that helped expel the Reeveses—had learned this bitter lesson in 1850. A man named Leonard Bowman had jumped Guye's claim, and because he was a member of the club and Guye was not, the club attempted to evict Guye by force. They were only stopped in this endeavor when Samuel Guye again mustered an armed extralegal band and forced the club to stand down.[57]

The beating that Cam Reeves visited upon François Guittar had now established in practice this precedent in the new territory. Claim law would be adjudicated by force. Ironically, Cam, the former horse thief, now found himself on the side of enforcing the law, informal as it may have been, as he settled his family on the western bank. Squatters soon organized similar groups at the other settlements that appeared along the western bank of the river. Some of these squatters, contending already through their clubs with the threat of jumpers, also began to vie to advance the profile of their settlements and increase the value of their claims. Speculation ran rampant. Cam Reeves's forcible retaking of Jones's claim had been the first recorded claim-related violence in the territory, but it would not be the last.

Alfred D. Jones was not the only ambitious seeker of fortune to brave the icy waters of the Missouri River in the winter of 1853–54. In early January 1854, another surveyor seized land to the north of Jones's claim. This surveyor's target was the site of the dilapidated Fort Atkinson and the Mormon Winter Quarters. There, he staked and blazed out the claim for a town. The Mormons had abandoned the camp, but the area saw high traffic from gold miners and others who ferried across the river at the site. The prospective town could service that traffic, and there was a chance the land could quickly rise in value once the territory officially opened for settlement. Satisfied with his work, the surveyor departed the area and returned to the eastern bank of the river and his home in Council Bluffs. James C. Mitchell had staked his claim.[58]

It had been a little under fourteen years since the Bellevue War when Mitchell surveyed the Winter Quarters area. With Mitchell having been spared legal repercussions for his killing of rapist James Thompson, he and his family had initially remained in Bellevue in the aftermath of the conflict. With the westward movement of the gold rush, though, Mitchell sensed opportunity and moved with his family to Iowa's western edge. They settled in Kanesville, where they operated two stores to sell provisions to the westward-slouching mass.[59]

As with Jones, it was not the Iowan town but the opportunities waiting on the Missouri's western bank that soon drove James Mitchell's interests. In 1853, Mitchell became involved in business efforts to build bridges across the Missouri River, one at Lone Tree Ferry between Council Bluffs and what would become Omaha, and one at the Elkhorn & Loup Fork Ferry. At the latter, he joined forces with an ambitious cohort of speculators that included brothers George and Abner Hollister, Andrew Jackson Poppleton, Hascall C. Purple, and Andrew Jackson Hanscom.[60]

Like Jones's "Omaha Township Claim Association," Mitchell and his allies formed into a squatter combination following the official establishment of the Nebraska Territory. On September 9, 1854, Mitchell's group met in Council Bluffs to organize the "Nebraska Winter Quarters Company." The prospective new town would have stiff competition from other rapidly developing settlements, such as Omaha and, further to the south, a familiar-sounding town by the name of Bellevue. Mitchell and his colleagues, hoping to push their town into dominance over these competitors—and turn their investments into returns—made provisions to establish a tavern, house, and warehouse, while securing ferry operations.[61] Mitchell, who had helped send one man accused of counterfeiting to his grave, now—perhaps unknowingly—entered into business with another as Alvarado C. Ford briefly joined the company.[62]

Mitchell renamed the prospective town "Florence," after his wife's granddaughter.[63] Political developments soon arose, however, that immediately threatened the site's prospects. President Franklin Pierce had selected a South Carolinian, Francis Burt, to serve as Nebraska's first territorial governor. Burt arrived on October 7, 1854, in the settlement of Bellevue to the south of Omaha. Eleven days later he was dead, felled by illness. Burt's successor was an ambitious twenty-seven-year-old territorial secretary by the name of Thomas B. Cuming. The new acting governor quickly threw his support behind Omaha's bid to become the territorial capital. Within five days of assuming office, Cuming ordered a territorial census and used the results to divide Nebraska into eight counties. Over cries of fraud, he then ensured that most of the seats went to Omaha and the counties north of the Platte River in an attempt to undercut the influence of Bellevue and its partisans. After quickly calling an election, Cuming announced on December 20 that the territory's first legislative session would be held in Omaha in the new year.[64]

Cuming's machinations infuriated Bellevue's and Florence's backers. The acting governor traveled to Bellevue to try to placate

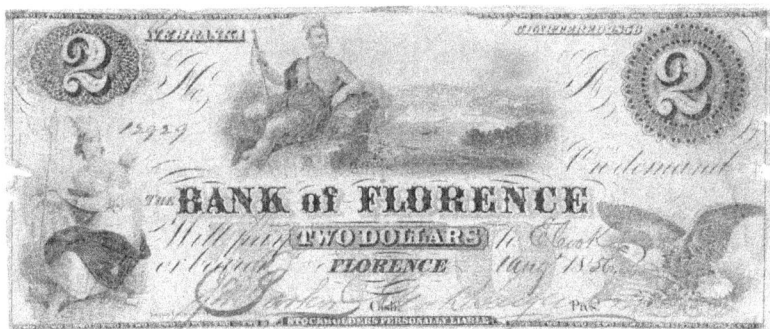

An 1856 bank note from Florence. From the Byron Reed Collection, owned by the City of Omaha and housed by the Durham Museum, Omaha, Nebraska.

the residents there, but Abner W. Hollister—Mitchell's former colleague on the bridge project—confronted Cuming with a letter purporting to expose his "lying, cheating, buying rascality." Hollister's actions infuriated Cuming, who denounced the letter as a forgery, derided Bellevue as "the deserted village," and stormed out of the meeting.[65] Bellevue supporters were not the only ones who felt cheated. On December 27, 1854, the writer of one article for Bellevue's *Nebraska Palladium* addressed Cuming directly and snarled, "You feared the independent citizens of Florence, and to overpower them, you brought the southern line of Washington to within a mile of Omaha, that importation might be easy." [66]

On December 30, Abner's younger brother George W. Hollister—who was also involved in the bridge project—served as secretary at a five-county delegate convention created to oppose Cuming. The convention produced a petition to President Pierce that stated that Cuming should be immediately removed from office.[67] Such threats were enough to prompt Cuming himself to write to Pierce directly, insisting that the "petitions have been prepared and are being distributed by speculators whose fortunes have been marred by the location of the capitol."[68] Pierce did not act, and the controversy continued to rage.

On January 9, 1855, Cuming's Florence and Bellevue foes again staged a convention. The attendees elected the fiery James C.

Mitchell as chairman. George W. Hollister was present, as was the ambitious Alvarado C. Ford, who had helped organize Bellevue in early 1854.[69] Mitchell delivered an inflammatory speech to the attendees, in which he accused Cuming of manipulating the results of his census with the help of the "*saloon brawlers* and street loafers of Council Bluffs." He also proclaimed that "if His Excellency should presume to approach him with bribes, he would whip him as he would whip a dog."[70]

With the temperature rising fast, the First Territorial Legislature met in Omaha on January 16. There was a palpable threat that the proceedings would devolve into violence. Omaha Claim Club member James Woolworth later recounted that the anti-Omaha representatives "arrayed themselves in the red blankets of savages, armed themselves with revolvers and knives, and loudly proclaimed their design of breaking up the Assembly."[71] George L. Miller, another Omaha Claim Club member and representative of the legislature, later recalled that "the excitement over the capital question was, at times, great. The lobbies, we remember, were once crowded with respective parties to the contest, armed with bludgeons, brick-bats, and pistols."[72]

Shrugging off the threat of violence, Omaha's partisans went to work. Hansom and Poppleton, two Omaha Claim Club members who shared the first and middle name of "Andrew Jackson," spearheaded a campaign that mixed bribery with physical intimidation.[73] The campaign paid dividends, and five previously anti-Omaha men defected to the Omaha side. Mitchell, who just weeks before had threatened to respond to bribery with flogging, was one of them. He had been swayed by an appointment as the sole commissioner for the selection of the capitol's site in Omaha.[74] Hansom and Poppleton had both been associated with Mitchell in the 1853 bridge project, and their influence may have also helped win him over. In any case, the legislature finally approved Omaha as the territorial capital on February 22, 1855.[75] Cam Reeves and Alfred Jones would also benefit from the establishment of the capitol in Omaha, with the two men furnishing the territorial government with the stone needed to construct the building.[76]

For Omaha's founders and backers like Alfred Jones, who had been present at the territorial legislature representing Omaha's Douglas County, it was a moment of triumph.[77] It seemed as though Omaha's rise was now assured, and the claims of its residents were destined to spike in value. The power and size of the Omaha Claim Club swelled, as squatters surged across the Missouri River and attempted to join in the speculatory whirl. For the most ambitious of the squatters, the claim club would serve as a vehicle for forcibly advancing their interests and undercutting their competitors.

The territory's leaders were not keen to miss out on the speculatory profits, and their own financial interests quickly became aligned with Omaha and its claim club. The reach of the organization stretched to the highest levels of power, and in short order even Thomas B. Cuming became a member of the Omaha Claim Club.[78] The club and its violence were not only tolerated but became institutionalized. As Murtazashvili argues, American claim clubs "were worthy competitors to the state in the provision of property institutions."[79] In Nebraska the state could not even compete. On March 6, 1855, the territorial legislature formally endorsed the regulations and activities of the claim clubs in flagrant violation of existing federal law. Such was the power of the clubs that even this went, for the moment, unchallenged. As Omaha Claim Club member Woolworth would write in 1857, "the law of the Territory conferring legislative authority on the clubs is unconstitutional. Still, public opinion is more than law."[80]

On April 3, 1855, Charles A. Henry killed Mitchell's old associate, George W. Hollister, with a shotgun blast. Hollister had continued to attempt to advance his interests in Bellevue even after the capital defeat, and had been surveying claims for the town's own club before his death. In the course of this work, Hollister became embroiled in a claim dispute that involved Henry and another man. Angry words flew. Henry's companion lashed out with a cudgel, and Hollister advanced holding a hatchet. Henry then lifted his shotgun, cocked the weapon, and fired. The duckshot disemboweled

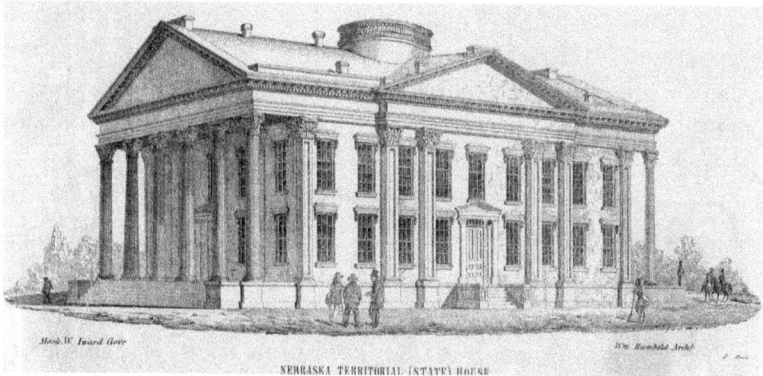

The Nebraska Territorial House. From the Byron Reed Collection, owned by the City of Omaha and housed by the Durham Museum, Omaha, Nebraska.

Hollister.[81] Hollister's fellow surveyor seized Henry and surrendered him to territorial authorities.

Hollister's friends in Bellevue, outraged by the killing, attempted to lynch Henry on the following night. Fenner Ferguson, the territory's chief justice, stopped them in this endeavor. Ferguson had surrounded the jail with guards, and the would-be vigilantes, unwilling to engage in what promised to be a bloody struggle over the prisoner, melted back into the night. While sympathetic to the deceased Hollister, Bellevue's *Palladium* denounced the attempted lynching, insisting to readers that "a resort to 'lynch law' is to be deplored in all cases, and particularly so where the reign of civil law has been established."[82] As the *Palladium* and its readers would soon discover, however, civil law reigned in Nebraska Territory in name only. For the moment, however, the proceedings ground to a halt. Authorities transferred Henry for detainment to the much more sympathetic Omaha. There, he waited until the fall months for his case to return to court.

Even as Chief Justice Ferguson and the formal legal system attempted to assert some control over the violent adjudication of claim disputes in the territory, participation in club-endorsed violence increasingly surfaced as a primary avenue of both garnering influence and securing wealth as the clubs emerged as a parallel system of informal governance. Cam Reeves, twice exiled from his home communities on account of his criminal escapades, suddenly found himself in Omaha, thrust into a state of respectability and public prominence. Other members of his family, including his mother, Elizabeth, and his brothers Preston, Jesse, and George, were—on account of their relationships to the Joneses and Cam—all able to establish themselves in the territory as decently respectable settlers.[83] Perhaps on account of this dramatic reversal in the family's situation, when Jesse Reeves and his wife Elizabeth Barlow Reeves welcomed a son on October 2, 1854, they christened him "William Nebraska."[84]

For Cam Reeves, the once-impoverished scion of the New River family network, this new standing would have been completely foreign. Reeves's personal propensity for violence had been the immediate trigger for the vigilante action against his family in Iowa. In Nebraska, Reeves's ability to threaten and engage in violence—an ability developed over the course of his own past experiences in dangerous and criminal action—had settled the first recorded claim dispute in Omaha. That violence established the credibility of his network to violently enforce its claims—an especially important precedent as Alfred Jones emerged at the center of the Omaha Claim Club's early leadership. With shotgun and fist, Reeves had secured a claim for his brother-in-law and local renown and prestige for himself.

Cam Reeves was willing to engage in violence. He possessed rare and valuable personal experience in braving such action. With moments of crisis emerging in the territory that necessitated in the minds of the settlers a forceful response, Cam Reeves suddenly presented himself not as a threat to local property rights but as a resolute and dependable leader capable of preserving those rights. Such was the case in June 1855, a little over two months after Henry's killing of Hollister. Pawnee parties, resisting the encroachment of the White settlers, raided a "good many cattle" from Omaha and the surrounding area. According to Grenville M. Dodge, this cattle raid was a deliberate act of provocation and not theft for material gain alone. "After they had killed the cattle,"

Dodge wrote, "they had placed their heads on mounds with the horns facing the settlement, which was an act of defiance and I understood it."[85]

The furious White settlers, anxious to respond, looked to Reeves for leadership. Cam Reeves, who had been expelled from two communities for his own alleged ties to the thieving of livestock, now found himself charged with organizing the response to that very offense. Reeves led a band of thirty Omaha residents to strike the Pawnees. En route, he and his party attempted to induce Dodge and a ferry operator named Samuel Newell Fifield to accompany the band. The two men refused, insisting that the Pawnees would kill Reeves and his men. Dodge noted that Reeves and his party "thought we were cowards." They would have, Reeves insisted, "cattle or blood." Despite Reeves's bravado, the counterraid quickly fell apart when, according to Dodge, five hundred Pawnees ambushed Reeves's band. Luckily for Reeves and his men, the Pawnees spared the party. They contented themselves with turning the would-be raiders into a humiliating spectacle, depriving them of "all their arms" and "most of their clothes." With the defeated and almost-naked party retreating and crying out for the ferry, Fifield mockingly inquired, "Which they got, cattle or blood?"[86]

Reeves's humiliation at the hands of the Pawnees did not, though, spell the end of his rise to prominence in the territory. On July 30, 1855, Reeves secured an officer's commission in the territorial militia and became the second lieutenant in the 2nd Company of the 1st Regiment Nebraska Volunteers. Exactly one month later, he found himself promoted to first lieutenant following the resignation of fellow Omaha Claim Club member Alfred D. Goyer.[87] Nebraska's early militia was tightly connected to the Omaha Claim Club, with many of the officers—including commanding officer Brigadier General John M. Thayer—holding positions of influence within the extralegal body.[88]

By infiltrating so thoroughly this ostensibly territorial institution, the claim club was able to use the militia to openly provision its members for violent action. According to Joseph Barker, a mercurial former Methodist preacher of English descent and a leader within the Omaha Claim Club, the club met in at least one instance in response to allegations of claim jumping "and decided to remove the jumpers by force of arms. All who had not guns or pistols of their own were furnished by an officer of the General Government with United States muskets."[89] Public arms performed private violence, and perhaps more importantly demonstrated to any witnesses that even the institutions of the constitutional territorial government were subservient to the Omaha Claim Club.

With the influence they held over territorial institutions emboldening club members, the use of violent and even lethal force in the settling of land claim disputes did not abate with the arrest of Charles Henry. On August 29, 1855, James Mitchell and a group of some thirty other armed men marched on Charles Davis's cabin. Davis's dwelling was located on the Fort Calhoun town claim, and Mitchell's party proclaimed that Davis had "jumped" their already existing claim on the site. Accompanying Mitchell were prominent Omaha and Council Bluffs men, including Addison Cochran, Hadley D. Johnson, J. P. Casady, Hascall C. Purple, A. V. Larimer, Andrew Jackson Poppleton, Sherman Goss, and others.[90] When they arrived at the claim to evict Davis, however, they found the cabin manned by an armed party, roughly seventeen strong. Davis's force consisted of men from the settlement of De Soto who had little love for Omaha and a vested interest in preventing the organization of a rival town in the area.[91]

The parties confronted each other. Cochran informed Davis that he would have to vacate the claim, to which Davis retorted that he would never leave it alive. "You will leave it," Cochran replied pointedly.[92] According to one newspaper account, "Hard words passed."[93] A shot rang out. Both parties began to fire wildly. A defender's bullet pierced through the heart of Sherman Goss, who crumpled dead, while another shot shattered Hascall Purple's arm.[94] A resident of Florence by the name of Theodore Thompson—a member of the attacking party—was wounded in the thigh.[95] From inside the cabin Davis cried out, "You are murdering my family!"[96] Bloodied, the attacking party retreated, vowing to return with a larger contingent and "have Davis alive or dead."[97]

News of the fight caused an uproar in Omaha. This outrage, though, was directed not against the extralegal nature of the destructive violence but against Davis for daring to resist. Andrew Jackson Hansom, a prominent member of the Omaha Claim Club, began to rally "a force to rout Davis at all hazards." Many of the men who joined Hansom swore "never to return while a live man remains in the house."[98] This was enough for Davis, who sued for peace and soon vacated the claim.[99] Calls for blood soon abated, and Davis, perhaps because he had ultimately complied, was socially rehabilitated. He soon joined many of the men who had tried to kill him as an officer in the territorial militia, and was commissioned on October 22 as the captain of the "De Soto Minute Men."[100]

The deadly fracas at Fort Calhoun did not occur somewhere along the periphery of territorial political life. The affair implicated several prominent leaders in both the territorial militia and legislature. That those men resorted to extralegal violence both prior to and in response to the killing at Davis's cabin indicated clearly that there was little to no appetite among the members of that group to cede the power of the claim clubs to constitutional entities or to cease the extralegal adjudication of land claims. It was in this environment when, in late October, Ferguson called for a grand jury in the Henry case. Killing over claims was going to court. [101]

The jury was assembled from Omaha's own Douglas County. With the Omaha Claim Club consisting of "almost all of the male residents of the town in 1854 and 1855," the organization easily dominated the jury. Cam Reeves was one of the "good and lawful men" called to serve on that grand jury. Jesse Lowe, who was an early member of the Omaha Claim Club and who would later admit to serving as "captain of the club" for most of its existence, was appointed foreman of the jury.[102] The club's presence extended beyond the jury itself. Influential club leader and legislature member Andrew J. Poppleton, who had been present at the Fort Calhoun firefight, emerged as one of Henry's two lawyers. Henry's second lawyer, Oliver Perry Mason, would eventually come to bitterly oppose the claim clubs, but because he had known Henry personally prior to their coming to Nebraska, he sought to defend Henry on that account.[103]

George W. Hollister had been a Bellevue partisan who had helped organize the bitter political maneuvering against the Omaha faction during the capital controversy. George Hollister had partaken in the attempt to convince the president of the United States to replace the powerful club member Thomas Cuming, while his brother, Abner, had personally insulted the acting governor in Bellevue. The late Hollister was not mourned in Omaha. So, while Henry had plainly and in the clear sight of witnesses shot Hollister, the Omaha club men actively endeavored to make sure that he faced no legal repercussions for the killing. Just two days after Ferguson assembled the grand jury, Lowe reported to the court that the jury had failed to "agree or find a Bill" against Henry.[104]

Denying the motion of Henry's lawyer to dismiss the case, Ferguson responded by calling for a second grand jury to serve at a special term starting in late November. This second jury included prominent leaders within the Omaha Claim Club, including Alfred D. Goyer.[105] Again, the jury refused to find a bill of indictment against Henry. On December 1, 1855, Chief Justice Ferguson, unable to so much as bring the case to trial, released Henry and terminated the legal proceedings.[106]

That two subsequent grand juries stubbornly blocked Henry's case from so much as going to trial expanded a radical if informal new precedent in the territory. Cam Reeves at Jones's claim and James Mitchell's party at Fort Calhoun had established that the threat and use of force were acceptable means of adjudicating claim disputes so long as a powerful claim club backed the action. The acquittal of Henry widened this precedent by establishing that club-sponsored killing was itself not a crime to be prosecuted. Henry had plainly killed Hollister, and while he might have mounted a real defense on grounds of self-defense or accidental discharge, his case should have still gone to trial. In denying that trial, the Omaha Claim Club–dominated grand juries denied the formal legal system any regulatory control over club-related violence. There was no territorial institution in Nebraska that could challenge the operations of the Omaha Claim Club.

This precedent became even more dangerous in 1856. Rumors began to spread in the early months of the year that the federal government was finally preparing to open a land office in the territory. While such an office could furnish residents with deeds to the land they claimed, this rumor was not universally celebrated. Some residents feared that a land office would lead to even more claim jumping. They anticipated that an unprecedented wave of speculators would attempt to force their way onto land and quickly secure official title before the original squatters could respond.[107] Club leadership, which had thoroughly infiltrated territorial institutions and enjoyed extensive influence, undoubtedly recognized that the presence of a federal regulatory body would diminish their own power.

In response to these perceived threats, the Omaha Claim Club grew increasingly militant in its structure and rhetoric. At a February 5, 1856, meeting at the state house presided over by General Thayer, the club vowed to counter "new comers and land sharks" with a formal vigilante wing. The members resolved to "protect every lawful claimant in the peaceable possession of his claim, and that in a case of his claim being jumped we will when called upon by the 'Captain of the Regulators' turn out and proceed to the claim jumped."[108] Before disbanding, the assemblage unanimously elected Alfred D. Goyer to the captainship.

Cam Reeves, the first enforcer of claim law for what would become the Omaha Claim Club, might not have been present at the meeting. On the night of the assembly, an Irishman named Dennis Dee had "severely stabbed" Reeves in the arm.[109] Even if Reeves had attended the meeting, however, the leadership of Omaha's Douglas County would not have made him captain of the regulators. They had already selected him for a different, and no less important, role. Cam Reeves, of all people, had become the sheriff of Douglas County.

P. G. Peterson had been the county's first sheriff, appointed to the post by the then-acting governor Thomas Cuming. Peterson had still been the sheriff in late 1855, appearing on the court documents related to the Henry case. By early 1856, Reeves held the post. The newspaper account of the February 5 stabbing incident referred to him as "sheriff of this county."[110] Reeves's ironic rise to the station of leading county lawman coincided with mounting club anxieties regarding the opening of the land office. As sheriff, Reeves could continue to defend the perceived property rights of club members through formal mechanisms, while the regulators could protect club interests through more informal means. The installment of a pro-club man like Reeves to the office of sheriff, moreover, broadcast publicly to club targets that their legal avenues for recourse would be limited if not eliminated entirely.[111]

Cam Reeves had been immersed in criminality over the course of most of his life. His mother and father had partaken in the passing of counterfeit and the trafficking of stolen horses, while his youthful role models, like network member Robert Birch, roved across the region practicing a quasi-professional itinerant criminality. Cam had only been twenty years old when authorities arrested him for theft in Illinois and an armed mob subsequently expelled his family. And it had been his brazen violence in Iowa that served as the immediate trigger for not only an arrest but for yet another vigilante movement against his family. Indeed, Cam Reeves probably had more personal experience with law enforcement than any other potential candidate for the position.

Looking beyond the irony of the appointment, though, it becomes clear that Cam Reeves the lawman was only possible because of Cam Reeves the horse thief. Reeves's past experiences—both with extralegal violence and criminal action—had equipped him with the skills and knowledge necessary to succeed as a sheriff operating in an area dominated by extralegal interests. The flow of violence that had forced Reeves west had hardened him as a fighter, and it was this reputation of hard-fighting that caused his profile to be elevated among local elites concerned with—above all other material concerns—the preservation and advancement of their propertied interests.

Having been promoted to the position of sheriff, Reeves suddenly found himself required to respond to property rights violations beyond the jumping of land claims. The same patterns of criminality that had bedeviled settlers across the Middle West continued to do so in Nebraska, and Reeves was soon forced to confront the problem of horse theft in the area. Unlike most other sheriffs,

however, Cam Reeves knew from personal experience the cadence
of horse trafficking and possessed both the knowledge and skill to
ride down thieves. On August 27, Reeves arrested two young thieves
who had stolen horses a week prior. *The Nebraskian* attributed the
sheriff's success to his superior horsemanship.[112] On September 6,
the *Nebraska Advertiser* celebrated "the energy and perseverance of
our Sheriff" and recounted Reeves's successful pursuit and arrest
of another set of horse thieves. In this case, Reeves used his ability to credibly threaten violence to full effect. As the paper noted,
"Sheriff Reeves, who was already getting out of patience, and finding that words would not suffice, brought COLT to his assistance,
and that they gone fifty feet farther, all that would have been necessary for him to have returned, would have been their scalps, to
have shown his success in his energetic adventure."[113] On September 24, *The Nebraskian* reported that the "indefatigable sheriff" was
once again in pursuit of "speculators in horseflesh." Sure enough, he
arrested the two alleged thieves near Florence. "Sheriff Reeves has
justly obtained quite a notoriety for overtaking horse thieves," the
paper noted approvingly. "He has not failed in a single instance of
arresting any fugitive he has started in pursuit of."[114] It turned out it
took a horse thief to catch a horse thief.

Reeves was not the only one putting his past experience to use.
On July 14, 1856, James C. Mitchell attended an Omaha meeting of
claim club members as a representative of Florence. Leaders from
Bellevue and the Omaha Claim Club were present. While the territory's assorted clubs had traditionally attended to local matters and
even engaged in rivalries with one another, the perceived threat of
claim jumping, club leadership now believed, necessitated a unified
front. To sustain the "strong arms" of the farmers, as *The Nebraskian*
had explained back in February, an even greater capacity to organize
and enact extralegal violence was now deemed crucial.[115] Mitchell was familiar with organizing and engaging in vigilante violence from his earlier experiences in Bellevue, and quickly rose to
a position of prominence in these efforts. He was one of three men,
along with Charles Holloway and Andrew J. Poppleton, to serve on
a committee at the meeting that resolved to "protect and defend

each other in sustaining and upholding the respective regulations of such associations in case such aid should become necessary."[116] This new combined force could field up to three hundred armed men, equipped with US muskets from the arsenal and under the command of club leaders.[117]

As evidenced by such measures, the February claim club meeting that formally founded the Omaha Claim Club's vigilante wing had failed to calm rising anxieties about the coming of the land office. On May 18, 1856, a company of between seventy-five and one hundred regulators under Goyer's command had marched to the upper end of town and destroyed cabins belonging to George Smith, a man named Kline, and a few German migrants.[118] The victims, who had attempted to claim 160 acres of unimproved land as allowed under federal law, had initially refused to submit to the demands of Goyer's company.[119] Tempers flared, and the club men threatened to kill Smith. Goyer advised him to flee, which he promptly did. "Popular sovereignty is the law in this Territory," railed *The Nebraskian* in its reporting of the violence, "and popular sovereignty will see that every man has his rights, and all claims held by actual settlers and improvements in accordance with the requirements of the 'Claim Association' are just as secure if they had the fee simple from Uncle Sam."[120] The claim club had then met at the statehouse the very next day to further tighten its regulations. Later the next month, another meeting had warned against the plots of "divers evil-disposed persons" to secretly preempt club land. The meeting further empowered the regulators to "compel" club targets to deed contested land to club members.[121]

Outbursts of intermittent extralegal violence would continue through the final months of 1856. In November, club members threatened to seize one alleged jumper of Dutch extraction and "put him across the river" if he did not comply with their demands. "Thieves only submit," argued the *Nebraska Advertiser*, "when overtaken in their evil deeds, and are compelled to surrender."[122] As local rhetoric hardened and intensified, it was not only alleged claim jumpers who suffered. In November, a Pawnee party captured two alleged horse thieves and delivered them to Omaha. Although Cam

Reeves had been remarkably effective in hunting down such criminals, a local mob quickly formed and demanded the right to punish the prisoners themselves. William Lee, a Black resident and barbershop owner, shaved half of the alleged thieves' heads "in a highly artistic manner" before other members of the mob tied the two men to a liberty pole.[123] Chief Justice Ferguson attempted to stop the mob and dispatched US Marshall B. P. Rankin to secure the prisoners and halt the extralegal proceedings. The crowd paid no attention to Rankin, who for his part was wise enough not to push the matter.[124] Both Rankin and the mob knew that it was an informal legal system that possessed the real coercive power in the territory. The mob then administered forty-nine lashes to the alleged thieves, "well laid on," before banishing their victims east across the river.[125] In attempting to publicly justify the violent organizing of the claim clubs through arguments related to popular sovereignty and the efficacy of extralegal action, local leaders and their presses had primed the Nebraskan public to embrace such violence not merely as a matter of necessity but as an informal right.

On February 1, 1857, the land office finally opened in Omaha for squatters to file preemptions.[126] Hoping to intimidate "jumpers" out of filing, the claim clubs responded with a call to arms. On February 20, club leadership organized "the largest and most enthusiastic" assemblage of squatters in the territory to that date, with representatives from the Omaha, Florence, Elkhorn, Bellevue, and Papillion clubs in attendance. Mitchell, along with Thayer, Poppleton, and Cuming, made, according to *The Nebraskian*, "eloquent speeches." The paper failed to mention, though, that the men passed resolutions to hang any claim jumpers on the spot.[127] Mitchell in particular emerged as one of the fieriest speakers and advocates of vigilante action. Club member John Redick later contrasted Mitchell's rhetoric with the "reasonable, moderate" language of Andrew Hanscom, recalling that Mitchell "was very abusive of new people who were coming into the territory to break down local institutions."[128] Mitchell's combative and confrontational personality had helped to instigate the Bellevue War. Almost seventeen years later, his bluster began to again propel his faction toward open and violent confrontation.

John M. Newton, who was in attendance, wrote to John Kellogg that one hundred men were gathered into a regulator company on the spot and were armed with US muskets. The company immediately "went out to Catch the jumpers. When they found the cabin of any one on anothers land they burned it up and finding the jumper brought him before the committee and tried him and made him with draw his pre-emption file and promise never to jump any more." For five straight days, Newton noted, the vigilante company attacked alleged jumpers. Newton personally approved of the violence. "Great deal of whiskey has gone up," he wrote. "There has been no body killed as yet—only in talk. I think aside from jesting the proceeding has a very good effect on the stability of property here It renders them very secure."[129]

A campaign of violent terror had begun. The club attempted to infiltrate the new land office, as they had with most of the territory's own institutions. This task fell to William N. Byers, an ambitious young surveyor. Daniel Carr would later testify that "Byers was appointed to watch the filings at the land office, keep plats of the filings, and reporting the same to the club; and this duty he did."[130] Armed with this intelligence, the club lashed out at alleged jumpers, real or perceived. Shortly after the February 20 meetings, club vigilantes seized an Irish immigrant by the name of Michael Callahan who had filed on former governor Cuming's claim. The vigilantes dragged Callahan to the Missouri River and plunged him into the frozen waters. There they held him "until almost lifeless, when he consented to withdraw his filing."[131] Around the same time, club regulators also targeted Jacob Shull. They terrorized Shull with muskets tipped with bayonets, chasing him through the streets of Omaha and torching his residence.[132] In a separate episode of torture, regulators repeatedly hanged, cut down, and revived another Irish "jumper" before starving him into submission.[133] Most incidents of violence were undoubtedly never recorded as the club ruthlessly eliminated its targets. Olive Gass later documented the grim secrecy that dominated one affair that her parents had witnessed in Plattsmouth, Nebraska Territory. "Heavily armed" vigilantes arrested a family of alleged "claim-jumpers and horse thieves." The vigilantes banished most of the family east across the river, but four of the arrested men vanished. "No search was ever made for them," she wrote. "No Vigilante could be found who would tell what become of those four men."[134]

James Mitchell, who had helped set this campaign of extralegal violence and terror into motion, took an active role in organizing and leading Florence's own vigilantes. On May 29, 1857, a number of Florence residents met and organized the "Florence Committee of Vigilance." They immediately elected Mitchell as their captain. With his uncompromising personality, prominence in the claim clubs, and prior fighting experience from the Bellevue War, Mitchell must have seemed the natural pick for the role. Mitchell, the founder of Florence, attempted to strike a paternalistic tone in his captainship. On June 10, when vigilantes hauled an H. Leary before Mitchell for "outrage and trespass," Mitchell "gave him some most wholesome, and fatherly exhortation." Mitchell and the committee then turned their attention toward Florence's saloons, ordering them to "keep quiet and orderly houses." Eight days later, in response to a "riot" in the town, vigilantes arrested three men and brought them before the committee, where "they were thoroughly admonished by the Captain and dismissed." Two other men accused of carrying slingshots received a similar treatment, and the committee ordered all local saloons to close on the Sabbath and "neither sell or give away any liquor at any time to anyone who is drunk or a habitual drunkard." While the vigilantes' responses to these issues indicated a measure of restraint, the vigilance committee was not above the use of violence. On June 18, the committee heard the case of D. Downs. The man had struck a dog belonging to V. M. Seaton, who, incensed at the blow to his animal, bashed Downs in the head with a spade. The vigilance committee, on the motion of vigilante Robert Williamson Steele, sentenced Seaton to a $50 fine and "ten lashes upon his bare back."[135]

Mitchell also participated in at least one violent attempt to use extralegal force to evict an entire community of alleged "jumpers." Irish migrants under the leadership of Dennis Dee—the same Dennis Dee who had stabbed Cam Reeves that February—had established in northern Omaha a community known as "Gophertown." The community was so called because the impoverished inhabitants lived in dugout shanties.[136] A resident of Florence, however, claimed the land into which Gopherton was carved. The claim clubs often targeted immigrants, perhaps perceiving that such targets would be more isolated and easier to coerce. In July, James Mitchell organized a party to march into Gophertown and seize Dee, whom they planned "to take and punish . . . for buying land without their consent." Mitchell's party stormed Dee's dwelling, where they found only frightened women and children. The community's male residents, mostly laborers, were absent at the time of the attempted raid. Word reached them quickly, though, and the Irish laborers "armed themselves with guns and pistols" and cudgels and rushed back toward their homes. Mitchell's party, surprised by the fury of the response, fled into Omaha. The Florence band tried to attack Gophertown a second time around noon but were again forced to make a chaotic retreat after the inhabitants counterattacked. In a mocking reference to would-be club victim Dennis Dee, *The Nebraskian* quipped that "all that is necessary to rouse the anger of a man of Florence is to mention the fourth letter of the alphabet."[137]

While the residents of Gophertown had been able to successfully counter club violence through force, most Nebraskan squatters outside of club circles, even if they feared or disdained the clubs, lacked the networks or notions of community necessary to rally any sort of coherent mutual defense. Instead, the visible campaign of club-sponsored terror had an enormous effect on most of the territory's residents and cowed them into passivity. Erastus F. Beadle, on April 18, 1857, watched Omaha's own mayor Jesse Lowe lead a group of armed regulators and a victim to the Missouri River. "There is no law here," he wrote in his diary, "except club laws and vigilance committee to enforce them." Beadle's account reveals the extent to which the grisly practice had become part of the cadence of daily life. Lowe, an elected official, had led in broad daylight through the city's streets a victim that he undoubtedly intended to torture. It was a public demonstration of pure terror and power. Sheriff Reeves, himself a member of the Omaha Claim Club, would do nothing to stop it. No elected official would or could. "The party returned without the prisoner," Beadle continued, "and no questions asked." If Lowe's procession of his captive was meant to serve as an instructive demonstration, it worked. Beadle concluded, "I think I will be quiet and peacible."[138] Other residents would similarly later recount the fear that the club successfully managed to instill. "It was not considered safe," John N. Smith would later testify, "to incur the displeasure, in any way, of the said Omaha Claim Club."[139]

Even club members were not completely safe from the organization's wrath. In early 1857, club members accused John Redick—himself a member of the Omaha Claim Club—of engaging in the use of "treasonable language against the Claim Club" after Redick publicly noted the disparities between the federal and club laws regarding claim size. Redick felt the need to carry a revolver in his coat pocket until he later had a chance to address the club and deny what he claimed to have been a misrepresentation of his words.[140] Later that year, in July, another Omaha Claim Club member, Augustus Macon, attempted to rescue some alleged jumpers from the club and transport them to Illinois, away from the club's reach. Club member John A. Creighton and a few of his kin, all armed with revolvers, had one of those men in their charge. When Macon attempted to free the man, he recalled, "they said that if I interfered they would shoot me." While Macon eventually succeeded in rescuing the men and transporting them, club members issued threats of retaliation and he found himself forced to temporarily flee to Iowa.[141]

Corruption accompanied this terror. Some of the more unscrupulous leaders within the claim clubs understood the campaign of violence to be a cover by which to advance their own speculatory interests. A. Deyo, a resident of Cass County, complained in March 1857 that Thomas Patterson, a government surveyor, "had taken advantage of his position, as surveyor, to select many fine tracts of land, and availing himself of the influence he held over a certain class of community, and also trusting to the aid of the claim club association, he was holding . . . much more land than would have been sanctioned, even by the territorial law." The local claim club found Deyo and four others in violation of Patterson's claims. The club's vigilantes targeted them, and they were forced to flee into Iowa. Patterson, Deyo bitterly complained, "who had been dealing out United States muskets and whiskey to the ignorant and lawless, would have them in the spirit, and armed to perpetrate any deeds of villainy that he might dictate."[142] Others used their club affiliations to engage in brazen criminality. John McConihe wrote to his friend John Kellogg in August 1857 that he and his associates had stolen weapons meant for anti-slavery partisans embroiled in Bleeding Kansas. "We have 30 men on the ground and have formed a claim club," he reported, "having stolen 10 muskets at Nebraska City that belonged to Jim Lane who had stored them there. We went back to steal more but were stopped."[143]

The Omaha Claim Club employed extralegal violence to advance the financial interests of not only the organization's leading members but of wealthy speculators who lived outside the territory. While language about protecting "actual" settlers from the predations of outside speculators featured prominently in club rhetoric, leaders were more than happy to ignore the club's own established regulations if the situation proved financially advantageous. In early 1857, New York City real estate broker Roswell G. Pierce managed to obtain the protection of the Omaha Claim Club—in clear violation of the club's own laws—after purchasing 1,100 acres of land near the settlement.[144] When Alexander H. Baker and John W. Brown attempted to settle on and preempt the empty land, club members threatened the men's lives and ordered them to deed their claims to Pierce. Baker later testified that Heman Glass, a club member, told him that "uncle Roswell" had "got the money & the friends to bulge it through, and if I did not withdraw my fileing, or pre-empt the land and deed it to Mr. Pierce, that they would serve me as they had served lots of others; that is, throw me in the Missouri River." Baker knew he would have no recourse should the club take action against him, noting that he knew that "the secretary of the Territory, the sheriff of Douglas County, the mayor of the city of Omaha, and the register & receiver of the land office" [145] were all members of the organization. Baker's friends convinced him to save his own life and surrender the land. Ultimately, he did.[146] "I conveyed from fear of personal violence," he admitted. "I never received any consideration whatsoever."[147]

The power of the claim clubs, confederated through the efforts of Mitchell and others, resembled an informal leviathan. The opening of the land office had only seemed to embolden the clubs, who effectively governed the sale and purchase of land in the territory through increasingly brazen violence and intimidation. Then, just as their power seemed to reach a new zenith, the claim clubs imploded. The organizations that had infiltrated territorial institutions bent the proceedings of the formal legal system to their will and ruled with a strong arm over the inhabitants of the territory who suddenly buckled and collapsed with shocking speed. There had been but one force powerful enough to land such a mortal blow to the clubs: the loss of profitability. August marked the beginning of the Panic of 1857, a financial crisis that saw the value of western lands plummet.[148] The wild speculation that had fueled the rise of the Omaha Claim Club and similar organizations ceased, as members found their investments degraded in value. Most of Nebraska's banks failed by the end of the year, further battering the territory's economic health and driving land prices down even lower.[149] Stripped by the crisis of their core purpose, the claim clubs quickly withered and vanished as former members quietly obtained the deeds to their claims and saw little reason to continue banding together for "mutual defense."

Even as the claim clubs vanished from Nebraska, the legacy of their violence did not. Extralegal organizations like the Omaha Claim Club had inducted hundreds of new initiates into the practice of organizing and engaging in vigilante-style violence. As individuals witnessed, participated in, and suffered from that violence, they internalized lessons from men like Reeves and Mitchell, who had been able to rise to prominence on account of their own prior experience with violent action. Those lessons persisted long after the decline of the clubs. Local Nebraskan elites and pressmen, moreover, had advanced public justifications structured around the issue of property rights for both their violent actions and their brazen defiance of existing law. Fueling this justification was an extreme vision of popular constitutionalism that increasingly shed conventions of restraint and deference to republican institutions. Although no longer organized and executed at the scale of the claim clubs' 1857 campaign of violence, extralegal violence in Nebraska would not cease in the years that followed.

At around eight o'clock on the evening of January 8, 1859, Thomas Allen and a mob of vigilantes stormed Cam Reeves's home. It was not the first or even second time in Reeves's life that vigilantes had assailed his residence. For once, however, he was not the target. He was not even home. The mob of men, taking advantage of his absence, quickly snatched the cell keys from a nail protruding from an interior wall. Three women were present in the dwelling when the mob burst in, and the vigilantes "advised the ladies to be quiet and they should not be hurt." The intruders then descended into the basement, which served as Omaha's jail. Two men were being held there at the time: a pair of alleged horse thieves by the names of John Daly and Harvey Braden. Forcing the two prisoners from their cell, the vigilantes chucked the stolen keys back into the room from which they had been taken and disappeared into the dark. The women sounded an alarm and sent a messenger to find Cam Reeves, but it was too late.

Nothing more was heard until the next day. Then, two miles north of Florence, two corpses were discovered. Still wearing their shackles, Daly and Braden hung suspended from a tree. In a final act of cruelty, the vigilantes had not even granted Braden a clean death. They had, by accident or design, fastened the noose "in his mouth instead of under his chin." It made for a grisly sight. "The corps of Braden," reported one paper, "presented the most frightful spectacle of which it is possible to conceive." [150] As Braden's teeth clenched the cord, the noose drew his silenced mouth toward the winter sky.

It was a common history that had brought the principal actors in this macabre drama—lawman, vigilante, and victim—to this moment of final collision. All three men had once been residents of Illinois. Interconnected flows of extralegal violence had driven those men, along with thousands of others, west into Iowa and Nebraska. Harvey Whitlock Braden, who died with a noose between his teeth, had lived a short and turbulent life. As a child he had been a part of the Mormon party that was expelled following the siege of Far West, Missouri, in 1838, and had lived through the mob turbulence and killing of Joseph Smith as a later resident of Nauvoo. Braden's father had been among the members of the Mormon flight who settled in Iowa, but Harvey himself had moved on to Utah.[151] There, he had enlisted as a cavalryman in the Nauvoo Legion during the 1853 Walkara War. Braden served in the same regiment as the notorious "destroying angel" and horse thief William "Wild Bill" Hickman, who had been linked to the Mormon criminal networks that had been active in Illinois and Iowa.[152] Braden eventually left Utah and returned to Iowa. When he died, his pregnant wife, Hannah Nixon Braden, was just across the river. The widow would give birth just under three months later to a son, whom she named William Harvey.[153]

Sheriff Cam Reeves had himself belonged to a familial criminal network and had faced vigilante mobs in both Iowa and Illinois. Unlike Braden, Reeves survived those encounters and used the violent circumstances in Nebraska to refashion himself as a respectable community member and enforcer of both informal and formal systems of justice. Thomas Allen, who partook in the 1859 lynching, had himself been part of the same larger Mormon exodus from Illinois as Braden. He had helped establish the Mormon Summer Quarters and was later part of the three-man surveying party that saw Reeves's brother-in-law, Alfred D. Jones, stake his claim on the western bank of the Missouri River. By 1854, Allen had become a lawman, having been appointed by Governor Cuming as the sheriff for Washington County, Nebraska.[154]

To examine the human dimensions of extralegal violence in the Nebraska Territory is to make visible these unexpected connections and transformations. To view the violence through the prism of these individual experiences is to recognize that the killing on that January night was not some isolated affair but a node located within a cascading sequence of violent connection and collision. Without splaying out the tangled and twisting histories of the principal actors, the lynching is reduced to a trope—a clear and easily digestible story of thieves, lawmen, and vigilantes, each playing their expected role. It is only through a careful analysis of the lives, networks, and experiences of those implicated in the incident that the much more complicated realities are revealed. Horse thieves became sheriffs, sheriffs became lynchers, and a young boy who escaped from the clutches of one mob would die at the hands of another over two decades later and 146 miles away.

The lynching of Braden and Daly reflected a broader reality. Prior episodes of violent, criminal, and extralegal action indelibly marked the form and direction of such violence in early territorial Nebraska. Cam Reeves's work as an enforcer for what would become the Omaha Claim Club and later as a sheriff only takes on its full meaning when located alongside his violent criminal history. James Mitchell's bellicose leadership in the confederation of the claim clubs and their subsequent campaign of violence is best understood as an outgrowth of his earlier actions during the Bellevue War. The tragedy of Allen's lynching of Braden only emerges in full when the pair's shared past is recognized.

Individuals like Reeves and Mitchell carried experiences with violent action with them into Nebraska and used those experiences to navigate the realities and conditions of the time and place. Rather than following a straight westward march of order, this movement resulted in a fluid environment that mixed the influences of both organized criminality and vigilantism. Nebraska's claim clubs, and the hulking Omaha Claim Club in particular, used violence and subversion to advance the financial and political interests of their constituencies. In doing so, they championed an even more extreme vision of popular constitutionalism that built upon and then went beyond the Jacksonian rhetoric that had stirred earlier extralegal action. Popular will was not merely the source of law. It was, to borrow again from Omaha Claim Club member James Woolworth, "more than law." Such a vision not only justified the temporary use of force outside the bounds established by law, but the wholesale infiltration and subversion of territorial and legal institutions. While extralegal groups had worked through and with formal governmental structures and officials in the past—Thomas Ford being a notable example—the near-complete control that the claim clubs exercised over the early territorial government in Nebraska, and the subsequent brazenness and duration of their extralegal violence, was without precedent.

American attitudes toward law, justice, and violence were continuing to change. Allen and his companions did not punish Braden and Daly out of some grim frontier necessity. The two alleged thieves were already imprisoned. The vigilantes certainly did not need to kill them. But they did, and by early March, their fellow citizens acquitted them for that killing.[155] Allen, his fellow vigilantes, and the men who acquitted them insisted through these actions that formal institutions and systems not only lacked a monopoly on the ability to enforce "justice," but that extralegal killing was itself no longer merely an action of desperate resort. It was an increasingly common and widely accepted "right."

Americans, however, paid little attention to these developments in Nebraska Territory. All eyes were on the violence of Bleeding Kansas. Claim club leadership embraced this distraction. It allowed the club to operate with less scrutiny. Nebraska, wrote Omaha Claim Club member James Woolworth, "has enjoyed now nearly three years of successful, safe government. None of the turbulence of the frontier, none of the outrages of heated strife, have disgraced her; no anarchy, no public demoralization has afflicted her; and to-day she offers to the emigrant a home guarded by law, and the promise of large rewards to his honest labor."[156] Woolworth wrote those lines in 1857, at the height of the violent campaign against "claim jumpers." His words, intended to draw more settlers to the territory and drive land prices even higher, were a distortion, another lie in the service of club interests. That lie stuck, and the violence of early territorial Nebraska remained largely ignored.

If the legacy of Nebraska's extralegal violence was not noticed, it would be felt. The raw and far-reaching power of the claim clubs during their reign of dominance introduced thousands of settlers to the cadence and practice of extralegal organization and violence. With the Panic of 1857 and the subsequent discovery of gold in the Rocky Mountains in 1858, a stampede of Nebraskan settlers and former claim club members would drive farther west in search of fortune. They would carry the lessons learned from their violent experiences in Nebraska with them into the new settlements and mining camps. There, they emerged as leaders within increasingly brutal vigilante combinations. The campaigns of vigilante killing that they would help orchestrate would be among the bloodiest in American history.

CHAPTER 6

THE ROCKY MOUNTAINS, KANSAS AND IDAHO TERRITORIES

"A New Order of Things"

On September 4, 1860, Alvarado C. Ford boarded the Express coach out of Denver. Death had been weighing on his mind. On August 22, he had purportedly penned his last will and testament, which, according to local newspaper *The Western Mountaineer*, "was evidently written in great haste." In it he had deeded, in the event of his demise, a substantial amount of his property to Sarah Jane Vailes. She and Ford had "since the first day of January, 1860, lived together as husband and wife."[1] Ford had ample reason to fear for his life. A secretive vigilance committee had organized within the settlement. On September 2, committee members had lynched an alleged horse thief. The next night—the night before Ford's departure—the vigilantes targeted attorney, city council member, and hotelkeeper John Shear. Locals found his corpse dangling six feet in the air, suspended from a poplar tree. A note at the scene, left by the killers, read, "This man was hung. It was proven he is a horse thief." Evidence did not suggest a sloppy or rushed killing. "The work," noted *The Western Mountaineer*, "seemed to have been performed by experienced hands."[2]

A year or so prior, Ford had left his legal wife, Martha A. Ford, and his children in Council Bluffs, Iowa, to follow the mass 1859 westward migration sparked by the Pike's Peak Gold Rush. James C. Mitchell's former business partner had for years chased and attempted to profit off such human movements. His ambition had seen him caught up in counterfeiting in California, and later in both land speculation and political controversy in Iowa and Nebraska. Now, in the region known today as Colorado, he marketed his services as an attorney.

Ford quickly found himself caught up in more than pedestrian property disputes, however. With no formal legal system present in the region, informal and extrajudicial "People's Courts" or "Miners' Courts" adjudicated law in settlements like Denver. All punishment was extralegal. Ford, who from his time in Council Bluffs had experience in defending lynching targets, emerged as a capable defense attorney. Earlier that August, he had participated in a particularly notable and heated affair. His "ingenious and forcible" defense had played a critical role in securing the release of Carroll Wood after Wood had on July 31 kidnapped and threatened to kill former Nebraska claim club member William N. Byers.[3]

Ford, undoubtedly on account of his own experiences in California, Iowa, and Nebraska, thoroughly opposed the extralegal dispensation of justice. In addition to his work as a defense attorney, he had been among the Denver lawyers to threaten to cease the practice of law after August 31, "until such a time as regular and constitutional tribunals of Justice are established in our midst."[4] At the time of his departure, Ford was reportedly en route to Leavenworth, Kansas Territory, to mount a legal defense for Denver resident James Gordon. The twenty-three-year-old Gordon had killed another young man, John Gantz, in an unprovoked drunken rage.[5] The killing sparked public fury. Hard feelings among some of Denver's residents had grown even more hostile when Kansas authorities—who held flimsy jurisdiction over the mountain region—demanded Gordon be tried in Leavenworth rather than by Denver's informal courts. Disturbingly, the most recent set of vigilante killings had abandoned even the informal oversight and procedure of the People's Courts. Vigilantes now decided who in Denver deserved to die.

The Express coach made it no farther than seven miles outside of Denver. A mounted band of armed, disguised men intercepted the coach and demanded that Ford be given to them. Having secured their prisoner, the mounted party vanished. Nothing more, for the moment, was heard. The next day, Byers's *The Rocky Mountain News* implied that Ford had been "president of the horse thief gang" and noted, "Rumors are current on the street that he was summarily disposed of."[6] The mysterious disappearance, combined with the spate of recent lynchings, resulted in a pronounced sense of unease throughout the settlement. "All kinds of rumors of hangings, shootings, and lynchings are rife on the streets," reported *The Rocky Mountain News* dismissively on the day following Ford's disappearance. "At one time yesterday evening it was reported that seven men had been found hanging dead near the city. It is needless to say they were false."[7]

Several days later, reports claimed that human remains were found about a mile from where the armed men had seized Ford. Buckshot perforated the corpse. The killers had made no attempt to bury the body. It had remained exposed to the elements for several days. A golden watch and chain, identified as belonging to Ford, were found on the deceased victim. These quickly disappeared. Pinned to the decomposing body was a simple notice: "Executed by the Vigilance Committee."[8]

Vigilantes, as Alvarado C. Ford had been unfortunate enough to discover, increasingly employed extreme and oftentimes lethal methods to both defend perceived property rights and advance financial interests. The rate at which Americans resorted to lethal force in incidents of extralegal violence exploded in the years following 1848. In the entire sixty-five-year span between 1783 and 1848, recorded acts of extralegal violence had claimed the lives of at least 239 persons. In the decade following 1848 alone, well over twice that number would die because of such action.[9] In the West, this surge is most famously associated with Californian vigilantism and with the brutality of Bleeding Kansas. But from beyond the Great Plains, another sequence of deadly violence also pushed westward during this period. That strain, directed by propertied and speculative interests, emerged directly from the sequence of extralegal action that cascaded across the Middle West through the 1840s and '50s. Settlers who had experienced extralegal action had carried that tradition with them as they moved between Iowa and Illinois, and then into what would become the Nebraska Territory, in search of wealth through land speculation and development. Those individuals had helped orchestrate the rise of violent extralegal organizations like the Omaha Claim Club, whose reach and power inducted hundreds more into the practice of such violence. The allure of gold and collapse in land prices would by 1859 drive some of those settlers farther west and into the Rocky Mountain region. There, in what would later be known as Colorado and Montana, those settlers would employ the violence they had learned in the Middle West and on the plains in the organization of some of the deadliest instances of extralegal violent action in American history.

What follows is an analysis of the movement of people already experienced in extralegal violent action from Nebraska into Denver, and subsequently into the mining settlements of Bannack and Virginia City in what is now Montana. That movement made possible two notable campaigns of orchestrated, large-scale extralegal killing. One occurred in September 1860, and the other transpired in the winter of 1863–64. By focusing on the direct linkages that bound these clusters of violence together, this narrative reveals that the vigilante violence in the Mountain West was not simply the product of the supposedly exceptional or peculiar conditions of the region and place, as it has been traditionally portrayed.[10] The violence was also not structured primarily around combatting "lawlessness" or "civilizing" the West.[11] Rather, merchants who ascended to positions of leadership in both campaigns circumvented existing, if informal, legal systems and turned instead to prior experiences with extralegal collective violence to organize campaigns of lynching structured around the protection and advancement of their own financial interests.

Far from being exceptional or isolated killing affairs, the lynching campaigns in what is now Colorado and Montana were embedded within an interconnected web of extralegal action. Former Nebraskan claim club men were among the most prominent leaders of the vigilance committee in Denver. Veterans of that vigilance committee would then travel to mining settlements like Bannack and

Virginia City in what is now Montana, where they encountered and eventually operated with other former claim club members from Nebraska, vigilantes from California, and partisans from Bleeding Kansas, amalgamating in their combined actions the violent traditions from which they had emerged. This commingling would prove volatile and deadly. The mode of lethal violence, so hesitantly practiced in Bellevue just two short decades prior, now stretched into maturity.

The city of Denver was born from a threat. In November 1858, William Larimer and a party of companions jumped the claim established by the St. Charles Town Company on the northwest bank of Cherry Creek. Most of the St. Charles group had departed from the area after staking the claim to pursue a charter from the territorial Kansas government, which nominally held jurisdiction over the area.[12] Before the members of the group left, they had erected a small cabin and left a representative by the name of Charles Nichols to hold the claim in accordance with squatter law. Larimer, however, had formerly been a resident of Nebraska and a claim club man.[13] Larimer and his party confronted Nichols and, according to fellow former Nebraskan E. P. Stout—the first president of the Denver City Town Company—informed him "that at his next attempt to make trouble a rope and noose would be used on him"[14] Nichols, sufficiently intimidated, quickly transferred the land to the Denver City Town Company. And so it was that William Larimer founded the settlement of Denver.[15]

The Denver City Town Company, like the Auraria Company on the other side of the creek and the now-ousted St. Charles Company, was a venture in speculation. In the summer of 1858, prospectors had found gold in the area. By early 1859, the Pike's Peak Gold Rush had begun in earnest. An influx of miners and fortune seekers rushed into the region, eager to discover imagined deposits of untold wealth. Denver quickly swelled as thousands of mostly male "Fifty-Niners" poured into the region.[16] Merchants and speculators quickly established the mercantile infrastructure in order to service and profit from the settlement's booming migrant population.

Hotels, coach lines, banks, and other service and manufacturing enterprises quickly appeared. Saloons and gambling halls proved to be particularly popular establishments.[17] In April 1859, another Nebraskan and former claim club member, Willian N. Byers, established a newspaper, *The Rocky Mountain News*, in the settlement.[18] Back in Nebraska, Byers had been the man tasked with monitoring the government land office for filings and reporting them to the claim club. [19] Like Larimer, he arrived in the mountain region no stranger to extralegal action.

Arapahoe County, where Denver was located, was in 1859 ostensibly part of Kansas Territory. It was after Kansas Territory governor James William Denver that Larimer had named his settlement, unaware that Governor Denver resigned from that office in November 1858. Before he resigned, Governor Denver had appointed a handful of men to serve as officials in Arapahoe County. H. P. A. Smith was to serve as probate judge, Hickory Rogers as county supervisor, and E. W. Wynkoop as sheriff.[20] Residents of Arapahoe County, discontent with the distant authority of territorial Kansas, elected their own county officials in March 1859. By early April, some began to agitate for the establishment of their own state or territory that could be independent from Kansas.[21] While federal and territorial authorities largely ignored these early efforts, the undeterred residents of Arapahoe County went about establishing their own informal legal and regulatory structures. In the mold of earlier settlers in Nebraska, Iowa, and elsewhere, residents soon founded a claim club to regulate land claims and deter jumpers.[22] It mattered little that Denver had itself been founded on a jumped claim.

The preservation of public order was quickly tested. In early April, John Stuffle robbed and murdered his brother-in-law, Arthur Binegraff, while prospecting. Arapahoe County residents organized a "People's Court" to try Stuffle. While the court was informal, residents ensured that the accused received trial by jury and a defense attorney. Stuffle selected Larimer to defend him but soon confessed to the killing.[23] After the People's Court found Stuffle guilty, residents hanged him from a cottonwood tree on Cherry Creek. Although Larimer's son and fellow Denver settler, William H. H.

Larimer, later insisted that the killing "could not be considered as lynching," the reality was that the court that sentenced and executed Stuffle was informal and unsanctioned by any authority other than popular will. Stuffle's death marked Denver's first extralegal killing.[24]

The hanging had an immediate effect in Arapahoe County. When, on April 16, John Scudder shot and killed Peleg T. Bassett, both he and his alleged accomplice Carroll Wood fled the area to avoid meeting a similar fate to Stuffle.[25] Still, while local residents had through the People's Court responded decisively to Binegraff's murder, they proved less eager to wield extralegal force in response to alleged property rights violations.[26] The stealing of livestock in particular remained a persistent problem. The Rocky Mountain News reported on May 14, 1859, that no fewer than sixteen horses and mules had been stolen in the previous three days alone. In his paper, Byers raged that the perpetrators, when caught, would "be called to dance upon nothing," which was a euphemistic reference to lynching. "Our people have borne it until forbearance ceases to be a virtue," he wrote, "and desperate measures will be adopted."[27]

In late May, a People's Court tried James Hanna for horse stealing. The jury, for want of evidence, ordered Hanna released. This was insufficient for some residents, who, according to The Rocky Mountain News, "were satisfied he had other stolen property in his possession, and they threatened to hang him." Hanna allegedly confessed and offered to lead the vigilantes to his associates. When this "proved a fruitless search," the enraged vigilantes briefly hanged Hanna but relented and cut him down before he died. They then flogged him with fifty lashes and banished him from the region. Byers, no stranger to such violence, endorsed the vigilantism in his paper. "We hope this will be a warning to all who may feel disposed to take horses without leave," he wrote, "for depend upon it, the next one caught will not be dealt with so leniently."[28]

With their open proceedings, attorneys, and jury trials, the People's Courts represented a genuine expression of republican—if extrajudicial and informal—popular will.[29] Byers and the vigilantes who seized and whipped Hanna, however, belonged to a subset of the county's population that believed the courts provided insufficient protection of property rights. The People's Court was indeed, according to scholar Richard Hogan, "inclined toward acquittal when the evidence was not overwhelming."[30] On the Monday after the vigilantes flogged Hanna, a judge dismissed for want of evidence horse-stealing charges against two residents, Nathan Stuart and Asa Smith.[31]

Disputes over law and justice did not abate as 1859 wore on. Byers, in the May 28 issue of his paper, warned that counterfeit was in circulation. To this warning he added a threat. "We would advise the gentleman who is trying to pass them here to desist if he wishes himself well," Byers wrote, "as he is known and his movements are being watched."[32] On June 18, Byers again threatened vigilantism after two residents allegedly provided whiskey to Native Americans. "There is a Vigilance Committee, of long standing," he wrote, "in existence here, which is pledged to lynch any man found engaged in giving or selling intoxicating liquor to the Indians. . . . Once more, gents, and you will see the operation of the *people's* prohibitory law."[33] Denver resident Thomas Wildman similarly remarked in a June 20 letter to his brother that "some men will get hung up if they do not stop selling them liquor, as there is a secret Vigilance Committee in the city and the penalty is death."[34] In August, a bandit attempted to ambush and rob W. M. McRaw as he tried to travel from the Jackson diggings to Denver.[35] McRaw, though, managed to grab hold of his assailant's cudgel and beat him down with it.

Disturbed local elites continued to discuss the creation of a more formalized vigilante organization. Despite Byers's threats, Denver vigilantism appeared to have been mostly ad hoc action up to that point. The September 5 lynching of Edgar Vanover in nearby Golden City further animated the discussion surrounding the creation of a standing vigilance committee. Vanover—who had seen action in Nicaragua as one of William Walker's filibusters—had not actually killed anyone but had threatened to do so multiple times while committing a string of property rights violations. It was a preemptive lynching that immediately generated intense controversy. Dueling reports portrayed Vanover's lynching as a unanimous, democratic decision "necessary for the safety of the inhabitants," and alternatively as an "act of the mob" repudiated by "nine-tenths" of the locals.[36] Thomas Wildman referenced the lynching in a September 8 letter to his sister, noting that "the people" hung Vanover. Wildman apparently approved of such rough methods and continued that "there is to be a Vigilance Committee organized in this town this evening. All the leading men of town have signed the Constitution, and its object is a good one."[37]

Still, seemingly nothing of substance was organized. On September 17, Wildman complained in a letter to his sister and mother that a thief had stolen his blankets. Although he "applied to the Vigilance Committee for a search warrant," he was unable to locate his stolen property.[38] The same day, *The Rocky Mountain News* reported a further spate of property rights violations. On the previous Monday, a man had allegedly stolen and butchered another man's cattle. The next day, someone stole between $40 to $50 from a Denver resident. In a separate incident that same day, another person stole over $600 in gold and silver from a local saloon. A few days later, a man gambled away two pairs of cattle and a wagon that he had borrowed or rented and did not rightly own. In the first two incidents, the alleged criminals were arrested and forced to pay at least partial restitution. In the latter two, the injured parties were not so lucky. Byers again turned to printed bluster, warning the "light fingered gentry" that they "had better look out, or some of them will be suddenly called upon to perform on a tight rope."[39]

Violent crimes also continued to occur. On October 4, a man named Hall quarreled with his business partner, a man named Thompson. Hall drew a pistol and attempted to shoot Thomson, who managed to knock away the barrel of the weapon before Hall squeezed the trigger. The bullet embedded harmlessly into a wall, but the would-be killer proceeded to flee the scene and run through the streets "without hat or coat, and calling for the vigilance committee." Hall exclaimed to confused bystanders that "he had killed a man and wanted to be hung."[40] The odd incident ended without further violence. A more serious confrontation occurred on October 20, between Oliver Davis, a baker, and William J. Paine, a blacksmith and landowner. Both were Black men. After some trouble over the lease of Davis's bakery, Davis had attempted to assault Paine but lost the fight. Davis later armed himself with a double-barreled shotgun and announced that he was going to "kill Bill before the sun sets!" He had his chance when Paine later rode past the bakery. After demanding that Paine dismount his horse, Davis attempted to fire his shotgun, but the barrel failed to discharge. Paine drew his own revolver and advanced on his assailant. Davis attempted to fire again. The second barrel similarly failed. Paine, who had continued to advance, then fired his pistol and killed the baker. The next day, the People's Court "honorably acquitted" Paine for having acted in self-defense.[41]

Merchants, speculators, and town boosters, unsatisfied with the capacity of the People's Court to protect their interests, began to attempt to organize a government. [42] In November 1859, a coalition of speculators, merchants, and other local elites organized the unrecognized "Provisional Government of Jefferson Territory." Miners outside of Denver and Auraria, unwilling to recognize the authority of the Jefferson government, maintained their Miners' Courts.[43] Local popular support in Denver was lacking. The backers of the new government, recognizing the extralegal nature of their efforts, understood and portrayed their creation as a successor to earlier, ad hoc vigilance committees. The first "governor" of Jefferson was Robert Williamson Steele, another former Nebraskan who was no stranger to engaging in vigilante violence. Steele had belonged to James C. Mitchell's Florence vigilance committee. It had been on his motion that one unfortunate resident of Florence received ten lashes in 1857, although Steele had balked at performing the flogging himself after his fellow vigilantes voted to give him the honor.[44] Two years later, in a "gubernatorial" address published in *The Rocky Mountain News*, Steele lionized vigilance committees as "the first resource of an isolated and exposed community." While he admitted that "a more perfect form of government than was afforded by a vigilance committee was needed," Steele's language revealed the extent to which a belief in the legitimacy of vigilante violence was entrenched within elements of Denver's governing elite.[45] The fact that highly visible elites like Steele, Byers, and Larimer already possessed personal experience in extralegal action from their tenures in Nebraska Territory contributed to and amplified this position.

While a lack of popular support limited the power and influence of Jefferson, the "territory" quickly approved the establishment of municipal and county governments. As Hogan notes, local merchants, speculators, and boosters dominated Denver's own municipal government, which was established in December. "Twelve of the 13 elected officials were identified in local business directories," he notes. "Of these 12, 2 were lawyers, 2 were merchants, 4 were realtors or bankers, and 4 were shopkeepers or clerks."[46] Paramilitary outfits like the "Rocky Mountain Rangers" and "Jefferson Rangers" were also organized in the region.[47] The Rocky Mountain Rangers, formed in Mountain City, swore to "protect each other in their rights of property in this coming spring; and to resist any attempt at unlawful or unjust taxation," a declaration that reflected a broader distrust in the provisional Jefferson government.[48]

A more serious challenge to Arapahoe County's interlacing systems of informal law and governance arrived in early 1860. On January 30, a group of men jumped part of the Denver town claim and started erecting buildings. When eighty members of the claim club moved to evict the men from the location, the jumpers produced rifles and leveled them against the advancing club men. Mayor John C. Moore called for a parlay with the jumpers. He soon returned and reported that the jumpers had forty loaded weapons with them and had resolved to "fight to the death." The claim club, unwilling to storm the armed position, retreated.

The next day, as rumors spread that the jumpers were "fortifying their position," news arrived that a party had stolen several turkeys. Suspicion eventually fell on a group of five men known as the "Bummers," which consisted of Thomas Clemo, William "Chuck-a-luck" Todd, William Harvey, William McCarty, and William "Buckskin Bill" Karl. The Bummers and their friends, defiant in the face of the charges, carried arms and paraded through town. McCarty and Harvey allegedly fired shots at W. H. Middaugh, who was a witness in the affair, but missed. The Jefferson Rangers rushed to the scene and established a patrol, but were less effective than Auraria resident Thomas Pollock, who split open McCarty's head with the butt of his rifle and later intimidated Harvey into flight. Taking advantage of the chaos, a party of the claim club men demolished the jumper-erected buildings in Denver.[49]

The turbulence roiled on the next day, as jumpers threatened to kill the secretary of the Denver Town Company for his alleged role in destroying their construction. Meanwhile, a public meeting gave McCarty, Todd, Harvey, and Karl five hours to leave the area "under the penalty of hanging, if found here at the expiration of that time, or ever afterward." Armed but bloodless confrontations between the claim club and the jumpers continued. With rumors spreading about the jumpers' plans to burn Denver, armed patrols again took to the streets. The next day, the club and jumper parties finally reached a settlement where the jumpers agreed to vacate the land in return for reimbursement for their property destroyed over the course of the action. As if to further emphasize the inability of the region's assorted informal political and legal regimes to effectively govern, George Steele, who according to Byers had "been twice before ordered out of town" then appeared and "made violent threats against the lives of three or four citizens, swearing that he would kill them before morning."[50] An attempt was made to apprehend Steele, but to no avail. Harvey, McCarty, and Todd all reappeared in town after less than a week but were not lynched. Instead, a jury discharged them after dispensing "good advice and caution" and accepting from Todd a bond for good behavior.[51]

Informal groups elsewhere in the region experienced similar difficulty in maintaining order. On February 3, in Mountain City, a man by the name of William W. Atkins, better known as "Pennsyltuck," stormed along with a party of young men to a private dance. Panicked attendees leaped from the second story windows of the building, while Atkins "assaulted a gentleman" who was "regarded as a peaceable and unoffending citizen."[52] Atkins was not some fringe figure in the community, and had been just a few weeks prior named the Inspector of Arms for the settlement's Rocky Mountain Rangers.[53] Local residents organized a trial. Atkins remained defiant, spewing abusive language and threats. Still, the jury awarded Atkins a verdict of "not guilty." When Sheriff John H. Kehler, whom Atkins would have also known as the captain of the Rocky Mountain Rangers, admonished him to behave better, Atkins shoved him and exclaimed, "Don't shoot," then fired a pistol that was concealed under his coat. Atkins missed. Kehler shot him in the right breast. In response to the incident, Mountain City residents formed a vigilance committee, announcing in *The Rocky Mountain News* that they had "ropes for murderers, and all those who commit crimes of a high nature, and whips for thieves and fighting men, which will be freely used when they are found guilty." Ironically, the pronouncement was printed next to a news item announcing that a bill to abolish the death penalty had been introduced in New York.[54] When Atkins did not die as expected and began to slowly recover, a group of vigilantes seized him from the bed where he had been convalescing and lynched him.[55]

Denver's People's Court remained busy. In March, the court ordered the extralegal execution of Moses Young for the murder of William West, but that same month acquitted John Rucker for the killing of Jack O'Neil. In June, the People's Court sentenced Marcus Gredler to death for the murder of Jacob Roeder. Later that same month, it handed down a similar sentence to William Hadley for the murder of J. B. Card, but Hadley managed to escape.[56] On July 12, gambler Charles Harrison killed a formerly enslaved man by the name of E. D. "Professor" Stark, a barber and former resident of Omaha.[57] Byers denounced the killing as "wanton and unprovoked; in short a cold blooded murder."[58] Harrison walked without so much as a trial.[59]

On July 18, a young saloon owner, James A. Gordon, went on a drunken "spree." At a house of "ill-fame" on Arapahoe Street, he shot an eighteen-year-old barkeep by the name of James O'Neill, hitting his unfortunate target four times in the hip and leg. With few bystanders caring to respond to such an incident at such an establishment, an unrestrained Gordon continued his binge for the next two days, making violent threats and haphazardly discharging his pistol. On the night of Friday, July 20, Gordon and two companions slunk into the Louisiana saloon and demanded whiskey. Gordon again grew violent and struck without provocation a young man named John Gantz, knocking him down. Gantz did not want to fight back. He attempted to flee. Gordon pursued. He caught Gantz, knocking him down again and dragging him back. He then began to land vicious blows to Gantz's head before gripping him by the hair and sticking his pistol in Gantz's face. Gordon squeezed the trigger. Four times the weapon snapped harmlessly. On the fifth attempt, it fired.[60]

While inaction at the moment the murder took place allowed Gordon and his companions to escape, anger among the locals percolated through the night. The next day, Saturday, July 21, a party of men set out in pursuit of Gordon. They tracked him to Fort Lupton, but he managed to dash past them and cried out, "Shoot, you damned cowardly sons of bitches, and then follow me." One pursuer, Babcock, chased Gordon for ten miles before peppering Gordon and his horse with buckshot. The horse collapsed, but the bloodied Gordon managed to escape on foot.[61] During this drama, the pursuers also stumbled upon three alleged horse thieves. They seized one, Samuel K. Dunn. Another, Frank Mulligan, drowned as he attempted to escape, and the fate of the third man was unclear.[62] To cap off the anarchic weekend, barkeep Bill Bates accidently shot and killed his friend Mell Hadley on the evening of Sunday, July 22.[63]

For Denver's merchants, speculators, and boosters, things had again gone too far. Golden's *The Western Mountaineer* lamented that "the last week has been a very carnival of horrors.... There will be no safety for human life until this region is purged of some of the desperadoes who infest it."[64] The People's Court, in taking a cautious approach to sentencing, had failed, in their estimation, to adequately quell threats to both life and property in the settlement. Dunn, the horse thief captured on July 21, was not handed over to the People's Court, nor to municipal or Jefferson authorities. On Tuesday morning, July 24, Denver's elites again formed a vigilance committee. They held a session in the hall above Graham's Drug Store, enrolling some sixty members and electing Thomas Pollock—who had proved decisive in the Bummer affair—as marshal and

D. P. Wallingford as judge. The vigilance committee then tried Dunn, the alleged horse thief, and sentenced him to twenty-five lashes and banishment. Dunn only endured seventeen lashes before falling "nearly senseless," and the vigilantes remitted the remaining blows.[65] The vigilance committee also examined Bill Bates for his killing of Hadley, finding him "not guilty, but censurable for the careless use of fire-arms."[66] Byers, who no doubt had participated in the vigilante action, complimented the work of the vigilance committee by issuing the usual threats in his newspaper. "One more act of violence," he thundered, "will at once precipitate the inevitable fate; and the terrors that swept over the fields of California at various times, and first purified its society, will be re-enacted here with terrible results to outlaws and villains."[67]

The July actions of the vigilance committee did not appear radically different from the previous, fleeting instances of vigilantism experienced in Denver. The cycle of committee formation, nonlethal retribution, and the issuing of threats by Byers all matched the cadence of prior episodes. Many residents probably expected this iteration of the vigilance committee to prove just as ephemeral as the ones that came before. That might have proven the case, had it not been for Carroll Wood and George Steele. Wood and Steele had a rough reputation in the area. Wood had, in 1859, along with John Scudder, temporarily fled Denver after Scudder killed Peleg T. Bassett. Steele had been banished from Denver twice, and had most recently during the "Turkey War" emerged to make violent and bloody threats. Both men had been incensed by Byers's printed attacks against Harrison in the wake of the gambler's killing of E. D. Stark, and they sought to chasten or silence the newspaperman.

On July 31, Byers sat in his office at *The Rocky Mountain News* with Larimer, an old associate from Nebraska, along with Presbyterian minister Alexander T. Rankin.[68] It was Rankin's first day in Denver, and Larimer, a Presbyterian himself, had brought the minister to the office to have his appointment announced. In the middle of the meeting, Carroll Wood burst into the office with a pistol in hand and grabbed Byers by the collar. He informed the newspaperman that he intended to take him "to meet his friend, Charley Harrison."

Steele and another man, James Ennis, waited just outside. All three intruders were drunk. They brought Byers to the Harrison's Criterion saloon. The gambler had apparently not authorized the raid, and managed to spirit Byers out a back door before more serious harm could be done.[69] According to contemporary Denver resident Henry Pitzer, Harrison "was a gay, reckless devil, and a killer, but he had sense enough to know that if anything happened to Byers the town would clean out the Criterion and have a wholesale lynching party."[70] It was, a shaken Rankin wrote in his diary, "a pretty ruff introduction to Denver."[71]

The trouble did not end there. Wood, Steele, and some friends, upon learning of Byers's escape, armed themselves and made for the offices of *The Rocky Mountain News*. John Rucker, who had earlier that year been acquitted by the People's Court for the killing of James O'Neil, was part of the band. After some posturing and the making of "rude gestures" toward the office, a mounted Steele fired two shots into the building. The occupants, though, had also armed themselves. They returned fire. A bullet struck Steele in the right shoulder, piercing clean through his body, while a load of buckshot caused him to "reel to and fro in his seat." [72] Steele attempted to flee. Near a part of town called Bradford's Corner, vigilance committee marshal Thomas Pollock met him. Pollock opened fire, striking Steele in the face just below his right eye.[73] Wood and his other companions fled. Residents soon captured Rucker and Wood, the latter narrowly avoiding a summary lynching at the hands of the angry crowd.[74] Wood was, however, saved, and a People's Court trial was arranged for him. Perhaps encouraged by the earlier temper of the crowd, Byers felt confident that the People's Court would punish Wood. "It was a foregone conclusion," he wrote, "that the prisoner would be brought in 'Guilty.'"[75]

That did not happen. On Wednesday, August 1, a storm delayed the trial. The next day, Wood's lawyers launched a well-prepared defense. Among Wood's attorneys was Alvarado C. Ford. Although he had established his own residence in Council Bluffs, Ford had speculated in Nebraska and dabbled in Nebraskan politics, partaking in the pro-Bellevue campaign to see Omaha Claim Club member

Thomas Cuming recalled from his station as acting governor. Byers, Larimer, and other former inhabitants of Nebraska Territory were doubtless familiar with him. At Wood's trial, Ford, according to the account printed by *The Rocky Mountain News*, "spoke for the defense, in a very impressive and feeling manner, cautioning the fury against prejudice, outside influence, and undue excitement. His effort was well received, and considering that the great weight of testimony was against his client, very ingenious and forcible."[76] Ford's powerful defense, along with the similarly effective work of his fellow defense attorney J. C. Moore and the poor performance of the prosecution, saved Wood. The jury voted 11 guilty to 1 not guilty, and Judge G. W. Purkins subsequently put the matter to a crowd vote. The response was, according to *The Rocky Mountain News*, an "almost unanimous responsive 'Aye!'"[77] Wood went free. It had been, according to witness Rankin, a "tragedy & farce."[78]

Byers, publicly, attempted to maintain an outwardly calm and detached demeanor. "The sovereign people had their say, or at least were so represented," read an article referencing the Wood trial in the August 8 edition of *The Rocky Mountain News*. "With its result we have no objection to make, and shall indulge in no reflections thereupon."[79] It was a startling reversal for Byers, who had before loudly and repeatedly called for Lynch law in far less serious cases. More quietly, he adopted an armed posture, always carrying on his gun belt twenty-two shots whenever he was in Denver. "We noticed," wrote the editors of *The Western Mountaineer* on August 9, "that his belt bore the ominous label, in glaring capitals, 'Fire King.'"[80]

The Western Mountaineer was itself less hesitant to heap scorn upon the verdict, and wrote on August 9 that "we deplore these occurrences from the fact that their inevitable tendency is to produce uncontrollable excitements, and to weaken even the imperfect barriers which these informal courts interpose between the fury of the community, and the right of every man charged with crime to a calm and dispassionate trial by a jury of his peers."[81] The rest of August passed relatively quietly, punctuated by the announcement of William H. Middaugh's arrest of Gordon and the news that he would be tried not in Denver but in Leavenworth, Kansas

Territory.[82] Many of Denver's merchants, speculators, and boosters, meanwhile, remained unsatisfied with the capacity of the existing informal system to offer sufficient protection to their lives and property. Shootings, burglaries, and other violations of property rights continued.[83] The theft of livestock was particularly troublesome, with over one hundred horses and mules stolen from three separate ranches in the last week of the month.[84] On August 30, *The Rocky Mountain News* wrote, "We care not whether under the name of State, Territory, or Claim Club, only that we have laws that can, and will be enforced."[85]

On August 31, one of the ranchers whose livestock had been stolen, a man by the name of Bradley, and eight companions set out in pursuit of the thieves. Bradley and his men eventually returned, empty-handed. On September 1, however, James Hill caught a man named John B. Bishop allegedly attempting to steal horses from Henderson's ranch. Examined by the vigilance committee, Bishop confessed "to several horse thefts." During this examination, he supposedly gave up the names of several men who had joined forces for the purpose of stealing horses.[86] Horse thieves had previously been flogged by prior iterations of the Denver vigilance committee. This now changed.

On September 2, vigilantes summarily hanged an alleged horse thief, identified only as "Black Hawk," from a cottonwood tree. He was, despite his name, a White man. Contemporary Denver resident Henry Pitzer, who knew Black Hawk, later wrote that he "was not an Indian but certainly was a lot worse than the worse Redskin I ever heard of."[87] According to Pitzer, his friend and likely vigilante "Noisy Tom" Pollock had harbored personal animosity toward Black Hawk. Pollock "wanted a chance" to hurt Black Hawk, Pitzer would later write, "and finally got it."[88] Pitzer himself disliked Black Hawk, and noted that while he "didn't see Black Hawk lynched," he "wasn't sorry to hear about it."[89] Black Hawk and John B. Bishop may have been the same person or two separate individuals, but sources do not provide clarity.[90]

The vigilante campaign had begun. "Desperate diseases," read foreboding text in the September 3 edition of Byers's *The Rocky*

Mountain News, "require desperate remedies."[91] The night after the vigilantes lynched Black Hawk, they moved against their next target. On the morning of September 4, Denver residents discovered the suspended corpse of John Shear outside of the settlement. A note pinned to a stump, to which one end of the rope had been fastened, announced that Shear had supposedly been a horse thief and had been killed by the vigilance committee. It was an odd pronouncement. Shear was "big, fat, and rather dissipated," a former proprietor of the local hotel known as the Vasquez House, a city council member, and a founder of Denver's library.[92] He did not match the profile of the typical horse thief. The vigilantes had forced Shear from his bed at the Platte House.[93] The corpse, when examined, displayed no signs of any struggle, but Shear's hands had turned black from the tight cord the vigilantes had used to bind him. "Dead! Dead!" recorded a disturbed Rankin in his diary on the day of the corpse's discovery. "A Terrible penalty for stealing."[94]

On the same day that Shear's body was discovered, Alvarado C. Ford, who had defended Wood at his trial for the attack on Byers, disappeared. There were rumors that Ford was on his way to provide testimony or legal defense for Gordon in Leavenworth.[95] Ford may have also understood the danger in which he found himself and possibly attempted to flee from the settlement once he heard the news of the lynchings of Black Hawk or Shear. In any case, the vigilantes quickly seized him from the coach and liquidated him. While Ford's abandoned and perforated remains stayed undiscovered, rumors of the lynching campaign gripped public attention in the area. By the time *The Rocky Mountain News* went to press on September 4, unconfirmed reports of two additional hangings had already spread.[96]

Byers showed no sympathy to the deceased. *The Rocky Mountain News* immediately attacked the characters of both Shear and Ford. On September 5, the paper published rumors that Ford had been "president of the horse thief gang" and that Shear was "one of the principal men in the gang that infests the country." That intelligence, *The News* claimed, had been, in a probable reference to Bishop, sourced from "a confession made by a horse-thief caught almost in the very act."[97] The particulars of Ford's personal life lent credence, in the eyes of some, to such rumors. "Ford was formerly a Free Will Baptist preacher," noted Rankin in his diary, "but renounced the ministry & belief in the Christian religion, became an Infidel & grossly immoral. If the report prove true he will have paid dearly for his wickedness."[98]

The Rocky Mountain News explicitly endorsed the lynchings, proclaiming that "much as we deprecate mob violence, or the working of Lynch law—and no one can be more conscientiously or sincerely opposed to it—we can in the present juncture see no other alternative than to resort to the extreme measures that have been adopted." For Byers, the former claim club member who had spent the past year lobbying for the application of lethal extralegal violence, to portray himself as a true opponent of Lynch law was cynical at best. The paper, though, did not stop there. It proceeded to savage the People's Court, calling it "little better than a farce," before assuring readers that "every movement of the Vigilance Committee—or whatever it may be called, has been taken with calm deliberation; evidence has been amassed extending back for many months, and in cases only where it has been most conclusive has action been taken."[99]

Byers was playing coy, but the attempt to cover his own association with the vigilance committee was transparent. Denver's vigilance committee kept its activities and membership secret, but resident Henry Pitzer later claimed that the organization was one hundred members strong and governed by a council of ten. Pitzer believed Byers, Larimer, Pollock, Middaugh, Edwin Scudder, D. C. Oakes, and another former Nebraskan, Methodist minister John Chivington, all belonged to the organization. Chivington would soon rise to infamy for his role in the 1864 Sand Creek Massacre. While Pitzer claimed to not believe it personally, he also noted that rumors placed Byers, Larimer, and Chivington all within the leadership council.[100] Sheriff Middaugh would, for his part, have to later deny reports that he "accompanied the individuals that were instrumental in the death of A. C. Ford, about one year ago." As an alibi, he claimed to have spent the night with none other than Byers and three other men.[101]

Byers was one of the vigilance committee's most important leaders and boosters. He certainly was its most public one. Byers played an especially critical role in countering public outcry against the secretive lynching campaign. The vigilantes did not enjoy universal or potentially even popular support in Denver. According to Pitzer, Charles Harrison and his friends disparagingly referred to the vigilance committee as "the Stranglers."[102] Thomas Gibson, editor of *The Rocky Mountain Herald*, similarly opposed the dispensation of lethal extralegal judgment. He condemned both the vigilantes and Byers in his paper.[103] Meetings were held to protest the vigilantism, and residents signed a petition denouncing the extralegal action. As Hogan noted, some of those who signed the petition were associated with the vigilance committee itself, hinting at rifts within the movement over "tactics."[104]

Byers hit back. *The Rocky Mountain News* took to mixing faux regret at the lynchings with rhetoric that attempted to justify and legitimatize the action. On September 11, the paper responded to news of an anti-vigilante meeting by dismissing it as a failure and claiming that popular will remained firmly in favor of the vigilance committee. "We pray God that we may never again be called upon to record a hanging by Lynch law," wrote the editors, "but our faith is slight so long as owners of property are daily and nightly despoiled of their possessions. Human nature will not stand it."[105] Byers took aim at Gibson as well. When the editor of the *Herald* noted that he would not lament to see a certain horse thief hanged, *The Rocky Mountain News* immediately seized on his hypocrisy. "Oh! wicked *Herald*," read *The News* reply, "how horrid. Why don't the public '*vigies*' do it in daylight, and how can one of its committeemen venture to throw a shadow of endorsement on midnight proceedings."[106]

At the same time, the paper also continued to publish accounts of the "depredations" that threatened and violated property rights throughout the area.[107] While these accounts may well have been genuine, they served the dual purpose of attempting to legitimize in the public opinion the vigilante campaign by portraying the situation as out of control. Concurrently, the paper attempted to convince readers that the vigilantes were the only group capable of counter-ing the threat. The September 12 edition of *The Rocky Mountain News* claimed that the vigilantes had discovered the "rendezvous of the company of thieves." "A large party of the sufferers under their depredations have set out to 'correl' them," the report continued, "and we shall not be surprised to hear of a reduction in the number of gentry now in the horse business."

Meanwhile, the rumors that Byers spread about Ford and Shear took root. On September 13, *The Western Mountaineer* reported excitedly that Ford, Shear, and even Gordon were all implicated in "a gigantic horse-stealing association, embracing several men of hitherto fair repute in the community, comprising in all more than fifty members, bound together by a perfect organization, and a com-plete system of secret signs, grips, and pass-words, and its stations extending to the Missouri river." Ford was president of this criminal group, the *Mountaineer* claimed in a parroting of the September 5 claims of *The Rocky Mountain News*, while Gordon was captain and Shear a "chief director."[108] No further evidence indicates the exis-tence of such a large criminal conspiracy, but the allegations did the important work of creating a unified and justifying narrative of the vigilante lynchings.

The lynchings did not stop with Black Hawk, Shear, and Ford. Protests and petitions did not halt them, either. The killing cam-paign lurched on through September. On September 7, Rankin had noted in his diary, a man named Bently had disappeared. He had later resurfaced, still living. "It seems the committee had him in custody," Rankin wrote, "& that he saved his life by disclos-ing the names & designs of the party of horse thieves."[109] Vigilance committee operations had quietly carried on as members continued to attempt to hunt down targets. According to historian Stephen J. Leonard, between three to six additional men were also likely killed by the vigilance committee over the course of the month.[110] It was a silent campaign of organized terror, designed to protect property rights by instilling in residents the fear that a shadowy commit-tee could seize and lynch them at any time should they fall under suspicion.

The campaign wound down after September ended. The vigilantes handed extralegal power back to the People's Court, and when James Gordon was finally returned to Denver in October, it was a People's Court jury, not the vigilance committee, who tried and lynched him.[111] The vigilantes most likely believed that their rash of lynchings had been enough to sufficiently communicate to the broader community their resolve and willingness to kill should conditions return to their summer state. Denver's newspapermen seemed to believe that it worked. On November 1, *The Western Mountaineer* responded angrily to a joke about Denver's violent reputation that was published in the *Omaha Nebraskian*. "Two months ago there would have been some justice in the above," the paper wrote, "but of late, life and property have been safe in Denver as in any other city of its size west of the Mississippi. The summary punishment of Steele, Gordon, Ford, and Shear have produced a new order of things."[112]

This "new order" did not mean that crime, killing, and the violation of property rights ceased, nor did it mean the end of the application of extralegal violence in the region. Lynchings would continue in and around Denver, even after Congress finally organized Colorado Territory in February 1861. Still, the September killing campaign planned and executed by Denver's secretive committee of vigilance enabled resident merchants, speculators, and boosters to violently enforce an informal state of "public order" to counter perceived threats to their financial and propertied interests. While exact membership remains unknown, former members of the Nebraskan claim clubs, who came into the region already in possession of experience in organizing and justifying extralegal collective action, played a critical role in making the success of that campaign possible. Byers represented the most public apologist of vigilante violence, and his printed advocation for and defenses of Lynch law were crucial for a secretive vigilance committee that lacked the mandate of popular will.

The experience of that campaign would continue to shape Denver and the surrounding region for years to come, as residents evoked the memory of the campaign or resorted to vigilantism in response to perceived threats over the years and decades that followed. The memory of the September lynching campaign would not, however, be regulated to Denver. The fresh discovery of gold in the region now known as Montana, along with a desire to escape from the Civil War, would soon pull many miners and merchants north. There, merchants who had lived through the vigilantism in Denver would meet and engage with others schooled in extralegal violent action from their own experiences in Nebraska, California, and Kansas. When confronted with fresh threats to their property and mercantile operations, these men would use this combined experience to produce what would prove to be one of the bloodiest instances of vigilantism in American history to that date.

"It was a weird and chilly night," remarked John A. Nye, "and is so yet when I think of it, though forty years ago." Nye could not escape the memory of January 13, 1864. The mere thought of it wrenched him back to the cold and dark watch he kept that night on the west side ravines. He was alone, clutching a shotgun. A subcommittee of the vigilance committee had issued killing orders, and Nye's responsibility was to ensure that no target escaped through the ravines. Admonitions to "speak low and keep your gun handy" spread among the anxious vigilantes. They struck in the morning. Five men were lynched. Nye could not forget the faces of the condemned men. "I see, even now," he shared, "six foot six Jack Gallager, wriggle his neck in derision of the rope as he marched inside of the crowd, up the street." It was a grim sight. The stain of death made Nye uncomfortable. "I felt relieved," he confessed, "when they selected the cross of another unfinished building instead of mine to do the hanging on."[113]

The lynchings that John Nye witnessed took place in Virginia City, a mining settlement in what was then Idaho Territory but is now known as Montana. Those events marked the bloodiest day in an orchestrated campaign of vigilante killings that extinguished twenty-one lives throughout the region.[114] The vigilante action that Nye helped organize and in which he subsequently participated bore much in common with the September 1860 campaign orchestrated by Denver's vigilantes just a few years prior. As had been the case in Denver, merchants like Nye had banded together in a secretive vigilance committee. Those merchant–vigilantes similarly circumvented already established, informal legal bodies out of a belief that such systems failed to provide ample protection to their lives and property. The prominent participation of individuals who already possessed experience in the organization and execution of extralegal collective violence profoundly shaped the violence in Montana, just as it had in Denver.

Veterans of the Omaha Claim Club, Bleeding Kansas, and the San Francisco Committee of Vigilance would, alongside likely members of the secretive Denver Committee of Vigilance, lead the action in Montana. [115] Through their joint participation, the various genealogical flows of violent action these men represented and carried into the region twisted together, facilitating the extreme nature of the vigilante violence experienced during the episode. The violence that occurred in Montana during the winter of 1863–64 was not a testament to the peculiar or exceptional conditions of the time and place, but rather to the combined influence of the cascading flows of violence that crashed, through human movement, into the region and subsequently produced one of the bloodiest campaigns of vigilantism in American history.[116]

As had been the case in Denver, gold triggered this mass movement. In the summer of 1862, John White had struck gold at a stream that he named Grasshopper Creek, located on the eastern side of the Rocky Mountains.[117] News of the discovery spread like contagion, and a town quickly sprouted in the area. The miners named their new town Bannack, after the Bannock people. In the spring of 1863, a group of prospectors found more gold in a creek in Alder Gulch, some seventy miles east of Bannack. A "stampede" of miners, hoping to strike it rich, established a large settlement. Confederate sympathizers initially named the town Varina, in honor of Jefferson Davis's wife, but a Unionist miners' judge altered the paperwork to rename the settlement Virginia City. The mining towns swelled with new settlers drawn to the region by the allure of gold and a desire to escape the turbulence of the Civil War. By 1864, Virginia

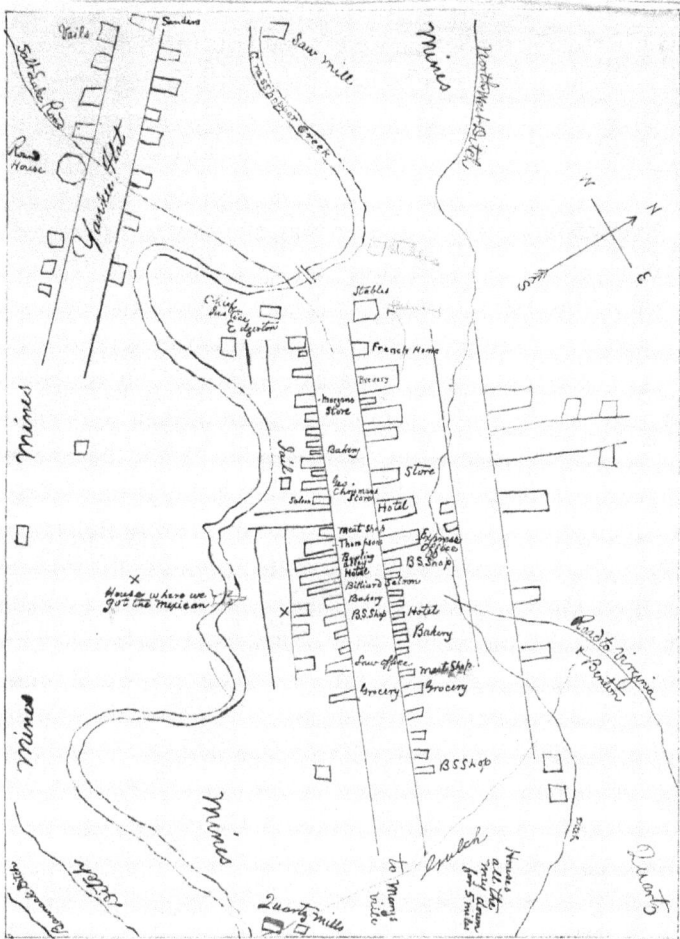

Map of Bannack City, Montana Territory, 1864, by Francis M. Thompson, Montana Historical Society Research Center, C-159, Archives, Helena, Montana.

City boasted a population of approximately five thousand residents, twice that of Denver.[118]

Such rapid population growth provided ample financial opportunities for merchants and speculators. Few people knew this better than John Nye. Nye had, during Nebraska's speculatory boom, opened and operated a hardware and stove store in Bellevue.[119] When gold was discovered in the Rocky Mountains, Nye and his business partner, John Kinna, were among the first settlers to arrive in what is now Denver, where they quickly established a mercantile operation to provide for the coming miners.[120] When miners began to surge into the northern reaches of the Rockies in search of gold, Nye followed.

As Nye was aware, mining gold was one way to extract wealth from the region, but this depended on a payable placer deposit and diligence in mining. A more profitable and dependable option was selling goods to the miners, taking from them their gold without needing a rich claim. Nye and other merchants quickly established a robust mercantile network that linked the remote new settlements to cities like Denver, Omaha, and Salt Lake City. While the new, gold-fueled market promised profits, establishing this commercial network came with considerable risk. Merchants had to freight goods long distances to reach the Montana settlements, and the slow travel left their investments vulnerable. The weather was unpredictable and hazardous. In the winter, snow obstructed travel, while powerful storms buffeted and stranded freight in the spring and summer. Freighters and travelers feared being attacked, noting their anxieties regarding possible Native American "depredations."[121] Some merchants adopted an armed posture—a siege mentality—before they even reached Montana. Settler Aaron T. Ford later recounted the measures enacted by former Nebraska resident, claim club member, and freighter John A. Creighton while on the road to the mountain diggings. "John Creighton was very careful," recalled Ford. "He would not let the stock be driven to water without plenty of men to guard them."[122]

For merchants willing to brave these risks, Montana promised substantial potential profits. The remote settlements produced enormous demand for supplies that could not be sourced locally. Butter, flour, tobacco, manufactured goods, and whiskey were among the many goods desired by miners that, due to scarcity and lack of competition, merchants could supply at a steep price. "Tobacco," recalled miner Robert Kirkpatrick, "had run up to $18.00 a pound the season we got to Bannock on account of scarcity. After we got there butter was 75 cents to 1.00 a pound and eggs 1.00 a dozen, cuts sold for 5.00 a piece, beef steers from 60.00 to 80.00 a head, hogs 40.00 a piece, sugar 30.00 a hundred pounds."[123] For comparison, the average price for a dozen eggs in 1863 Cincinnati was 20 cents, the same price as a pound of butter.[124]

Even wealthier residents like Mary Edgerton—wife of Sidney Edgerton, the chief justice of Idaho Territory—struggled to pay the merchants' prices. "I tasted butter for the first time since we came here," she reported to her sister in November 1863, "& it was a treat I can assure you but as long as it is ten & twelve shilling a pound I think we shall do without it most of the time. Everything is very high here."[125] By New Year's Day 1864, prices would rise even higher, with Edgerton writing to her sister that she "bought seven lbs of butter at $1.25 per lb & I expect it to last all winter, but precious little do I use about cooking, & have bought one doz of eggs at $1.50 per doz—have been without milk most of the time since we have been here; when I do get any I have to pay seventy five cents a quart."[126] Scarcity caused spikes in staple prices, with Kirkpatrick complaining that "flour that cost 2.50 in Utah cost 20.00 in Bannock."[127] Nye, eager to profit from such conditions, opened up his own tin and hardware shop in a small log cabin on Jackson Street, between Idaho and Wallace Streets in Virginia City.[128]

Buoyed by gold and hope, many miners proved willing to pay the inflated prices. Due in part to the dearth of familiar institutions and recreational opportunities, the goods and services offered by the merchants occupied a central place in the social world of the mining towns. Often bored and without their families, many miners, as they had in Denver, swarmed the local saloons and dance halls after the day's labor in search of companionship, diversion, and the numbing effects of liquor. "After supper," Kirkpatrick reminisced, "the miner hurried away to some gambling hell to smoke fill himself with blue ruin and gamble off his gold, and there were other vile ways that their gold went."[129] Nye's hardware and tin store stood opposite one such large gambling hall and saloon.[130] This behavior was not limited to the miners, and although merchant Thomas

Conrad assured his wife that he "neither gambled, visited the fan-
cies nor have I been drunk since I left home," he confessed that
"I chew more tobacco, smoke more and drink more whiskey."[131]

These comforts did not come cheap. Despite its abominable quality, a single drink of whiskey cost 25 cents. Kirkpatrick claimed
that the whiskey "was often made two barrels of water and a few
plugs of tobacco with a quantity of camphor and a little stricknine
to give it a tang to a barrel of pure whiskey, making three barrels of
red eye."[132] While this method boosted profits for the merchants,
it resulted in an inferior and dangerous product. Merchants even
came to dominate the Sabbath. With no churches or clerics yet
established in the mining towns, commerce became the primary
Sunday diversion. Conrad, a Roman Catholic, wrote to his wife that
"there is no Priest—no church—no Sunday here—I believe there is
more goods sold on Sunday than on all the balance of the week. The
miners appropriate Sunday to do their trading and merchants and
shop keepers, seem quite willing to accommodate them."[133] Conrad
sheepishly admitted that he too took part in the Sabbath-breaking
trade, and asked his wife to ask the priest back in their native Missouri for guidance. Although it pained his conscience to do so,
Conrad kept his doors open on Sundays. The sales were simply too
profitable to refuse.

Many settlers held property in the form of land or mining claims,
but ownership was difficult to establish and maintain, while value
oftentimes remained uncertain. Many settlers and potential inves-
tors did not immediately consider the region desirable for agricul-
ture, dampening the promise of speculatory profits from the sale
of land, and the absence of a government land office meant that
squatters could encroach on boundaries or jump claims.[134] Mining
claims suffered from similar vulnerability, and miners often found
themselves forced to contend with rival claimants as they attempted
to extract mineral wealth. In September 1862, miner James Henry
Morley recorded in his diary that he and his associates seized one
mining claim from alleged jumpers "'at the point of the bayonet.'"[135]
Even if a miner could establish and defend a claim, there was no
guarantee that the claim contained payable gold.

Merchants like Nye had better prospects than the prospectors. Lawyer Wilbur Fisk Sanders observed in 1863 that Virginia City was a place "where he who follows mining seldom pursues the most lucrative calling, but where the petty trader, and the great wealthy freighter . . . amassed his fortune and goes home contended or returns again with goods to gratify the insatiable demands of avarice."[136] The majority of prospectors did not find their fortunes through mining, but they still had to contend with the high prices the region's merchants could command. Miners' resentments rose with debts, and some began to grumble about real or imagined cheating on the part of the merchants. "Some of the gold scales were made to cheat with or rather the weights were," Kirkpatrick later claimed. This alleged duplicity added insult to the already inflated prices charged by the merchants. "Things were so expensive," he continued, "that we had all we could do to get along and run in debt besides."[137]

This environment of miner resentment, inflated prices, and valuable caravans of trade goods and wealth made the conditions ripe for banditry. The dynamics of trading meant that merchants had to remain somewhat mobile and able to transport property both into and out of Montana as well as between settlements. While merchants could more easily maintain ownership over their property from within the confines of walled shops and storehouses, their ability to control and defend their goods weakened along isolated trails. Highway bandits, commonly referred to as "road agents," took advantage of this vulnerability and ambushed wealthy merchants and miners during transit. Wealth could be accumulated in territorial Montana, but the inflated local economy devalued the worth of any capital accrued. Transporting that wealth out of Montana, however, would increase its value and present opportunities for profitable reinvestment. Merchants and successful miners had to therefore transport their earnings out of the remote settlements and make the long journey back to either their homes or to a trade hub. For desperate failed miners, banditry targeting these gold-laden travelers offered an opportunity to rapidly accrue wealth or reverse poor fortunes. "It is not safe now for men to travel alone if they have much money with them," Mary Edgerton wrote to her sister in December 1863. "There are too many highway robbers."[138]

This was not mere sensationalism. In October, bandits killed merchant Lloyd Magruder and stole $12,000 worth of gold dust after he left Virginia City. Over the following weeks, bandits robbed the Peabody & Caldwell stagecoach and the A. J. Oliver & Company stagecoach, and attempted to rob the wagons of freighter Milton S. Moody. Robbers also targeted merchant and butcher Conrad Kohrs and young Henry Tilden, an employee of both lawyer Wilbur Fisk Sanders and Idaho Territory chief justice Sidney Edgerton.[139] In December, the robbery and murder of Nicholas Tiebolt, an employee of merchant William Clark, led to the capture of George Ives. He was tried by a miners' court and executed by hanging. These robberies and killings drove the merchants into a deeper siege mentality. "Men engaged in business or in the possession of property," Wilbur Fisk Sanders later wrote, "were always armed and vigilant for the protection of their persons and possessions."[140] Not all thieves were bold enough to commit acts of banditry, and some limited themselves to the role of "the petty pilferer of sluice boxes or miners cabins," according to Hezekiah Hosmer, who became chief justice of territorial Montana's supreme court in 1864.[141] Such venial offenses, however, did not threaten the larger economic flows of the region or endanger the investments of the mercantile class. It was the highway bandits who most directly threatened the merchants' profits and consequently demanded a more resolute response.

On the night of December 20, 1863, a group of eight men gathered in John Nye's Virginia City dry goods store. Nye covered the windows with sheet iron, and when this failed to adequately veil the proceedings, he doused the lights. Assembled in the darkness of that furtive council were, in addition to Nye, Wilbur Fisk Sanders, Paris S. Pfouts, Nicholas Wall, John A. Creighton, Alvin V. Brookie, Frederick Root, and John S. Lott.[142] Six of the men—Creighton, Lott, Nye, Pfouts, Root, and Wall—were merchants. Sanders was the prosecuting attorney in the ongoing Ives trial. Whispered plots swirled in the cold, dark store. By the time the meeting was over, the men had formed a vigilance committee. The vigilantes quickly added to their ranks William Clark, James Williams, John X. Beidler, and others.[143]

That merchants and freighters formed the overwhelming majority of the vigilance committee's founders reflects the acute threat posed to mercantile interests by highway banditry. For these men, vigilantism was a means to secure their property. While banditry threatened the ability of the territory's wealthier settlers to protect their property, the stakes were highest for merchants. A lucky miner, having only needed to invest capital in a claim, tools, and supplies, could make a profit after accruing a modest sum of gold. Should a merchant's venture prove profitable, though, they would have to first recoup the cost of their initial cargo and transport. For John Creighton and other freighters, this included the cost of multiple wagons, animals, teamsters, and guards in addition to the cargo itself. A profitable merchant attempting to move his wealth out of Montana would therefore be transporting a much more substantial sum of wealth than even a modestly wealthy miner. This made merchants highly vulnerable to theft. A single robbery could reduce an entire investment to ruin. John Nye stated this when he gave his own account of the founding of the vigilance committee. "We might guard our dust with shotguns in the cabins," he wrote, "but how about getting it out to the States. It was doubtful then which were in the majority, outlaws or miners. We resolved to see others and make a call for a meeting and that was the initiation of the far reaching Vigilance Committee."[144]

Montanan vigilantism, like Denver vigilantism, was not a struggle against lawlessness. While the formal legal system had not established itself in Montana before the outbreak of vigilantism, the settlers established informal legal bodies known as miners' courts to adjudicate claim disputes and respond to crimes. While extrajudicial, miners' courts were, much like Denver's People's Court, presided over by judges and offered trial by jury. The healthy presence of lawyers in the territory, including Wilbur Fisk Sanders, speaks to the existence of a robust legal culture, informal as it may have been. This informal nature, however, left the miners' courts at times ineffectual or liable to outside influence. Other settlers complained about the ability of skilled or simply unscrupulous attorneys to sway decisions in their favor. "There was a Lawyer came to Bannack," later recalled Aaron T. Ford, "by the name of Smith. He was a very smart man but was in sympathy with the Rough Characters. If the Roughs wanted a miners claim he would jump it would call a miners meeting, have Shenanagan Smith and he was shure to get it."[145] Smith, a former Denver resident, had experience in navigating such systems. Still, it had been a miners' court that found George Ives guilty—even with the benefit of a legal defense mounted by H. P. A. Smith—and sentenced him to death.

Legal mechanisms, informal and flawed as they may have been, did exist in Montana before the outbreak of vigilantism. That the vigilantes elected not to involve the miners' courts in their campaign of lynching speaks to priorities organized not around combating "lawlessness," but rather, as had been the case in Omaha and Denver, around making a bloody example out of those who threatened the financial interests of vigilante leadership. High concepts of law and justice were not the prime motivators for the vigilante leadership. Even Sanders showed the limits of his own respect for the law when he later claimed in a speech that, a few weeks before the founding of the vigilance committee, Sheriff Henry Plummer approached him to secure legal counsel. Plummer planned to assassinate one of his own deputies. "I am afraid," Sanders admitted, "I encouraged him in his purpose."[146] Rather than being concerned with "lawlessness," the nascent vigilantes were more concerned about the deficiencies of the miners' courts when it came to securing their property. Extralegal and violent methods offered a much surer means of protecting wealth and of broadcasting a clear and resolute message of power and control.

There were risks, though, in conspiring to engage in vigilante action. Should the violence be performed sloppily or indecisively, the vigilantes would find their own lives at risk as wounded parties or even the broader community sought retribution. As had been the case in Denver, the Virginia City vigilance committee did not enjoy a mandate of popular will. The vigilance committee represented, primarily, the financial interests of the resident merchants.[147] Operating from this position, any vigilante action would need to be so decisive that a response would be unthinkable. Experience among leaders would be key.

At least three of the vigilance committee's founding members had prior experience with orchestrated campaigns of extralegal collective violence. Pfouts and Nye had come to the Montana camps from Denver. While the secrecy surrounding the Denver vigilance committee's membership makes it impossible to verify, it is possible if not probable that both men had been associated with the vigilantes there. Both had recorded ties to likely vigilantes. Pfouts and Nye belonged to Denver's Masonic circle, along with many of the rumored leaders of the vigilance committee. One 1862 Masonic festival, for instance, saw Pfouts serve on a small committee of arrangements with William N. Byers and John M. Chivington, alleged leaders within Denver's vigilante circle. Nye served on the same festival's committee of invitation.[148] If nothing else, Nye and Pfouts had the experience of seeing a small band of vigilantes successfully use a lynching campaign to defend their property rights. This alone would have been valuable, but the prominence of both men in the initial work of organizing the vigilance committee in Virginia City indicates a deeper level of experience.

John A. Creighton's prior experience in extralegal collective action was more extensively documented. Creighton had been a member of the Omaha Claim Club and had violently enforced its prerogatives. Eyewitness Augustus Macon later testified that Creighton and some of his relatives formed a party that arrested a club target in nearby Iowa. "Four of the members of the Claim Club had one of the men in charge," recounted Macon, "& had brought him by force, all of them being armed with revolvers." When Macon challenged the authority under which the arrest was made, the Creightons "said that if I interfered they would shoot me."[149] This experience enabled John Creighton to play a decisive role in the early formation of the Montanan vigilante ring. Having been a member of the Omaha Claim Club, he was no stranger to the use of force. Creighton had provided an armed guard to Sanders during the Ives trial and had later, in his store, personally protected Sanders against an assault.[150]

As the vigilance committee enlisted more men into its ranks, the organization added even more individuals with prior experience in extralegal collective action. William Clark, the merchant employer of the murdered Nicholas Tiebolt, had been a member of one of the San Franciscan committees of vigilance. According to the eyewitness account of William Herron, who knew the old merchant well after two years in his employ while in Colorado, Clark had declared, following Tiebolt's disappearance, that "I helped organize the vigilance committee in California and I am going to do the same here, and I will make it hot for them before I die."[151] Clark had led the posse that arrested George Ives on suspicion of having killed Tiebolt. It was also Clark who, before the posse attempted the arrest, had drafted written accusations against the suspects in Lott's store—a move that carried no legal validity but reflected the common vigilante practice of pantomiming the legal system.[152]

John X. Beidler and James Williams were themselves both in "Bleeding Kansas" as fighters for the anti-slavery, Free State cause. Mobile young men in search of wealth, Beidler and Williams quickly engaged in the fighting. Beidler fought at the Battle of Hickory Point, where Free-Staters besieged a blacksmith's shop where pro-slavery forces had taken refuge. Beidler recounted filling a howitzer with ersatz grapeshot consisting of type from a sacked printing press, joking that the wounds inflicted by the artillery presented the pro-slavery men with means through which "they first learned to read."[153] Beidler may have sustained wounds at fighting near Osawatomie in 1856.[154] Elsewhere, James Williams, in the words of his son, took part in "very exciting and many seeming desperate adventures." Williams led fighters during the conflict, developing an intense and unswerving style of command. Describing his father's actions in Bleeding Kansas, the younger Williams later wrote that "as a leader of men he always studied the situation well before issuing an order after an order was issued he seldom or never changed it he would make no explanation why the order was made he seemed to have no trouble in having his orders carried."[155] With Williams in the ranching and livery trade and Beidler a merchant and miner, both men had a personal interest in aligning with the vigilante cause.[156]

While neither Beidler nor Williams were part of the council that founded the vigilance committee, both had played prominent roles in the arrest and subsequent execution of George Ives. Beidler had stood guard at the Ives trial, where he publicly encouraged Sanders to take no mercy. He participated both in the subsequent hanging and in the vigilante campaign that followed. Williams had, along with Clark, led the posse that originally arrested Ives.

The killing campaign began on January 4, 1864. A group of vigilantes under the command of James Williams moved against Rattlesnake Ranch in search of associates of the late Ives. They arrested and summarily executed Erastus "Red" Yeager and George Brown, but not before supposedly eliciting confessions implicating a whole, organized gang of road agents led by Bannack's sheriff, Henry Plummer.[157] Like the rumors of the sophisticated horse-thieving ring spread by Byers and the members of Denver's committee of vigilance, this was likely a fabrication by either the vigilantes' desperate captives or the vigilantes themselves to justify a large-scale campaign of killing.[158] On January 10, vigilantes in Bannack lynched Sheriff Plummer and two of his deputies: Ned Ray and Buck Stinson.[159] The next day, vigilantes hanged "Dutch John" Wagner and attempted to arrest Joe Pizanthia, a Mexican or Mexican American miner.

The attempt to move against Pizanthia immediately went sideways. Rather than surrendering to the vigilantes, Pizanthia barricaded himself inside his cabin. When vigilantes George Copley and Smith Ball attempted to force their way inside, he opened fire and hit both. Copley would die shortly thereafter. A mob of White miners much larger than the vigilance committee soon descended on the cabin. The killing of an Anglo by a Mexican had added a racial dimension to the violence. Some men produced a howitzer from Chief Justice Sidney Edgerton and began firing into the cabin. Resident Robert Kirkpatrick was swept up in the mob. He later recalled the frenzied atmosphere that accompanied the moment, recollecting that "the miners boys and all turned out with a rush, droping all kinds of work. Father my brothers and I running with the rest, Some had guns and pistols, most had no arms. The boon of the howitzer

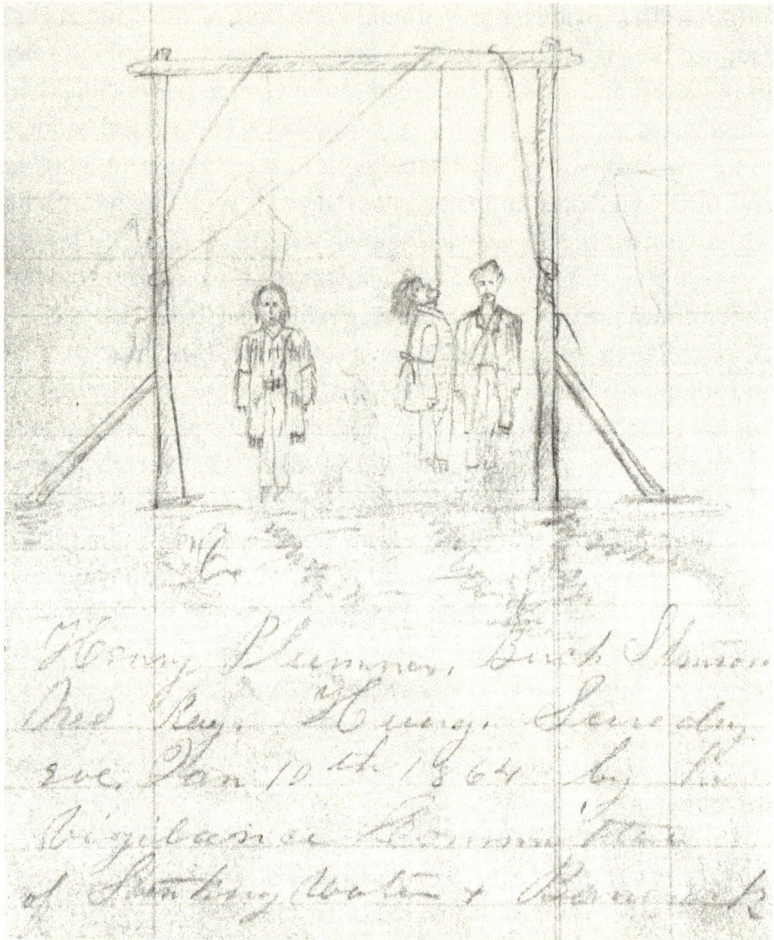

Pencil sketch showing Henry Plummer, Buck Stinson, and Ned Ray hanged by the vigilantes. Henry Plummer collection, 1863–1864 and [undated], SC 651, Montana Historical Society Research Center, Archives, Helena, Montana.

hurried us along."[160] Once the howitzer ran out of shells, members of the crowd continued to wildly shoot into the structure. Eventually, one man carefully approached the cabin, weapon drawn. He would have no use for it. Pizanthia was dead. "The Mexican had died bravely," Kirkpatrick noted. "He had torn down a partition of boards inside the cabin and piled them up in front of the bed as a breast-work and had laid behind that under the bed while the shells were fired through the cabin." After one shell had launched a large splinter into his chest, Pizanthia, Kirkpatrick claimed, shot himself in the head to deny the mob the satisfaction of killing him themselves.[161]

The violence against Pizanthia, however, did not end there. The racial dimensions of the violence ensured that Pizanthia, even in death, received far crueler and more abusive treatment than any other victim of the killing campaign. In California, Anglo miners had, starting in the late 1840s, engaged in a sweeping extralegal campaign mainly directed against Mexican, Mexican American, and other Latino miners and camp residents. Scores died in the years that followed, as lynch mobs summarily executed an unprecedented number of victims in what was oftentimes a cynical means of eliminating competition in the mines.[162] The attitudes behind that violence traveled with miners into the Montana camps. Even before the vigilante campaign had begun, Kirkpatrick noted that Pizanthia had been subject to extreme violence on account of his race. In one instance, he had drunkenly smashed a window in Darrant's saloon. Pizanthia's White associates had frequently done the same thing without consequence, but he would have no such fortune. "He was starting in for a general frolic," Kirkpatrick recalled, "when Darrant took the six shooter, a heavy self acting revolver, away from him, knocked him down with it, and beat his head up frightfully nearly killing him."[163] The killing of an Anglo had only amplified such racially motivated hatreds. The mob hanged Pizanthia's corpse from a clothesline and riddled it with bullets and shot. They then proceeded to light his cabin on fire and burned his remains.[164] The mob lynching of Pizanthia, which resembled no other killing during the vigilante campaign, undoubtedly represented the influence of yet another genealogical flow. With many of the miners having come from California, the tradition of extreme extralegal violence against Mexicans and Mexican Americans had now intertwined itself into the grisly affair.

Following the January 11 lynchings, the action moved to Virginia City. As John Nye noted, orders were issued on the night of January 13

Pencil sketch showing the burning of Pizanthia's body. Henry Plummer collection, 1863–1864 and [undated], SC 651, Montana Historical Society Research Center, Archives, Helena, Montana.

and decisively executed the following morning. Not a single shot was fired. William Clark, the old veteran of the San Francisco Committee of Vigilance, personally captured one target, Jack Gallagher, at gunpoint.[165] Nye and his fellow vigilantes hanged Gallagher, Frank Parish, Boone Helm, "Clubfoot George" Lane, and Hayes Lyon before the day was done.[166] The vigilante campaign had now overseen the killing of twelve men. And the violence continued. Vigilantes under the command of Bleeding Kansas veteran James Williams summarily lynched Steve Marshland and Bill Bunton on January 16 and 18, respectively. Williams quickly developed a reputation as a killer. Sanders later recalled that "at times when others shrank from the task he would put the halter around the neck of the victim with absolute coolness, and I think it might be said he performed this unwelcome duty with greater frequency than any other member, although X. Beidler was a close second." Both Bleeding Kansas veterans were hard-hearted men with few qualms about the taking of human life. Sanders noted that Williams believed, concerning the road agents, that "the only remedy was their destruction, he thought the best way was to destroy, holding for a while in abeyance sentiments of squeamishness or even of mercy."[167] Williams's posse then lynched Cyrus Skinner, Aleck Carter, and Johnny Cooper at Hellgate on January 24, before similarly dispatching Bob Zachary and George Shears the next day and "Whiskey Bill" Graves on the one thereafter. Williams's entourage tore through this bloody spree with even less oversight and procedure than the Virginia City and Bannack companies. On February 3, vigilantes lynched their final target, Bill Hunter.[168]

While their initial campaign against the alleged "road agents" had concluded, the vigilantes continued to sporadically lynch residents over the weeks and months that followed. As had been the case elsewhere, the legacy of the violence persisted. John Nye, for his part, did not stick around the see the killing work concluded. His mind had returned to mercantile matters. He left for Salt Lake City on January 19, on "the first trip out that promised any safety for trade." Still, even as he left Montana and the lynchings behind him, those events would not leave him. "Hundreds and hundreds have been telling for the last forty years of what occurred that day," he later remarked, "and no one can likely forget it while they live."[169] The violence would reverberate, and not just in memory. Settlers who had experienced the vigilantism in Bannack and Virginia City carried the lessons of that episode with them as they moved on to other mining camps, organizing in 1865 a "Committee of Safety" in the newly founded settlement of Helena. Vigilantes in that town would kill at least a dozen men by the end of 1870.[170] The bloody cascade would continue.

*   *   *

On the night of January 30, 1866, an unknown party posted small pieces of white paper, cut into the shape of coffins and marked in the center with a cross, "upon the windows and doors of nearly every house in Denver."[171] *The Rocky Mountain News* reported on the mysterious event in biblical terms. In a reference to the Passover, when Israelites painted lamb's blood above their doors to escape from the Angel of Death, the paper warned those "whose windows are not thus ornamented" that they were in "the most danger." The next day, people traveling in a wagon train discovered three corpses suspended from the branches of a cottonwood tree near Fort Lupton to the north of Denver. On the chests of each of the bodies was marked a black coffin, with a red cross painted in the center. "It is evident that the Vigilantes had been at work," reported wagon boss John G. Stevens in a letter to *The Rocky Mountain News*. "From the horse tracks we concluded that they had come from and departed in the direction of your city."[172]

Earlier in January, *The Rocky Mountain News* had reported that Montana's own vigilantes had been active around Denver. They had been in search of Frank Williams, a stagecoach driver who had, earlier in 1865, allegedly driven his passengers into a trap for the purpose of robbing and killing them.[173] The Montanan vigilantes had tracked Williams to Godfrey's station between Denver and Julesburg, arresting him on January 2. According to Denver historian Jerome Smiley, the Montanans then brought Williams to Denver and contacted the members of that city's own committee of vigilance.

Williams's trial was, tellingly, held in the second story of the store, belonging to none other than John A. Nye.[174] The stagecoach driver allegedly confessed and revealed the names of his co-conspirators. The Denver vigilantes then handed him over to their Montanan counterparts. On January 4, the Montanans lynched him. According to an excerpt from the *Montana Post* republished in *The Rocky Mountain News*, "the other members of the gang are being hotly pursued, and will no doubt be overtaken."[175] The lynchings of three men near Fort Lupton, and of an additional two men just a few days later, followed.[176]

The extralegal collective violence experienced in mining settlements like Denver, Bannack, and Virginia City did not exist in isolation. They were not spawned whole from the supposedly unique or peculiar conditions of their respective times and places. While local conditions were certainly important, so too were the webs of hidden human linkage and connection that tethered each episode of violence to extralegal action elsewhere. That the Coloradan and Montana vigilantes cooperated so easily in the Williams affair speaks to this level of conscious interconnection, with the trial at Nye's store representing a shared node that bound both organizations together.

Such connections stretched far beyond the shadows of the Rocky Mountains. The vigilantism in Colorado and Montana was embedded within a far larger network of violent extralegal action. Human beings already experienced in the organization and execution of vigilante violence moved into both regions from Nebraska, Kansas, and California. When such persons perceived threats to their lives and property, they did not invent a novel response but rather fell back on the rough education they had already received elsewhere. It is no accident that the leaderships of the Denver and Montanan vigilance committees were populated by former members of the Omaha Claim Club, alongside veterans of Bleeding Kansas and old vigilantes from San Francisco. For men like Byers and Creighton, the violent experience of membership in the Omaha Claim Club had provided the instruction that molded them into ready-made vigilante leaders by the time they reached Colorado and Montana. Recognizing these linkages is key to understanding the bloody development of both the 1860 vigilante movement in Denver and the subsequent winter 1863–64 campaign in Bannack and Virginia City.

An acknowledgement of these human linkages is important not only for a deeper and broader understanding of what happened in Colorado and Montana. It is a necessary component in developing a fuller understanding of the shifting forms and mechanics of American extralegal violence itself. The extreme violence of those two lynching campaigns did not occur by accident or on account of local conditions alone. They represented a much longer development, stretching across decades and hundreds of miles, through which American extralegal violence had slowly grown more lethal and more concerned with the defense of private interests. That shift started long before gold had been discovered in the Rocky Mountains. It developed over an unbroken chain of human interconnection, exchange, and collision.

As the 1866 Williams affair demonstrated, neither the September 1860 lynching campaign in Denver nor the 1863–64 campaign in what is now Montana put an end to crime or killing. The existence of an informal legal system did not prevent the action of the vigilantes, and the establishment of regular territorial governments did not prompt their dissolution. The "new order of things" heralded by Golden's *The Western Mountaineer* in 1860 was, for most, not defined by order. No republican definition of order could include shadowy committees and subcommittees issuing death warrants without a trace of transparency or oversight. Nor was it new. This order, one of force and fear, was older than Denver itself. It had emerged slowly and unevenly over the course of decades, slouching across an interconnected and expanding web. It was the type of order that had seen William W. Brown, the Driscolls, and Joseph Smith shot dead. It was the order that allowed claim clubs to rule in Nebraska. Now, in the mountain region, it saw scores of people lynched. This violence was more extreme in scope and execution but emerged from the same flow. It was an order grounded in the notion that small groups of Americans could use violence to enforce their will beyond the bounds established by formal and constitutional law, even to the point of mass killing. It was Lynch law, triumphant.

Conclusion

"Iknow there was a place called Bellevue," testified Thomas J. Babcoke. He stood before the committee appointed by the Missouri State House of Representatives to investigate the charges that he had not only orchestrated the lynching of Judge Wright and his four sons the previous year but had formerly been a counterfeiter and caught up in the bloodletting of the Bellevue War. It was February 19, 1866. Twenty-six years prior, there were in Bellevue, Babcoke continued, "some counterfeiters and horse-thieves taken and roughly treated by the vigilance committee, and I know that two of these horse-thieves ran to Farmington and concealed themselves inside of Heaight's house. That much I know, but further I know not."[1]

The hated Heaight was none other than Silas Heaight, who had two decades prior secured indictments against Babcoke's cousin, Edward Bonney, on charges of counterfeiting and murder.[2] That legal effort had failed in part thanks to the efforts of then-Illinois governor Thomas Ford.[3] Bonney had been in the process of betraying members of the New River family network when Heaight initiated legal proceedings against him. This betrayal had itself been borne out of desperation, after Governor Ford's earlier actions had led to the killing of Bonney's former associate, Mormon prophet Joseph Smith, and sparked Bonney's subsequent fall from grace in Nauvoo. That web of action and association had taken decades to untangle.

On February 14, the committee charged with investigating Babcoke had summoned Heaight to provide testimony. He was now fifty-four years old, and while still a resident of Iowa, he did his business in St. Louis.[4] Heaight relayed that he had first met Babcoke in 1839, when Heaight was just twenty-seven years old. Both men were residents of the small community of Farmington. Babcoke, then still known as Babcock, had been Heaight's preacher. It had been on the way to church, Heaight testified, that Babcock first attempted to induce him to join the counterfeiting business. The reverend, he claimed, had confided to him that "if he had the means to buy material with, there could be plenty of money made at" counterfeiting. Babcock had further confided to Heaight that he "expected to get a circuit to ride to preach, in a short time, as soon as the quarterly conference met." That circuit would provide the preacher with a cover for widely disseminating the spurious currency while avoiding detection. Edward Bonney was also in Farmington and "had a press for making bogus coin."[5] The alleged plan certainly matched the roving cadence of experienced counterfeiting operations. Heaight had insisted that he could not accept the entreaty. Soon after, a mob of locals "under arms" arrested Babcock and his confederates. When the excitement had sufficiently cooled, Babcock and his family fled the area.[6]

Babcoke soon had his chance to respond to the testimony. It was Heaight, he claimed, who had enjoyed the connections to the network of counterfeiters and horse thieves. Twisting the timeline, Babcoke insisted that when Bonney first came to Iowa, they "covenanted together to use every means that was possible, counseling with each other, to detect and hunt out" the Mormon Hodges brothers for the Miller–Leiza murders. Cousin Bonney, he admitted, "was the most active one" in this pursuit.[7] That the Miller–Leiza murders did not take place until 1845 mattered little. It was Heaight, according to Babcoke's inverted account, who first attempted to induct the then-reverend into the passing of bogus currency. Babcoke testified that he would have arrested Heaight "immediately" had Bonney not counseled him "to keep all still" while his efforts to arrest the alleged killers remained underway. It was on account of his efforts to combat criminality in Farmington, Babcoke maintained, that he found himself forced to flee the town.[8]

Babcoke then went on the offensive, claiming that Heaight was confederated in a criminal enterprise with Nathaniel Paschall of *The Daily Missouri Republican*, the paper that had originally printed the charges against Babcoke. "I have tracked him from the stable in St. Louis where he helped to burn a mulatto man," Babcoke raged in reference to Paschall. "I have traced him to Lovejoy's, where he gave his influence in encouraging the mob that murdered Lovejoy.... I have traced him to the bushwhackers in the field."[9] Babcoke understood the danger of being implicated within such genealogical sequences of extralegal action, and attempted to construct for Paschall his own narrative of criminality and violence.

Faced with contradictory narratives, the committee solicitated further witnesses and testimonies. Edward Bonney could not testify. He had died in early 1864.[10] Many others did testify, however, offering conflicting reports regarding both the killing of the Wrights and the alleged counterfeiting in Iowa. Even Babcoke and Bonney's shared maternal aunt, Mary Webster, sent from Ohio a communication claiming that Bonney "was at my house several times during the period that he was trying to detect rogues. I heard him speak of Thomas J. Babcoke being in Iowa, and that he had assisted him (Bonney) in his work of detection."[11] The dueling stances advanced two distinct realities: one where Babcoke had selflessly spent decades combating criminal groups, culminating with the shooting of the guerrilla Wrights as they attempted to escape, and one where he had spent much of his life on the run from lynch mobs, only to ultimately lead one himself.

The committee finally issued its verdict on March 17. The majority report, penned by four members of the committee, reflected an embrace of the former version of reality. "There is no evidence," their report read, "to support the charge that Colonel Babcoke is guilty of the murder of Judge Wright and his four sons, nor accessory to the killing of the same." The report, in its final paragraph, also responded to the allegations connected to the crime and violence at Farmington and Bellevue over twenty years prior. "Hon. Thomas J. Babcoke," the majority concluded, "was not engaged in making or uttering counterfeit coin there as charged . . . he did not belong to any lawless or disorderly secret society there . . . his standing was good and his character fair in that community."[12]

Only one member of the committee, T. J. O. Morrison, dissented. "The minority of your committee," Morrison wrote in his report, "can but find that there are strong grounds for the belief that the said Thomas J. Babcoke was, on or about the years 1830 and 1840–41, in criminal complicity with a band of counterfeiters operating in the then territory of Iowa." Morrison insisted, moreover, that Babcoke was similarly guilty of murder, or at least accessory to murder, for his role in the killing of the Wrights. "It is clear he is guilty," the minority report concluded, "of the charges preferred against him in the *Missouri Republican*."[13] Outnumbered 4 to 1, Morrison could do little more than formally protest, however. Babcoke, exonerated, had escaped once again.

But Thomas J. Babcoke did know Bellevue. He knew and had done business with William W. Brown. He had been caught up in the turbulent violence of the Bellevue War and had barely escaped a flogging. With his cousin, Edward Bonney, he had engaged in criminal and counterfeiting operations, and his "pivot" toward detective work had been fabricated out of Bonney's desperate gambit of self-preservation through betrayal. His wife, Lovina West Babcoke, was the sister to the same Charles West who had belonged to a triumvirate leading Lee County, Illinois's organized criminal element, until he too turned state's evidence. The treachery of Babcoke's cousin and brother-in-law had pushed those they had betrayed, the surviving members of the New River family network, westward. Thomas J. Babcoke had been deeply and intimately embedded within this web of violent extralegal and criminal activity. A knowledge of that web of violent action, and of the connections that bound each incident into a sequence, reveals a truth that the majority of the committee could not or would not see.

Identifying the human linkages that bound together seemingly disparate instances of extralegal collective violent action leads to new insights into both singular violent episodes and into the larger sequences of action to which those episodes belonged. The Reverend

Col. Thomas J. Babcock was just one of the many human beings who were at the center of the action explored in this book. The Driscolls responded to vigilantism in Ogle as they did because of what happened to Babcock's associate, Brown, in Bellevue. Governor Thomas Ford, in turn, perceived the mob at Carthage through the lens of the violence against the Driscolls. Vigilantes fell upon the New River families after the combined weight of the foregoing episodes of extralegal violence led to desperation and shattered bonds of trust and association. Cam Reeves and James C. Mitchell rose to prominence in Nebraska because those prior episodes of violence had taught them how to use force outside of the law. And, in the rarified air of the Rocky Mountains, men like William Larimer, William Byers, and John Creighton used their prior experience with extralegal action to organize and execute two bloody campaigns of lynching, including one of the largest ever organized in the United States to that date. All of these episodes, all of that bloodletting, were interconnected. These events cannot be fully understood independent of the sequence to which they belonged. This is a human history, and the narratives of individuals and their networks are integral to the narrative of extralegal collective violence in the United States.

The findings of this book insist that it is not enough to study violence as self-contained outbursts detached from the influence of human networks. Human movements and networks created the avenues along which exchange, connection, and collision occurred. As individuals experienced extralegal violent action, they transported that experience across such avenues. If they engaged in further extralegal action, they did so informed by that prior experience, creating linkages between the incidents of violence themselves. In understanding violence in this way, genealogies of extralegal violent action emerge. Recognizing the existence of those genealogies and examining violence in relation to the action that helped produce it enable a fuller comprehension of the dynamics of both individual episodes and longitudinal stretches of extralegal action. None of this would be discernable, though, without acknowledging the centrality of the experiences, activities, and networks of individuals.

Knowledge of the linkages they forged, this book contends, is indispensable for developing a wider and deeper understanding of the history of and mechanics behind violence.

There is more work to be done. Beholden to the records that were produced, survived, located, and accessed, I undoubtedly only captured a small percentage of the linkages that bound together the acts of violence in this cascading sequence, and connected that violence to movements and episodes elsewhere. Constrained, moreover, by the self-imposed delimiters of its narrative arc, this work does not pursue every identified linkage related to this sequence of violent action. The sequence this book traces is only a single thread in a much larger web. More research is needed to explore those threads that intersect or run parallel to the action studied here. While this account makes visible the transregional flows and interconnections behind the production and transportation of extralegal collective violence, it does not explore the global dimensions of such movement. The human linkages along which violence flowed across transnational boundaries are in need of study, especially because historians have already noted that immigrant groups like the Irish brought distinct traditions of and experiences with extralegal violence with them into the United States.[14] More work also needs to be done on extralegal violence related to the struggle over freedom and enslavement in the Middle West, and on the human connections that linked episodes of extralegal collective violence to violence against Native peoples.

The history of extralegal violence is bound up in the larger history of the United States. The sequence of extralegal collective violence studied in this book alone led directly to the rise of prominent western urban hubs. Salt Lake City emerged after the Mormon flight following Joseph Smith's killing and the subsequent fighting in Hancock County. Omaha rose through the machinations of the Omaha Claim Club. Denver grew on land seized through threats issued by former Nebraskan claim club members. This sequence of events contributed to the rise and acceptance of a practice of violence that was both increasingly lethal and centered around the interests of the few. That practice commingled with the desire among some to enforce or restore desired racial and class hierarchies to help produce the horrific deluge of lynchings in the postbellum United States. At the same time, the practice established a romanticized vigilante legend that continues to occupy an especially prominent position in the popular memory of the American West. Its legacy is both clear and distorted.

The American tradition of extralegal collective violence has not disappeared. Even as the Civil War and Reconstruction transformed the relationship between Americans and the state, and ushered in a wave of accompanying legal and constitutional changes, the use of extralegal collective violence endured. Americans continued to group together in attempts to violently reshape society outside the bounds of the formal legal system. They continued to riot, to lynch, to engage in vigilantism, and to terrorize. Such disorder was not simply a product of the political turbulence of the moment. It was the ongoing manifestation of a long, violent history. That history endures. To fully reckon with extralegal collective violence, its origins, and the dynamics behind its movement and development, it is critical to recognize the human beings at the center of each violent collision. It is this human dimension that lends durability and adaptability to the practice of violence, allowing for the maintenance and transmission of knowledge that can be adapted to the situations, crises, and conflicts of the day. To engage with the history of extralegal collective violence through that prism is to make visible the means by which violence moves across ranges both spatial and temporal—not as a series of isolated bursts, but as sequences threading through a great web of human activity and interconnection. Blood does not spill. It flows.

NOTES

Introduction

1. *Appendix of the House Journal of the Adjourned Session of the Twenty-Third General Assembly of the State of Missouri* (Jefferson City, MO: Emory S. Foster, 1865–66), 2: 774.

2. Despite its name, the *Republican* was not a Republican paper. "Murder of the Wright Family," *The Daily Missouri Republican,* August 27, 1865.

3. "Horrible Outrage in Phelps County," *The Daily Missouri Republican,* August 21, 1865.

4. *Appendix of the House Journal of the Adjourned Session of the Twenty-Third General Assembly of the State of Missouri,* 775.

5. "Babcoke in the House," *The People's Tribune,* November 29, 1865.

6. "Babcoke, Alias Babcoe, Alias Babcock," *The Daily Missouri Republican,* December 20, 1865.

7. "Colonel Babcoke and the Missouri Republican," *Missouri State Times,* January 26, 1866.

8. *Appendix of the House Journal of the Adjourned Session of the Twenty-Third General Assembly of the State of Missouri,* 634.

9. See Frederick Jackson Turner, *The Frontier in American History* (New York: Henry Holt and Company, 1921), 212.

10. Richard Maxwell Brown, *Strain of Violence: Historical Studies of American Violence and Vigilantism* (New York: Oxford University Press, 1975), 100.

11. Brown, *Strain of Violence,* 100.

12. As Michael Pfeifer argues, the "transformation of the United States during the Civil War and Reconstruction was a complex, fitful process, with interconnected local, regional, and national dimensions" not confined to the former Confederacy. See Michael Pfeifer, *The Roots of Rough Justice: Origins of American Lynching* (Urbana: University of Illinois Press, 2011), 67.

13. Pfeifer, *The Roots of Rough Justice,* 3. As Pfeifer notes, this is a legacy of the origins of lynching scholarship, which began as anti-lynching activism. That activism focused on exposing and combating the postbellum southern lynchings designed to enforce racial hierarchies. See Michael Pfeifer,

"Introduction," in *Lynching Beyond Dixie: American Mob Violence Outside the South*, edited by Michael J. Pfeifer (Urbana: University of Illinois Press, 2013). 2. Other scholars, like Edward L. Ayers, have also explored violence in the South through the lens of a southern honor culture. I attempt to build on this earlier research by exploring how certain practices, such as "gouging" and even references to extralegal punishment as "lynching," crossed regional boundaries. See Edward L. Ayers, *Vengeance & Justice: Crime and Punishment in the 19th-Century American South* (Oxford: Oxford University Press, 1984): 9–33.

14. Pfeifer, "Introduction," 8.

15. The Middle West is defined here as the states of the Old Northwest Territory, as well as Iowa and Minnesota.

16. Susan K. Lucke, *The Bellevue War: Mandate of Justice or Murder by Mob? A True—and Still Controversial—Story of Iowa as the Wild West* (Ames: McMillen Publishing, 2002).

17. Christopher Waldrep notes that Thomas Dimsdale's 1866 book on the Montana vigilantes, while a distorted justification of the vigilantism, was and remains massively influential. Christopher Waldrep, *The Many Faces of Judge Lynch: Extralegal Violence and Punishment in America* (New York: Palgrave Macmillan, 2002), 65; and Thomas J. Dimsdale, *The Vigilantes of Montana, or, Popular Justice in the Rocky Mountains* (Virginia City, MT: D.W. Tilton, 1882).

18. Laura J. Arata, *Race and the Wild West: Sarah Bickford, the Montana Vigilantes, and the Tourism of Decline, 1870–1930* (Norman: University of Oklahoma Press, 2020).

19. See, for example, Iver Bernstein, *The New York City Draft Riots: Their Significance for American Society and Politics in the Age of the Civil War* (Oxford: Oxford University Press, 1990); and Robert M. Senkewicz, *Vigilantes in Gold Rush San Francisco* (Stanford: Stanford University Press, 1985).

20. Richard Maxwell Brown, Paul Gilje, David Grimsted, Ashraf Rushdy, Christopher Waldrep, and Michael Pfeifer are among the scholars who have used this approach to study national patterns in antebellum extralegal violence. Each of these scholars developed their own arguments for why extralegal violence—be it in the form of lynching, vigilantism, or mobbing—developed as it did in the antebellum United States. Brown argues that American extralegal violence was "socially conservative" and "used to support the cohesive, three-tiered structure of the American community . . . and its underlying social values of law and order and the sanctity of property." Brown, *Strain of Violence*, 4. Gilje argues that the changing conditions and realities of four discrete periods representing "key changes in American society" shaped extralegal violence in the United States. Paul A. Gilje, *Rioting in America* (Bloomington: Indiana University Press, 1996), 9. Grimsted understood extralegal violence between 1828 and 1861 to be tied to the issue of enslavement, with mobbing—and the response to that mobbing—taking different forms in the North and the South. David Grimsted, *American Mobbing,*

1828–1861: Toward Civil War (Oxford: Oxford University Press, 1998), viii. Pfeifer held the view in 2011 that lynching occurred in the early-to-mid- nineteenth century in response to "alterations in law and social values," including "the shift from a penology of retribution and deterrence to one centered on reform of the criminal, the rise of the adversarial system and aggressive defense lawyering, the shift from private to public criminal prosecution, and the professionalization of criminal justice." White Americans, Pfeifer argued, saw lynching as the surest way to uphold racial and class hierarchies in the face of such change. See Pfeifer, *The Roots of Rough Justice*, 4–5. Ashraf Rushdy argues in his 2012 book, *American Lynching*, that lynching is tied to enslavement and the very foundations of the American state. "Lynching," he writes, "is not an aberration in American history . . . but a result of the fundamental contradictions that faced the nation at its origins." Rushdy, *American Lynching*, xii. Each of these arguments provides valuable insight, but, in arguing for the importance of human movements and flows to explain the development of extralegal violent action, I do diverge somewhat from these earlier theses. Other scholars, like Stephen Leonard, Ken Gonzales-Day, Clive Webb, and William Carrigan, have explored regional and statewide patterns in violence through a slightly narrower lens. See Stephen J. Leonard, *Lynching in Colorado, 1859–1919* (Louisville, CO: University Press of Colorado, 2002); Ken Gonzales-Day, *Lynching in the West 1850–1935* (Durham, NC: Duke University Press, 2006); and William D. Carrigan and Clive Webb, *Forgotten Dead: Mob Violence against Mexicans in the United States, 1848–1928* (Oxford: Oxford University Press, 2013).

21. Patrick Hoehne, Riot Acts, https://www.riotacts.org/.
22. Waldrep, *The Many Faces of Judge Lynch*, 12.
23. Gilje, *Rioting in America*, 6.
24. Waldrep, *The Many Faces of Judge Lynch*, 17.
25. Senechal de la Roche identified four major manifestations of collective violence: lynching, rioting, vigilantism, and terrorism. See Roberta Senechal de la Roche, "Collective Violence as Social Control," *Sociological Forum* 11, no. 1 (March 1996): 97–128; and Roberta Senechal de la Roche, "Why is Collective Violence Collective?" *Sociological Theory* 19, no. 2 (July 2001): 126–44.
26. Gilje, *Rioting in America*, 4. Gilje's definition is as follows: "a riot is any group of twelve or more people attempting to assert their will immediately through the use of force outside the normal bounds of law."
27. Farah Peterson, "Constitutionalism in Unexpected Places," *Virginia Law Review* 106, no. 3 (May 2020): 559–609; and Pfeifer, *The Roots of Rough Justice*, 4.
28. See Larry D. Kramer, *The People Themselves: Popular Constitutionalism and Judicial Review* (Oxford: Oxford University Press, 2004), 8; and Christian G. Fritz, *American Sovereigns: The People and America's Constitutional Tradition Before the Civil War* (Cambridge: Cambridge University Press, 2008), 3.
29. David Grimsted notes that "the most distinctive trait of ante-bellum vigilante groups compared to <<mobs>> was this tendency to prate." David Grimsted,

"Né D'Hier: American Vigilantism, Communal Rebirth and Political Traditions," in *People and Power: Rights, Citizenship and Violence,* ed. Loretta
Valtz Mannucci (Milan: Grafiche Vadacca, 1992; brackets in the original), 79.
30. Waldrep, *The Many Faces of Judge Lynch,* 64.
31. Carol Kammen, *On Doing Local History* (Walnut Creek, CA: AltaMira Press,
    2003), 24.
32. The racial component of extralegal violence meant that violence against non-
    White actors took a more extreme form than the violence generally suffered
    by White victims. As Rushdy notes, enslaved victims of extralegal violence
    "seemed to suffer more grotesque lynchings than white victims, and often
    suffered immolation in a way that white victims simply did not." See Rushdy,
    American Lynching, 55. While not limited to the South, violence was most
    acute in slaveholding areas. In Mississippi, Joshua Rothman points out,
    extreme violence offered White slaveholders the "only reliable mechanism
    for enforcing control." See Joshua D. Rothman, *Flush Times & Fever Dreams:
    A Story of Capitalism and Slavery in the Age of Jackson* (Athens, GA: The Uni-
    versity of Georgia Press, 2012), 99.
33. Transcript of Record, Supreme Court of the United States, no. 117, 1870, *Baker
    v. Morton,* 79 U.S. 150. 12 Wall. 150, file date: December 6, 1869, 14; Joseph
    Barker, "American Reminiscences," *Barker's Review* 2, no. 38 (May 24, 1862),
    598; and Earl G. Curtis, "John Milton Thayer," *Nebraska History* 28, no. 4
    (October–December 1947): 228. See also Edgar S. Dudley, "Notes on the Early
    Military History of Nebraska," *Transactions and Reports, Nebraska State His-
    torical Society* 3 (1887): 189.
34. Gregory Ablavsky, *Federal Ground: Governing Property and Violence in the
    First U.S. Territories* (Oxford: Oxford University Press, 2021), 141.
35. Lucke, *The Bellevue War,* 42.

Chapter 1

1. William A. Warren, *The Bellevue Leader,* March 8, 1876, as printed in Lucke,
   The Bellevue War, 117. As an eyewitness participant and writer, Warren is a key
   source for this account. He is also a biased, unreliable narrator. His account is
   riddled with errors, contradictions, and discrepancies. Warren's writing also
   tends to treat Brown as the local root of all evil, and connects him to every real
   or imagined crime in Jackson County prior to 1840. Warren had to defend
   his role in the attack on Brown and had a motive to paint Brown as a villain. This analysis attempts to triangulate a more accurate understanding of
   Brown's actual activity by reading Warren's eyewitness account against the—
   admittedly still inflammatory and questionable—charges against Brown
   published by his enemies immediately following the attack. This material is
   then weighed against the reminiscences published by others such as Henrie
   and Wilson, the evidence left by Brown himself, and the broader collection
   of material concerning the other actors caught up in the action. This body of
   primary evidence is further leavened by the secondary historical literature.
   As a consequence, this account leaves out allegations and narratives that do

not make sense in the historical context, that do not align with the primary evidence, and that introduce new, sensational accusations against Brown decades after Warren, Cox, and members of their party published the "Statement of Facts" immediately following the Bellevue War.

2. William A. Warren, "A Warrant Issued for the Arrest of Brown and His Gang," *The Bellevue Leader*, February 9, 1876, in Lucke, *The Bellevue War*, 111.

3. "A Warrant Issued for the Arrest of Brown and His Gang."

4. Given the high number of fatalities alone, this lack of scholarly interest is surprising. Paul Gilje and David Grimsted both neglected the Bellevue War in their longitudinal studies of extralegal collective violence in the United States. See Gilje, *Rioting in America* and Grimsted, *American Mobbing 1828–1861*. Michael J. Pfeifer paid some brief attention to the Bellevue War in his own work, but his analysis largely aligned with the standard revisionist position. See Michael J. Pfeifer, "Law, Society, and Violence in the Antebellum Midwest: The 1857 Eastern Iowa Vigilante Movement," *Annals of Iowa* 64, no. 2 (Spring 2005): 149–51. Jonathan Obert referenced W. W. Brown in his work on violence in American politics but in doing so relied entirely on traditionalist sources and simply branded Brown as a criminal. See Jonathan Obert, *The Six-Shooter State: Public and Private Violence in American Politics* (Cambridge: Cambridge University Press, 2018), 77. Richard Maxwell Brown briefly references the Bellevue War in his study of vigilantism in the United States, but his analysis too remained uncritical of the traditionalist narrative of law overcoming frontier disorder. Brown identified the Bellevue War as one of the earliest episodes in what he deemed the "second wave" of American vigilantism but provided no further analysis of the incident. See Brown, *Strain of Violence*, 100. The most thorough study of the Bellevue War to date was written by Susan K. Lucke, a local historian and resident of Bellevue. Lucke painstakingly accumulated and reproduced the extant sources regarding the episode in her book, making her work undoubtedly the most valuable resource for those interested in the Bellevue War. Lucke's analysis was profoundly influenced by the traditionalist narrative.

5. The Bellevue War was not a genesis for this sequence of violence but was itself influenced by prior incidents of violence, as will be explored later in this chapter.

6. Lucke, *The Bellevue War*, 10.

7. There is some controversy over the prior residence of the Brown family. Some cite Elkhart, Indiana, and others Coldwater, Michigan. As Lucke notes, the two locations were not especially far apart. However, the Elkhart argument is more likely, given that Brown's network included known prior residents of Elkhart, like Thomas J. Babcock. Lucke, *The Bellevue War*, 42.

8. Lucke, *The Bellevue War*, 42.

9. *The Territorial Papers of the United States*, ed. John Porter Bloom (Washington, D.C.: US Government Printing Office, 1969), 27:120; and *The Bellevue War*, 42.

10. J. W. Ellis, "A. H. Wilson on the Bellevue War," in *Annals of Jackson County, Iowa* (Maquoketa, IA: The Jackson County Historical Society, 1906), 2:95. Joseph Henrie, who settled in Bellevue in 1835, gave a similar report. See J. W. Ellis, "Another Old Pioneer Gives Something of Interest," in *Annals of Jackson County, Iowa*, 2:78.

11. This language, appearing in the 1879 *History of Jackson County* was paraphrased from a no-longer extant article penned by William A. Warren in 1875. See *History of Jackson County, Iowa* (Chicago: Western Historical Company, 1879), 359; and Lucke, *The Bellevue War*, 61.

12. "Brown, William W." Jackson County Probate Records 1848–65, (Iowa City, IA: State Historical Society of Iowa), in "Iowa, County Marriages, 1838–1934," database, FamilySearch, https://familysearch.org/ark:/61903/3:1:9392-S5DL -8?cc=1805551&wc=M6TC-4NL%3A149396001 : 12 April 2016, 004707896 > image 1,216 of 1,559; county courthouses, Iowa. The Brown Probate files were seemingly mistakenly filed with later material, or else the material was improperly labeled. Lucke calculated the number to be $7,204.30, with $2,479.50 in "notes or balances with interest" and $4,724.80 in "open accounts." See Lucke, *The Bellevue War*, 43. My own count returned a total of $7,622.10, with $2,951.08 in the former category and $4,671.02 in the latter.

13. George K. Holmes, *Wages of Farm Labor. Nineteenth Investigation, in 1909, Continuing a Series That Began in 1866* (Washington: Government Printing Office, 1912), 18.

14. Lucke, *The Bellevue War*, 76.

15. Lucke, *The Bellevue War*, 48, 156.

16. William A. Warren, *Jackson Sentinel*, August 5, 1875, in Lucke, *The Bellevue War*, 90.

17. Ellis, "A. H. Wilson on the Bellevue War," 2:95; and Ellis, "Another Old Pioneer Gives Something of Interest," 2:78.

18. James Ellis, *History of Jackson County, Iowa* (Chicago: S. J. Clarke Publishing Co., 1910), 1:474.

19. These sums come from both loans with interest and open accounts. "Brown, William W." Jackson County Probate Records 1848–65. See also Lucke, *The Bellevue War*, 156–58.

20. Ellis, "Another Old Pioneer Gives Something of Interest," 78. Some of the residents who joined in on the attack on Brown's hotel would later claim to have long known that Brown was a criminal himself or in league with criminals. Brown's own account books, however, show no interruptions in normal trade immediately prior to the outbreak of violence. James C. Mitchell, for example, would later testify that Brown divulged his criminal activity to him on October 15, 1839. On October 21, 1839, though, records show Mitchell providing Brown with three loans totaling $230. This would have been a very questionable loan had Mitchell actually possessed any concrete evidence of Brown's criminality. See "Statement of Facts Connected with the Late Tragical Occurrence at Bellevue, I.T.," in *North Western Gazette and Galena*

Advertiser, May 1, 1840, in Lucke, *The Bellevue War,* 146; and Lucke's commentary in Lucke, *The Bellevue War,* 147.

21. Stephen Mihm, *A Nation of Counterfeiters: Capitalists, Con Men, and the Making of the United States* (Cambridge, MA: Harvard University Press, 2007), 199. For more on the Panic of 1837, see David Walker Howe, *What Hath God Wrought: The Transformation of America, 1815–1848* (Oxford: Oxford University Press, 2007), 502–8.

22. See *History of Johnson County, Iowa* (Iowa City: n.p., 1883), 208–12. See also Paul W. Black, "Lynchings in Iowa," *The Iowa Journal of History and Politics* 10, no. 2 (April 1912): 171.

23. Such networks and stations will be discussed at greater detail in the following chapter. For a good contemporary description of these operations, see J. Lamborn, *Illinois State Register,* Oct. 15, 1841. See also Obert, *The Six-Shooter State,* 75.

24. *History of Johnson County, Iowa,* 206–9.

25. William A. Warren, *Jackson Sentinel,* April 15, 1875, in Lucke, *The Bellevue War,* 66–68.

26. *Annals of Jackson County, Iowa,* 3:34.

27. "The trial of Samuel Groff," *Iowa News,* May 11, 1839.

28. "Much excitement," *North Western Gazette and Galena Advertiser,* May 17, 1839.

29. William A. Warren would decades later suggest that Brown played some role in this affair, but this accusation was not found among the claims against Brown published immediately following the attack on his hotel. J. W. Ellis, "Groff Commits Murder and Is Acquitted," in *Annals of Jackson County, Iowa,* 3:34–35; William A. Warren, "Mysteries of a Butcher Shop—A Pious Cattle Thief, etc.," *Jackson Sentinel,* Jun. 3, 10, 17, in Lucke, *The Bellevue War,* 76–83.

30. Cluse, "Confession of Samuel B. Cluse."

31. Kramer, *The People Themselves,* 199–200.

32. Kramer, *The People Themselves,* 200.

33. Peterson, "Constitutionalism in Unexpected Places," 559–609.

34. Pfeifer, *The Roots of Rough Justice,* 4.

35. Stuart Banner, *The Death Penalty: An American History* (Cambridge, MA: Harvard University Press, 2002), 131–32.

36. Pfeifer, *The Roots of Rough Justice,* 13–14.

37. Grund goes on to mock the sensibilities of "'the *learned* in the law'" while extolling the virtues of Lynch law. Francis Grund, *The Americans, in their Moral, Social, and Political Relations* (Boston: Marsh, Capen and Lyon, 1837), 180. It should be noted that Jackson himself denounced the "spirit of mob-law," even as he contributed to the rhetoric behind its rise. See Andrew Jackson to Amos Kendall, August 9, 1835.

38. Gilje, *Rioting in America,* 16.

39. Gilje, *Rioting in America,* 27.

40. Waldrep, *The Many Faces of Judge Lynch,* 29.

41. Waldrep, *The Many Faces of Judge Lynch*, 15–19.
42. Waldrep, *The Many Faces of Judge Lynch*, 25.
43. For more on Jacksonian rioting, see David Grimsted, "Rioting in its Jacksonian Setting," *The American Historical Review* 77, no. 2 (April 1972): 361–97; Carl E. Price, "The Great 'Riot Year': Jacksonian Democracy and Patterns of Violence in 1834," *Journal of the Early Republic* 5, no. 1 (Spring 1985): 1–19; Grimsted, *American Mobbing*, 3–32; Gilje, *Rioting in America*, 72–86; and Howe, *What Hath God Wrought*, 430–39.
44. Waldrep, *The Many Faces of Judge Lynch*, 33–35.
45. Pfeifer, *The Roots of Rough Justice*, 19.
46. "Mob and Murder in Alton, Illinois," *Vermont Phœnix*, November 24, 1837.
47. Patrick Hoehne, "'Murderous, Unwarrantable, and Very Cold': Mapping the Rise of Extralegal Killing in the United States, 1783–1865," *Journal of Digital History* 2 (2022), https://journalofdigitalhistory.org/en/article/8pGzPyTDKBjR?idx=74&layer=narrative.
48. Paul W. Black, "Lynchings in Iowa," 167–72.
49. Farmington residents arrested Babcock and others for counterfeiting sometime between 1839 and 1841. Accounts differ on the exact date of the arrest, but they are clear that suspicion began in 1839. It bears noting that Babcock would later lie and attempt to conceal his involvement in the Bellevue War in later testimony. See "Reports of Committee Appointed to Investigate Charges Against Col. T. J. Babcoke," in *Appendix to the House Journal of the Adjourned Session of the Twenty-Third General Assembly of the State of Missouri*, 627–832.
50. Ellis, "Another Old Pioneer Gives Something of Interest," in *Annals of Jackson County, Iowa*, 2:78.
51. *History of Jackson County*, 359.
52. Ellis, "A. H. Wilson on the Bellevue War," 2:95.
53. Ellis, "Another Old Pioneer Gives Something of Interest," 2:78; and Ellis, "A. H. Wilson on the Bellevue War," 2:95.
54. Harvey Reid, *Thomas Cox* (Iowa City: State Historical Society of Iowa, 1909), xi.
55. Lucke, *The Bellevue War*, 63.
56. Ellis, "A. H. Wilson on the Bellevue War," 96.
57. *Annals of Jackson County, Iowa*, 7:3.
58. *Annals of Jackson County, Iowa*, 2:61.
59. Ellis, *History of Jackson County, Iowa*, 1:445.
60. *History of Jackson County, Iowa*, 361.
61. *History of Jackson County, Iowa*, 361.
62. *History of Jackson County, Iowa*, 361.
63. Cox may have maintained an outwardly friendly disposition toward Brown, at least temporarily. Brown lent Cox $16.10 on July 31, 1839. See "Brown, William W." Jackson County Probate Records 1848–65.
64. "A Leaf from the Early History of Jackson County," *Maquoketa Excelsior*, September 6, 1879 in *Annals of Jackson County, Iowa*, 2:61.

65. Warren, *Jackson Sentinel,* April 15, 1875, in Lucke, *The Bellevue War,* 68.

66. Brown, *Strain of Violence,* 309.

67. William Newnham Blane, *An Excursion Through the United States and Canada During the Years 1822-23 by an English Gentleman* (London: Baldwin, Cradock, and Joy, 1824), 235.

68. "Bloody Business," *Illinois Gazette,* May 17, 1823.

69. The name of Dennis Collins is given by Warren in his later reminiscences, but not the name of his wife. It appears that the two Collinses who were assaulted in 1839 were the Dennis and Mary Collins appearing in the 1850 Census. The 1840 "Statement of Facts" lists the Collinses as living on Deep Creek. The 1850 Census shows the Collinses as inhabiting Fairfield Township, which is located on Deep Creek. If Mary was Dennis's wife at the time of the assault, she did indeed survive the ordeal. See US Census Bureau, *Free Inhabitants in Fairfield Township in the County of Jackson, State of Iowa,* 1850.

70. Lucke, *The Bellevue War,* 75.

71. Lucke, *The Bellevue War,* 52–53.

72. "Statement of Facts," *North Western Gazette and Galena Advertiser,* May 1, 1840.

73. "Statement of Facts."

74. Warren, in his later account, connects the harassment of Levi Brown to raids against Sand Prairie livestock in the winter of 1839–40, yet strangely does not explicitly draw a connection to the Donner case. Donner too lived in Sand Prairie, and he too had his cattle stolen that winter, but Warren discusses his case elsewhere. In the account that ends with the searching of Levi Brown's home, Warren instead mentions "The Messrs. Hunts, Peletts, and others" as victims of the theft. Donner may well have been one of these "others" in Warren's mind, and certainly was one in reality. See William A. Warren, *Jackson Sentinel,* September 2, 1875, in Lucke, *The Bellevue War,* 97.

75. According to the 1840 US Census, 172 free Black people resided in Iowa Territory. Additionally, sixteen enslaved people were recorded as living in Dubuque County. The total population of the territory at that time was, according to the census, 43,112. See US Census Bureau, *Compendium of the Enumeration of the Inhabitants and Statistics of the United States as Obtained at the Department of States, From the Returns of the Sixth Census* (Washington: Thomas Allen, 1841), 101–2. For the detail on the location of the Brown home, see William A. Warren, *Jackson Sentinel,* July 15, 1875, in Lucke, *The Bellevue War,* 87.

76. "Brown, William W." Jackson County Probate Records 1848–65.

77. *The Statute Laws of the Territory of Iowa* (Du Buque: Russel & Reeves, 1839), 404.

78. M. Scott Heerman, "'Reducing Free Men to Slavery': Black Kidnapping, the 'Slave Power,' and the Politics of Abolition in Antebellum Illinois, 1830–1860," *Journal of the Early Republic* 38, no. 2 (Summer 2018): 263.

79. White supremacy was a key facet of Jacksonian democracy. See Howe, *What Hath God Wrought,* 510.

80. Pfeifer claims that racial lynchings in the South began in the 1830s, if not earlier. See Pfeifer, *The Roots of Rough Justice*, 35.

81. "A Horrid Murder at Du Buque," *North Western Gazette and Territorial Advertiser*, September 11, 1840.

82. William A. Warren, "The Robbery of J. C. Mitchell's House by Thompson and His Confederates," *Jackson Sentinel*, November 4, 1875, in Lucke, *The Bellevue War*, 101.

83. Marian G. Miles, "The Founding Florence, Nebraska, 1854–1860," MA Thesis (University of Nebraska at Omaha, 1970), 57.

84. "Brown, William W." Jackson County Probate Records 1848–1865; and Lucke, *The Bellevue War*, 147.

85. "Trial of James C. Mitchell," *North Western Gazette and Territorial Advertiser*, July 3, 1840.

86. Lucke, *The Bellevue War*, 84; and Ellis, "Another Old Pioneer Gives Something of Interest," 79. One of the Samuel Burtises had also served on the Groff trial jury.

87. "Trial of James C. Mitchell."

88. "Trial of James C. Mitchell."

89. "Statement of Facts."

90. Brian P. Luskey, *On the Make: Clerks and the Quest for Capital in Nineteenth-Century America* (New York: New York University Press, 2010), 195. For more on the early history of rape in America, see Sharon Block, *Rape and Sexual Power in Early America* (Chapel Hill: The University of North Carolina Press, 2006).

91. "Statement of Facts."

92. "Trial of James C. Mitchell."

93. William A. Warren, "Bandits Attempt to Lynch Mitchell," *Bellevue Leader*, November 10, 1875, in Lucke, *The Bellevue War*, 104.

94. Ellis, "Another Old Pioneer Gives Something of Interest," 2:79.

95. "Historical Document," *Bellevue Leader*, December 7, 1911, in Lucke, *The Bellevue War*, 248.

96. "Statement of Facts."

97. Lucke, *The Bellevue War*.

98. Ellis, "Another Old Pioneer Gives Something of Interest," 2:79.

99. "A Warrant Issued for the Arrest of Brown and His Gang."

100. Ellis, "A. H. Wilson on the Bellevue War," 2:95.

101. "A Warrant Issued for the Arrest of Brown and His Gang;" and Harvey Reid, "The Bellevue War–A Review," in *Annals of Jackson County*, 2:85–92.

102. Ellis, "Another Old Pioneer Gives Something of Interest," 2:80.

103. William A. Warren, *The Bellevue Leader*, March 8, 1876, in Lucke, *The Bellevue War*, 114–17.

104. Ellis, "Another Old Pioneer Gives Something of Interest," 2:79.

105. Warren and Henrie agree on the misfire, but Warren, ever dramatic, claims that the ball went through Cox's coat. See "A Warrant Issued for the Arrest of Brown and His Gang;" and Ellis, "Another Old Pioneer Gives Something

of Interest," 2:79. Henrie claimed to be an eyewitness to the event, standing sixty-six feet from Brown's hotel when the fighting commenced.

106. There is controversy over who shot first and who killed Brown. The "Statement of Facts" claimed that Brown himself intentionally began the firefight. Warren and Henrie both claim misfire, but Warren says Brown's men shot first, while Henrie claims Cox and Warren's men immediately killed Brown. "A Warrant Issued for the Arrest of Brown and His Gang;" and Ellis, "Another Old Pioneer Gives Something of Interest," 2:79.

107. "A Warrant Issued for the Arrest of Brown and His Gang."

108. Henrie and Wilson both describe this attempted summary execution.

109. William A. Warren, *The Bellevue Leader,* March 8, 1876.

110. William A. Warren, *The Bellevue Leader,* March 8, 1876.

111. William A. Warren, *The Bellevue Leader,* March 8, 1876.

112. "Statement of Facts."

113. William A. Warren, *The Bellevue Leader,* March 8, 1876.

114. "Statement of Facts." This contradicts some of the details in Warren's later account, but the "Statement of Purpose," being published just a month after the violence, is given precedence here.

115. William A. Warren, *The Bellevue Leader,* March 8, 1876.

116. J. V. Berry to Robert Lucas, April 4, 1840, in Reid, *Thomas Cox,* 159.

117. John King to Robert Lucas, April 6, 1840, in Reid, *Thomas Cox,* 159–62.

118. "Resistance of Civil Authority in Jackson County. Great Loss of Life." *Iowa Territorial Gazette,* April 4, 1840.

119. "The Bellview Tragedy," *North Western Gazette and Galena Advertiser,* April 10, 1840.

120. Robert Lucas to J. V. Berry, April 7, 1840, in Reid, *Thomas Cox,* 162–63.

121. Ellis, "Another Old Pioneer Gives Something of Interest," 2:80.

122. Reid, *Thomas Cox,* 192.

123. Lucke, *The Bellevue War,* 158.

124. Lucke, *The Bellevue War,* 162.

125. Ellis, "A. H. Wilson on the Bellevue War," 2:96.

126. Peterson maintains that scholars should recognize the Boston Tea Party as a legal event. They should do the same with the Bellevue War and similar extralegal events. See Peterson, "Constitutionalism in Unexpected Places," 561.

Chapter 2

1. "Destruction of the New Court House at Oregon City," *The Illinois Free Trader,* April 2, 1841.

2. Ogle County Record Book A, Ogle County Courthouse, Oregon, Illinois, 270.

3. "Destruction of the New Court House at Oregon City."

4. Ogle County Record Book A, 330.

5. Ogle County Record Book A, 340.

6. Ogle County Record Book A, 359–60.

7. "Destruction of the New Court House at Oregon City."

8. J. F. Snyder "Governor Ford and his Family," *Journal of the Illinois State Historical Society* 3, no. 2 (July 1910): 45–51; and Usher F. Linder, *Reminiscences of the Early Bench and Bar of Illinois* (Chicago: The Chicago Legal News Company, 1879), 107.

9. Ford later denied making such statements, but given that his name appears repeatedly in multiple accounts of the subsequent regulator action as a facilitator of extralegal violence, the paper was most likely reporting the truth. See "Rock River Affairs," *The Illinois Gazette*, July 21, 1841.

10. Thomas Ford, *A History of Illinois, from its Commencement as a State in 1818 to 1847* (Chicago: S. C. Griggs & Co., 1854), 247.

11. This information regarding Ford's advice apparently came from Ralph Chaney, a lyncher. See Charles A. Church, *Past and Present of the City of Rockford and Winnebago County, Illinois* (Chicago: The S. J. Clarke Publishing Co., 1905), 41.

12. John Dean Caton, *Early Bench and Bar of Illinois* (Chicago: Chicago Legal News Company, 1893), 54; and Stuart Rulan Black, "How Governor Ford's Background, Choices, and Actions Influenced the Martyrdom of Joseph Smith in Carthage Jail," MA Thesis (Brigham Young University, 2020), 37.

13. Ford, *A History of Illinois*, 250.

14. *The History of Ogle County, Illinois* (Chicago: H. F. Kett & Co., 1878), 351; and Grimsted, "Né D'Hier," 81.

15. William Cullen Bryant, *Letters of a Traveller; or, Notes of Things Seen in Europe and America* (New York: George P. Putnam, 1851), 64.

16. *The History of Ogle County, Illinois*, 353; and Obert, *The Six-Shooter State*, 78.

17. "Astonishing Discoveries," *The Rockford Star*, Dec. 12, 1840.

18. "After all the rascally thief," *The Rockford Star*, Dec. 12, 1840.

19. "Jail," *The Rockford Star*, Feb. 27, 1841.

20. Ford, *A History of Illinois*, 247.

21. Obert, *The Six-Shooter State*, 85–95.

22. Obert, *The Six-Shooter State*, 13.

23. See Joyce Lee Malcom, *To Keep and Bear Arms: The Origins of an Anglo-American Right* (Cambridge, MA: Harvard University Press, 1994).

24. See Peterson, "Constitutionalism in Unexpected Places," 562.

25. Obert, *The Six-Shooter State*, 13.

26. Ford, *A History of Illinois*, 250.

27. "Horrible Proceedings," *Chicago American*, June 30, 1841, as printed in *Jeffersonian Republican*, July 28, 1841.

28. Henry L. Boies, *History of DeKalb County, Illinois* (Chicago: O. P. Bassett, 1868), 82.

29. *The History of Ogle County, Illinois*, 356; and "The Ogle County Volunteer Company," *The Rockford Star*, June 17, 1841. Pro-lyncher accounts often claim that Hearl joined the lynchers after his flogging, but his name does not appear in the list of 106 lynchers in the 1841 murder indictment.

30. *The History of Ogle County, Illinois*, 359.

31. Church, *Past and Present of the City of Rockford and Winnebago County,* 41.

32. "The Ogle County Volunteer Company," *The Rockford Star,* June 17, 1841.

33. Henry R. Boss, *Sketches of the Story of Ogle County, Ill. and the Early Settlement of the Northwest* (Polo, Il: Henry R. Boss, 1859), 58.

34. "The Ogle County Volunteer Company."

35. *The History of Ogle County, Illinois,* 339.

36. Ford, *A History of Illinois,* 245.

37. *The History of Ogle County, Illinois,* 341.

38. Obert, *The Six-Shooter State,* 96.

39. *The History of Ogle County, Illinois,* 352. For another account of John Driscoll's background and upbringing, see Ken Lizzio, *Pirates of the Prairie: Outlaws and Vigilantes in America's Heartland* (Guilford, CT: Lyons Press, 2018), 1–15.

40. See "Early Marriages in Jefferson County, Ohio, Found in Deed Book A," in *Early Records of Jefferson County, Ohio 1788–1851* (Steubenville, OH: Public Library of Steubenville and Jefferson County, 1999), 42. "Driscoll" is spelled in a variety of manners throughout different accounts. It has been written as Driskell, Driskall, Driscall, Driskil, and so on. This account, for the sake of clarity, will use "Driscoll" throughout. John's children Pierson, Sarah, and Mercy all appeared to have married Brodies, as did John's brother, William.

41. See Tax & Exoneration Lists, 1762–94. Series No. 4.61; Records of the Office of the Comptroller General, RG-4. Pennsylvania Historical & Museum Commission, Harrisburg, Pennsylvania. *Ancestry,* https://www.ancestry.com/family-tree/person/tree/75320502/person/34314463446/facts : 2011.

42. Slaughter, *The Whiskey Rebellion,* 11, 113.

43. "Appendix" in Alfred Creigh, *History of Washington County from its First Settlement to the Present Time* (Harrisburg, PA: B. Singerly, 1871), 108.

44. Columbiana County Marriage Records 1803–18, Volume 1. Columbiana County Courthouse. Retrieved from "Ohio, County Marriages, 1789–2016," database with images, FamilySearch, https://familysearch.org/ark:/61903/3:1:9392-S5ZM-X?cc=1614804&wc=ZR3D-GP8%3A121347301%2C121347302 : 15 July 2014.

45. See Wayne County Court of Common Pleas Journal (Columbus, OH: Ohio Historical Society, 1980), 1:40, 94, 235, 238, 283; and Wayne County Court of Common Pleas Appearance Dockett Journal (Columbus, OH: Ohio Historical Society, 1980), 1:17.

46. A. A. Graham, *History of Richland County, Ohio: Its Past and Present* (Mansfield, OH: A. A. Graham & Co., 1880), 240.

47. Ben Douglass, *History of Wayne County, Ohio, from the Days of the Pioneers and First Settlers to the Present Time* (Indianapolis, IN: Robert Douglass, 1878), 724.

48. William Newnham Blane, *An Excursion Through the United States and Canada During the Years 1822–23 by an English Gentleman* (London: Baldwin, Cradock, and Joy, 1824), 161.

49. James Flint, *Letters from America* (Edinburgh: W. & C. Tait, 1822), 114.

50. Elliot J. Gorn, "'Gouge and Bite, Pull Hair and Scratch': The Social Significance of Fighting in the Southern Backcountry," *The American Historical
Review* 90, no. 1 (Feb. 1985): 19.

51. Ryan L. Dearinger, "Violence, Masculinity, Image, and Reality on the Antebellum Frontier," *Indiana Magazine of History* 100, no. 1 (Mar. 2004): 40.

52. Wayne County Court of Common Pleas Journal (Columbus, OH: Ohio Historical Society, 1980), 3:315, 362.

53. On November 2, 1830, Brody was indicted for both larceny and stabbing with
intent to wound. Wayne County Court of Common Pleas Journal (Columbus, OH: Ohio Historical Society, 1980), 5:369, 382.

54. The Wayne Court of Common Pleas repeatedly continued the larceny indictment against Benjamin Wellington, alias Benjamin Worthington. This went
on from 1831 to at least through 1835.

55. Douglass, *History of Wayne County*, 723.

56. *Joseph Morrison v. The State of Ohio*, Supreme Court of Ohio, Dec. 1832, in
Condensed Reports of Decisions in the Supreme Court of Ohio, ed. P. B. Wilcox (Columbus, OH: I. N. Whiting, 1836), 275–76.

57. Wayne County Court of Common Pleas Journal (Columbus, OH: Ohio Historical Society, 1980) 5: 455, 504; and Wayne County Court of Common Pleas
Journal (Columbus, OH: Ohio Historical Society, 1980) 6: 5, 42, 115, 162, 214,
249, 442, 311, and 374.

58. Douglass, *History of Wayne County*, 723.

59. Graham, *History of Richland County*, 602.

60. Graham, *History of Richland County*, 605.

61. Wayne County Court of Common Pleas Journal, 5:81.

62. Wayne County Court of Common Pleas Journal, 5:125.

63. A. J. Baughman, *History of Ashland County, Ohio* (Chicago: The S.J. Clarke
Publishing Co., 1909), 118.

64. *The History of Ogle County, Illinois*, 350.

65. William A. Warren, *Jackson Sentinel*, July 15, 1875, in Lucke, *The Bellevue
War*, 87.

66. Boies, *History of DeKalb County*, 85.

67. *The Territorial Papers of the United States*, ed. John Porter Bloom (Wash-
ington, D.C.: US Government Printing Office, 1969), 27:209. That "Stephen
Brawdy" is the Stephen Brody in question is verified by the presence of David
Wilson. When the Brody family would later migrate to Linn and later Benton
Counties, Iowa Territory, they would be joined by none other than David
Wilson. See *The History of Benton County, Iowa* (Chicago: Western Historical
Company, 1878), 337.

68. Lizzio, *Pirates of the Prairie*, 24–25; *The History of Ogle County, Illinois*, 375;
Lewis M. Goss, *Past and Present of DeKalb County, Illinois* (Chicago: The
Pioneer Publishing Company, 1907), 1:129; and Luther Brewer and Barthin-
ius L. Wick, *History of Linn County Iowa* (Chicago: The Pioneer Publishing
Company, 1911), 1:46.

69. Hannah Brody's name is mistranscribed here as "Brady," but the original handwriting clearly reads "Brody." "Iowa, County Marriages, 1838–1934," database, FamilySearch, https://familysearch.org/ark:/61903/1:1:KC42–16L : 6 November 2017, James Leverich Jr. and Hannah Brady, February 19, 1842, Marion, Linn, Iowa, United States; citing reference, county courthouses, Iowa; FHL microfilm 1, 710, 786, accessed December 7, 2022, https://www.familysearch .org/ark:/61903/1:1:KC42–16L.

70. "Confession of Samuel B. Cluse."

71. *Acts and Resolutions Passed at Several Sessions of the Territorial Legislature of Iowa 1840–1846* (Des Moines, IA: Emory H. English, 1912), 49.

72. "Confession of Samuel B. Cluse."

73. Brewer and Wick, *History of Linn County Iowa*, 301.

74. Boss, *Sketches of the History of Ogle County, Ill.*, 58.

75. *The History of Ogle County, Illinois*, 362.

76. *The History of Ogle County, Illinois*, 83–84.

77. Goss, *Past and Present of DeKalb County, Illinois*, 1:67.

78. Boss, *Sketches of the History of Ogle County, Ill.*, 58; and *The History of Ogle County, Illinois*, 360.

79. *The History of Ogle County, Illinois*, 360.

80. Church, *Past and Present of the City of Rockford and Winnebago County*, 41.

81. *The History of Ogle County, Illinois*, 360.

82. *The History of Ogle County, Illinois*, 361.

83. See Boies, *History of DeKalb County*, 84.

84. Boies, *History of DeKalb County*, 85.

85. Isaac N. Arnold, *Reminiscences of the Illinois Bar Forty Years Ago: Lincoln and Douglas as Orators and Lawyers* (Chicago: Fergus Printing Company, 1881), 27.

86. Boies, *History of DeKalb County*, 85.

87. This account of the violence in northern Illinois is unique for the sympathetic treatment of William Driscoll in particular. It was undoubtedly written by a close associate of William Driscoll, or at the very least based on the account of one. This is supported by the author's knowledge of William's whereabouts in the settlement of Sycamore on the day of Campbell's death. See Boies, *History of DeKalb County*, 84. The Iowa connection was also made by contemporary newspaper accounts. See, for instance, "Rock River, June 30, 1841," *Lacon Illinois Gazette*, July 14, 1841.

88. See "Rock River, June 30, 1841;" and *The History of Ogle County, Illinois*, 362; and Boss, *Sketches of the History of Ogle County, Ill.*, 59; and Arnold, *Reminiscences of the Illinois Bar Forty Years Ago*, 27.

89. *The History of Ogle County, Illinois*, 361.

90. Church, *Past and Present of the City of Rockford and Winnebago County*, 42.

91. *The History of Ogle County, Illinois*, 363.

92. "Murder—Lynching of the murderers, &c." *The Illinois Free Trader*, July 9, 1841.

93. *The History of Ogle County, Illinois*, 364.

94. Arnold, *Reminiscences of the Illinois Bar Forty Years Ago*, 28.
95. "Murder—Lynching of the murderers, &c."
96. "Murder—Lynching of the murderers, &c."
97. The *History of DeKalb County* and *The History of Ogle County, Illinois* diverge on their accounts of the "trial." The Ogle account tends to paint the lynchers as orderly and professional, while the DeKalb account portrays them as more of a drunken mob.
98. "Murder—Lynching of the murderers, &c."
99. "Murder—Lynching of the murderers, &c." See Boies, *History of DeKalb County*, 92.
100. *The History of Ogle County, Illinois*, 366.
101. *The History of Ogle County, Illinois*, 366; and Boies, *History of DeKalb County*, 92.
102. Boies, *History of DeKalb County*, 92.
103. *The History of Ogle County, Illinois*, 366; and Boies, *History of DeKalb County*, 93; and "Illinois Lynch Law," *The Southport Telegraph*, July 20, 1841.
104. "Illinois Lynch Law."
105. This was Grimsted's contention. See Grimsted, "Né D'Hier: American Vigilantism, Communal Rebirth and Political Traditions," 85.
106. Boies, *History of DeKalb County*, 92.
107. Caton, *Early Bench and Bar of Illinois*, 99.
108. "Illinois Lynch Law."
109. "Horrible Proceedings."
110. "Horrible Proceedings."
111. "Illinois Lynch Law."
112. "Ogle County—Lynch Law," July 27, 1841.
113. *Peoria Register* as published in *Lacon Illinois Gazette*, July 21, 1841.
114. Most distant newspapers republished articles from the *Chicago American*. See "Lynch Law on Rock River," *Litchfield Enquirer*, July 22, 1841; "Lynch Law on Rock River," *Alexandria Gazette*, July 16, 1841; "Horrible Proceedings," *Chicago American*, June 30, 1841, as printed in *New-York Tribune*, July 13, 1841; "Horrible Proceedings," *Chicago American*, June 30, 1841, as printed in *The Middlebury People's Press*, July 20, 1841.
115. Most sources say that there were 112 men indicted for murder, but counting the names in the court records returns 106 defendants. Ogle County Record Book A, 411.
116. Ford, *A History of Illinois*, 249.
117. Ogle County Record Book A, 363.
118. Grimsted, "Né D'Hier: American Vigilantism, Communal Rebirth and Political Traditions," 84.
119. Caton, *Early Bench and Bar of Illinois*, 97.
120. "Lynchers," *The Southport Telegraph*, October 5, 1841.
121. Thomas Ford, "To the people of Illinois" *Peoria Register*, August 5, 1842; and Rodney O. Davis, "Judge Ford and the Regulators, 1841–1842," in *Selected*

Papers in Illinois History 1981, ed. Bruce D. Cody (Springfield, IL: Illinois State Historical Society, 1982), 31.

122. *The History of Ogle County, Illinois,* 379.

123. Caton, *Early Bench and Bar of Illinois,* 99.

124. A Spectator, "One Hundred and Twelve Men tried at the Ogle County Court for Murder," *The Illinois Free Trader,* October 1, 1841.

125. Caton, *Early Bench and Bar of Illinois,* 99.

126. Rebecca H. Kauffman, "Governor Thomas Ford in Ogle County," in *Transactions of the Illinois State Historical Society for the Year 1911* (Springfield, IL: Illinois State Journal Co., 1913), 16:110.

127. William Blackstone, *Commentaries on the Laws of England* (London: A. Strahan, 1800), 3:4.

128. Amor Legum, "The Rock River Tragedy," *The Illinois Free Trader,* October 8, 1841.

129. A Spectator, "One Hundred and Twelve Men tried at the Ogle County Court for Murder."

130. A Spectator, "The Rock River Affair," *The Illinois Free Trader,* October 15, 1841.

131. "The Rock River Affair," *The Illinois Free Trader,* October 22, 1841.

Chapter 3

1. John Francis Snyder, *Adam W. Snyder, and His Period in Illinois History, 1817–1842* (Virginia, IL: E. Needham, Bookseller and Stationer, 1906), 395; and Davis, "Judge Ford and the Regulators, 1841–1842," 31; and "Judge Ford—Public Opinion," *The Illinois Free Trader,* June 03, 1842.

2. The Church of Jesus Christ of Latter-day Saints has, since 2018, discouraged the use of the label "Mormon." Many historians who have written on Mormon history have continued, however, to use the term. See Benjamin E. Park, *Kingdom of Nauvoo: The Rise and Fall of a Religious Empire on the American Frontier* (New York: Liveright Publishing Corporation, 2020), 288. Spencer McBride wrote in his 2021 book that he used "'Mormons,' 'Latter-day Saints,' and 'Saints' interchangeably, just as church members of the 1830s and 1840s did." See Spencer W. McBride, *Joseph Smith for President: The Prophet, the Assassins, and the Fight for American Religious Freedom* (Oxford: Oxford University Press, 2021).

3. Stuart Rulan Black, who penned a 2020 master's thesis on Thomas Ford, argued that the governor's background within the formal legal system—including his actions as judge in 1841 Ogle County—had a profound impact on Ford's actions. Black argues that Ford, though a legalist at heart, would at times tolerate extralegal collective violence both out of necessity and because it allowed justice to be done even when the formal legal system was powerless. Black analyzes Ford's actions at Carthage critically, postulating that Ford's actions enabled the mob violence against Smith. This account builds on Black's analysis by providing a more detailed account of Ford and Smith's relationship between 1842 and 1844, with special attention paid to

both men's previous experiences with extralegal collective violence. It also diverges from Black's analysis of Ford's actions in Carthage. I do not agree that Ford was primarily guided by a love of law or justice. Rather, I argue that the governor came to view violence as inevitable and believed, because of his own past experience, that he was powerless to stop it. Fear and perceived pragmatism guided Ford. His choices, therefore, were structured around directing the flow of that violence to best manage the consequences. See Black, "How Governor Ford's Background, Choices, and Actions Influenced the Martyrdom of Joseph Smith in Carthage Jail." Grimsted similarly noted the connection between the killing of the Driscolls and the killing of the Smiths. Referencing the Carthage mob, he wrote that "if Ford was not in cahoots with this mob, he had a fatal propensity to take vigilante words at face value." See Grimsted, "Né D'Hier: American Vigilantism, Communal Rebirth and Political Traditions," 86.

4. "Democratic Candidate for Governor," *The Illinois Free Trader*, June 03, 1842.
5. Chicago Democrat, June 29, 1842, as quoted in Davis, "Judge Ford and the Regulators, 1841–1842," 31.
6. Davis, "Judge Ford and the Regulators, 1841–1842," 31.
7. "Judge Ford at Home," *Peoria Register*, July 29, 1842.
8. "Circular of Judge Ford to the People of the State of Illinois," *Peoria Register*, July 29, 1842.
9. Executive Order 44, October 27, 1838, Missouri Secretary of State Records and Archives, accessed August 31, 2022, https://www.sos.mo.gov/cmsimages /archives/resources/findingaids/miscMormRecs/eo/18381027_ExtermOrder .pdf.
10. Park, *Kingdom of Nauvoo*, 55.
11. "Mr. S. A. Douglass," *Quincy Whig*, July 2, 1842.
12. Park, *Kingdom of Nauvoo*, 80–81.
13. "The Question is Often Asked," *Quincy Whig*, July 16, 1842.
14. "Further Mormon Developments!!" *Sangamo Journal*, July 15, 1842.
15. Thomas Ford, "Circular of Judge Ford to the People of the State of Illinois," *Peoria Register*, July 29, 1842.
16. "Murder and Lynching," *Times and Seasons*, August 16, 1841.
17. "For the Whig," *Quincy Whig*, July 30, 1842.
18. Andrew M. Hedges, "Thomas Ford and Joseph Smith, 1842–1844," *Journal of Mormon History* 42, no. 4 (October 2016): 100; and Park, *Kingdom of Nauvoo*, 82.
19. Thomas Ford, "To the people of Illinois," *Peoria Register*, August 5, 1842.
20. *Journal of the Senate of the Thirteenth General Assembly of the State of Illinois at their Regular Session, Begun and Held at Springfield December 5, 1842* (Springfield, IL: William Walters, Public Printer, 1842), 44.
21. Vortex, "For the Wasp," *The Wasp*, May 26, 1842.
22. Hedges, "Thomas Ford and Joseph Smith," 101; and "Lilburn W. Boggs, Affidavit, 20 July 1842, William Clayton Copy [Extradition of JS for Accessory to Assault]," p. 6, The Joseph Smith Papers, accessed July 25, 2022, https://www

.josephsmithpapers.org/paper-summary/lilburn-w-boggs-affidavit-20-july-1842-william-clayton-copy-extradition-of-js-for-accessory-to-assault/1.

23. Park, *Kingdom of Nauvoo*, 127.

24. "Letter from Wilson Law, 17 August 1842," p. 171, The Joseph Smith Papers, accessed July 25, 2022, https://www.josephsmithpapers.org/paper-summary/letter-from-wilson-law-17-august-1842/1.

25. Park, *Kingdom of Nauvoo*, 128.

26. Park, *Kingdom of Nauvoo*, 129.

27. "Letter from Thomas Ford, 17 December 1842," p. 1, The Joseph Smith Papers, accessed July 25, 2022, https://www.josephsmithpapers.org/paper-summary/letter-from-thomas-ford-17-december-1842/1.

28. Hedges, "Thomas Ford and Joseph Smith, 1842–1844," 104.

29. "Letter to Justin Butterfield, 16 January 1843," p. 1, The Joseph Smith Papers, accessed July 25, 2022, https://www.josephsmithpapers.org/paper-summary/letter-to-justin-butterfield-16-january-1843/1.

30. Hedges, "Thomas Ford and Joseph Smith," 107.

31. "Journal, December 1842–June 1844; Book 2, 10 March 1843–14 July 1843," p. 289–90, The Joseph Smith Papers, accessed June 23, 2025, https://www.josephsmithpapers.org/paper-summary/journal-december-1842-june-1844-book-2-10-march-1843-14-july-1843/297.

32. "History, 1838–1856, volume E-1 [1 July 1843–30 April 1844]," p. 1,694, The Joseph Smith Papers, accessed June 23, 2025, https://www.josephsmithpapers.org/paper-summary/history-1838-1856-volume-e-1-1-july-1843-30-april-1844/66.

33. Hedges, "Thomas Ford and Joseph Smith," 111.

34. "History, 1838–1856, volume E-1 [1 July 1843–30 April 1844] [addenda]," p. 4–6 [addenda], The Joseph Smith Papers, accessed August 5, 2022, https://www.josephsmithpapers.org/paper-summary/history-1838-1856-volume-e-1-1-july-1843-30-april-1844/429.

35. "History, 1838–1856, volume E-1 [1 July 1843–30 April 1844] [addenda]," p. 6.

36. It is important to recognize that anti-Mormon bias amplified rumors and unfounded accusations, and as Bill Shepard correctly notes of the region's Mormons and non-Mormons, "the majority of people in both camps were law-abiding." Still, the very real problem of property rights violations and criminality that emanated from Nauvoo cannot be minimized. Organized bands of thieves did operate out of Nauvoo, and a criminal element certainly took advantage of the city to evade apprehension. Shepard, who maintains that "it is my sense there were fewer Mormon thieves proportionally in Nauvoo prior to the deaths of the Smiths than there were Gentile thieves in neighboring towns," still agrees that "stealing at pre-martyrdom Nauvoo was a serious problem." That such criminality went largely undetected by Mormon authorities is not evidence of a crime-free utopia, but speaks rather to the deficiencies of a Nauvoo legal system more attenuated to stymying potential persecution than criminality. See Kenneth W. Godfrey, "Crime and Punishment in Mormon Nauvoo, 1839–1846," *Brigham Young University Studies*

32, nos. 1/2 (Winter and Spring 1991): 195–227; and Bill Shepard, "Stealing at Mormon Nauvoo," The *John Whitmer Historical Association Journal* 23 (2203): 91–110.

37. "Edward Bonney," *The Columbia Democrat,* July 30, 1842. Mary Ann Clements, "Nauvoo Counterfeiting: Meet Edward Bonney," *Wheat and Tares,* July 27, 2021, accessed August 6, 2022, https://wheatandtares.org/2021/07/27/nauvoo-counterfeiting-meet-edward-bonney/.

38. Trumbull County Common Pleas Journal (Warren, OH: Trumbull County Court of Common Pleas, 1841–1842), 13: 445–47.

39. Trumbull County Common Pleas Journal, 13: 487–88.

40. Edward Bonney Requestion for Extradition, January 26, 1844, Indiana State Archives, Accession # 2007199, Box # 3, AAIS 40378.

41. Doris M. Reed, "Edward Bonney, Detective," *The Indiana University Bookman* 2 (1957): 8.

42. "Minutes and Discourse, 4 April 1844," p. 74, The Joseph Smith Papers, accessed August 10, 2022, https://www.josephsmithpapers.org/paper-summary/minutes-and-discourse-4-april-1844/1.

43. "Military Appointment of Edward Bonney, 18 June 1844," p. 1, The Joseph Smith Papers, accessed August 10, 2022, https://www.josephsmithpapers.org/paper-summary/military-appointment-of-edward-bonney-18-june-1844/1.

44. Shepard, "Stealing at Mormon Nauvoo," 95.

45. Mormons later insisted that Danite leader Sampson Avard had taught his men that "the riches of the Gentiles shall be consecrated to my people, the house of Israel; and thus you will waste away the Gentiles by robbing and plundering them of their property; and in this way we will build up the Kingdom of God." "History, 1838–1856, volume B-1 [1 September 1834–2 November 1838]," p. 843, The Joseph Smith Papers, accessed June 23, 2025, https://www.josephsmithpapers.org/paper-summary/history-1838-1856-volume-b-1-1-september-1834-2-november-1838/297.

46. "Journal, December 1842–June 1844; Book 2, 10 March 1843–14 July 1843," p. 62–65, The Joseph Smith Papers, accessed June 23, 2025, https://www.josephsmithpapers.org/paper-summary/journal-december-1842-june-1844-book-2-10-march-1843-14-july-1843/71.

47. See Alex D. Smith, "Untouchable: Joseph Smith's Use of the Law as a Catalyst for Assassination," *Journal of the Illinois State Historical Society* 112, no. 1 (Spring 2019): 8–42.

48. Park, *Kingdom of Nauvoo,* 179; and "Affidavit from Philander Avery, 20 December 1843, Willard Richards Copy," p. 1, The Joseph Smith Papers, accessed June 23, 2025, https://www.josephsmithpapers.org/paper-summary/affidavit-from-philander-avery-20-december-1843-thomas-bullock-copy/1.

49. Park, *Kingdom of Nauvoo,* 179; and Smith, "Untouchable," 21.

50. Hedges, "Thomas Ford and Joseph Smith," 117.

51. Ford, *A History of Illinois,* 320.

52. Hedges, "Thomas Ford and Joseph Smith," 117.

53. Hedges, "Thomas Ford and Joseph Smith," 117.

54. Thomas Ford, "Letter from Governor Ford in relation to our difficulties with the Mormons," *The Warsaw Signal*, February 14, 1844.

55. Park, *Kingdom of Nauvoo*, 223–24.

56. Park, *Kingdom of Nauvoo*, 178, 223–24.

57. Park, *Kingdom of Nauvoo*, 63.

58. Park, *Kingdom of Nauvoo*, 63.

59. McBride, *Joseph Smith for President*, 182.

60. "Preamble," "Affidavits," and "We have received the last number of the 'Warsaw Signal,'" *Nauvoo Expositor*, June 7, 1844.

61. Park, *Kingdom of Nauvoo*, 231.

62. "UNPARRALLED OUTRAGE AT NAUVOO," *The Warsaw Signal*, June 12, 1844.

63. Park, *Kingdom of Nauvoo*, 232.

64. Ford, *A History of Illinois*, 324.

65. Ford, *A History of Illinois*, 332.

66. "Letter from Thomas Ford, 21 June 1844," p. 1, The Joseph Smith Papers, accessed August 12, 2022, https://www.josephsmithpapers.org/paper-summary/letter-from-thomas-ford-21-june-1844/1.

67. "Letter from Thomas Ford, 22 June 1844," p. 6, The Joseph Smith Papers, accessed August 12, 2022, https://www.josephsmithpapers.org/paper-summary/letter-from-thomas-ford-22-june-1844/6 : 12 August 2022.

68. Park, *Kingdom of Nauvoo*, 234.

69. Ford, *A History of Illinois*, 338.

70. Dallin Harris Oaks and Marvin S. Hill, *The Carthage Conspiracy: The Trial of the Accused Assassins of Joseph Smith* (Urbana: University of Illinois Press, 1977), 18; and Eudocia Baldwin Marsh, "When the Mormons Dwelt Among Us," *The Bellman* 20, no. 507–8 (April 1916), 378.

71. Samuel Otho Williams to John Prickett, July 10, 1844, in *Cultures in Conflict: A Documentary History of the Mormon War in Illinois*, ed. John E. Hallwas and Roger D. Launius (Logan, UT: Utah State University Press, 1995), 222–26.

72. Samuel Otho Williams to John Prickett, July 10, 1844.

73. General Deming denied that an arrest order was ever issued. See M. R. Deming, "To the editor of the Warsaw Signal," *The Warsaw Signal*, July 10, 1844. Ford issued a similar denial in his history. See Ford, *A History of Illinois*, 343.

74. Ford, *A History of Illinois*, 338.

75. Oaks and Hill, *The Carthage Conspiracy*, 18.

76. Ford, *A History of Illinois*, 339.

77. Ford, *A History of Illinois*, 340.

78. Minor Deming to Stephen, Sarah, and Sarah Deming, June 26, 1844, University of Illinois Library Digital Collections, accessed June 23, 2025. https://digital.library.illinois.edu/items/6c1aed70-57fd-0137-6caa-02d0d7bfd6e4-8.

79. Samuel Otho Williams to John Prickett, July 10, 1844.

80. Minor Deming to Stephen, Sarah, and Sarah Deming, June 26, 1844.

81. Ford claimed that he left two companies in Nauvoo, but Eudocia Baldwin Marsh, an eyewitness, maintained that "there was but one company left at

Carthage. At least, all that afternoon there were no soldiers in sight but the Carthage Greys." See Marsh, "When the Mormons Dwelt Among Us," 378.

82. Ford, *A History of Illinois*, 342.

83. Ford, in his history, claims that Deming urged him to leave the Carthage Greys as the guard. Given Lieutenant Williams's account of the hostile behavior of the Carthaginians toward Deming even before Ford's arrival, the notion that Deming would advocate for the Greys is odd. Deming had also, on June 26, noted to his family the inexperienced and mutinous nature of the militia, identifying his own men as the greatest threat. Deming was long dead by the time Ford published his history. See Minor Deming to Stephen, Sarah, and Sarah Deming, June 26, 1844; and Ford, *A History of Illinois*, 344.

84. Marsh, "When the Mormons Dwelt Among Us," 378.

85. James W. Woods, "At the request of the friends of Joseph and Hyrum Smith," *Times and Seasons*, July 1, 1844.

86. Ford, *A History of Illinois*, 340; and Keith Huntress, "Governor Thomas Ford and the Murderers of Joseph Smith," *Dialogue* 4, no. 2 (1969): 49.

87. Ford, *A History of Illinois*, 344.

88. Black, "How Governor Ford's Background, Choices, and Actions Influenced the Martyrdom of Joseph Smith in Carthage Jail," 73.

89. Black, "How Governor Ford's Background, Choices, and Actions Influenced the Martyrdom of Joseph Smith in Carthage Jail," 78

90. Ford, *A History of Illinois*, 251.

91. Ford, *A History of Illinois*, 249.

92. Ford, *A History of Illinois*, 249.

93. *Cultures in Conflict: A Documentary History of the Mormon War in Illinois*, ed. John E. Hallwas and Roger D. Launius (Logan, UT: Utah State University Press, 1995), 203.

94. In his later *History*, Ford details his calculus regarding his military prospects. He was not confident that he could achieve any success in a limited campaign, much less a broader war. See Ford, *A History of Illinois*, 341.

95. Ford, *A History of Illinois*, 345.

96. Given his subsequent strong and shocked reaction to the killings, it is certain that the governor did not want any killing. It is difficult to determine precisely what outcome at the Carthage jail Ford anticipated when he left for Nauvoo. Given the governor's legal philosophy as judge and growing personal impatience with Joseph Smith, Ford might have hoped for the application of some form of nonlethal violence.

97. Ford, *A History of Illinois*, 346.

98. Samuel Otho Williams to John Prickett, July 10, 1844.

99. Ford, *A History of Illinois*, 346.

100. Minor Deming to Stephen, Sarah, and Sarah Deming, July 26, 1844, University of Illinois Library Digital Collections, accessed August 19, 2022.

101. Samuel Otho Williams to John Prickett, July 10, 1844.

102. William R. Hamilton, "A Youth's Recollection of the Smith Murders," in *Cultures in Conflict: A Documentary History of the Mormon War in Illinois*, ed.

John E. Hallwas and Roger D. Launius (Logan, UT: Utah State University Press, 1995), 228.

103. Hamilton, "A Youth's Recollection of the Smith Murders," 229.

104. Hamilton, "A Youth's Recollection of the Smith Murders," 229.

105. Marsh, "When the Mormons Dwelt Among Us," 402.

106. John Hay, "The Mormon Prophet's Tragedy," *The Atlantic Monthly* (Dec. 1869): 674.

107. George Rockwell to Thomas H. Rockwell, August 3, 1844, in *Cultures in Conflict: A Documentary History of the Mormon War in Illinois*, ed. John E. Hallwas and Roger D. Launius (Logan, UT: Utah State University Press, 1995), 234.

108. Ford, *A History of Illinois*, 353.

109. Hay, "The Mormon Prophet's Tragedy," 674.

110. Ford, *A History of Illinois*, 354.

111. Samuel Otho Williams to John Prickett, July 10, 1844.

112. Oaks and Hill, *The Carthage Conspiracy*, 21.

113. Samuel Otho Williams to John Prickett, July 10, 1844.

114. William R. Hamilton, "The Statement of William R. Hamilton," in *Historical Encyclopedia of Illinois and History of Hancock County*, ed. Newton Bateman, Paul Selby, and J. Seymour Currey (Chicago: Munsell Publishing Company, 1921), 845.

115. Ford, *A History of Illinois*, 347.

116. Ford, *A History of Illinois*, 348.

117. Ford, *A History of Illinois*, 349.

118. Marsh, "When the Mormons Dwelt Among Us," 403.

119. Samuel Otho Williams to John Prickett, July 10, 1844.

120. Marsh, "When the Mormons Dwelt Among Us," 403.

121. Ford, *A History of Illinois*, 351.

122. "Awful assassination of JOSEPH AND HYRUM SMITH!—The pledged faith of the state of Illinois stained with innocent blood by a Mob!" *Times and Seasons*, July 1, 1844.

123. Park, *Kingdom of Nauvoo*, 238.

124. "Awful assassination of JOSEPH AND HYRUM SMITH!"

125. Park, *Kingdom of Nauvoo*, 238.

126. "Awful assassination of JOSEPH AND HYRUM SMITH!"

127. Vilate Kimball to Herber C. Kimball, June 30, 1844, in *Cultures in Conflict: A Documentary History of the Mormon War in Illinois*, ed. John E. Hallwas and Roger D. Launius (Logan, UT: Utah State University Press, 1995), 216.

128. Ford, *A History of Illinois*, 354.

129. Thomas Ford, "To the People of the State of Illinois," *Times and Seasons*, July 1, 1844.

130. W. W. Phelps, "The Joseph/Hyrum Smith Funeral Sermon," ed. Richard Van-Wagoner and Steven C. Walker, *BYU Studies Quarterly* 23, no. 1 (1983): 17.

131. "Awful assassination of JOSEPH AND HYRUM SMITH!"

132. *History of the Church* (Salt Lake City, UT: Deseret News, 1912), 6:542.

133. Ford, *A History of Illinois*, 360.

134. Thomas Ford, "To the People of Warsaw, in Hancock County," *Nauvoo Neighbor*, July 31, 1844.

135. "The above communication from Governor Ford," *The Warsaw Signal*, July 31, 1844.

Chapter 4

1. "Execution of the Murderers of Col. Davenport," *Universalist Watchman and Christian Repository*, December 6, 1845.

2. See Bill Shepard, "The Notorious Hodges Brothers: Solving the Mystery of Their Destruction at Nauvoo," *The John Whitmer Historical Association Journal* 26 (2006): 260–86; and Bill Shepard, "The Tragedy of William Hodges," *The John Whitmer Historical Association Journal* 38, no. 1 (Spring/Summer 2018): 142–67.

3. "Council of Fifty, Minutes, March 1844–January 1846; Volume 1, 10 March 1844–1 March 1845," p. 74, The Joseph Smith Papers, accessed June 23, 2025, https://www.josephsmithpapers.org/paper-summary/council-of-fifty-minutes-march-1844-january-1846-volume-1-10-march-1844-1-march-1845/76; "Military Appointment of Edward Bonney, 18 June 1844," p. 1, The Joseph Smith Papers, accessed November 8, 2022, https://www.josephsmithpapers.org/paper-summary/military-appointment-of-edward-bonney-18-june-1844/1; and "Bonney, Edward William," The Joseph Smith Papers, accessed November 8, 2022, https://www.josephsmithpapers.org/person/edward-william-bonney.

4. Bonney is given as "Bonny" in the newspaper account, but I have corrected the spelling for clarity.

5. "Murder—Lynching of the Murderers, &c" *The Illinois Free Trader*, July 9, 1841.

6. In *The History of Ogle County*, the author mistakenly asserts that Bridge fled to the home of Redden in Marshall County. See *The History of Ogle County, Illinois* (Chicago: H. F. Kett & Co., 1878), 369. The Redden in question is undoubtedly Return Jackson Redden, who converted to Mormonism in 1841 and possessed his own ties to horse stealing networks. It was the Reeves family, however, not the Redden family, who lived in Marshall County. Return Jackson Redden is recorded as living in DeKalb County in 1842, and had married his wife, Laura Trask, in 1838 in McLean County. See Ancestry.com, *DeKalb County, Illinois, U.S., Land Records, 1838–1927*, Lehi, UT, USA: Ancestry.com Operations, Inc., 2021; and Ancestry.com, *Illinois, U.S., Compiled Marriages, 1791–1850*, Provo, UT, USA: Ancestry.com Operations Inc, 1997. Furthermore, an 1845 newspaper account identifies Reeves as the man who sheltered Bridge. See "More Developments," *The Ottawa Free Trader*, September 19, 1845.

7. Spencer Ellsworth, *Records of the Olden Time; or Fifty Years on the Prairies* (Lacon, IL: Home Journal Steam Printing Establishment, 1880), 532–53.

8. *The History of Ogle County, Illinois*, 369.
9. "More Developments," *The Ottawa Free Trader,* September 19, 1845.
10. Ellsworth, *Records of the Olden Time,* 533.
11. "The Old Settlers Picnic and Reunion at Lacon" *Henry Republican,* June 15, 1871; "Pioneerism," *Henry Republican,* August 24, 1876; and "The Old Settlers Picnic and Reunion at Lacon," *Henry Republican,* June 15, 1871, as published on "Marshall County Illinois Old Settler's Association Meetings," Illinois Genealogy Trails, geneaologytrails.com, accessed September 27, 2021, http://genealogytrails.com/ill/marshall/old_settlers_index.html.
12. Josiah Lamborn, "For the State Register," *Illinois State Register,* October 15, 1841.
13. Galena Illinois General Land Office, Certificate No. 8992, issued November 10, 1841.
14. A local newspaper would complain in 1843 that George Reeves "has always succeeded in evading conviction or even commitment or bail; except in a late instance he was held to bail for threatening to kill one of his neighbors." See "Greet Meeting—Expulsion of Geo. Reeve and Family—Arrest of Thieves," *Lacon Illinois Gazette,* June 24, 1843.
15. Mihm, *A Nation of Counterfeiters,* 199.
16. "The Times," *The Lacon Illinois Gazette,* February 13, 1841.
17. Ellsworth, *Records of the Olden Time,* 532.
18. Ellsworth, *Records of the Olden Time,* 182.
19. Ellsworth, *Records of the Olden Time,* 185.
20. Ashe County Records of Deeds Book V (Raleigh, N.C.: North Carolina Dept. of Archives and History, 1966), 268–69, FamilySearch, accessed September 21, 2022, https://www.familysearch.org/search/catalog/143704?availability=Family%20History%20Library; and Grayson County Deed Book 3 (Grayson Co., VA: Clerk of the Circuit Court), 59, FamilySearch, accessed September 21, 2022, https://www.familysearch.org/ark:/61903/3:1:3Q9M-CSKJ-M9YX-T?cat =401551. Descendants of the Reeves family have organized an effort to create a digital chronicle of the genealogical records of the family. That project, The Reeves Project, has been instrumental in tracing lineages and locating primary sources. For Polly Reeves, see "Reeves, Mary Ann 'Polly,'" The Reeves Project, accessed September 21, 2022, https://thereevesproject.org/data/tiki -index.php?page=Reeves_Mary_3171.
21. "Reeves, George," The Reeves Project, accessed September 21, 2022, https:// thereevesproject.org/data/tiki-index.php?page=Reeves_George_3331; and Bureau of the Census. Fourth Census of the United States, 1820. Washington, D.C.: National Archives and Records Administration, 1820. M33, 14, Ancestry, accessed September 21, 2022, https://www.ancestry.com/family-tree /person/tree/7045735/person/6944987501/facts?_phsrc=MLc63&_phstart =successSource.
22. "Reeves, George Sr.," The Reeves Project, accessed September 21, 2022, https:// thereevesproject.org/data/tiki-index.php?page=Reeves_George_Sr_3168. Reeves had his roots in Orange County, a hotbed for regulator action.

23. Arthur L. Fletcher, *Ashe County, a History* (Jefferson, N.C.: Ashe County Research Association, 1963), 18–19.

24. Minute Dockett of the Ashe County Superior Court, 1807–18 (Ashe, N.C.: Ashe County Superior Court) FamilySearch, accessed September 21, 2022, https://www.familysearch.org/search/film/008248476?cat=405596.

25. Minute Dockett of the Ashe County Superior Court, 1807–18.

26. Grayson County Superior Court Order Book, 1809–32 (Grayson, VA: Grayson County Clerk of the Circuit Court), 80, FamilySearch, accessed September 21, 2022, https://www.familysearch.org/search/film/008249403?i=5&cat=782338.

27. Vincennes Indiana General Land Office, Certificate No. 1357, issued April 10, 1829. See also Beverly Watson, "The Wayfarer—William Reeves of Ashe County," Reeves, Reaves, and More Rives: A Genealogy Blog for Researchers of the Surname Reeves in All of Its Flavors, usreeves.blogspot.com, accessed October 17, 2022, http://usreeves.blogspot.com/2012/11/the-wayfarer-william-reeves-of-ashe.html; and "Reeves, William," The Reeves Project, accessed December 10, 2022, https://thereevesproject.org/data/tiki-index.php?page=Reeves_William_3054.

28. US Census Bureau, Fifth Census of the United States, 1830, Greene, Indiana, p. 310, Ancestry, accessed September 21, 2022, https://www.ancestry.com/discoveryui-content/view/1778422:8058?tid=&pid=&queryId=0e7ada09904030692bfa0560c79b68d4&_phsrc=MLc108&_phstart=successSource.

29. *Counties of Clay and Owen, Indiana,* ed. Charles Blanchard (Chicago: F. A. Battey & Co., 1884), 583.

30. Grayson County Deed Book 3 (Grayson Co., VA: Clerk of the Circuit Court), 59, FamilySearch, accessed September 21, 2022, https://www.familysearch.org/ark:/61903/3:1:3Q9M-CSKJ-M9YX-T?cat=401551.

31. Minute Dockett of the Ashe County Superior Court, 1807–18.

32. *Counties of Clay and Owen,* Indiana, 742.

33. State Historical Society of Iowa; Des Moines, Iowa; Iowa Death Records, 1888–1904, Ancestry, accessed October 12, 2022, https://www.ancestry.com/discoveryui-content/view/750051918:61442; and "Indiana Marriages, 1811–2019," database with images, FamilySearch, https://www.familysearch.org/ark:/61903/1:1:XXJM-6VH : 3 August 2022 Phipps in entry for Washington Phipps and Elizabeth Griffith, citing Owen, Indiana, United States, Marriage Registration, Indiana Commission on Public Records, Indianapolis; FHL microfilm 004170562, accessed October 12, 2022.

34. US Census Bureau, "United States Census, 1850," database with images, FamilySearch, https://www.familysearch.org/ark:/61903/1:1:MHJ1–2KC : 19 December 2020, Jesse Long, Marion Township, Owen, Indiana, United States; citing family, NARA microfilm publication (Washington, D.C.: National Archives and Records Administration, n.d.), accessed October 12, 2022, and US Census Bureau, "United States Census, 1830," database with images, FamilySearch, https://familysearch.org/ark:/61903/1:1:XHPB-7RQ : 20 February 2021, Owen Long, Owen, Indiana, United States; citing 273, NARA

microfilm publication M19, (Washington, D.C.: National Archives and Records Administration, n.d.), roll 29; FHL microfilm 7,718, accessed October 12, 2022.

35. See Galena Illinois General Land Office, Certificate No. 8513, issued May 20, 1841; and Galena Illinois General Land Office, Certificate No. 8512, issued May 20, 1841.

36. Ellsworth, *Records of the Olden Time,* 532.

37. Ellsworth, *Records of the Olden Time,* 532.

38. "Biographical Notices," in *Transactions and Reports of the Nebraska State Historical Society* (Lincoln, NE: State Journal Company, 1892), 4: 270.

39. William Travis, *A History of Clay County, Indiana* (New York: The Lewis Publishing Company, 1909), 1: 235.

40. Ellsworth, *Records of the Olden Time,* 532.

41. Ellsworth, *Records of the Olden Time,* 184–85.

42. Edward Bonney, *The Banditti of the Prairies; or, The Murderer's Doom* (Philadelphia: T. B. Peterson and Brothers, 1855), 79.

43. *Counties of Clay and Owen, Indiana,* 742.

44. Howe, *What Hath God Wrought,* 504.

45. Bonney, *The Banditti of the Prairies,* 97.

46. Although the older and bolder John seems like the more likely Long present during the Bellevue War, for identification of the Long in question as Aaron Long, see *The History of Jackson County, Iowa,* 378. Newspaper articles as early as 1845 connect a Long with Brown.

47. US Census Bureau, "United States Census, 1830," database with images, FamilySearch, https://familysearch.org/ark:/61903/1:1:XHPB-M17 : 20 February 2021, John Fox, Washington, Wayne, Indiana, United States; citing 77, NARA microfilm publication M19, (Washington, D.C.: National Archives and Records Administration, n.d.), roll 29; FHL microfilm 7,718, accessed October 14, 2022.

48. "Life at the West—Extensive Organization of Murderers and Thieves," *New York Daily Herald,* October 12, 1845.

49. *The History of Jackson County, Iowa,* 403.

50. *Annals of Jackson County, Iowa,* 2:62.

51. "Execution of the Murderers of Col. Davenport," *Universalist Watchman and Christian Repository,* December 6, 1845.

52. "Gang of Counterfeiters and Robbers taken up," *The Atlas,* June 19, 1841.

53. *Counties of Clay and Owen, Indiana,* 742

54. Travis, *A History of Clay County, Indiana,* 1: 235.

55. *History of Crawford and Clark Counties, Illinois,* edited by William Henry Perrin (Chicago: O. L. Baskin & Co., 1883), 427.

56. *History of Crawford and Clark Counties, Illinois,* 427.

57. See Bonney, *The Banditti of the Prairies,* 77, 80, 151, 157, 195.

58. See Bonney, *The Banditti of the Prairies,* 59; and "Execution of the Murderers of Col. Davenport."

59. Bonney, *The Banditti of the Prairies,* 17.

60. Park, *Kingdom of Nauvoo*, 226.
61. Shepard, "Stealing at Mormon Nauvoo," 95.
62. "Execution of the Murderers of Col. Davenport."
63. Shepard, "The Notorious Hodges Brothers," 261–63.
64. Shepard, "The Notorious Hodges Brothers," 262; and Godfrey, "Crime and Punishment in Mormon Nauvoo, 1839–1846," 204–5.
65. Shepard, "The Notorious Hodges Brothers," 271.
66. *The History of Ogle County, Illinois*, 305.
67. Letta Brock Stone, *The West Family Register* (Washington, D.C.: W. F. Roberts Company, Inc., 1928), 297–98; and Clements, "Nauvoo Counterfeiting: Meet Edward Bonney."
68. I would like to thank historian Michael Leroy Oberg for generously helping to decipher the handwriting on that envelope. See "Brown, William W." Jackson County Probate Records 1848–65.
69. Ellsworth, *Records of the Olden Time*, 533.
70. "Execution of the Murderers of Col. Davenport."
71. Mihm, *A Nation of Counterfeiters*, 199.
72. "Burglary," *The Lacon Illinois Gazette*, May 27, 1843.
73. "Increase of Crime," *The Lacon Illinois Gazette*, June 10, 1843.
74. "Mr. Coutlett," *The Lacon Illinois Gazette*, June 24, 1842.
75. "STEALING," *The Lacon Illinois Gazette*, June 17, 1843.
76. Thomas Ford, "To the People of Illinois," *Peoria Register*, August 5, 1842.
77. "STEALING."
78. "GREAT MEETING—EXPULSION OF GEORGE REEVES AND FAMILY—ARREST OF THIEVES," *The Lacon Illinois Gazette*, June 24, 1842.
79. "GREAT MEETING—EXPULSION OF GEORGE REEVES AND FAMILY—ARREST OF THIEVES."
80. Robert Boal, "Reeves the Outlaw," *Henry Republican*, March 27, 1873.
81. Boal, "Reeves the Outlaw."
82. Boal, "Reeves the Outlaw."
83. "GREAT MEETING—EXPULSION OF GEORGE REEVES AND FAMILY—ARREST OF THIEVES."
84. Boal, "Reeves the Outlaw."
85. "GREAT MEETING—EXPULSION OF GEORGE REEVES AND FAMILY—ARREST OF THIEVES."
86. "The Season," *The Lacon Illinois Gazette*, June 10, 1843.
87. "Great Meeting," *The Lacon Illinois Gazette*, June 24, 1843. There is some confusion regarding who actually torched the Reeves home. Boal does not mention Elizabeth Reeves setting the fire in his account. As that was written some thirty years later, however, I will defer to the contemporary report of the affair, which insists that Elizabeth did indeed set the blaze.
88. "GREAT MEETING—EXPULSION OF GEORGE REEVES AND FAMILY—ARREST OF THIEVES" and Ellsworth, *Records of the Olden Time*, 534.
89. "GREAT MEETING—EXPULSION OF GEORGE REEVES AND FAMILY—ARREST OF THIEVES."

90. "GREAT MEETING—EXPULSION OF GEORGE REEVES AND FAMILY— ARREST OF THIEVES."

91. "GREAT MEETING—EXPULSION OF GEORGE REEVES AND FAMILY— ARREST OF THIEVES."

92. "ESCAPE OF REEVES AND ALLISON," *The Lacon Illinois Gazette,* July 1, 1843.

93. "ESCAPE OF REEVES AND ALLISON."

94. "GREAT MEETING—EXPULSION OF GEORGE REEVES AND FAMILY— ARREST OF THIEVES."

95. "For the Gazette," *The Lacon Illinois Gazette,* July 8, 1843.

96. It is possible that Bonney fabricated Royce and Bridge's continued cooperation with the New River men as a means of potentially eliminating witnesses to his own criminal past. Bonney, *Banditti of the Prairies,* 131, 138.

97. "A store at Rockford," *The Southport Telegraph,* October 3, 1843; and Frank E. Stevens, *History of Lee County Illinois* (Chicago: S. J. Clarke Publishing Company, 1914), 1:372.

98. This incident is likely the robbery referred to in "The mail stage," *Belleville Advocate,* October 26, 1843. See also Stevens, *History of Lee County Illinois,* 372.

99. "Execution of the Murderers of Col. Davenport."

100. William Clayton, *William Clayton's Journal* (Salt Lake City, UT: The Deseret News, 1921), 281.

101. "Trial Report, 19–21 June 1844 [State of Illinois v. JS et al. for Riot–B]," p. 1, The Joseph Smith Papers, accessed June 23, 2025, https://www.josephsmithpapers .org/paper-summary/trial-report-19-21-june-1844-state-of-illinois-v-js-et-al -for-riot-b/1.

102. "Execution of the Murderers of Col. Davenport." Long's reference to the "exasperation" of "the people," given the timeline of Bonney's subsequent fall from proverbial grace and departure from Nauvoo, indicates that Long was speaking in reference to the 1844 march on Nauvoo.

103. "Bonney, Edward William" The Joseph Smith Papers, accessed June 23, 2025, https://www.josephsmithpapers.org/person/edward-william-bonney.

104. For more on Young's rise to power, see Park, *Kingdom of Nauvoo,* 244–45.

105. Bonney, *Banditti of the Prairies,* 30.

106. "Execution of the Murderers of Col. Davenport."

107. "Pioneer Woman Tells the Truth," *The Gazette,* January 7, 1910.

108. J. M. Reid, *Sketches and Anecdotes of the Old Settler and New Comers, Mormon Bandits, and Danite Band* (Keokuk, IA: R. B. Ogden, 1876), 36.

109. Reid, *Sketches and Anecdotes,* 36.

110. Lee County Circuit Court, *The People vs. Adolphus Bliss* (Dixon, IL: Lee County Circuit Court, 1841) provided by Illinois Regional Archives Depository.

111. Bonney, *Banditti of the Prairies,* 15.

112. Shepard, "The Tragedy of William Hodges," 146.

113. Redden might have been present at the murder itself. See Shepard, "The Tragedy of William Hodges," 144–45.

114. "Execution of the Murderers of Col. Davenport."
115. Reid, *Sketches and Anecdotes*, 36.
116. Bonney, *The Banditti of the Prairies*, 30.
117. Bonney, *The Banditti of the Prairies*, 30.
118. Shepard, "The Notorious Hodges Brothers," 264.
119. John Taylor, "The John Taylor Nauvoo Journal: January 1845—September 1845," edited by Dean C. Jesse, *BYU Studies Quarterly* 23, no. 3 (Summer 1983): 48.
120. "The Iowa Murder," *The Nauvoo Neighbor*, May 21, 1845.
121. Bonney, *The Banditti of the Prairies*, 43. The actual court documents themselves are missing.
122. "Trial for Murder," *Burlington Hawk-Eye*, June 26, 1845; and Common Law Record C, Des Moines County Courthouse, Des Moines, Iowa, 447.
123. Taylor, "The John Taylor Nauvoo Journal," 53.
124. Bonney, *The Banditti of the Prairies*, 137.
125. Taylor, "The John Taylor Nauvoo Journal," 53; and Shepard, "The Notorious Hodges Brothers," 269.
126. Taylor, "The John Taylor Nauvoo Journal," 58.
127. Zina Diantha Huntington Jacobs, "'All Things Move in Order in the City': The Nauvoo Diary of Zina Diantha Huntington Jacobs," edited by Maureen Ursenbach Beecher, *BYU Studies Quarterly* 19, no. 3 (1979): 314.
128. Shepard, "The Notorious Hodges Brothers," 270; and "Irvine Hodges," *Warsaw Signal*, July 23, 1845.
129. "The Execution," *Burlington Hawk-Eye*, July 17, 1845.
130. "Fiendish Outrage," *Burlington Hawk-Eye*, July 10, 1845.
131. B., "Rock Island, July 8, 9 A.M.," *Illinois State Register*, July 25, 1845.
132. Timothy Mahoney, "'A Common Band of Brotherhood': Male Subcultures, the Booster Ethos, and the Origins of Urban Social Order in the Midwest of the 1840s," *Journal of Urban History* 25, no. 5 (July 1999): 623.
133. Bonney, *The Banditti of the Prairies*, 60.
134. "Astonishing Disclosers!" *The Ottawa Free Trader*, July 25, 1845.
135. "Pioneer Woman Tells the Truth," *The Gazette*.
136. Bonney, *The Banditti of the Prairies*, 98.
137. Bonney would claim that Fox bribed Johnson. Bonney, *The Banditti of the Prairies*, 183.
138. Bonney, *The Banditti of the Prairies*, 181.
139. Bonney, *The Banditti of the Prairies*, 193.
140. Bonney, *The Banditti of the Prairies*, 188, 195.
141. Bonney, *The Banditti of the Prairies*, 189.
142. Bonney, *The Banditti of the Prairies*, 205.
143. Bonney, *The Banditti of the Prairies*, 196.
144. *Appendix to the House Journal of the Adjourned Session of the Twenty-Third General Assembly of the State of Missouri*), 637. Heaight also appears as a prankish member of Keokuk's middle-class male subculture in Mahoney, "'A Common Band of Brotherhood,'" 639.
145. Bonney, *The Banditti of the Prairies*, 199.

146. "Outlaw John Long to be buried 133 years after being hanged," *The Decatur Daily Review,* July 14, 1978.

147. Bonney, *The Banditti of the Prairies,* 208.

148. Bonney, *The Banditti of the Prairies,* 205.

149. Bonney, *The Banditti of the Prairies,* 222.

150. *A Catalogue of the Everett D. Graff Collection of Western Americana,* edited by Colton Storm (Chicago: The University of Chicago Press, 1968), 348.

151. William Beckman, "An Interesting Letter from an Old Resident of Illinois," *Journal of the Illinois State Historical Society* 7 no. 1 (April 1914): 131; and Reed, "Edward Bonney, Detective," 12.

152. According to Bonney, Birch identified the handwriting as that of Hiram Long's. Bonney, *The Banditti of the Prairies,* 212–15.

153. Ford, *History of Illinois,* 411; and Hallwas and Launius, *Cultures in Conflict,* 245.

154. Susan Eaton Black et al., *Property Transactions in Nauvoo, Hancock County, Illinois and Surrounding Communities (1839–1859)* (Wilmington, DE: World Vital Records, Inc., 2006), 5: 3,041–3,046; and "The Phipps Twins at Nauvoo," Phipps Genealogy, accessed December 10, 2022, https://phippsgenealogy .wordpress.com/2017/09/29/the-phipps-twins-at-nauvoo/.

155. Thomas Ford, "Governor Ford Gets Involved," *Cultures in Conflict,* edited by Hallwas and Launius, 345–47.

156. *History of Crawford and Clark Counties, Illinois,* 430.

157. Travis, *A History of Clay County,* Indiana, 536.

158. Polk County Probate Court, Estate of Owen Long, filed November 16, 1846.

Chapter 5

1. Will Porter, *Annals of Polk County, Iowa, and City of Des Moines* (Des Moines, IA: Geo. A. Miller Printing Company, 1898), 507.

2. "James Phipps to Eliza Hart," September 15, 1847, Polk County Marriage Index A, Polk County Courthouse, 20.

3. A. J. Hoisington, "The Reeves War," in *History of Madison County, Iowa, and its People,* ed. Herman A. Mueller (Chicago: The S. J. Clarke Publishing Company, 1915), 1:134.

4. Hoisington, "The Reeves War," 134.

5. Hoisington, "The Reeves War," 134.

6. Hoisington, "The Reeves War," 134.

7. Sources disagree on both the impetus for this flight and which members of the family fled. Hoisington states that "all young men of the Reeves crowd" fled into the settlement, with the old men staying in their homesteads. He also states that the flight happened after the shooting. *The History of Polk County,* on the other hand, claims that the flight had already occurred following the initial vigilante threat, and that the entire family fled. See Hoisington, "The Reeves War," 135; and *The History of Polk County, Iowa* (Des Moines, IA: Union Historical Company, 1880), 518.

8. Hoisington, "The Reeves War," 135.

9. A few historians have written about extralegal violence in early Nebraska Territory. See James E. Potter, "Wearing the Hempen Neck-Tie: Lynching in Nebraska 1858–1919," *Nebraska History* 93 (2012); Sean M. Kammer, "'Public Opinion is More Than Law:' Popular Sovereignty and Vigilantism in the Nebraska Territory," *Great Plains Quarterly* 31, no. 4 (Fall 2011): 309–24; and Byron T. Parker, "Extra-Legal Law Enforcement on the Nebraska Frontier," MA Thesis (University of Nebraska, 1931). I diverge from previous approaches, however, in that I focus here on the human linkages that bound the violence in Nebraska to both prior and subsequent incidents of violence elsewhere.

10. Turner wrote: "The frontiersman was impatient of restraints. He knew how to preserve order, even in the absence of legal authority. If there were cattle thieves, lynch law was sudden and effective: the regulators of the Carolinas were the predecessors of the claims associations of Iowa and the vigilance committees of California. But the individual was not ready to submit to complex regulations." See Turner, *The Frontier in American History*, 212.

11. Hoisington, "The Reeves War," 134.

12. Hoisington, "The Reeves War," 135.

13. Ellsworth, *Records of the Olden Time*, 532.

14. J. M. Dixon, *Centennial History of Polk County, Iowa* (Des Moines: State Register, 1876), 24, 110, 317.

15. Hoisington, "The Reeves War," 135.

16. Dixon, *Centennial History of Polk County, Iowa*, 311.

17. Hoisington, "The Reeves War," 135.

18. *The History of Polk County, Iowa*, 519.

19. Hoisington, "The Reeves War," 135–36.

20. Hoisington, "The Reeves War," 136.

21. Hoisington, "The Reeves War," 136.

22. Hoisington, "The Reeves War," 137.

23. Hoisington, "The Reeves War," 137.

24. "Robinson v. Jones," in *Reports of Cases in the Supreme Court of Nebraska. September Term, 1890-January Term, 1891.* (Lincoln, NE: State Journal Company, 1892), 31:24.

25. The National Archives in Washington, D.C.; Record Group: Records of the Bureau of the Census; Record Group Number: 29; Series Number: M432; Residence Date: 1850; Home in 1850: Madison, Iowa; Roll: 187; Page: 152a, *Ancestry*, accessed January 9, 2023, https://www.ancestry.com/discoveryui-content/view/1425394:8054?tid=&pid=&queryId=245abe3168f84e7c908d31b833ee02c9&_phsrc=MLc123&_phstart=successSource.

26. "Robinson v. Jones," 26.

27. *History of Cass County, Iowa* (Springfield, IL: Continental Historical Company, 1884), 625.

28. See *History of Cass County, Iowa*, 834. Sources differ on the date of George Reeves's death. The *History of Cass County* locates the passing in 1855. Ellsworth, alternately, claims that George died in 1852. See Ellsworth, *Records of the Olden Time*, 535.

29. "Reeves, Joseph Cameron," The Reeves Project, accessed January 9, 2023, https://thereevesproject.org/data/tiki-index.php?page=Reeves_Cameron _3865; and the National Archives in Washington, D.C.; Record Group: Records of the Bureau of the Census; Record Group Number: 29; Series Number: M432; Residence Date: 1850; Home in 1850: Madison, Iowa; Roll: 187; Page: 152a, Ancestry, accessed January 9, 2023, https://www.ancestry.com/discoveryui -content/view/1425394:8054?tid=&pid=&queryId=245abe3168f84e7c908d3 1b833ee02c9&_phsrc=MLc123&_phstart=successSource; and the National Archives in Washington, D.C.; Record Group: Records of the Bureau of the Census; Record Group Number: 29; Series Number: M432; Residence Date: 1850; Home in 1850: Benton, Osage, Missouri; Roll: 408; Page: 452b, Ancestry, accessed January 9, 2022, https://www.ancestry.com/discoveryui-content/view /3954006:8054?tid=&pid=&queryId=a132343f16d97e994e91fd29d16c6a77& _phsrc=MLc126&_phstart=successSource.

30. John F. Dillon, *Cases Determined in the United States Circuit Courts for the Eighth Circuit* (Davenport, IA: Egbert, Fidlar, and Chambers, 1880), 5:549.

31. John Doyle Lee, *Journals of John D. Lee 1846–47 and 1859*, ed. Charles Kelly (Salt Lake City, UT: Western Printing Company, 1938), 141.

32. William G. Hartley, "Council Bluffs/Kanesville, Iowa: A Hub for Mormon Settlements, Operations, and Emigration, 1846–1852," *The John Whitmer Historical Association Journal* 25 (2006): 30.

33. Hartley, "Council Bluffs/Kanesville, Iowa: A Hub for Mormon Settlements, Operations, and Emigration, 1846–1852," 37.

34. Hartley, "Council Bluffs/Kanesville, Iowa," 17–47.

35. Jean Trumbo, "Orson Hyde's Frontier Guardian: A Mormon Editor Chronicles the Westward Movement Through Kanesville, Iowa," *Iowa Heritage Illustrated* 77, no. 2 (Summer 1996): 83; and Douglas C. McMurtrue, "The First Printing at Council Bluffs," *Annals of Iowa* 18, no. 1 (July 1931): 9.

36. "Alvarado C. Ford," *Palmer Journal*, November 16, 1850. See also Mihm, *A Nation of Counterfeiters*, 409.

37. Edward L. Kimball and Kenneth W. Godfrey, "Law and Order in Winter Quarters," *Journal of Mormon History* 32, no. 1 (Spring 2006): 197; and Norton Jacob, *The Record of Norton Jacob*, ed. C. Edward Jacob and Ruth Jacob (Salt Lake City, UT: The Norton Jacob Family Association, 1949), 35.

38. Kimball and Godfrey, "Law and Order in Winter Quarters," 197.

39. *History of Pottawattamie County, Iowa.* (Chicago: O. L. Baskin & Co., 1883), 102; and Black, "Lynchings in Iowa," 182–83; and Pfeifer, *The Roots of Rough Justice*, 99.

40. John D. Lee recorded "Allen, Wm. and T." as farmers at Summer Quarters. See John D. Lee, *Journals of John D. Lee*, 144.

41. *Omaha: The Gate City, and Douglas County Nebraska*, ed. Arthur C. Wakeley (Chicago: The S. J. Clarke Publishing Company, 1917), 1:75.

42. *Omaha: The Gate City*, 1:76.

43. "Robinson v. Jones," 22.

44. Kammer, "Public Opinion is More Than Law," 311.

45. *Omaha: The Gate City,* 1:77.

46. William Pleasant Snowden and Rachel Snowden settled in Nebraska in June 1854. In an 1897 interview, they gave the name of the jumper as "Van Saw," and noted that he ran a grocery in Council Bluffs. Sorenson gives his name as "Veanseau" and notes that he was French. Both Van Saw and Veanseau appear to be misspellings of "François." François Guittar had lived in the area since the 1820s and operated a general store in Council Bluffs. See Rachel Snowden and William Snowden, "W. P. Snowden and Wife Recall Many Incidents of Pioneer Days Here," *Sunday World-Herald,* September 12, 1897; and Alfred Sorenson, *The Story of Omaha from the Pioneer Days to the Present Time* (Omaha: National Printing Company, 1923), 115; and Benjamin F. Gue, *History of Iowa from the Earliest Times to the Beginning of the Twentieth Century* (New York City: The Century Historical Company, 1903), 4:114.

47. Gue, *History of Iowa,* 4:113.

48. Snowden and Snowden, "W. P. Snowden and Wife Recall Many Incidents of Pioneer Days Here."

49. Snowden and Snowden, "W. P. Snowden and Wife Recall Many Incidents of Pioneer Days Here."

50. Charles Collins, *Collins' Omaha Directory.* (Omaha: Charles Collins, 1866), 32.

51. J. Sterling Morton et al., *Illustrated History of Nebraska: A History of Nebraska from the Earliest Explorations of the Trans-Mississippi Region* (Lincoln, NE: Jacob North & Company, 1905), 1:231–32.

52. James M. Woolworth, *Nebraska in 1857* (New York: A. S. Barnes, 1857), 50.

53. Ilia Murtazashvili, *The Political Economy of the American Frontier* (Cambridge: Cambridge University Press, 2013), 2. They were, as Murtazashvili continues, both "bandits within the state" and "perhaps the most impressive examples of private-order specification and enforcement of property institutions in the political economic history of the United States, as well as one of the most important examples of rent-seeking organizations of the nineteenth century."

54. The signature reads "N. Reeves," but Lenoir went by Noah. See *The History of Polk County, Iowa,* 389.

55. Allan G. Bogue, "The Iowa Claim Clubs: Symbol and Substance," *The Mississippi Valley Historical Review* 45, no. 2 (Sept. 1958): 237.

56. Bogue, "The Iowa Claim Clubs," 253.

57. *History of Madison County, Iowa, and its People,* 1:132.

58. Miles, "The Founding of Florence, Nebraska, 1854–1860," 8.

59. *Annals of Jackson County Iowa,* 2:92.

60. "Elk Horn & Loup River Fork Ferry Bridge Company" in RG 1547 Mitchell, James C., History Nebraska.

61. Miles, "The Founding of Florence, Nebraska, 1854–1860," 11.

62. Miles, "The Founding of Florence, Nebraska, 1854–1860," 9.

63. Miles, "The Founding of Florence, Nebraska, 1854–1860," 60.

64. James B. Potts, "The Nebraska Capital Controversy, 1854–59," *Great Plains Quarterly* 8, no. 3 (Summer 1988): 173.

65. "The Governor—His Acts—Their Consequence," *Nebraska Palladium*, December 27, 1854; and Morton et al., *Illustrated History of Nebraska*, 1:182.

66. "The Governor—His Acts—Their Consequence."

67. Morton et al., *Illustrated History of Nebraska*, 1:186.

68. Thomas B. Cuming to Franklin Pierce, December 13, 1854, as quoted in Morton et al., *Illustrated History of Nebraska*, 1:186.

69. Sorenson, *The Story of Omaha From the Pioneer Days to the Present Time*, 39.

70. "Mitchell's Speech," *Nebraska Palladium*, January 10, 1855.

71. Woolworth, *Nebraska in 1857*, 18.

72. George L. Miller as quoted in Alfred Sorenson, *Early History of Omaha: Or, Walks and Talks Among the Old Settlers* (Omaha: The Daily Bee, 1876), 68.

73. Miller as quoted in Sorenson, *Early History of Omaha*, 68.

74. Miles, "The Founding of Florence, Nebraska, 1854–1860," 48.

75. Potts, "The Nebraska Capital Controversy, 1854–59," 173.

76. Alfred Sorenson, *History of Omaha from the Pioneer Days to the Present* (Omaha: Gibson, Miller, and Richardson, 1889), 57.

77. *Compendium of History Reminiscence and Biography of Western Nebraska* (Chicago: Alden Publishing Company, 1909), 63.

78. *Omaha: The Gate City*, 1:81.

79. Murtazashvili, *The Political Economy of the American Frontier*, 132.

80. Woolworth, *Nebraska in 1857*, 50.

81. "Murder of Hollister," *Nebraska Palladium*, April 11, 1855. For a longer analysis of the case, see Patrick Hoehne, "'In Union There is Strength': Claim Clubs, the Law, and the First Murder Case Brought to Court in the Nebraska Territory," *Great Plains Quarterly* 40, no. 4 (Fall 2020): 305–24.

82. "Threatening Excitement," *Nebraska Palladium*, April 11, 1855.

83. Albert Watkins, *History of Nebraska from the Earliest Explorations to the Present Time* (Lincoln, NE: Western Publishing and Engraving Company, 1913), 3:549–50.

84. This may also have been because they believed this son was the first White child born in Omaha. See "Reeves, William Nebraska," The Reeves Project, accessed February 7, 2023, https://thereevesproject.org/data/tiki-index.php?page=Reeves_William_Nebraska_4818.

85. Grenville M. Dodge, *Biography of Major General Grenville M. Dodge from 1831 to 1871 Written and Compiled by Himself at Different Times and Completed in 1914* (Des Moines: State Historical Society of Iowa, 1914), 26.

86. It is possibly relevant that Dodge had supported one of the Hollister brothers politically and was potentially happy to report on the humiliation of the Omaha settlers. Dodge, *Biography of Major General Grenville M. Dodge*, 22, 27.

87. Dudley, "Notes on the Early Military History of Nebraska," 189.

88. *Omaha: The Gate City*, 1:81; and James W. Savage and John T. Bell, *History of the City of Omaha Nebraska* (New York: Munsell & Company, 1894), 98.

89. Barker, "American Reminiscences," 598. See also Curtis, "John Milton Thayer," 228.

90. Homer H. Field and Joseph R. Reed, *History of Pottawattamie County, Iowa* (Chicago: The S. J. Clarke Publishing Co., 1907), 25.

91. John Rives, "Nebraska Contested Election," *Appendix to the Congressional Globe: Containing Speeches and Important State Papers, Etc., of the First Session, Thirty-Fourth Congress* (Washington, D.C.: John C. Rives, 1856), 964.

92. "From Nebraska," *Chronicle & Sentinel*, September 20, 1855.

93. "Fatal Affray at Calhoun," *Semi-Weekly Bugle*, September 4, 1855.

94. "Fatal Affray at Calhoun."

95. "Border Fighting," *National Intelligencer*, September 21, 1855. Newspapers refer to the Thompson in question merely as "Thompson." Theodore Thompson appeared on the list of votes cast in Florence in 1857, and with the papers identifying Thompson as a Florence resident, Theodore Thompson appears to be the identity of the combatant in question. See "Bird D. Chapman vs. Fenner Ferguson," Mis. Doc No. 5, 35th Congress, 1st Session, 40, in *A List of Reports to be Made to Congress During the First Session of the Thirty-Fifth Congress by Public Officers.* (Washington, D.C.: Cornelius Wendell, Printer, 1857).

96. "Squatter Claims in Nebraska," *Daily Missouri Republican*, September 24, 1855.

97. "Border Fighting."

98. "From Nebraska," *Chronicle & Sentinel*, September 20, 1855.

99. John Thomas Bell, *History of Washington County, Nebraska* (Omaha: The Herald Steam Book and Job Printing House, 1876): 32.

100. Dudley, "Notes on the Early Military History of Nebraska,"190.

101. My interest in the Henry–Hollister case was first sparked by Allison Buser's display at Omaha's Durham Museum. Buser collected many of the primary sources related to the trial for a temporary display and provided insightful written analysis. Allison Buser, "'Public Opinion is More Than Law:' The First Murder Brought to Court in the Nebraska Territory," Byron Reed Gallery, Durham Museum, Omaha, Nebraska.

102. Transcript of Record, *Baker v. Morton*, 12; and Douglas County Court Record, October 22, 1855, TEMP276, Byron Reed Collection, The Durham Museum. Allison Buser assembled these documents for public view as part of her exhibit at The Durham.

103. Sorenson, *History of Omaha*, 85.

104. Douglas County Court Record, October 24, 1855, TEMP274, Byron Reed Collection, The Durham Museum.

105. Douglas County Court Record, November 27, 1855, TEMP519, Byron Reed Collection, The Durham Museum.

106. Douglas County Court Record, December 1, 1855, TEMP273, Byron Reed Collection, The Durham Museum.

107. Kammer, "Public Opinion is More Than Law," 312.

108. "Meeting of the Omaha Claim Association," *The Nebraskian*, February 6, 1856.

109. "Stabbing Affray," *The Nebraskian*, February 6, 1856.

110. "Stabbing Affray." Reeves would win the election for sheriff.

111. Alexander Baker, in later testimony, specifically noted that the sheriff of Douglas County was a member of the Omaha Claim Club in his discussion of club power and influence. This knowledge, combined with what he knew about the strength and violence of the club, left Baker afraid and feeling helpless, and he surrendered his land to a club member. See Transcript of Record, *Baker v. Morton*, 24.

112. "Horse Thieves Caught," *The Nebraskian*, August 27, 1856.

113. "For the Nebraska Advertiser," *The Nebraska Advertiser*, September 6, 1856.

114. "More Horse Thieves," *The Nebraskian*, September 24, 1856.

115. "Claim Meeting," *The Nebraskian*, February 6, 1856.

116. "Claim Association Meeting," *The Nebraskian*, July 16, 1856.

117. Transcript of Record, *Baker v. Morton*, 14.

118. "Claim Jumping," *The Nebraskian*, May 21, 1856.

119. Sorenson, *History of Omaha*, 103.

120. "Claim Jumping."

121. "Claim Meeting," *The Nebraskian*, July 2, 1856.

122. "Correspondence of the Nebraska Advertiser," *The Nebraska Advertiser*, November 29, 1856.

123. Sorenson, *Early History of Omaha*, 115. A "W. Lee" ran advertisements for his Omaha barbershop in the Bellevue Gazette. See "W. Lee's," *Bellevue Gazette*, February 4, 1858.

124. Sorenson, *Early History of Omaha*, 116.

125. "Correspondence of the Advertiser," *The Nebraska Advertiser*, November 8, 1856.

126. "Notice to Pre-Emptors," *The Nebraska Advertiser*, February 5, 1857.

127. "The Squatters Meeting," *The Nebraskian*, February 25, 1857.

128. *Omaha: The Gate City*, 83.

129. John M. Newton to John B. Kellogg, February 24, 1857, John McConihe Papers, MS 308, Box 1, Folder 2, Archives and Special Collections, University of Nebraska–Lincoln Libraries.

130. Transcript of Record, Supreme Court of the United States, no. 270, *Shields et al., vs. Root*, file date: April 6, 1868, 158.

131. Transcript of Record, *Shields et al., vs. Root*, 158.

132. Transcript of Record, *Baker v. Morton*, 28, 32.

133. Sorenson, *Early History of Omaha*, 110.

134. Olive Gass, "The Vigilantes, Nebraska's First Defenders," *Nebraska History Magazine* 14, no. 1 (1933): 6–8.

135. "Minutes of Vigilance Committee, Florence, Nebraska, May 29-July 30, 1857," ed. Charles W. Shull, *Nebraska History* 58 (1977): 76–80.

136. In the words of *The Nebraskian*, the community was "called Gophertown, because the inhabitants thereof dwell in houses made in the ground, like unto the burrows of the gophers of the prairies." See "The True and Veracious History of the War between the citizens of the Town of Florence and the citizens of Gophertown," *The Nebraskian*, October 7, 1857.

137. "The True and Veracious History of the War between the citizens of the Town of Florence and the citizens of Gophertown."

138. Erastus F. Beadle, *Hams, Eggs, & Corn Cake: A Nebraska Territory Diary* (Lincoln, NE: University of Nebraska Press, 2001), 41.

139. Transcript of Record, *Baker v. Morton*, 52.

140. *Omaha: The Gate City*, 83.

141. Transcript of Record, *Baker v. Morton*, 30–31.

142. A. Deyo, "To the Public," *The Nebraskian*, March 11, 1857.

143. John McConihe to John B. Kellogg, August 2, 1857, John McConihe Papers, MS 308, Box 1, Folder 1, Archives and Special Collections, University of Nebraska–Lincoln Libraries.

144. Kammer, "Public Opinion is More Than Law," 320.

145. Transcript of Record, *Baker v. Morton*, 23–24.

146. Kammer, "Public Opinion is More Than Law," 320.

147. Transcript of Record, *Baker v. Morton*, 24.

148. Charles W. Calomiris and Larry Schweikert, "The Panic of 1857: Origins, Transmission, and Containment," *The Journal of Economic History* 51, no. 4 (Dec., 1991): 881.

149. Kammer, "Public Opinion is More Than Law," 319.

150. "Shocking Murder" *The Daily Milwaukee News*, January 19, 1859.

151. 1870; Census Place: Cass, Harrison, Iowa; Roll: M593_395; Page: 14A, from Ancestry.com. *1870 United States Federal Census* [database online]. Lehi, UT, USA: Ancestry.com Operations, Inc., 2009. Images reproduced by FamilySearch, accessed February 13, 2023, https://www.ancestry.com/discoveryui -content/view/21257232:7163?tid=&pid=&queryId=66c71d46387afbce23998962 82d7ca9c&_phsrc=MLc157&_phstart=successSource.

152. *The Latter-Day Saints Millennial Star,* edited by Franklin D. Richards (Liverpool: Franklin D. Richards, 1854) 16: 730; *The Nauvoo High Council Minute Books of the Church of Jesus Christ of Latter-Day Saints,* edited by Fred C. Collier (Hanna, UT: Collier's Publishing Co., 2005), 180; "United States Census, 1850," database with images, FamilySearch, https://familysearch.org /ark:/61903/3:1:S3HY-DRB7-1LR?cc=1401638&wc=95R8-BZ3%3A1031298601 %2C1031390201%2C1031390202, April 9 2016; Harvey Braden, 21 Aug 1853, in "Utah, Territorial Militia Records, 1849–1877," database with images, FamilySearch, https://familysearch.org/ark:/61903/1:1:Q231-PMH4; and Shepard, "The Tragedy of William Hodges," 144.

153. "Idaho, Southeast Counties Obituaries, 1864–2007," database with images, FamilySearch, https://familysearch.org/ark:/61903/3:1:3QS7-99V3-469P?cc =1876879 : 23 July 2014, > image 1 of 1; Idaho Falls Regional Family History Center, Idaho Falls.

154. *History of Dodge and Washington Counties, Nebraska, and Their People* (Chicago: The American Historical Society, 1921), 355.

155. "As Expected," *The Nebraskian*, March 17, 1859.

156. Woolworth, *Nebraska in 1857*, 19.

Chapter 6

1. "A. C. Ford Still Missing.—His Last Will and Testament.—A Most Remarkable Document," *The Western Mountaineer,* September 13, 1860.

2. "A Man Hung," *The Western Mountaineer,* September 6, 1860.

3. Wood's first name is also given as "Carl." Leonard, *Lynching in Colorado, 1859–1919,* 21–22; and "Postscript," *The Rocky Mountain News,* August 1, 1860.

4. "Notice," *The Rocky Mountain News,* August 31, 1860.

5. Leonard, *Lynching in Colorado,* 24.

6. "More of the Tragedy," *The Rocky Mountain News,* September 5, 1860.

7. "Local Matters," *The Rocky Mountain News,* September 5, 1860.

8. "Local Matters," *The Rocky Mountain News,* September 8, 1860; and "A. C. Ford," *The Rocky Mountain News,* October 29, 1860.

9. Patrick T. Hoehne, "'Murderous, Unwarrantable, and Very Cold': Mapping the Rise of Extralegal Collective Killing in the United States, 1783–1865" *Journal of Digital History* 2, (2022), https://journalofdigitalhistory.org/en/article/8pGzPyTDKBjR.

10. This sense of regional exceptionalism is pronounced in many retellings of vigilantism in the American West. The notion that the violence was tied primarily to local conditions, however, was part of a deliberate narrative first crafted to justify the actions of the vigilantes and later as a tool for promoting tourism and a sense of local identity. For examples of the first, see Nathaniel P. Langford, *Vigilante Days and Ways* (Chicago: A. C. McClurg & Co., 1912), xiv–xv; and Dimsdale, *The Vigilantes of Montana,* 6. For more on the later role of using the "vigilante legend" to encourage local tourism, see Arata, *Race and the Wild West.*

11. For more on the latticing legal system that existed in what is now Colorado, see also Darlene A. Cypser, "Myth of the Wild West: Law and Justice Prior to the Organization of the Territory of Colorado," MA Thesis (University of Colorado, 2017).

12. Richard Hogan, *Class and Community in Frontier Colorado* (Lawrence, KS: University Press of Kansas, 1990), 19.

13. "Meeting at Bellevue," *Bellevue Gazette,* February 26, 1857.

14. *History of Denver with Outlines of the Earlier History of the Rocky Mountain County,* edited by Jerome C. Smiley (Denver: The Denver Times, 1901), 213.

15. Leonard, *Lynching in Colorado,* 16.

16. Leonard, *Lynching in Colorado,* 16.

17. Hogan, *Class and Community in Frontier Colorado,* 20.

18. "Salutatory," *The Rocky Mountain News,* April 23, 1859.

19. Transcript of Record, *Shields et al., vs. Root,* 158.

20. *History of Denver,* 530.

21. Hogan, *Class and Community in Frontier Colorado,* 24–25.

22. "At a meeting," *The Rocky Mountain News,* August 13, 1859; and Cypser, "Myth of the Wild West," 68–69.

23. William H. H. Larimer, *Reminiscences of General William Larimer and of his Son William H. H. Larimer: Two of the Founders of Denver City,* edited by Herman S. Davis (Lancaster, PA: The New Era Printing Company, 1918), 148.

24. Leonard, *Lynching in Colorado,* 17.

25. Leonard, *Lynching in Colorado,* 20; and "Shooting Affair," *The Rocky Mountain News,* April 23, 1859.

26. Hogan, *Class and Community in Frontier Colorado,* 25.

27. "Horse Thieves," *The Rocky Mountain News,* May 14, 1859.

28. "Horse Thief," *The Rocky Mountain News,* May 28, 1859.

29. See more in Andrea G. McDowell, *We the Miners: Self-Government in the California Gold Rush* (Cambridge: Harvard University Press, 2022), 12.

30. Hogan, *Class and Community in Frontier Colorado,* 24.

31. "Local Items," *The Rocky Mountain News,* May 28, 1859.

32. "Local Items," *The Rocky Mountain News,* May 28, 1859.

33. "Caution," *The Rocky Mountain News,* June 18, 1859.

34. *Reports from Colorado: The Wildman Letters 1859–1865,* edited by LeRoy R. Hafen and Ann W. Hafen (Glendale, CA: The Arthur H. Clark Company, 1961), 39.

35. "Highwayman," *The Rocky Mountain News,* August 13, 1859.

36. "Full Particulars of the Late Lynching Case at Golden City," *The Rocky Mountain News,* September 10, 1859; and "For the Rocky Mountain News," *The Rocky Mountain News,* September 17, 1859.

37. *Reports from Colorado,* 59–60.

38. *Reports from Colorado,* 65–67.

39. "Theft," *The Rocky Mountain News,* September 17, 1859.

40. "Almost a Tragedy," *The Rocky Mountain News,* October 6, 1859.

41. "Fatal Affray," *The Rocky Mountain News,* October 27, 1859.

42. Hogan, *Class and Community in Frontier Colorado,* 27; and Leonard, *Lynching in Colorado,* 19. See also James Grafton Rogers, "The Beginnings of Law in Colorado," *Dicta* 36, no. 2 (March–April 1959): 114–15.

43. Hogan, *Class and Community in Frontier Colorado,* 27; and Leonard, *Lynching in Colorado,* 27.

44. Shull, "Minutes of Vigilance Committee, Florence, Nebraska, May 29–July 30, 1857," 80.

45. "Governor's Message," *The Rocky Mountain News,* November 10, 1859.

46. Hogan, *Class and Community in Frontier Colorado,* 27.

47. "Military," *The Rocky Mountain News,* February 8, 1860.

48. "Mountain City," *The Rocky Mountain News,* December 29, 1859.

49. "Exciting Times," *The Rocky Mountain News,* February 3, 1860.

50. "Exciting Times," *The Rocky Mountain News,* February 8, 1860.

51. "Local and Miscellaneous," *The Rocky Mountain News,* February 15, 1860; and Hogan, *Class and Community in Frontier Colorado,* 28.

52. "The Difficulty at Mountain City," *The Rocky Mountain News,* February 15, 1860.

53. "Mountain City."
54. "The Difficulty at Mountain City," and "Our Eastern Correspondence," *The Rocky Mountain News,* February 15, 1860.
55. "The Hanging of Pennsyl Tuck at Missouri City," *The Rocky Mountain News,* March 14, 1860; and "Mountain City Correspondence," March 7, 1860.
56. Leonard, *Lynching in Colorado,* 20–21.
57. "Three Day's News," *The Rocky Mountain News,* July 18, 1860. While most sources only give the victim's name as "Professor" Stark, an E. D. Stark advertised his services as a barber in Omaha, where the *News* reported that Stark had previously lived and worked. See "E. D. Stark," *The Omaha Nebraskian,* September 30, 1857.
58. "Death of Stark," *The Rocky Mountain News,* July 25, 1860.
59. Leonard, *Lynching in Colorado,* 21.
60. "A Modern Dick Turpin—Three Days in the Life of a Villain," *The Rocky Mountain News,* July 25, 1860; and "Revolting Tragedies," *The Western Mountaineer,* July 26, 1860.
61. "A Modern Dick Turpin—Three Days in the Life of a Villain."
62. "Horse Thieves Arrested," *The Rocky Mountain News,* July 25, 1860.
63. "Another Man Shot," *The Rocky Mountain News,* July 25, 1860.
64. "The last week," *The Western Mountaineer,* July 26, 1860.
65. "Vigilance Committee Organized—The Horse Thief Punished," *The Western Mountaineer,* July 26, 1860.
66. "Examination of Bates," *The Western Mountaineer,* July 26, 1860.
67. "Words of Caution," *The Rocky Mountain News,* July 25, 1860.
68. Edward Creighton may also have been present. See "Life in the American Gold Diggings," *Lloyd's Weekly London Newspaper,* September 2, 1860; "Attack Upon the 'News' Office!" *The Rocky Mountain News,* August 1, 1860; and "Another Week of Bloodshed," *The Western Mountaineer,* August 2, 1860.
69. "Attack Upon the 'News' Office!"
70. Henry L. Pitzer, *Three Frontiers: Memories, and a Portrait of Henry Little Pitzer as Recorded by his Son Robert Claiborne Pitzer,* Robert Claiborne Pitzer, ed. (Muscatine, IA: The Prairie Press, 1938), 103.
71. Alexander T. Rankin, *Alexander Taylor Rankin: His Diary and Letters,* edited by Nolie Mumey (Boulder, CO: Johnson Publishing Company, 1966), 86.
72. "Another Week of Bloodshed."
73. "Another Week of Bloodshed."
74. "Another Week of Bloodshed."
75. "Postscript," *The Rocky Mountain News,* August 1, 1860.
76. "Postscript."
77. "Postscript."
78. Rankin, *Alexander Taylor Rankin,* 87.
79. "Last Week's Troubles," *The Rocky Mountain News,* August 8, 1860.
80. "An Editorial Call," *The Western Mountaineer,* August 9, 1860.
81. "The Recent Trial," *The Western Mountaineer,* August 9, 1860.

82. "James A. Gordon Captured," *The Rocky Mountain News,* August 29, 1860.
83. "Shooting Affray," *The Rocky Mountain News,* August 31, 1860; and "Robbery," *The Rocky Mountain News,* August 31, 1860.
84. "Horse Stealings," *The Rocky Mountain News,* September 3, 1860; and *History of Denver,* 347.
85. "State Organization," *The Rocky Mountain News,* August 30, 1860.
86. "The Vigilance Committee," *The Western Mountaineer,* September 13, 1860; and *History of Denver,* 347.
87. Pitzer, *Three Frontiers,* 73.
88. Pitzer, *Three Frontiers,* 98.
89. Pitzer, *Three Frontiers,* 103.
90. Denver historian Jerome C. Smiley and those who quoted him refer to this victim only by the nickname of "Black Hawk." As both were allegedly arrested on September 1 and gave damning confessions, it is possible that "Black Hawk" was the John B. Bishop referenced in the contemporary press. Still, a John Bishop was later lynched in Apex for livestock stealing in 1861, and this may also have been the John B. Bishop mentioned here.
91. "Horse Stealings."
92. Leonard, *Lynching in Colorado,* 22; and *History of Denver,* 347.
93. "The Vigilance Committee."
94. Rankin, *Alexander Taylor Rankin,* 100.
95. "From Pike's Peak," *The New York Times,* September 20, 1860.
96. "A Man Hung."
97. "John Shear," *The Rocky Mountain News,* September 5, 1860; and "More on the Tragedy."
98. Rankin, *Alexander Taylor Rankin,* 100.
99. "John Shear."
100. Pitzer does mistakenly refer to the vigilance committee as the people's court. Pitzer, *Three Frontiers,* 102; and Leonard, *Lynching in Colorado,* 23.
101. "A Card," *The Rocky Mountain News,* November 27, 1861.
102. Pitzer, *Three Frontiers,* 102.
103. Hogan, *Class and Community in Frontier Colorado,* 31.
104. Hogan, *Class and Community in Frontier Colorado,* 31–32.
105. "That Meeting," *The Rocky Mountain News,* September 11, 1860.
106. "Local Matters, *The Rocky Mountain News,* September 15, 1860.
107. See "Local Matters," *The Rocky Mountain News,* September 11, 1860; "Attempt at Highway Robbery," *The Rocky Mountain News,* September 11, 1860; and "More Thieves," *The Rocky Mountain News,* September 12, 1860.
108. "The Vigilance Committee."
109. Rankin, *Alexander Taylor Rankin,* 101.
110. Leonard, *Lynching in Colorado,* 24.
111. Leonard, *Lynching in Colorado,* 25.
112. "Jocular, but Unjust," *The Western Mountaineer,* November 1, 1860.
113. Untitled Typescript Document by John A. Nye, p. 2, Box 5, Fldr 8, MC 53, Wilbur Fisk Sanders Papers, MHS.

114. Mark C. Dillon, *The Montana Vigilantes 1863–1870: Gold, Guns, & Gallows* (Logan: Utah State Univ. Press, 2013), 156.

115. Much of this section was first submitted to *Montana The Magazine of Western History*. See Patrick T. Hoehne, "Apostles of Disorder: Montana Merchants, Vigilantes, and the Interconnectivity of Extralegal Collective Violence," *Montana* 72, no. 3 (Autumn 2022).

116. Influential early accounts, like those by Langford and Dimsdale, advanced a romanticized and distorted depiction of the vigilantes and their violence. These writers presented the action of 1863 and 1864 as a morality tale, with the vigilantes playing the champions of order and justice. These early accounts insisted that the vigilantism in territorial Montana was a consequence of the exceptionalism of that time and place. It was Montana's supposedly peculiar attributes—the allure of gold and the rough, isolated mining camps nestled in the mountains—that shaped the contours of the violence. See Langford, *Vigilante Days and Ways* and Dimsdale, *The Vigilantes of Montana*. R. E. Mather and F. E. Boswell challenged such depictions of Plummer in their 1998 *Hanging the Sheriff: A Biography of Henry Plummer*. The authors argued for the sheriff's good character and innocence, maintaining that Plummer's "downfall is therefore a true tragedy in the literary sense of the word, brought on mainly by his being too tolerant for his times." See R. E. Mather and F. E. Boswell, *Hanging the Sheriff: A Biography of Henry Plummer* (Missoula, MT: Historic Montana Publishing, 1998), 185. While Mather and Boswell's assertion that Plummer was innocent has not taken root in the recent literature, the scholars' more critical assessment of the vigilantes has proven influential.

117. The vigilante action that took place during the winter of 1863–64 technically occurred within the political container of Idaho Territory. For the sake of clarity, though, this chapter uses "Montana" to refer to the region as it is now known.

118. Frederick Allen, *A Decent Orderly Lynching: The Montana Vigilantes* (Norman: University of Oklahoma Press, 2004), 6–9; and Dillon, *The Montana Vigilantes*, 1–11.

119. "It is pleasant to behold," *Bellevue Gazette*, April 30, 1857.

120. *History of Denver*, 231–32.

121. Thomas Conrad relayed such anxieties to his wife in 1864, when he arrived in Montana before his goods did. "There are rumors of indian troubles in the neighborhood where our goods must have been," he wrote from Virginia City, "and we are fearful that some truth may attach to the rumor." Thomas Conrad to Mary Conrad, Aug. 7, 1864, MC 30 Box 1, Thomas Conrad Papers, MHS. For more on the dramatic impact that bad weather could have on freighting and commodity prices, see Harrison A. Trexler, *Flour and Wheat in the Montana Gold Camps, 1862–1870* (Missoula, MT: Dunstan, 1918), 4–6.

122. Aaron T. Ford, Life and History of A. T. Ford, p. 7, SC 702, MHS.

123. Robert Kirkpatrick, "From Wisconsin to Montana and Life in the West, 1863–1889: The Reminiscences of Robert Kirkpatrick," ed. Michael Gee McLatchey, (M.A. thesis, Montana State University, 1961), 85.

124. *Seventeenth Annual Report of the Bureau of Labor Statistics to the 71st General Assembly of the State of Ohio for the Year 1893* (Norwalk, OH: The Laning Printing Co., State Printers, 1894), 807.

125. Mary Wright Edgerton to Martha Wright Carter, Nov. 29, 1863, fldr 5, MC 26, Sidney Edgerton Papers, MHS.

126. Mary Wright Edgerton to Martha Wright Carter, Jan. 1, 1864, fldr 5, MC 26, Sidney Edgerton Papers, MHS.

127. Kirkpatrick, "From Wisconsin to Montana and Life in the West, 1863–1889," 85.

128. Untitled Document by Wilbur Fisk Sanders, p. 9, MC 53, Box 5, Folder 3, Wilbur Fisk Sanders Papers, MHS.

129. Kirkpatrick, "From Wisconsin to Montana and Life in the West, 1863–1889," 83.

130. Untitled Document by Wilbur Fisk Sanders, p. 9, MC 53, Box 5, Folder 3, Wilbur Fisk Sanders Papers, MHS.

131. Thomas Conrad to Mary Conrad, Feb. 12, 1865, MC 30 Box 1, Thomas Conrad Papers, MHS.

132. Kirkpatrick, "From Wisconsin to Montana and Life in the West, 1863–1889," 84.

133. Thomas Conrad to Mary Conrad, Jul. 23, 1864, MC 30 Box 1, Thomas Conrad Papers, MHS.

134. Alton B. Oviatt, "Steamboat Traffic on the Upper Missouri River, 1859–1869," *Pacific Northwest Quarterly* 40, no. 2 (April 1949): 93.

135. Such disputes were widespread, and even implicated future vigilantes like George Copley, whom Morley suspected in January 1863 of preparing to jump one of his claims. James Henry Morley, *Diary of James Henry Morley in Montana, 1862–1865*, SC 533, MHS, 48, 73.

136. Virginia City or Varina Idaho Territory December 15, 1863, by Wilbur Fisk Sanders, p. 2, MC 53, Box 5, Folder 8, Wilbur Fisk Sanders Papers, MHS.

137. Kirkpatrick, "From Wisconsin to Montana and Life in the West, 1863–1889," 85. Overland commerce, according to historian Alton B. Oviatt, initially flowed into Montana from the already-established trade routes from Omaha and St. Joseph to Salt Lake City. See Alton B. Oviatt, "Pacific Coast Competition for the Gold Camp Trade of Montana," *Pacific Northwest Quarterly* 56, no. 4 (October 1965): 168. Additionally, the pack trains from Portland and Walla Walla and steamboats from St. Louis serviced the camps. Trade via steamboat, however, only accounted for a small share of commerce in the first half of the 1860s, and according to Oviatt steamboats, only transported 2,100 tons of freight into Montana between 1859 and 1865. See Oviatt, "Steamboat Traffic on the Upper Missouri River, 1859–1869," 94. With no local agricultural or manufacturing sector to support the swelling mining towns, settlers were then forced to rely on the overland trade for provisions. This reliance contributed to the high prices experienced by Kirkpatrick and others. Historian Harrison A. Trexler highlighted the "tedious and dangerous" nature of freighting, the "lack of competition," and the Civil War as

factors that contributed to extremely high prices of staple goods in the mining camps. See Trexler, *Flour and Wheat in the Montana Gold Camps*, 4–6. This total reliance on freighting left consumers vulnerable to shortages and sudden price fluctuations. These issues manifested most dramatically in the spring of 1865, when snow prevented freighters from reaching the Montanan settlements. The price of flour skyrocketed, prompting a "flour riot" in which almost five hundred armed men scoured the town for hoarded flour. The rioters targeted the stores of the merchants who had attempted to sell the flour at massively inflated prices, including vigilante leader John Creighton. The vigilantes, though, did not respond to this violation of merchant property rights, perhaps on account of the popular support enjoyed by the rioters. See W. M. Underhill, "Historic Bread Riot in Virginia City," *The Washington Historical Quarterly* 21:3 (Jul. 1930): 189–94.

138. Correspondence from Mary Wright Edgerton to Martha Wright Carter, Dec. 27, 1863, MC 26, Folder 5, Sidney Edgerton Papers, MHS.

139. Dillon, *The Montana Vigilantes 1863–1870*, 60–74.

140. *Org of the Com. 1903 in Historical Writings* by Wilbur Fisk Sanders, p. 1, MC 53, Box 5, Folder 2, Wilbur Fisk Sanders Papers, MHS.

141. *Handwritten Biographical Sketch Revised by J. A. Hosmer*, p. 4, SC 104, Hezekiah L. Hosmer Papers, MHS.

142. One of the strangest discrepancies in accounts of the formation of the vigilance committee is the minimization or erasure of the very prominent role played by John A. Creighton. Both Nye and Sanders identify Creighton as a founding member of the committee. Sanders repeatedly references Creighton and stresses his importance. Pfouts, strangely, does not mention Creighton in his account. See Paris Swazy Pfouts, *Four Firsts for a Modest Hero: The Autobiography of Paris Swazy Pfouts*, ed. Harold Axford (Portland: Dunham Printing Company, 1968), 98. Dimsdale and Langford similarly fail to note Creighton's contributions. The reasons for this are difficult to determine, but it is possible that Creighton himself wished to avoid advertising his involvement in published material. This chapter leans on Sanders's and Nye's eyewitness accounts. *Org of the Com. 1903 in Historical Writings by Wilbur Fisk Sanders*, p. 10, MC 53, Box 5, Folder 2, Wilbur Fisk Sanders Papers, MHS.

143. The vigilantes would also include in their ranks Jeremiah M. Fox, Adriel B. Davis, John C. Guy, Nelson Story, Joseph Hinckley, J. S. Daddow, C. F. Keyes, Charles Brown, Elkanah Morse, J. H. Balch, W. C. Maxwell, Nelson Kellock, S. J. Ross, Charles Beehrer, Thomas Baume, William H. Brown Jr., John Brown Jr., Enoch Hodson, Hans J. Holst, Anton Holter, John Triff, Alex Gillon Jr., A. D. Smith, William Palmer, Luther Leebold, and M. S. Warner. Dillon, *The Montana Vigilantes, 1863–1870*, 122–23.

144. Untitled Typescript Document by John A. Nye, p. 2, Box 5, Fldr 8, MC 53, Wilbur Fisk Sanders Papers, MHS.

145. Aaron T. Ford, "Life and History of A. T. Ford," 28–29, SC 702, MHS.

146. Untitled Speech by Wilbur Fisk Sanders, 10–11. Box 4, Fldr 4, MC 53, Wilbur Fisk Sanders Papers, MHS.

147. Prior experience shaped some of the vigilantes themselves, but this experience also motivated opposition to vigilantism. Henry Plummer was in California during the reign of the 1856 vigilance committee, and his opposition to vigilante justice while he was there influenced his reaction toward the vigilantes in Montana. Plummer was not alone in his dislike for the San Francisco committee of vigilance, with Sanders himself admitting that Californians living in Montana's mining camps "did not sympathize with that organization, information concerning it was difficult to obtain and that which was obtainable was not encouraging." *Org of the Com. 1903 in Historical Writings by Wilbur Fisk Sanders*, p. 4, Box 5, Fldr 2, MC 53, Wilbur Fisk Sanders Papers, MHS.
148. "Masonic Festival!" *The Weekly Commonwealth*, Dec. 11, 1862.
149. Transcript of Record, *Baker v. Morton*, 30.
150. Address Delivered by Llewellyn L. Callaway, Past Grand Commander, At Dillon, Montana, June 8, 1938, James E. Callaway Family Papers, SC 1215, MHS; and Patrick Aloysius Mullens, S. J., *Creighton* (Omaha: Creighton University, 1901), 40.
151. Given the secrecy of the vigilance committee in San Francisco, it is impossible to verify Clark's claims. Even if Clark was lying, his desire to link himself to a prior, familiar episode of violence underscores the consciously interconnected nature of extralegal collective violence during this period. John X. Beidler, *X. Beidler: Vigilante,* ed. Helen Fitzgerald Sanders and William H. Bertsche, Jr. (Norman: University of Oklahoma Press, 1957), 37.
152. Allen, *A Decent Orderly Lynching*, 10.
153. Beidler, *X. Beidler*, 4.
154. Matt W. Alderson, "X. Beidler: Evangelist to the Montana Road Agent Manuscript," Matt W. Alderson Manuscripts, SC 115, [Undated], MHS.
155. John M. Williams, "Biographical Sketches" (n.d.), 1–4, SC 1418, James "Cap" Williams papers, MHS.
156. Beidler, *X. Beidler*, 32–33; Wilbur Fisk Sanders, Untitled Manuscript, 3, Box 5, Fldr 2, MC 53, Wilbur Fisk Sanders Papers, MHS.
157. Dillon, *The Montana Vigilantes, 1863–1870*, 135–36.
158. While sophisticated criminal networks did exist, as seen earlier in this book, there is no evidence outside of these claims that any such network operated in this area. Criminality and association occurred, but the footprint of the sort of organized operations seen earlier in the Middle West is absent.
159. Dillon, *The Montana Vigilantes, 1863–1870*, 142.
160. Kirkpatrick, "From Wisconsin to Montana and Life in the West, 1863–1889," 99.
161. Kirkpatrick, "From Wisconsin to Montana and Life in the West, 1863–1889," 100.
162. See Carrigan and Webb, *Forgotten Dead*, 21.
163. Kirkpatrick, "From Wisconsin to Montana and Life in the West, 1863–1889," 91–92.
164. Kirkpatrick, "From Wisconsin to Montana and Life in the West, 1863–1889," 101.
165. C. Barbour, "Two Vigilance Committees," *Overland Monthly and Out West Magazine* vol. 10 (1887): 289.

166. Dillon, *The Montana Vigilantes, 1863–1870*, 157.
167. Untitled Manuscript by Wilbur Fisk Sanders, p.3, MC 53, Box 5, Folder 2, Wilbur Fisk Sanders Papers, MHS.
168. Dillon, *The Montana Vigilantes, 1863–1870*, 162–66.
169. Untitled Typescript Document by John A. Nye, 3.
170. Several prominent members of the 1863–64 committee of vigilance, including Sanders, Biedler, and Holter, all relocated to Helena. See Dillon, *The Montana Vigilantes 1863–1870*, 199–200; and Allen, *A Decent Orderly Lynching*, 366.
171. "To-Day's Wonder—The Passover," *The Rocky Mountain News*, January 31, 1866.
172. "The Passover Again," *The Rocky Mountain News*, February 1, 1866.
173. Leonard, *Lynching in Colorado*, 34.
174. *History of Denver*, 429.
175. "Montana Vigilantes in Colorado, *The Rocky Mountain News*, January 13, 1866
176. Leonard, *Lynching in Colorado*, 35.

Conclusion

1. *Appendix to the House Journal of the Adjourned Session of the Twenty-Third General Assembly of the State of Missouri*, 662.
2. Bonney, *The Banditti of the Prairies*, 196.
3. Bonney, *The Banditti of the Prairies*, 196–222.
4. *Appendix to the House Journal of the Adjourned Session of the Twenty-Third General Assembly of the State of Missouri*, 636.
5. *Appendix to the House Journal of the Adjourned Session of the Twenty-Third General Assembly of the State of Missouri*, 635.
6. *Appendix to the House Journal of the Adjourned Session of the Twenty-Third General Assembly of the State of Missouri*, 637.
7. *Appendix to the House Journal of the Adjourned Session of the Twenty-Third General Assembly of the State of Missouri*, 661.
8. *Appendix to the House Journal of the Adjourned Session of the Twenty-Third General Assembly of the State of Missouri*, 661–62.
9. The first incident is likely a reference to the 1836 lynching of Francis McIntosh. See "Horrible Tragedy," *National Banner and Nashville Whig*, May 11, 1836; and *Appendix to the House Journal of the Adjourned Session of the Twenty-Third General Assembly of the State of Missouri*, 663.
10. Doris Reed, "Edward Bonney, Detective," *The Indiana University Bookman*, no. 2 (1957): 12.
11. *Appendix to the House Journal of the Adjourned Session of the Twenty-Third General Assembly of the State of Missouri*, 825.
12. *Appendix to the House Journal of the Adjourned Session of the Twenty-Third General Assembly of the State of Missouri*, 629.
13. *Appendix to the House Journal of the Adjourned Session of the Twenty-Third General Assembly of the State of Missouri*, 632–33.
14. Pfeifer, *The Roots of Rough Justice*, 5.

Bibliography

Archival Collections

Church History Catalog, The Church of Jesus Christ of Latter-day Saints
Allen J. Stout Reminiscences and Journal, 1845–89

The Durham Museum, Omaha, Nebraska
Byron Reed Collection

Illinois Regional Archives Depository
The People vs. Adolphus Bliss, Lee County Circuit Court

Indiana State Archives
Pardons and Paroles

History Nebraska
James C. Mitchell Papers

Montana Historical Society
Aaron T. Ford Reminiscence
Hezekiah L. Hosmer Papers
James "Cap" Williams papers
James E. Callaway Family Papers
James Henry Morley Diary
John G. Overton Letter
Matt W. Alderson Manuscripts
Sidney Edgerton Papers
Thomas Conrad Papers
Wilbur Fisk Sanders Papers

University of Nebraska–Lincoln Libraries Archives and Special Collections
John McConihe Papers

Databases, Digital Collections, and Web Projects

Ancestry. ancestry.com.
Bureau of Land Management General Land Office Records. glorecords.blm.gov.
Chronicling America. chroniclingamerica.loc.gov.
Colorado Historic Newspapers Collection. coloradohistoricnewspapers.org.
FamilySearch. familysearch.org.
Gale Primary Sources. go-gale-com.
Nebraska Newspapers. nebnewspapers.unl.edu.
Newspapers.com. newspapers.com.
Hoehne, Patrick. Riot Acts. riotacts.org.
The Joseph Smith Papers. josephsmithpapers.org.
Phipps Genealogy. phippsgenealogy.wordpress.com.
The Reeves Project. thereevesproject.org.
Reeves, ,Reaves, and More Rives: A Genealogy Blog for Researchers of the Surname Reeves in All of Its Flavors. usreeves.blogspot.com.
University of Illinois Library Digital Collections. digital.library.illinois.edu.

Government Publications

Acts and Resolutions Passed at Several Sessions of the Territorial Legislature of Iowa 1840–1846. Des Moines, IA: Emory H. English, 1912.
Appendix to the Congressional Globe: Containing Speeches and Important State Papers, Etc., of the First Session, Thirty-Fourth Congress. Washington, D.C.: John C. Rives, 1856.
Appendix to the House Journal of the Adjourned Session of the Twenty-Third General Assembly of the State of Missouri. Jefferson City, MO: Emory S. Foster, 1865–66.
Bloom, John Porter, ed. *The Territorial Papers of the United States.* Washington, D.C.: US Government Printing Office, 1969.
Dillon, John F. *Cases Determined in the United States Circuit Courts for the Eighth Circuit.* Davenport, IA: Egbert, Fidlar, and Chambers, 1880.
Early Records of Jefferson County, Ohio 1788–1851. Steubenville, OH: Public Library of Steubenville and Jefferson County, 1999.
Holmes, George K. *Wages of Farm Labor. Nineteenth Investigation, in 1909, Continuing a Series That Began in 1866.* Washington: Government Printing Office, 1912.
Journal of the Senate of the Thirteenth General Assembly of the State of Illinois at their Regular Session, Begun and Held at Springfield December 5, 1842. Springfield, IL: William Walters, Public Printer, 1842.
A List of Reports to be Made to Congress During the First Session of the Thirty-Fifth Congress by Public Officers. Washington, D.C.: Cornelius Wendell, Printer, 1857.
Reports of Cases in the Supreme Court of Nebraska. September Term, 1890–January Term, 1891. Lincoln, NE: State Journal Company, 1892.
Seventeenth Annual Report of the Bureau of Labor Statistics to the 71st General Assembly of the State of Ohio for the Year 1893. Norwalk, OH: The Laning Printing Co., State Printers, 1894.
The Statute Laws of the Territory of Iowa. Du Buque: Russel & Reeves, 1839.

US Census Bureau. *Compendium of the Enumeration of the Inhabitants and Statistics of the United States as Obtained at the Department of States, From the Returns of the Sixth Census.* Washington: Thomas Allen, 1841.

Wilcox, P. B., ed. *Condensed Reports of Decisions in the Supreme Court of Ohio.* Columbus, OH: I. N. Whiting, 1836.

Courthouse Records

Ashe County (NC) Records of Deeds Book
Columbiana County (OH) Marriage Records
Common Law Record C, Des Moines (IA) County Courthouse
Grayson County (VA) Deed Book
Grayson County (VA) Superior Court Order Book
Jackson County (IA) Probate Records
Minute Dockett of the Ashe County (NC) Superior Court
Ogle County (IL) Record Book A
Polk County (IA) Marriage Index A
Polk County (IA) Probate Court Records
Trumbull County (OH) Common Pleas Journal
Wayne County (OH) Court of Common Pleas Appearance Dockett Journal
Wayne County (OH) Court of Common Pleas Journal

United States Supreme Court Cases and Documents

Baker v. Morton. 79 U.S. 150. 12 Wall. 150. December Term, 1870.
Shields et al., vs. Root (not heard). Filed April 6, 1868.

Newspapers

Alexandria (VA) *Gazette*
The Atlas
Belleville (IL) *Advocate*
Bellevue (IA) *Gazette*
The Bellevue (IA) *Leader*
Burlington (IA) *Hawk-Eye*
Chicago (IL) *American*
Chicago (IL) *Democrat*
Chronicle & Sentinel
The Columbia (OH) *Democrat*
The Daily Milwaukee (WI) *News*
Daily Missouri Republican
The Decatur (IL) *Daily Review*
The Gazette
Henry (IL) *Republican*
The Illinois Free Trader and LaSalle County Commercial Advertiser
Illinois Gazette
Illinois State Register
Iowa Territorial Gazette

Iowa News
Jackson (IA) *Sentinel*
Jeffersonian Republican
The Lacon Illinois Gazette
Litchfield (CT) *Enquirer*
Lloyd's Weekly London Newspaper
Maquoketa (IA) *Excelsior*
The Middlebury (VT) *People's Press*
Missouri State Times
National Banner and Nashville (TN) *Whig*
National Intelligencer
Nauvoo (IL) *Expositor*
Nauvoo (IL) *Neighbor*
The Nebraska Advertiser
Nebraska Palladium
The Nebraskian
New York Daily Herald
The New York Times
New-York Tribune
North Western Gazette and Galena (IL) *Advertiser*
The Ottawa (IL) *Free Trader*
Palmer Journal
The People's Tribune
Peoria (IL) *Register*
Quincy (IL) *Whig*
The Rockford (IL) *Star*
The Rocky Mountain News
Sangamo (IL) *Journal*
Semi-Weekly Bugle
The Southport (WI) *Telegraph*
Sunday World-Herald
Times and Seasons
Universalist Watchman and Christian Repository
Vermont Phoenix
The Warsaw (IL) *Signal*
The Wasp
The Weekly Commonwealth
The Western Mountaineer

Dissertations, Theses, and Unpublished Articles

Black, Stuart Rulan. "How Governor Ford's Background, Choices, and Actions Influenced the Martyrdom of Joseph Smith in Carthage Jail." MA Thesis. Brigham Young University, 2020.

Cypser, Darlene A. "Myth of the Wild West: Law and Justice Prior to the Organization of the Territory of Colorado." MA Thesis. University of Colorado, 2017.

Kirkpatrick, Robert. "From Wisconsin to Montana and Life in the West, 1863–1889: The Reminiscences of Robert Kirkpatrick," Edited by Michael Gee McLatchey. MA Thesis. Montana State University, 1961.

Miles, Marian G. "The Founding of Florence, Nebraska, 1854–1860." MA Thesis. University of Nebraska at Omaha, 1970.

Parker, Byron T. "Extra-Legal Law Enforcement on the Nebraska Frontier." MA Thesis. University of Nebraska, 1931.

County and Local Histories

Annals of Jackson County, Iowa. Maquoketa, IA: The Jackson County Historical Society, 1906.

Bateman, Newton, Paul Selby, and J. Seymour Currey, eds. *Historical Encyclopedia of Illinois and History of Hancock County.* Chicago: Munsell Publishing Company, 1921.

Baughman, A. J. *History of Ashland County, Ohio.* Chicago: The S.J. Clarke Publishing Co., 1909.

Bell, John Thomas. *History of Washington County, Nebraska.* Omaha: The Herald Steam Book and Job Printing House, 1876.

Blanchard, Charles, ed. *Counties of Clay and Owen, Indiana.* Chicago: F. A. Battey & Co., 1884.

Boies, Henry L. *History of DeKalb County, Illinois.* Chicago: O. P. Bassett, 1868.

Boss, Henry R. *Sketches of the Story of Ogle County, Ill. and the Early Settlement of the Northwest.* Polo, Il: Henry R. Boss, 1859.

Brewer, Luther, and Barthinius L. Wick. *History of Linn County Iowa.* Chicago: The Pioneer Publishing Company, 1911.

Church, Charles A. *Past and Present of the City of Rockford and Winnebago County, Illinois.* Chicago: The S. J. Clarke Publishing Co., 1905.

Creigh, Alfred. *History of Washington County from its First Settlement to the Present Time.* Harrisburg, PA: B. Singerly, 1871.

Dixon, J. M. *Centennial History of Polk County, Iowa.* Des Moines: State Register, 1876.

Douglass, Ben. *History of Wayne County, Ohio, from the Days of the Pioneers and First Settlers to the Present Time.* Indianapolis, IN: Robert Douglass, 1878.

Ellis, James. *History of Jackson County, Iowa.* Chicago: S. J. Clarke Publishing Co., 1910.

Ellsworth, Spencer. *Records of the Olden Time; or Fifty Years on the Prairies.* Lacon, IL: Home Journal Steam Printing Establishment, 1880.

Field, Homer H., and Joseph R. Reed. *History of Pottawattamie County, Iowa.* Chicago: The S. J. Clarke Publishing Co., 1907.

Goss, Lewis M. *Past and Present of DeKalb County, Illinois.* Chicago: The Pioneer Publishing Company, 1907.

Graham, A. A. *History of Richland County, Ohio: Its Past and Present.* Mansfield, OH: A. A. Graham & Co., 1880.

The History of Benton County, Iowa. Chicago: Western Historical Company, 1878.

History of Cass County, Iowa. Springfield, IL: Continental Historical Company, 1884.
The History of Cedar County, Iowa. Chicago: Western Historical Company, 1878.
History of Dodge and Washington Counties, Nebraska, and Their People. Chicago: The American Historical Society, 1921.
The History of Jackson County, Iowa. Chicago: Western Historical Company, 1879.
History of Johnson County, Iowa. Iowa City: n.p., 1883.
The History of Ogle County, Illinois. Chicago: H. F. Kett & Co., 1878.
The History of Polk County, Iowa. Des Moines, IA: Union Historical Company, 1880.
History of Pottawattamie County, Iowa. Chicago: O. L. Baskin & Co., 1883.
Mueller, Herman A., ed. *History of Madison County, Iowa, and its People.* Chicago: The S. J. Clarke Publishing Company, 1915.
Perrin, William Henry, ed. *History of Crawford and Clark Counties, Illinois.* Chicago: O. L. Baskin & Co., 1883.
Porter, Will. *Annals of Polk County, Iowa, and City of Des Moines.* Des Moines, IA: Geo. A. Miller Printing Company, 1898.
Reid, J. M. *Sketches and Anecdotes of the Old Settler and New Comers, the Mormon Bandits, and Danite Band.* Keokuk, IA: R. B. Ogden, 1876.
Savage, James W., and John T. Bell. *History of the City of Omaha Nebraska.* New York: Munsell & Company, 1894.
Smiley, Jerome C., ed. *History of Denver with Outlines of the Earlier History of the Rocky Mountain County.* Denver: The Denver Times, 1901.
Sorenson, Alfred. *Early History of Omaha: Or, Walks and Talks Among the Old Settlers.* Omaha: The Daily Bee, 1876.
——*History of Omaha from the Pioneer Days to the Present.* Omaha: Gibson, Miller, and Richardson, 1889.
——*The Story of Omaha from the Pioneer Days to the Present Time.* Omaha: National Printing Company, 1923.
Stevens, Frank E. *History of Lee County Illinois.* Chicago: S. J. Clarke Publishing Company, 1914.
Travis, William. *A History of Clay County, Indiana.* New York: The Lewis Publishing Company, 1909.
Wakeley, Arthur, ed. *Omaha: The Gate City, and Douglas County Nebraska.* Chicago: The S. J. Clarke Publishing Company, 1917.

Primary Source Publications

Arnold, Isaac N. *Reminiscences of the Illinois Bar Forty Years Ago: Lincoln and Douglas as Orators and Lawyers.* Chicago: Fergus Printing Company, 1881.
Barker, Joseph. "American Reminiscences." *Barker's Review* 2, no. 38 (May 24, 1862): 597–600.
Beadle, Erastus F. *Hams, Eggs, & Corn Cake: A Nebraska Territory Diary.* Lincoln, NE: University of Nebraska Press, 2001.
Beckman, William. "An Interesting Letter from an Old Resident of Illinois." *Journal of the Illinois State Historical Society* 7 no. 1 (April 1914): 127–32.
Beidler, John X. *X. Beidler: Vigilante.* Edited by Helen Fitzgerald Sanders and William H. Bertsche, Jr. Norman: University of Oklahoma Press, 1957.

Blackstone, William. *Commentaries on the Laws of England*. London: A. Strahan, 1800.

Blane, William Newnham. *An Excursion Through the United States and Canada During the Years 1822–23 by an English Gentleman*. London: Baldwin, Cradock, and Joy, 1824.

Bonney, Edward. *The Banditti of the Prairies; or, The Murderer's Doom*. Philadelphia: T. B. Peterson and Brothers, 1855.

Bryant, William Cullen. *Letters of a Traveller; or, Notes of Things Seen in Europe and America*. New York: George P. Putnam, 1851.

Caton, John Dean. *Early Bench and Bar of Illinois*. Chicago: Chicago Legal News Company, 1893.

Clayton, William. *William Clayton's Journal*. Salt Lake City: The Deseret News, 1921.

Collier, Fred C., ed. *The Nauvoo High Council Minute Books of the Church of Jesus Christ of Latter-Day Saints*. Hanna, UT: Collier's Publishing Co., 2005.

Collins, Charles. *Collins' Omaha Directory*. Omaha: Charles Collins, 1866.

Dimsdale, Thomas J. *The Vigilantes of Montana, or, Popular Justice in the Rocky Mountains*. Virginia City, MT: D.W. Tilton, 1882.

Dodge, Grenville M. *Biography of Major General Grenville M. Dodge from 1831 to 1871 Written and Compiled by Himself at Different Times and Completed in 1914*. Des Moines: State Historical Society of Iowa, 1914.

Flint, James. *Letters from America*. Edinburgh: W. & C. Tait, 1822.

Ford, Thomas. *A History of Illinois, from its Commencement as a State in 1818 to 1847*. Chicago: S. C. Griggs & Co., 1854.

Gass, Olive. "The Vigilantes, Nebraska's First Defenders." *Nebraska History Magazine* 14, no. 1 (1933): 3–18.

Grund, Francis. *The Americans, in their Moral, Social, and Political Relations*. Boston: Marsh, Capen and Lyon, 1837.

Hafen, LeRoy R., and Ann W. Hafen, eds. *Reports from Colorado: The Wildman Letters 1859–1865*. Glendale, CA: The Arthur H. Clark Company, 1961.

Hay, John. "The Mormon Prophet's Tragedy." *The Atlantic Monthly* (Dec. 1869).

An Interesting Account of the Organization and Mode of Operations of the Celebrated Horde of Robbers Known as the Markham Gang. Toronto: Scobie & Balfour, 1846.

Jacob, Norton. *The Record of Norton Jacob*. Edited by C. Edward Jacob and Ruth Jacob. Salt Lake City: The Norton Jacob Family Association, 1949.

Jacobs, Zina Diantha Huntington. "'All Things Move in Order in the City': The Nauvoo Diary of Zina Diantha Huntington Jacobs." Edited by Maureen Ursenbach Beecher. *BYU Studies Quarterly* 19, no. 3 (1979): 285–320.

Langford, Nathaniel P. *Vigilante Days and Ways*. Chicago: A. C. McClurg & Co., 1912.

Larimer, William H. H. *Reminiscences of General William Larimer and of his Son William H. H. Larimer: Two of the Founders of Denver City*. Edited by Herman S. Davis. Lancaster, PA: The New Era Printing Company, 1918.

Lee, John Doyle. *Journals of John D. Lee 1846–47 and 1859*. Edited by Charles Kelly. Salt Lake City: Western Printing Company, 1938.

Linder, Usher F. *Reminiscences of the Early Bench and Bar of Illinois*. Chicago: The Chicago Legal News Company, 1879.

Marsh, Eudocia Baldwin. "When the Mormons Dwelt Among Us." *The Bellman* 20, no. 507–8 (April 1916): 373–78, 401–6.

Pearson, Jonathan. *Diaries of Jonathan Pearson Volume 2*. Union College Schaffer Library Digital Projects and New York Heritage Digital Collections. https://arches.union.edu/do/coc2d526-eaf4-4e3e-942a-3b0974b421a3.

Pfouts, Paris Swazy. *Four Firsts for a Modest Hero: The Autobiography of Paris Swazy Pfouts*. Edited by Harold Axford. Portland, OR: Dunham Printing Company, 1968.

Phelps, W. W. "The Joseph/Hyrum Smith Funeral Sermon." Edited by Richard Van-Wagoner and Steven C. Walker. *BYU Studies Quarterly* 23, no. 1 (1983): 3–18.

Pitzer, Henry L. *Three Frontiers: Memories, and a Portrait of Henry Little Pitzer as Recorded by his Son Robert Claiborne Pitzer*. Edited by Robert Claiborne Pittzer. Muscatine, IA: The Prairie Press, 1938.

Rankin, Alexander T. *Alexander Taylor Rankin: His Diary and Letters*. Edited by Nolie Mumey. Boulder, CO: Johnson Publishing Company, 1966.

Richards, Franklin D., ed. *The Latter-Day Saints Millennial Star*. Liverpool, UK: Franklin D. Richards, 1854.

Shull, Charles W., ed. "Minutes of Vigilance Committee, Florence, Nebraska, May 29–July 30, 1857." *Nebraska History* 58 (1977): 73–87.

Stone, Letta Brock. *The West Family Register*. Washington, D.C.: W. F. Roberts Company, Inc., 1928.

Taylor, John. "The John Taylor Nauvoo Journal: January 1845–September 1845." Edited by Dean C. Jesse. *BYU Studies Quarterly* 23, no. 3 (Summer 1983): 1–105, 107–24.

Woolworth, James M. *Nebraska in 1857*. New York: A. S. Barnes, 1857.

Secondary Source Publications

Ablavsky, Gregory. *Federal Ground: Governing Property and Violence in the First U.S. Territories*. Oxford: Oxford University Press, 2021.

Allaman, John Lee. "Policing in Mormon Nauvoo." *Illinois Historical Journal* 89, no. 2 (Summer 1996): 85–98.

Allen, Frederick. *A Decent Orderly Lynching: The Montana Vigilantes*. Norman: University of Oklahoma Press, 2004.

Arata, Laura J. *Race and the Wild West: Sarah Bickford, the Montana Vigilantes, and the Tourism of Decline, 1870–1930*. Norman: University of Oklahoma Press, 2020.

Arculus, Paul. *Mayhem to Murder: The History of the Markham Gang, Organized Crime in Canada in the 1840s*. Port Perry, ON: Observer Publishing, 2003.

Ayers, Edward L. *Vengeance & Justice: Crime and Punishment in the 19th-Century American South*. Oxford: Oxford University Press, 1984.

Bailyn, Bernard. *The Ideological Origins of the American Revolution*. Cambridge, MA: Harvard University Press, 1967.

Banner, Stuart. *The Death Penalty: An American History.* Cambridge, MA: Harvard University Press, 2002.

Barbour, C. "Two Vigilance Committees." *Overland Monthly and Out West Magazine* 10 (1887): 285–91.

Bernstein, Iver. *The New York City Draft Riots: Their Significance for American Society and Politics in the Age of the Civil War.* Oxford: Oxford University Press, 1990.

Black, Paul W. "Lynchings in Iowa." *The Iowa Journal of History and Politics* 10, no. 2 (April 1912): 151–254.

Black, Susan Eaton, et al. *Property Transactions in Nauvoo, Hancock County, Illinois and Surrounding Communities (1839–1859).* Wilmington, DE: World Vital Records, Inc., 2006.

Block, Sharon. *Rape & Sexual Power in Early America.* Chapel Hill: The University of North Carolina Press, 2006.

Bogue, Allan G. "The Iowa Claim Clubs: Symbol and Substance." *The Mississippi Valley Historical Review* 45, no. 2 (Sept. 1958): 231–53.

Brown, Richard Maxwell. *Strain of Violence: Historical Studies of American Violence and Vigilantism.* New York: Oxford University Press, 1975.

Calomiris, Charles W., and Larry Schweikert. "The Panic of 1857: Origins, Transmission, and Containment." *The Journal of Economic History* 51, no. 4 (Dec. 1991): 807–34.

Carrigan, William D. and Clive Webb. *Forgotten Dead: Mob Violence against Mexicans in the United States, 1848–1928.* Oxford: Oxford University Press, 2013.

Clements, Mary Ann. "Nauvoo Counterfeiting: Meet Edward Bonney." *Wheat and Tares.* July 27, 2021. Accessed August 6, 2022. https://wheatandtares.org/2021/07/27/nauvoo-counterfeiting-meet-edward-bonney/.

Collins, Randall. *Violence: A Micro-sociological Theory.* Princeton: Princeton University Press, 2008.

Compendium of History Reminiscence and Biography of Western Nebraska. Chicago: Alden Publishing Company, 1909.

Curtis, Earl G. "John Milton Thayer." *Nebraska History* 28, no. 4 (Oct.–Dec. 1947): 225–38.

Davis, Rodney O. "Judge Ford and the Regulators, 1841–1842." *Selected Papers in Illinois History 1981.* Edited by Bruce D. Cody. Springfield, IL: Illinois State Historical Society, 1982.

Dearinger, Ryan L. "Violence, Masculinity, Image, and Reality on the Antebellum Frontier." *Indiana Magazine of History* 100, no. 1 (March 2004): 26–55.

Dillon, Mark C. *The Montana Vigilantes 1863–1870: Gold, Guns, & Gallows.* Logan: Utah State University Press, 2013.

Dudley, Edgar S. "Notes on the Early Military History of Nebraska." *Transactions and Reports, Nebraska State Historical Society* 3 (1887): 166–96.

Fletcher, Arthur L. *Ashe County, a History.* Jefferson, N.C.: Ashe County Research Association, 1963.

Fritz, Christian G. *American Sovereigns: The People and America's Constitutional Tradition Before the Civil War.* Cambridge: Cambridge University Press, 2008.

Gilje, Paul. *Rioting in America*. Bloomington: Indiana University Press, 1996.

Godfrey, Kenneth W. "Crime and Punishment in Mormon Nauvoo, 1839–1846." *Brigham Young University Studies* 32, nos. 1/2 (Winter and Spring 1991): 195–227.

Gonzales-Day, Ken. *Lynching in the West 1850–1935*. Durham, NC: Duke University Press, 2006.

Gorn, Elliot J. "'Gouge and Bite, Pull Hair and Scratch': The Social Significance of Fighting in the Southern Backcountry." *The American Historical Review* 90, no. 1 (Feb. 1985): 18–43.

Grimsted, David. *American Mobbing, 1828–1861: Toward Civil War*. Oxford: Oxford University Press, 1998.

———"Né D'Hier: American Vigilantism, Communal Rebirth and Political Traditions." *People and Power: Rights, Citizenship and Violence*. Edited by Loretta Valtz Mannucci. Milan: Grafiche Vadacca, 1992.

———"Rioting in its Jacksonian Setting." *The American Historical Review* 77, no. 2 (April 1972): 361–97.

Gue, Benjamin F. *History of Iowa from the Earliest Times to the Beginning of the Twentieth Century*. New York City: The Century Historical Company, 1903.

Hallwas, John E. and Roger D. Launius, eds. *Cultures in Conflict: A Documentary History of the Mormon War in Illinois*. Logan, UT: Utah State University Press, 1995.

Hartley, William G. "Council Bluffs/Kanesville, Iowa: A Hub for Mormon Settlements, Operations, and Emigration, 1846–1852." *The John Whitmer Historical Association Journal* 25 (2006): 17–47.

Hedges, Andrew M. "Thomas Ford and Joseph Smith, 1842–1844." *Journal of Mormon History* 42, no. 4 (Oct. 2016): 97–124.

Heerman, M. Scott. "'Reducing Free Men to Slavery': Black Kidnapping, the 'Slave Power,' and the Politics of Abolition in Antebellum Illinois, 1830–1860." *Journal of the Early Republic* 38, no. 2 (Summer 2018): 261–91.

History of the Church. Salt Lake City: Deseret News, 1912.

Hoehne, Patrick. "Apostles of Disorder: Montana Merchants, Vigilantes, and the Interconnectivity of Extralegal Collective Violence." *Montana The Magazine of Western History* 72, no. 3 (Autumn 2022): 3–21.

———"'In Union There Is Strength': Claim Clubs, the Law, and the First Murder Case Brought to Court in the Nebraska Territory." *Great Plains Quarterly* 40, no. 4 (Fall 2020): 305–24.

———"'Murderous, Unwarrantable, and Very Cold': Mapping the Rise of Extralegal Killing in the United States, 1783–1865." *Journal of Digital History* 2 (2022).

Hogan, Richard. *Class and Community in Frontier Colorado*. Lawrence: University Press of Kansas, 1990.

Howe, David Walker. *What Hath God Wrought: The Transformation of America, 1815–1848*. Oxford: Oxford University Press, 2007.

Huntress, Keith. "Governor Thomas Ford and the Murderers of Joseph Smith." *Dialogue* 4, no. 2 (1969): 41–52.

Kammen, Carol. *On Doing Local History*. Walnut Creek, CA: AltaMira Press, 2003.

Kammer, Sean M. "'Public Opinion is More Than Law:' Popular Sovereignty and Vigilantism in the Nebraska Territory." *Great Plains Quarterly* 31, no. 4 (Fall 2011): 309–24.

Kauffman, Rebecca H. "Governor Thomas Ford in Ogle County," in *Transactions of the Illinois State Historical Society for the Year 1911.* Springfield: Illinois State Journal Co., 1913.

Kimball, Edward L. and Kenneth W. Godfrey. "Law and Order in Winter Quarters." *Journal of Mormon History* 32, no. 1 (Spring 2006): 172–218.

Kimmel, Michael S. *Manhood in America: A Cultural History.* New York: The Free Press, 1996.

Kramer, Larry D. *The People Themselves: Popular Constitutionalism and Judicial Review.* Oxford: Oxford University Press, 2004.

Leonard, Stephen J. *Lynching in Colorado, 1859–1919.* Louisville: University Press of Colorado, 2002.

Lizzio, Ken. *Pirates of the Prairie: Outlaws and Vigilantes in America's Heartland.* Guilford, CT: Lyons Press, 2018.

Lucke, Susan K. *The Bellevue War: Mandate of Justice or Murder by Mob? A True—and Still Controversial—Story of Iowa as the Wild West.* Ames: McMillen Publishing, 2002.

Luskey, Brian P. *On the Make: Clerks and the Quest for Capital in Nineteenth-Century America.* New York: New York University Press, 2010.

Mahoney, Timothy. "'A Common Band of Brotherhood': Male Subcultures, the Booster Ethos, and the Origins of Urban Social Order in the Midwest of the 1840s." *Journal of Urban History* 25, no. 5 (July 1999): 619–46.

Malcom, Joyce Lee. *To Keep and Bear Arms: The Origins of an Anglo-American Right.* Cambridge, MA: Harvard University Press, 1994.

Mather, R. E., and F. E. Boswell. *Hanging the Sheriff: A Biography of Henry Plummer.* Missoula: Historic Montana Publishing, 1998.

McBride, Spencer W. *Joseph Smith for President: The Prophet, the Assassins, and the Fight for American Religious Freedom.* Oxford: Oxford University Press, 2021.

McDowell, Andrea G. *We the Miners: Self-Government in the California Gold Rush.* Cambridge: Harvard University Press, 2022.

McMurtrue, Douglas C. "The First Printing at Council Bluffs." *Annals of Iowa* 18, no. 1 (July 1931): 3–11.

Mihm, Stephen. *A Nation of Counterfeiters: Capitalists, Con Men, and the Making of the United States.* Cambridge, MA: Harvard University Press, 2007.

Morton, J. Sterling, et al. *Illustrated History of Nebraska: A History of Nebraska from the Earliest Explorations of the Trans-Mississippi Region.* Lincoln, NE: Jacob North & Company, 1905.

Mullens, Patrick Aloysius. *Creighton.* Omaha: Creighton University, 1901.

Murtazashvili, Ilia. *The Political Economy of the American Frontier.* Cambridge: Cambridge University Press, 2013.

Oaks, Dallin Harris and Marvin S. Hill. *The Carthage Conspiracy: The Trial of the Accused Assassins of Joseph Smith.* Urbana: University of Illinois Press, 1977.

Obert, Jonathan. *The Six-Shooter State: Public and Private Violence in American Politics.* Cambridge: Cambridge University Press, 2018.

Oviatt, Alton B. "Pacific Coast Competition for the Gold Camp Trade of Montana," *Pacific Northwest Quarterly* 56, no. 4 (Oct. 1965): 168–76.

——"Steamboat Traffic on the Upper Missouri River, 1859–1869." *Pacific Northwest Quarterly* 40, no. 2 (April 1949): 93–105.

Park, Benjamin E. *Kingdom of Nauvoo: The Rise and Fall of a Religious Empire on the American Frontier.* New York: Liveright Publishing Corporation, 2020.

Peterson, Farah. "Constitutionalism in Unexpected Places." *Virginia Law Review* 106, no. 3 (May 2020): 559–609.

Pfeifer, Michael J. "Law, Society, and Violence in the Antebellum Midwest: The 1857 Eastern Iowa Vigilante Movement." *Annals of Iowa* 64, no. 2 (Spring 2005): 139–66.

——ed. *Lynching Beyond Dixie: American Mob Violence Outside the South.* Edited by Michael J. Pfeifer. Urbana: University of Illinois Press, 2013.

——*The Roots of Rough Justice: Origins of American Lynching.* Urbana: University of Illinois Press, 2011.

Potter, James E. "Wearing the Hempen Neck-Tie: Lynching in Nebraska 1858–1919." *Nebraska History* 93 (2012), 138–53.

Potts, James B. "The Nebraska Capital Controversy, 1854–59." *Great Plains Quarterly* 8, no. 3 (Summer 1988): 1732–832.

Price, Carl E. "The Great 'Riot Year': Jacksonian Democracy and Patterns of Violence in 1834." *Journal of the Early Republic* 5, no. 1 (Spring 1985): 1–19.

Price, Eliphalet. "The Trial and Execution of Patrick O'Conner at the Dubuque Mines in the Summer of 1834." *The Palimpsest* 1 (1920): 86–97.

Quinn, D. Michael. "National Culture. Personality, and Theocracy in the Early Mormon Culture of Violence." *The John Whitmer Historical Association Journal.* 2002 Nauvoo Conference Special Edition (2002): 159–86.

Reed, Doris M. "Edward Bonney, Detective." *The Indiana University Bookman* 2 (1957): 5–17.

Reid, Harvey. *Thomas Cox.* Iowa City: State Historical Society of Iowa, 1909.

Richards, Leonard L. *Shays's Rebellion: The American Revolution's Final Battle.* Philadelphia: University of Pennsylvania Press, 2002.

Rindfleish, Bryan C. "'What it Means to be a Man': Contested Masculinity in the Early Republic and Antebellum America." *History Compass* 10, no. 11 (Nov. 2012): 852–65.

Rogers, James Grafton. "The Beginnings of Law in Colorado." *Dicta* 36, no. 2 (March–April 1959): 111–20.

Rushdy, Ashraf H. A. *American Lynching.* New Haven: Yale University Press, 2012.

Senechal de la Roche, Roberta. "Collective Violence as Social Control." *Sociological Forum* 11, no. 1 (March 1996): 97–128.

——"Why is Collective Violence Collective?" *Sociological Theory* 19, no. 2 (July 2001): 126–44.

Senkewicz, Robert M. "The Inflation of an Overdose Business: Economic Origins of San Francisco Vigilantes." *The Pacific Historian* 23, no. 3 (1979): 63–75.

———*Vigilantes in Gold Rush San Francisco.* Stanford: Stanford University Press, 1985.

Shepard, Bill. "The Notorious Hodges Brothers: Solving the Mystery of Their Destruction at Nauvoo." *The John Whitmer Historical Association Journal* 26 (2006): 260–86.

———"Stealing at Mormon Nauvoo." *The John Whitmer Historical Association Journal* 23 (2003): 91–110.

———"The Tragedy of William Hodges." *The John Whitmer Historical Association Journal* 38, no. 1 (Spring/Summer 2018): 142–67.

Slaughter, Thomas P. *The Whiskey Rebellion: Frontier Epilogue to the American Revolution.* Oxford: Oxford University Press, 1986.

Smith, Alex D. "Untouchable: Joseph Smith's Use of the Law as a Catalyst for Assassination." *Journal of the Illinois State Historical Society* 112, no. 1 (Spring 2019): 8–42.

Snyder, John Francis. *Adam W. Snyder, and His Period in Illinois History, 1817–1842.* Virginia, IL: E. Needham, Bookseller and Stationer, 1906.

———"Governor Ford and his Family." *Journal of the Illinois State Historical Society* 3, no. 2 (July 1910): 45–51.

Storm, Colton, ed. *A Catalogue of the Everett D. Graff Collection of Western Americana.* Chicago: The University of Chicago Press, 1968.

Transactions and Reports of the Nebraska State Historical Society. Lincoln, NE: State Journal Company, 1892.

Trexler, Harrison A. *Flour and Wheat in the Montana Gold Camps, 1862–1870.* Missoula, MT: Dunstan, 1918.

Trumbo, Jean. "Orson Hyde's Frontier Guardian: A Mormon Editor Chronicles the Westward Movement Through Kanesville, Iowa." *Iowa Heritage Illustrated* 77, no. 2 (Summer 1996): 74–85.

Turner, Frederick Jackson. *The Frontier in American History.* New York: Henry Holt and Company, 1921.

Underhill, W. M. "Historic Bread Riot in Virginia City." *The Washington Historical Quarterly* 21:3 (July 1930): 189–94.

Waldrep, Christopher. *The Many Faces of Judge Lynch: Extralegal Violence and Punishment in America.* New York: Palgrave Macmillan, 2002.

Watkins, Albert. *History of Nebraska from the Earliest Explorations to the Present Time.* Lincoln, NE: Western Publishing and Engraving Company, 1913.

Index